D1007328

Beethoven at the age of forty-nine (1819)

From a portrait by Josef Stieler

BEETHOVEN'S LETTERS

WITH EXPLANATORY NOTES
BY
DR. A. C. KALISCHER

TRANSLATED WITH PREFACE BY
J. S. SHEDLOCK, B.A.

SELECTED AND EDITED BY
A. EAGLEFIELD-HULL, MUS. DOC. (OXON.)

ILLUSTRATED

DOVER PUBLICATIONS, INC.
NEW YORK

Published in Canada by General Publishing Company, Ltd., 30 Lesmill Road, Don Mills, Toronto, Ontario.

Published in the United Kingdom by Constable and Company, Ltd., 10 Orange Street, London WC 2.

This Dover edition, first published in 1972, is an unabridged republication of the work originally published by J. M. Dent & Sons, Ltd., London & Toronto (in New York by E. P. Dutton & Co.), in 1926. The present edition is published by special arrangement with J. M. Dent & Sons, Ltd., London.

International Standard Book Number: 0-486-22769-3
Library of Congress Catalog Card Number: 73-159687

Manufactured in the United States of America
Dover Publications, Inc.
180 Varick Street
New York, N. Y. 10014

INTRODUCTION

MR. SHEDLOCK's English translation of Dr. Kalischer's *Complete Collection of Beethoven's Letters* has now unfortunately been out of print for many years. I therefore willingly accepted the publishers' proposal for a handier and less expensive form of this work, to be brought about by a selection of those letters which, bearing more particularly on the music of Beethoven or more directly on his character, are of great interest to the general lover of music. Having first sought the approval of Mr. Shedlock's executrix, Mrs. Manning, I immediately availed myself of some corrections which Mr. Shedlock sent me some years ago for another work.

The present selection in one volume is a book for the general reader, rather than for the musical researcher and historian. I feel sure that every music-lover who has not Dr. Kalischer's German collection (1220 letters) will be thankful for this condensation, which contains all that is most valuable as a search-light on the music and the character of Beethoven.

A. EAGLEFIELD-HULL.

PREFACE

"THIS appears to be the special task of biography: to present the man in relation to his times, and to show how far as a whole they are opposed to him, in how far they are favourable to him, and how, if he be an artist, poet, or writer, he reflects them outwardly." Thus wrote Goethe in his *Wahrheit und Dichtung*, and, as regards Beethoven, his letters offer a unique biography, for studying the man in relation to his times, while such works as the *Eroica* and *Choral* symphonies certainly reflect them outwardly. We also see clearly from his letters how deeply he was affected by the times. He did not suddenly decide to write a work and dedicate it to Napoleon, for that was his original intention with respect to the *Eroica*, nor did he suddenly think the Schiller *Ode to Joy* would be a fine poem to set to music; but the one work was the outcome of strong sympathy with the man whom he thought was about to establish a republican millennium, the other of ardent desire for peace and goodwill to reign upon earth. Reichardt tells us of the ideals after which men were aiming at the end of the eighteenth century. The victories of the republican armies specially impressed Beethoven soon after his arrival in Vienna, for his native country suffered thereby, while the *Ode to Joy* of Schiller, though the setting was a late one, occupied his thoughts from a very early period. Of the horrors of war he had personal experience. In 1801 we find him taking part in a concert for the benefit of the wounded Austrian soldiers at the battle of Hainau; in 1805 Vienna was occupied by French troops, and again in 1809 the city of Vienna was bombarded and then occupied by Napoleon. The events of 1805 were unfavourable to the success of his opera *Fidelio*, while those of 1809 greatly worried him. "What a disturbing wild life all around me, nothing but drums, cannons, men, misery of all sorts." So he writes in a graphic letter to his publishers, Breitkopf and Härtel (26 July, 1809). How far these and other events may have interfered with his art-creations is difficult to determine; but the great works which he produced were surely in part owing to the excitement of those times. Had Beethoven lived a quiet, peaceful life, such as that of Haydn at Esterház, it is very doubtful whether we should now possess the *Eroica*, C minor, and the later Symphonies.

Much could be said about Beethoven and the times in which he lived, and many quotations could be given from the Letters, but for the moment we wish to say something about them as showing what kind of a man he was. In these Letters we get at the very heart of the composer, and his thoughts and feelings are expressed in strong characteristic terms, yet quite naturally. From their general character one is convinced that Beethoven had absolutely no thought of their ever being published. For the most part, they are anything but models of style, yet, and not unfrequently, there are sentences which seem, as it were, inspired. A few have been often quoted. Here is one less familiar. In Letter 254 he writes to his friend and helper, Nanette Streicher, who is at Baden: "If you go to the old ruins, think that Beethoven lingered there; if you wander through the mysterious fir-forests, think it was there Beethoven often poetised, or, as it is called, composed."

By reading Berlioz's *Mémoires* one gets a very good idea both of the man and the musician; of his likes and dislikes, of his excitability, and at times of his despondency, of his high ideals, of his outspokenness, and of his art career generally. Berlioz had a powerful pen, and drew a strong picture of himself. Yet there is a literary polish about the whole thing: while writing, Berlioz had the public in mind. Therein lies the difference between his *Mémoires* and the Letters of Beethoven. Setting aside the dedication letter to the Prince Elector of Cologne, in which his father no doubt had the larger share, the rest of the correspondence gives a natural picture of the man. Many, nay, probably most, were written in a great hurry; *in der Eile* was the composer's usual ending to his letters, and of haste the letters bear many traces: the same words are constantly repeated; the structure of the sentences is frequently very loose, and at times it is, indeed, hard to find out what he meant. For punctuation he cared little. With him, the comma did duty for comma, semicolon, also full stop. At times, indeed, he hurries on to a fresh sentence without any kind of stop, and does not even trouble to begin a new one with a capital letter. Nouns, which in German always begin with a capital, seldom have it, and on the other hand, words not needing one have one. Again, there is constant confusion with the pronouns *sie*, *ihr* and *ihnen*, which seldom have a capital initial letter when such is required. Another proof of haste will be found in the spelling of proper names; very few of them are correct. They have been left in the Letters as he wrote them. It is a characteristic feature which I felt ought to be represented. It is curious to note that in a letter to Schindler, he says: "But you are a bad speller." And, finally, hurry is shown in his handwriting, which often puzzled even Jahn, Schindler, Nohl and others who had seen and studied very many of the composer's autograph letters. In informing Neate of the conditions on which he would accept a proposal of the Philharmonic Society, he states that he got someone to write the letter, so that "it might be easier to read." And in a letter to Streicher he describes how one day at the post office he handed in a letter, and was asked by the official whither it was to be sent. And he adds that he himself, like his writing, is often misunderstood.

The Letters, then, offer a true reflection of the man. His words only express the state of his feelings at certain times, and in reading the letters this must ever be borne in mind. The scene with Stephan Breuning (see Letter 53) offers a case in point: the composer was angry, and on Stephan he poured the vials of his wrath; but this must be compared with the letter of reconciliation (No. 58). Another outburst of anger, for which, however, Beethoven seemed to have just cause, was with Artaria about the quintet (see Letter 39). Artaria was a "rascal"—a favourite word with the composer—of the first water; yet, and to his cost, Beethoven afterwards learnt that he had been somewhat hasty in his judgment; and soon after we find him doing business with the "rascally" firm.

There is, however, no doubt that Beethoven loved truth and justice, and that at heart he was one of the kindest of men. To understand his true character, these outbursts, while they show the impressionable nature of the man, must not be taken as normal specimens. Many and many a letter might be adduced in favour of his noble-mindedness, of his contempt for all that was mean and wicked. And his charity was great. He was always ready to benefit "suffering humanity."

From many of Beethoven's works one can perceive that he was a man of varied moods, also of sudden changes of mood. In one letter we find him speaking of a person in the most friendly manner, while in another no words are too strong to condemn that same person. Such was the case notably with his friend and benefactor, the Archduke Rudolph. So these letters seem to contain a mass of contradictions. But on closer examination one finds that Beethoven's feelings were at times so strong that he seemed incapable of listening to reason. He felt he had been badly treated, and nothing would for the time being convince him that his view of the matter was wrong. But if his anger was great, his apology afterwards was equally so; in fact, both the one and the other were exaggerated.

In speaking of Clive, Lord Macaulay remarked that exceptional men must not be judged by ordinary standards. And never more necessary is it to bear this in mind than when studying Beethoven's character. He was a perfectly sincere man: his moods were not assumed, but genuine; and in judging any of his statements one has to consider under what circumstances they were made. When *Fidelio* was revived in 1806 there seemed a chance of Beethoven's winning both fame and fortune, but he fancied he was being swindled, and withdrew his score after the third performance. Then for Schindler, who was Beethoven's Boswell, at one time no words could express Beethoven's contempt for him, but we find this was only a momentary explosion of anger; the clouds rolled by, and friendship was restored.

Letters to v. Zmeskall and Nanette Streicher offer substantial proof that Beethoven did not know himself; for more than once in his letters he declares that he disliked giving trouble to other people. Yet Zmeskall was constantly helping, for he well knew that Beethoven was a genius; while Nanette Streicher was indeed a good Samaritan, for she saw in what a deplorable state the composer was in all household matters. The letters to Zmeskall when Beethoven wanted fresh quills, or a looking-glass, or a hat changed on account of a slit in it, are at any rate most amusing, whereas those to Streicher are one long jeremiad about servants, dusters, tin spoons, scissors, neckties, stays, etc. And in reading them, one cannot but marvel at the man who, while worried by servants and having to look after trivial matters, could compose works which now afford the highest rapture. For some of his worries he blamed the Austrian Government, as, for instance, when he found it difficult to get an honest servant; or when the chimney in his room smoked.

Beethoven, like Mozart, was not in the habit of writing much about his art, yet there are some striking thoughts and comments in these letters. In one (No. 262), for instance, he speaks of *Allegro*, *Andante*, etc., those "senseless terms," in that the music often expresses something quite contrary to them. Beethoven, in another, declares it the duty of composers to be generally acquainted with ancient and modern poets, so as, for vocal music, to be able to choose the best. And here is a remarkable sentence. Beethoven is writing to his friend Andreas Streicher (Letter 381) about the *Missa Solemnis*, and he says that in writing this great work "it was my chief aim to awaken, and to render lasting, religious feeling as well in the singers as in the hearers." In similar spirit, Handel, speaking of *The Messiah*, said: "I should be sorry if I only entertained them [i.e. the audience], I wish to make them better." And

one more specimen referring to the redundant bars in the Scherzo
of the C minor Symphony: "You [Breitkopf and Härtel] will
receive to-morrow a list of small improvements which I made
during the performance of the symphonies—when I gave them
to you I had not heard a note of either. One must not pretend to
be so divine as not to make improvements here and there in one's
creations." And once again, in a letter to the Archduke Rudolph
referring to the bad state of his health, he regrets "that for only
a few hours in the day can I give myself up to Heaven's noblest
gift, my art, and to the Muses."

The references to great composers are most interesting. Our
composer's veneration for Bach and Handel was great; of the
ancients, indeed, he declared in a letter to the Archduke Rudolph,
that they alone possessed genius. He made early acquaintance with
Bach's *clavier* music, for before he was twelve years of age his
teacher Neefe sent a notice to *Cramer's Magazine* about his talented
pupil who "played the greater part of Bach's *Well-tempered Clavier*."
Then there is the Letter (No. 29) to Hofmeister, in which Beethoven
speaks of the high art of Bach, "the forefather of harmony," and
one to Breitkopf and Härtel, 8 April, 1803, in which he thanks
them for the beautiful things of Bach, which "I intend to keep and
study." A reference to the *Mass in B minor* deserves particular
note. It occurs in a letter to Breitkopf and Härtel (No. 107), in
which he asks for all the works of Carl Ph. Em. Bach, also "a Mass
of J. Sebastian Bach in which is a *Crucifixus* with a *Basso ostinato*,"
and of which he quotes the first four bars; it is the *Crucifixus* from
the *Hohe Messe* in B minor. Again, Dr. Bach was the barrister who
helped Beethoven in the lawsuits connected with the Kynsky estate,
and with the guardianship of the nephew. In one letter to him,
the composer writes the letters of J. S. Bach's name in musical notes.

Great, too, was his admiration of Handel. Of several references
to this composer I give a special one. The genuine joy which he felt
when Stumpff, the harp manufacturer, sent him the edition of
Handel's works, has been often spoken of. These volumes came,
however, too late for use; the composer was then on his death-bed.
But he had among his music Handel's Harpsichord Suites, and
then in a letter to Breitkopf and Härtel we learn of his having a
copy of *The Messiah*, for before the bombardment of Vienna by
Napoleon in 1809, he had gatherings at his rooms for the practising
of choral works.

The letter to Abbé Stadler *re* the Mozart *Requiem* shows how he
respected that composer. There are, also, references to *Don Giovanni*
and to the *Magic Flute* which prove that, whatever he may have

thought of the morality, or rather immorality, of the book of the former opera, he fully appreciated the music. The second opera furnished him with nicknames for his depraved sister-in-law, also for Schindler: the one was Queen of Night, while the other was surnamed Papageno. Haydn is spoken of in a way which shows, at any rate, that in spite of all the natural antagonism between the old and the rising master, they were on a friendly footing. When Beethoven wrote (Letter 73) to Prince Esterhazy that he should, with much fear and trembling, send him his *Mass in C*, seeing that "You, most serene prince, are accustomed to hear the inimitable masterpieces of the great Haydn," he was, perhaps, smiling in his sleeve. Of Handel, Haydn and Mozart, in the charming letter to Emilie M. (Letter 131) he says: "Do not snatch the laurel wreaths from them; they are entitled to them, as yet I am not."

A fragment of a letter from Weber is given *re* performance of *Fidelio* under his direction. And not only is it a fragment, but unfortunately all that remains of a "lively correspondence" between the two composers. Let us hope that documents of such great interest will one day be discovered.

Haydn and Schubert took great interest in folk melodies, and made frequent use of them in their works. So with Beethoven. The theme in the fifth movement of the Septet, according to Ries, is a Rhenish folk melody, and the Trio of the Presto of the Seventh Symphony appears to be an Austrian Hymn to the Virgin; moreover there are the Russian national melodies introduced into the "Rasumowsky" Quartets. In the Letters we have further proof of Beethoven's interest in such music. In a letter to George Thomson, in referring to the Scottish nation, he speaks of "le génie de ses chansons." But in Letter 322 are given two Austrian folk-songs, music and words. The first, *Das liebe Käzchen*, appears to have been in the composer's mind when he wrote the *Allegro molto* of the pianoforte Sonata in A flat (Op. 110). The second is entitled *Der Knabe auf dem Berge*. Beethoven sent them to Simrock, and says: "The accompaniment is my own"; then he adds: "You could have many things of the kind from me." It is not at all unlikely that other folk-tunes than those known may still be traced in his works.

Beethoven was a great reader. The only regular instruction he received was at a public school at Bonn, but this ceased when he was thirteen. It was at the house of the Breunings that he became acquainted not only with German literature, but most probably with Homer and Plutarch. Voss's translation of the *Odyssey* must have formed part of the library of this highly-cultured family. In one of his letters, speaking of Homer, Beethoven says: "Whom I know, unfortunately, only in translation." Plutarch's *Lives* was another of Beethoven's favourite books. This we know from Schindler, and in the letters there is more than one sign that he was familiar with it.

Of Shakespeare there are only indirect traces in the Letters; from what Schindler has told us, there is, however, abundant evidence of his acquaintance with the poet's works. As regards Goethe, Beethoven says he knew him, i.e. his poems, almost from childhood, and here again we trace the influence of the Breuning family. To Goethe and his plays and poems there are, of course, many references. The meeting of the poet and tone-poet at Teplitz was a disappointment on both sides. Goethe pitied Beethoven on account of his rough manners and deafness, and naturally the polished courtier was not in sympathy with the composer's radical opinions. The impression which the man Goethe made on Beethoven is graphically expressed in the words: "One cannot laugh much at the ridiculous things that *virtuosi* do, when poets, who ought to be looked upon as the principal teachers of the nation, forget everything else amidst this glitter."

But a word must be said about the Bible. Grove, in his article, says: "It is strange that the Bible does not appear to have been one of his favourite books"; also that references to it are very rare. There are, however, many signs, some direct, some indirect, that Beethoven was a Bible reader. The direct references may be rare, but there are many sentences which are practically paraphrases of Bible words. The statement of Grove, viz., that Beethoven's deeply religious feeling "is shown by many and many a sentence in his letters," is more than confirmed in the new letters published in this edition, especially those addressed to the magistrates in the lawsuits respecting the guardianship of his nephew.

Of puns and various plays upon words there is abundance—one might say superabundance. And with regard to these it is evident that in translation, except in some instances where equivalent terms have been found, either the idea of reproducing the pun or play on word had to be abandoned; or, as has been done here in other instances, the German words have been inserted in square brackets. To take a simple example. Beethoven speaks of a person named Traeg as *traeg*, i.e. slow. The mere fact of having to explain such mild specimens of humour is, of course, fatal; yet as this punning propensity runs through the whole of the letters, some attempt had to be made to show it in translation. Of Beethoven's puns, as one can well imagine, some were very good, others very bad. He never missed an opportunity with names of composers.

We need not call attention to familiar jokes, but would note two in connection with Bach. The composer hears that Anna Regina Bach, the last surviving child of the great composer, is in distress, and in writing to Hofmeister expresses the hope that something may be done for this "brook" before it dries up. The play upon the word "Bach" is explained in the notes to that letter. The other is a play upon the *basso ostinato* of the *Crucifixus* in Bach's *B minor Mass*. Beethoven tells his publisher, Steiner, that this *basso* resembles him, i.e. in his obstinacy with regard to terms. He writes to Ries that he hears J. B. Cramer does not approve of his (Beethoven's) music, and so calls him a Counter-subject; the Society of Musical Friends (*Gesellschaft der Musikfreunde*) is a Society of Fiends, and so on.

Much has been written about Wagner's dogs and love of animals generally. Of Beethoven the only reference hitherto as to animals was the story of the horse presented to the composer by Count Browne. In this edition three letters are published for the first time in which we hear about dogs. In the one describing the scene at Artaria's about the quintet in C, Beethoven mentions that in the confusion his brother lost his pet dog; while in two others (Nos. 68 and 69) is an account of "Gigaud," which belonged to the Gleichensteins, and which followed Beethoven home and proved a pleasant companion.

By permission of Dr. A. C. Kalischer, his notes have been compressed. Many refer to the German text, to various readings of the original letters, criticisms of those readings, all of which, in the absence of the German text, would be meaningless. Again, Dr. Kalischer often gives a paraphrase of the contents of letters, and in many instances, actual quotations from them. In compressing I have omitted nothing that seemed of importance. Beethoven's Letters have, of course, been translated in full.

In conclusion, I have to express my warmest thanks to Viscount Althorp, Stephen Lewis Courtauld, Esq., Sir George Donaldson, Dr. Theodor Frimmel, Alfred Morten, Esq., Sir George Henschel, Arthur F. Hill, Esq., Professor Dr. Knickenberg (Bonn), Mrs. J. A. Fuller Maitland, Dr. Joseph Mantuani (Vienna), Sir Hubert Parry, Dr. Erich Prieger, Herr Adolf Schlösser, M. Julien Tiersot (Paris), and Miss E. A. Willmott, for allowing me to copy unpublished letters, and to publish the facsimiles described in the lists of Illustrations. I have also to thank the publishers, Herren Schuster and Loefler and Herren Georg Müller, Munich, for granting permission to take facsimiles of portraits from *Die Musik* and from Dr. Th. Frimmel's *Beethoven Studien*, vol. ii. My thanks are like-

Beethoven's Birthplace
From a drawing by Herbert Railton

wise due to F. G. Edwards, Esq., William Barclay Squire, Esq., for kind assistance, also to Dr. Julius Reusch, whom I consulted with regard to Austrian dialect words, imperfect, ungrammatical and obscure sentences.

J. S. SHEDLOCK.

London, 1909.

The miniature reproduced in facsimile by the kind permission of Sir George Henschel (see *facing page* 4) was identified by Ritter von Breuning as the work of a young Bonn painter, Gerhard von Kügelgen.

LIST OF ILLUSTRATIONS

BEETHOVEN'S LETTERS

1. Dedication Letter to the Prince Elector, MAX FRIEDRICH of Cologne

Most illustrious!

Music from my fourth year began to be the first of my youthful occupations. Thus early acquainted with the gracious muse who tuned my soul to pure harmonies, I became fond of her, and, as it often seemed to me, she of me. I have already reached my eleventh year; and since then often has my muse whispered to me in inspired hours: "Try for once and write down the harmonies of thy soul!" Eleven years old—methought—and how would an author's air become me? And what would masters of the art probably say to it? I almost became diffident. Yet my muse so willed—I obeyed, and wrote.

May I now venture, most illustrious Prince, to place at the foot of your throne the first-fruits of my youthful works? And may I venture to hope that you will bestow on them the benevolent paternal look of your encouraging approval? Oh yes! the arts and sciences have always found in you a wise protector, a generous patron, and budding talent has prospered under your noble, paternal care.—

Full of this encouraging assurance, I venture to approach Your most serene Highness with these youthful attempts. Accept them as a pure offering of childlike homage, and look graciously on them, and on their young author.

The above appears on the reverse side of the title-page of the first publication. The title is as follows :

"Three Sonatas for pianoforte dedicated to the Most worthy Archbishop and Prince Elector of Cologne, Maximilian Friedrich, my most gracious Lord.

"Dedicated and composed by Ludwig van Beethoven,
"Aged eleven."

Published by Councillor Bossler, Spires.

No. 21.   Price 1 fl. 30 kr.

1

[According to the original edition of the three pianoforte sonatas in E flat, F minor, and D, published in 1783. In that year Beethoven was not eleven, but thirteen years old. Not only the composer, but many of his friends, maintained for a long time that he was born in 1772. Even Joh. Aloys Schlosser, in the first small Beethoven Biography, which appeared in 1828, wrote: "Ludwig van Beethoven was born in the year 1772."]

2. To Councillor Dr. Von SCHADEN, Augsburg

September 15th,
Bonn, 1787.

WELL AND NOBLY BORN AND SPECIALLY WORTHY FRIEND,

I can easily imagine what you think of me; and I cannot deny that you have good cause for not entertaining a good opinion of me. In spite of that, I will not offer any excuse until I have shown the causes, whereby I venture to hope that my excuses will be accepted. I must acknowledge that since I left Augsburg, my happiness, and with it my health, began to fail; the nearer I approached my native city, the more frequent were my father's letters urging me to travel faster than I should have done under ordinary circumstances, as my mother's state of health was far from satisfactory. I hurried as fast as I could, for I myself, indeed, became unwell. The longing once more to see my sick mother caused me to make light of all obstacles, and helped me to overcome the greatest difficulties. I found my mother still alive, but in the weakest possible state; she was dying of consumption, and the end came about seven weeks ago, after she had endured much pain and suffering. She was to me such a good, lovable mother, my best friend. Oh! who was happier than I, when I could still utter the sweet name of mother, and heed was paid to it; and to whom can I say it now? —to the dumb pictures resembling her, the creations of my imagination? Since I have been here, I have enjoyed only a few pleasant hours; during the whole time I have been troubled with asthma, and I much fear that it will lead to consumption. I also suffer from melancholy which for me is almost as great an evil as my illness itself. Imagine yourself now in my place, and I hope that you will forgive my long silence. As you showed extraordinary kindness and friendship at Augsburg in lending me three carolins, I must beg of you to be still patient with me. My journey was expensive, and here I have not the slightest hope of earning anything; the fates have not been favourable to me here in Bonn.

Please excuse my having detained you so long with my prattling, but was it absolutely necessary to vindicate myself. I hope you will not refuse still to extend to me your honoured friendship; I have

no greater desire than to prove myself to some degree worthy
of it.

   I am, with all respect,
     Your most obedient servant and friend,
          L. v. BEETHOVEN,
      Organist to the Prince Elector of Cologne.
A MONSIEUR,
   MONSIEUR DE SCHADEN
    Conseilièr d'augspurg
    à augspurg.

[This, the first real letter by Beethoven which we possess, first appeared
in the *Vossische Zeitung*, 21 August, 1845, at the time of the inauguration
of the Beethoven monument at Bonn.]

3. TO FRL. ELEONORE VON BREUNING

         [BONN, *about* 1791]
           Fragment.

  . . The neckcloth worked with your own hand came to me
as a great surprise. It awoke in me feelings of sadness, however
pleasant the thing in itself. It reminded me of former times; also
your magnanimous behaviour filled me with shame. In truth, I
did not think that you still considered me worthy of your remembrance. Oh! if only you could have seen how this incident affected
me yesterday, you certainly would not accuse me of exaggeration,
if I now say to you, that your token of remembrance caused me to
weep and feel very sad. I entreat you, however little I deserve
faith in your eyes, to believe, *my friend* (let me still ever call you
thus), that I have deeply suffered, and still suffer, through the loss
of your friendship. Never shall I forget you and your dear mother.
Your kindness was so great that it will be long ere I can make
good my loss. I know what I have forfeited, and what you were to
me, but—to fill up this blank I should have to recall scenes unpleasant for you to hear, and for me to describe. As a small return
for your kind remembrance of me, I take the liberty of sending you
herewith these Variations and the Rondo with violin. I am very
busy, otherwise I would have copied for you the long-promised
Sonata. In my manuscript it is little more than a sketch, and it
would have been difficult even for Paraquin, clever as he is, to copy
it out. You can have the Rondo copied and then the score returned
to me. I am sending you the only one of my compositions of which

you could probably make any use; and as, besides, you are going away to Kerpen, I thought this trifle might give you some pleasure.

Farewell, my friend. It is impossible for me to call you otherwise; and however indifferent I may be to you, pray believe that I honour you and your mother just as much as formerly. Moreover, if it be in my power to please you in any way, I beg you not to ignore me; it is the only means left for me to show gratitude for the friendship which I have enjoyed.

A pleasant journey, and bring your dear mother back fully restored to health. And think sometimes of one who still always esteems you.   Your friend,

BEETHOVEN.

4. To the Prince Elector, MAX FRANZ, Cologne

[VIENNA, *end of April or beginning of May*, 1793.]

MOST REVEREND AND ILLUSTRIOUS PRINCE ELECTOR, MOST GRACIOUS
     SOVEREIGN,

A few years ago it pleased your Highness to pension off my father, the court tenor singer, van Beethoven; also, by a most gracious decree, to assign to me 100 rix-thalers of that pension, so that I might be able to clothe, feed, and educate my two younger brothers, also to discharge our father's debts.

I wished to place this decree before your chief land-steward, but my father earnestly begged me not to do it, so that it might not publicly appear as if he himself were incapable of providing for his family. And he added that he himself would hand over to me twenty-five rix-thalers every quarter, and that promise was always duly kept.

Now after his death (which followed last year in December) I wished to make use of your most gracious kindness by presenting the above-named decree, when I was startled to find that my father had made away with it.

With highest respect, I therefore beg your Serene Highness most graciously to renew this decree, and to instruct your land-steward to hand over to me the gracious salary for the quarter just elapsed (due at the beginning of February).

Your Serene Highness's most dutiful and faithful

LUD. V. BEETHOVEN
(Court Organist).

[Both writers consulted the Rhenish archives at Düsseldorf. This petition, circumspect as it is, gives a clear insight into the sad relationship between Beethoven and his unfortunate father, who died suddenly on 18 December,

Beethoven at the age of twenty-one (1791)

From a miniature by Gerhard von Kügelgen, in the
possession of Sir George Henschel

1792—very soon, therefore, after his son's arrival in Vienna. The petition was answered. According to Deiters, Beethoven received fifty thalers every quarter up to March 1794. With that, all connection between Beethoven and the Electorate ceased.]

5. To Frl. ELEONORE Von BREUNING, Bonn

VIENNA, *November* 2, 1793.

HONOURED ELEONORE, MY DEAREST FRIEND,

I shall soon have been in this capital a whole year, yet only now do you receive a letter from me, but you were certainly constantly in my thoughts. Frequently, indeed, did I hold converse with you and your dear family, but, for the most part, not with the tranquillity of mind which I should have liked. Then it was that the fatal quarrel hovered before me, and my former behaviour appeared to me so abominable. But the past cannot be undone, and what would I not give if I could blot out of my life my former conduct so dishonouring to me, so contrary to my character. Many circumstances, indeed, kept us at a distance from each other, and, as I presume, it was especially the insinuations resulting from conversations on either side which prevented all reconciliation. Each of us believed that he was convinced of the truth of what he said, and yet it was mere anger, and we were both deceived. Your good and noble character is indeed a guarantee that I have long since been forgiven. But true repentance consists, so it is said, in acknowledging one's faults, and this I intended to do. And now let us draw a curtain over the whole story, and only learn from it the lesson that when friends fall out it is always better to have no go-between, but for friend to turn directly to friend.

Herewith you receive a dedication from me to yourself, and I only wish that the work were more important, more worthy of you. I have been worried here to publish this small work, and I make use of this opportunity to give you, my adorable Eleonore, a proof of my high esteem and of my friendship towards you, and of my constant remembrance of your family. Accept this trifle, and realise that it comes from a friend who holds you in high esteem. Oh, if it only gives you pleasure, I am fully rewarded. Let it be a small re-awakening of that time in which I spent so many and such happy hours in your home; it may, perhaps, keep me in your remembrance, until one day I return, but that will not be for a long time. Oh, how we shall then rejoice, my dear friend. You will then find your friend a more cheerful being, for whom time and his better fortune have smoothed down the furrows of the horrid past. If you happen to see B. Koch, please tell her that it is not nice of her

not to have sent me a single line. For I have written twice; to Malchus
I wrote three times—and no answer. Tell her that if she would not
write, she ought to have urged Malchus to do so.

As conclusion to my letter, I add a request; it is that I may be
lucky enough, my dear friend, again to possess a waistcoat worked
by you in goat's wool. Forgive this indiscreet request from your
friend. It arises from the great preference I have for anything
coming from your hands, and as a secret I may say to you that in
this there is at bottom a little vanity, viz., to be able to say that
I possess something given to me by one of the best, most worthy
young ladies in Bonn. I still have the first one which you were
kind enough to give me in Bonn, but it is now so out of fashion
that I can only keep it in my wardrobe as a precious gift from
you. If you would soon write me a nice letter, it would afford me
great pleasure. If perchance my letters give you pleasure, I certainly
promise that I will willingly send news as often as I can. For everything is welcome to me whereby I can show you in what esteem
you are held by

Your true friend,
L. v. BEETHOVEN.

P.S.—The V[ariations] will be somewhat difficult to play,
especially the shakes in the Coda. But don't let that alarm you. It
is so arranged that you need only play the shake; the other notes
you leave out, as they are also in the violin part. I never would have
written anything of the kind, but I had already frequently noticed
that there was some one in V. who generally, when I have been
improvising of an evening, noted down next day many of my
peculiarities in composing, and boasted about them. Now as I
foresaw that such things would soon appear in [print], I resolved
to be beforehand with them. And there was another reason for
perplexing the pianists here, viz., many of them are my deadly
enemies, so I wished in this way to take vengeance on them, for
I knew beforehand that here and there the Variations would be
put before them, and that these gentlemen would come off badly.

[This first letter of Beethoven to his honoured friend, about a year after
his arrival in Vienna, offers to us a last glimpse of the great quarrel between
him and the Breuning family in Bonn, where already harmony had been
restored; of this the above-mentioned Album offers substantial proof. The
Variations mentioned in the above letter are those for pianoforte and violin
on the well-known theme *Se vuol ballare*, from Mozart's *Figaro*. They were
published, with dedication to Frl. von Breuning, in 1793, by Artaria as
Op. 1, but afterwards as No. 1, when the three Trios were marked as Op. 1.
B. Koch was Barbara Koch, who afterwards became Countess Belderbusch,
one of the most distinguished women of her day.]

6. To the Music Publisher N. SIMROCK, Bonn

VIENNA, *August 2*, 1794.

DEAR SIMROCK,

I deserved a bit of a scolding from you, for having kept back your Variations so long, but I am telling you no lie when I say that pressing business prevented me from correcting sooner. What is still amiss, you will find out yourself. For the rest, I must congratulate you on your printing, which is beautiful, clear, and readable; in fact, if you continue thus, you will become chief in the art of printing—I mean, of course, music-printing.

In my last letter I promised to send you something of mine, and you interpreted it as *cavalier* talk; why, then, have I deserved this *predicate*? Faugh! who in these democratic times would accept such language? In order to forfeit the *predicate* you have dubbed me with, as soon as I have completed the grand *Revue* of my compositions, and that will not take me long, you shall have something that you certainly will print. I have been on the look-out for a *Commissionaire*, and have found a first-rate, able man. His name is Traeg. You have only to write to him or to me what terms you will accept. He wants from you a third *discount*. Only the devil would understand business of that sort.

It is very warm here; the Viennese are afraid that it will soon be impossible for them to have any *ice-creams*; for as the winter was mild, ice is rare. Many persons of *importance* have been arrested; they say there was fear of a *revolution* breaking out—but it is my belief that so long as an Austrian can get his brown beer and sausages there will be no revolution. The gates in the suburbs are ordered to be closed at ten o'clock at night. The soldiers have loaded guns. One dare not speak too loud, otherwise the police will accommodate you for the night.

Are your daughters already grown up, train one to be my bride, for if I am in Bonn unmarried I shall certainly not stop so long. You also must really have an anxious time of it!

What is good Ries doing? I will soon write to him. He must surely have a bad opinion of me, but that cursed writing is always a trouble to me.

Have you already performed my part [*Partie*]? Write to me occasionally.

Your,

BEETHOVEN.

Please send me also some copies of the first Variations.

[The tone of the letter shows us that in Beethoven's fiery mind revolutionary ideas had already found the right soil in which they could continue unceasingly to develop. The variations in question are most probably the " Waldstein " Variations for four hands in C and the thirteen variations for pianoforte solo in A on *Es war einmal ein alter Mann,* both of which were published by Simrock in 1794 without opus number.]

7. To Dr. FRANZ WEGELER, Vienna

Between 1794–1796.

MY DEAREST, MY BEST ONE!

What a horrid picture you have drawn to me of myself. I recognise it; I do not deserve your friendship. You are so noble, so kindly disposed, and now for the first time I do not dare to compare myself with you; I have fallen far below you. Alas! for weeks I have given pain to my best, my noblest friend. You believe I have ceased to be kind-hearted, but, thank heaven, 'tis not so. It was not intentional, thought-out malice on my part, which caused me to act thus; but my unpardonable thoughtlessness, which prevented me from seeing the matter in the right light. I am thoroughly ashamed for your sake, also for mine. I scarcely venture to beg you to restore your friendship. Ah! Wegeler, *my only consolation is that you knew me almost from my childhood,* and—oh, let me say it myself—I was really always of good disposition, and in my dealings always strove to be upright and honest; how, otherwise, could you have loved me! Could I, then, in so short a time have suddenly changed so terribly, so greatly to my disadvantage? Impossible that these feelings for what is great and good should all of a sudden become extinct. My Wegeler, dear and best one, venture once again to come to the arms of your B. Trust to the good qualities which you formerly found in him. I will vouch for it that the pure temple of holy friendship which you will erect on it will for ever stand firm; no chance event, no storm will be able to shake its foundations—firm—eternal— our friendship—forgiveness—forgetting—revival of dying, sinking friendship. Oh, Wegeler! do not cast off this hand of reconciliation; place your hand in mine—O God!—but no more—I myself come to you and throw myself in your arms, and sue for the lost friend, and you will give yourself to me full of contrition, who loves and ever will be mindful of you.

BEETHOVEN.

I have just received your letter, on my return home.

[Wegeler only gives a fragment of this letter just to show that after passionate outbursts, Beethoven's "prayer for forgiveness was *out of all proportion* to the fault committed." This letter, however, has acquired great importance in the history of our composer, in that it upsets Thayer's statement that it was only *after* his first journey to Vienna that he made the acquaintance of Wegeler and of the Breuning family.]

8. To his Brother NIKOLAUS JOHANN Von BEETHOVEN

PRAGUE, *February* 19, 1796.

DEAR BROTHER,

Now that you may at any rate know where I am and what I am doing, I must write you a letter. First of all, I am getting on well, very well. My art wins for me friends and esteem. What more can I want. I am also earning this time a fair amount of money. I shall stay here for a few weeks, and then travel to *Dresden, Leipzig* and *Berlin*; it will be at least six weeks before I return. I hope your residence in Vienna will please you more and more—only beware of the whole tribe of bad women. Have you already been to see cousin Elss [?]? You might write me a letter if you have time and inclination. F. Lichnowski will probably soon return to Vienna; he has already gone away from here. In case you want money, you can boldly go to him, for he still owes me some. For the rest, I hope that you may become more and more prosperous, also that I may aid in bringing this about. Farewell, dear brother, and sometimes think of

Your true, faithful brother,

L. BEETHOVEN.

Greetings to brother Caspar [*scratched out with a thick stroke of the pen, but afterwards* ~~~~~~~~~ *placed under it*].

My address is the Golden Unicorn at the Kleinseite.

[The letter is addressed: "To be delivered to my brother, Nicholaus Beethoven, at the apothecary's shop at the Kärnthner Thor. Herr v. Z. is requested to hand this letter to the wig-maker, who will deliver it." "Herr von Z." must be the court secretary, N. Zmeskall von Domanovecz, to whom are addressed the following and many other letters.]

9. To the I.R. Court Secretary, N. ZMESKALL Von DOMANOVECZ

[1796–1798.]

MY VERY CHEAP BARON,

Tell the *guitarist* to come to me this very day. *Amenda* instead of an *Amende*, which he sometimes deserves for his bad pauses, shall get me this most welcome *guitarist*. If possible, let the so-named come to me at five o'clock; if not, to-morrow morning at five or six o'clock, but if I should be asleep, he must not wake me.

Adieu, mon ami à bon Marché, perhaps we may see each other at the Swan.

[Probably 120 letters and notes to the very musical Baron Nicolaus Zmeskall (Zmeskall von Domanovecz und Lestynie) have been preserved, ranging from 1796 through the whole of Beethoven's life. The court secretary, a distinguished violoncellist, was one of the most trustworthy friends of the composer, and about ten years his senior; and, all things considered, his influence was most beneficial. At an early stage, convinced of his friend's greatness, Zmeskall collected everything he received from Beethoven; even the smallest note he thought worthy of preservation. Beethoven's bursts of humour, even the roughest jokes, he accepted without ill-will or vexation, like a true "pious sheep." The proof of the high esteem in which he was held by the composer is to be found in the dedication to him of the Quartet in F minor (Op. 95).—Amenda, on whose name Beethoven gives a specimen of his favourite habit of playing upon words, a priest in Courland, also a musician, was one of Beethoven's earliest friends in Vienna; letters soon to be given show that he left that city even before 1800. The "guitarist" was the fellow-student of Amenda, the theologian G. H. Mylich, who excelled in singing and as a performer on the guitar.—The "Swan" inn, a favourite resort of the friends, is frequently mentioned in these letters.]

10. To Baron ZMESKALL

[1796.]

The Music Count from to-day is dishonoured and cashiered. The first violin will be sent *as an exile* to Siberia. For a whole month the Baron is *forbidden to ask questions*; he must not be *over-hasty*, and he must only concern himself about his *ipse Miserum*.

[Wegeler already speaks about the performances of music, quartet parties at the house of Prince Lichnowsky during his second stay in Vienna (1794–6). The first violin is most probably Ignaz Schuppanzigh. The "Music Count" is Zmeskall; Wegeler, in connection with these musical meetings, mentions an "amateur Zmeskall."]

11. To LENZ Von BREUNING (IN HIS ALBUM)

October 1797.

Die Wahrheit ist vorhanden für den Weisen,
Die Schönheit für ein fühlend Herz;
Sie beide gehören für einander.[1]

DEAR, GOOD BREUNING,

Never shall I forget the days which I spent with you, both formerly in Bonn as well as here. Continue to be my friend, as you will always find me yours.

Your true friend,
L. v. BEETHOVEN.

[The lines at the head are not, as commonly thought, Beethoven's, but Schiller's, as I found out by chance some years ago. They are the words of the Marquis of Posa to the Queen in the fourth act of *Don Carlos*. This album-leaf was first communicated by Wegeler. Lenz—or more exactly, Lorenz von Breuning—was the youngest of the Breuning children. Like Wegeler he studied medicine, but died in the following year at Bonn (10 April, 1798), at the early age of twenty-one. He was more than six years younger than his pianoforte-teacher and friend Beethoven.]

12. To THE COURT SECRETARY VON ZMESKALL

[1798.]

DEAREST SCAVENGER OF A BARON,

Je vous suis bien obligé pour votre faiblesse de vos yeux. For the rest, take care in future when I am in a jolly mood, as is sometimes the case, not to spoil it; for yesterday, through your Zmeskall-domanovezian chatter, I became quite sad. The devil take you; I don't want to know anything about your whole system of ethics. *Power* is the morality of men who stand out from the rest, and it is also mine. And if you begin again to-day, I will worry you until you find everything I do, good and praiseworthy, for I am coming to the Swan; I should prefer the Ox, but that depends upon your *Zmeskalian Domanovezian* decision (*réponse*). Adieu, Baron Ba . . . ron ron | nor | orn | rno | onr | .

[1] The Schiller lines may be translated thus:

Wisdom is for the wise,
Beauty for a feeling heart;
And both belong to each other.

(*Voilà quelque chose* out of the pawnbroker's shop.)

[Of Beethoven's "pawnbroker's shop" (*Versatzamt*), i.e. transposition of letters and syllables, we have many specimens.]

13. TO THE SAME

[1798?]

BEST MUSIC COUNT,

Do please send me one or several pens, as I am really in great want of them. As soon as I find out where really good ones are to be had, I will buy some.

I hope to see your at the Swan to-day.

Adieu, dearest Music Count,

Your, etc.

[The Music Count generally saw that he had quills properly cut; and these Beethoven used for copying music. This continued for about ten years. For him the count was "the best quill-man in the world."]

14. DEDICATION OF OP. 9 TO COUNT BROWNE

VIENNA, *July* 20, 1798.

Monsieur, l'auteur, vivement pénétré de votre munificence aussi délicate que libérale, se réjouit, de pouvoir le dire au monde, en vous dédiant cette œuvre. Si les productions de l'art, que Vous honorez de Votre protection en Connoisseur, dépendaient moins de l'inspiration du génie, que de la bonne volonté de faire de son mieux, l'auteur aurait la satisfaction tant désirée, de présenter au premier Mécène de sa Muse la meilleure de ses œuvres.

[The above was the Dedication in the earliest edition of the Three String Trios in G, D, and C minor (Op. 9).

There are two special points to notice in this dedication: firstly that Beethoven names Count Browne *le premier Mécène de sa Muse*; and secondly that he describes the Three String Trios (Op. 9) as the best of his (early) works. The slightly demonstrative character of this dedication leads one to conclude that about this time Beethoven had become somewhat uneasy in Lichnowsky's house, so that he was compelled to lead a trump-card against him, first Lichnowsky, then Browne. To the same count was dedicated the great Sonata in B flat (Op. 22), and to his wife, an excellent pianist, among other things, the three sonatas (Op. 10). From 1805, however, no more is heard of this artistic pair in connection with Beethoven.]

15. TO BARON ZMESKALL

[1799–1800?]

DEAREST CONTE DI MUSICA,

May you be the better for your sleep, and for to-day we wish you a good appetite and good digestion, which is all that is necessary for a man's existence; and yet for everything we have to pay such a high price. Yes, dearest *Conte*, trusty *amico*, times are bad, our treasury is empty, our income low, and we, most gracious lord, are compelled to humble ourselves, and to beg of you a loan of 5 gulden which we will return to you within the next few days. —With regard to the documents, we order the strictest inquiry, since in the case of any cheatings we are resolved to severely punish the criminal.

Farewell, dearly beloved *amico* and *conte di musica*.

Your most affectionate

L. v. BHVN.

Given in our Composition Cabinet.

16. To the Same

[*c.* 1799.]

DEAR ZMESKALL,

I shall probably be unable to come to Countess Deym's to-day, as since last night I have been suffering from a bad cold. I therefore commend her to your care at the rehearsal. As for the rendering of the music, I was there yesterday, and you will have scarcely anything to tell her, except about the *tempi*. But *do* tell me whether or not the name of the *captain who whistled several times at Tost's house is Gilg*? I particularly want to know.

[Countess Josephine Deym, like her sister Therese Brunswick and Countess Guicciardi, was a pianoforte pupil of Beethoven's. In the album of the two sisters Beethoven wrote Variations for four hands. The little work based on Beethoven's setting of Goethe's *Ich denke dein* was dedicated to them, and appeared in 1805, when Countess Dehm was already a widow. Her second husband was the Russian Baron von Stackelberg. Between the years 1800–3 Beethoven and his circle of intimate friends were frequent visitors at the house of Count Deym.]

17. To the Composer J. N. HUMMEL

[VIENNA, *c.* 1799.]

Do not come any more to me. You are a false fellow, and the knacker take all such.

BEETHOVEN.

18. To the Same

[*The next day.*]

GOOD FRIEND NAZERL,

You are an honourable fellow, and I see you were right. So come this afternoon to me. You will also find Schuppanzigh, and both of us will blow you up, thump you, and shake you, so you will have a fine time of it.

Your Beethoven, also named Mehlschöberl, embraces you.

[These two characteristic notes to Johann Nepomuk (— Natzerl) Hummel are here given according to Thayer. At the time Hummel was studying with Albrechtsberger and Salieri, and the notes show how intimate was the friendship between Beethoven and Hummel. It is interesting to see how the amusing nickname "Mehlschöberl" appeared already at this period to be current among the composer's friends. In a favourite burlesque, *Das lustige Beilage*, the cook Mehlschöberl plays a prominent part. Ignaz v. Seyfried tells us that Beethoven, during the last period of his earthly pilgrimage, being altogether dissatisfied with his kitchen fairy, took into his head to be his own cook, and to invite his friends to the culinary delicacies which he himself had prepared, and thus humorously entitled himself "Cook Mehlschöberl."]

19. To Fräulein GERARDI

[1798?]

My dear Frl. G.,

If I told you that the verses you just sent me did not perplex me, I should be telling a lie. It is a peculiar sensation to see, to hear one's self praised, and then to be conscious of one's weakness, as I am. I always look upon such opportunities as warnings to approach nearer, however difficult it may be, to the unattainable goal which art and nature set before us. These verses are really beautiful, but they have just the one fault, which, indeed, it is customary to find in poets; for *that which they wish to see and to hear*, they actually do see and hear, however far it may be, at times, below their ideal. You can readily understand that I should be glad *to make the acquaintance of the poet, or poetess*, and now also I tender my thanks to you for the kindness shown

to your admirer,

BEETHOVEN.

À Mademoiselle,
    Mademoiselle de Gerardi.

[The family of the excellent amateur vocalist, Christine Gerardi (Gerhardi) to whom the letter was addressed, came from Tuscany to Vienna, and the young lady, who was spoken of as "the greatest singer of Vienna," married the physician, Dr. Joseph von Frank, most probably in 1798. Their house became a centre of intellectual life in the Austrian capital.]

20. To the Same

[1798?]

Dear Chr.,

You let me hear something yesterday about a portrait of myself. I wish you to proceed somewhat carefully in the matter. I fear if we return it through F., the disagreeable B. or the arch-fool Joseph might interfere, and then the affair might be intended as a mean trick played on me, and that would be really most annoying. I should have to avenge myself, and the whole *populasse* does not deserve it. Try to get hold of the thing as well as you can. I assure you that after this I should put a notice in the newspaper, requesting all painters not to take my portrait without my consent, were I not afraid of falling into perplexity, over my own countenance. As to the matter of taking off my hat, it is altogether stupid, and at the same time too impolite for me to retaliate. Pray explain to him the truth about the walk.

Adieu. The devil take you.

[So far as can be made out, some painter had taken Beethoven's portrait, so to speak, from behind. There had been more talk about the portrait—by no means a successful one—than was pleasant to Beethoven, so that he had to protest against it, without wishing to give offence to the artist. The "disagreeable B." was probably the physician, Dr. Bolderini, a friend of Beethoven; and the "arch-fool Joseph," Christine's admirer, Joseph Frank, afterwards her husband. Beethoven appears to have been annoyed at the jealousy of Joseph Frank, evidently the favoured one.]

21. To CARL AMENDA

[1799.]

To-day I received a letter inviting me to Mödling in the country; I have accepted it, and start off this very evening to spend a few days there. It was all the more welcome to me, for my lacerated heart would have suffered all the more, although the main attack has again been repelled; but I am not yet quite certain whether my plan will prevent it. Yesterday a journey to Poland in September was proposed to me, and as I shall not be put to any travelling or other expenses, and as I shall be able to earn money, I have accepted.

Farewell, dear A., and give me speedy news from the places you stop at on the way, and also when you have arrived home. Pleasant journey, and do not forget

Your

BEETHOVEN.

[The happy period of this friendship was about 1798–9. The "lacerated heart" is probably connected with Beethoven's first attempt at marriage. He had lost his heart, easily susceptible of love, to the excellent vocalist Magdalene Willmann,[1] then in Vienna; he made a serious offer to her, which, however, met with no response. In that same year she married Herr Galvani. Nothing came of the projected journey to Poland.]

22. TO THE SAME

[1799.]

I lose not a moment in giving you what Prince L[ichnowsky] sent for you. It is only a small sum, but he is now about to start on a journey, and you, of course, know what one wants at such a time.

Yes, dear, good Amenda, again I must repeat that I am extremely sorry that you did not let me know sooner how you were situated. Things could have been arranged quite differently, and I should not now be anxious lest you might be in want of something while travelling. For the moment I am so situated that I can spare nothing, but this cannot last very long, so I earnestly beg of you, wherever you may be, and whenever you find yourself in want of anything, at once to let me know; for you can rest assured that I will help you without delay. As I do not know whether you may not be starting off to-morrow, I felt I must say all this to you.

In haste,
Your,
BTHVN.

[When the enthusiastic friends were forced to part in June 1799, Beethoven honoured his theological and musical friend with a carefully written copy of the parts of the F major quartet (Op. 18, No. 1).]

23. TO THE SAME

June 25, 1799.

DEAR AMENDA,

Accept this quartet as a small remembrance of our friendship, and as often as you play it, think of the days we spent together, and at the same time of the genuine affection which I felt towards you, and which I shall ever continue to feel.

Your sincere and warm friend,
LUDWIG.

VIENNA, 1799.

[1] The fact that Beethoven made an offer to Magdalene Willmann was told to Thayer by a daughter of her brother Max.—TR.

[The above words were written by Beethoven on the work marked by him "Quartetto II." Amenda himself was an able violinist. The designation "Quartetto II." rectifies an error to which Nohl had already called attention. The statement of Ries that of the six quartets, Op. 18, the one in D was composed first, and the one in question third, was accepted. From the inscription on the presentation copy to Amenda, there is, however, no doubt that the quartet in D was the first, and the one in F the second.]

24. To CARL AMENDA, WIRBEN IN COURLAND

[VIENNA, *June* 1, 1800.]

MY DEAR, MY GOOD AMENDA, MY HEARTILY BELOVED FRIEND,

With deep emotion, with mixed pain and pleasure did I receive and read your last letter. To what can I compare your fidelity, your attachment to me. Oh! how pleasant it is that you have always remained so kind to me; yes, I also know that you, of all men, are the most trustworthy. You are no *Viennese friend*; no, you are one of those such as my native country produces. How often do I wish you were with me, for your Beethoven is most unhappy, and at strife with nature and Creator. The latter I have often cursed for exposing His creatures to the smallest chance, so that frequently the richest buds are thereby crushed and destroyed. Only think that the noblest part of me, my sense of hearing, has become very weak. Already when you were with me I noted traces of it, and I said nothing. Now it has become worse, and it remains to be seen whether it can ever be healed. The primal cause of it is the state of my bowels. So far as the latter are concerned, I am almost well, but I much fear that my hearing will not improve; maladies of that kind are the most difficult of all to cure. What a sad life I am now compelled to lead; I must avoid all that is near and dear to me, and then to be among such wretched egotistical beings such as * * *, etc. I can say that among all, Lichnowski has best stood the test. Since last year he has settled on me 600 florins, which, together with the good sale of my works, enables me to live without anxiety. Everything I write, I can sell immediately five times over, and also be well paid. I have composed a fair quantity, and as I hear that you have ordered pianofortes from * * *, I will send you many things in one of the packing-cases, so that it will not cost you so very much. Now to my consolation, a man has come here with whom intercourse is a pleasure, and whose friendship is free from all selfishness. He is one of the friends of my youth. I have often spoken to him about you, and told him that since I left my native country, you are the one whom my heart has chosen. Even he does not like * * *, the latter is and remains too weak for friendship. I consider him and * * * mere instruments on which, when it pleases me, I play; but they can never become noble witnesses of my inner and outer activity, nor be in true sympathy with me; I value them according as they are useful to me. Oh! how happy should I now be if I had my perfect hearing, for I should then hasten to you. As it is, I must in all things be behindhand; my best years will slip away without bringing forth what, with my talent and my strength, I ought to have accomplished. I must now have recourse to sad resignation. I have, it is true, resolved not to worry about all this, but how is it possible? Yes, Amenda, if, six months hence, my malady is beyond cure, then I lay claim to your help. You must leave everything and come to me. I will travel (my malady interferes least with my playing and composition, most only in conversation), and you must be my companion. I am convinced good fortune will not fail me. With whom need I be afraid of measuring my strength? Since you went away I have written music of all kinds except operas and sacred works.

Yes, do not refuse; help your friend to bear with his troubles, his infirmity. I have also greatly improved my pianoforte playing. I hope this journey may also turn to your advantage; afterwards you will always remain with me. I have duly received all your letters, and although I have only answered a few, you have been always in my mind, and my heart, as always, beats tenderly for you. *Please keep as a great secret what I have told you about my hearing ; trust no one, whoever it may be, with it.* Do write frequently; your letters, however short they may be, console me, do me good. I expect soon to get another one from you, my dear friend. Don't lend out my Quartet any more, because I have made many changes in it. I have only just learnt how to write quartets properly, as you will see when you receive them.

Now, my dear good friend, farewell! If perchance you believe that I can show you any kindness here, I need not, of course, remind you to first address yourself to

Your faithful, truly loving,
L. v. BEETHOVEN.

25. TO DR. F. WEGELER, BONN

[VIENNA, *June* 29, 1800.]

MY GOOD, DEAR WEGELER,

I am most grateful to you for thinking of me; I have so little deserved it, or sought to deserve it at your hands. And yet you are so very good, and are not kept back by anything, not even by my unpardonable negligence, but always remain a faithful, good, honest friend. That I could ever forget you, and especially all of you who were so kind and affectionate to me, no, do not believe it; there are moments in which I myself long for you—yes, and wish to spend some time with you.—My native land, the beautiful country in which I first saw the light of the world, is ever as beautiful and distinct before mine eyes as when I left you. In short, I shall regard that time as one of the happiest of my life, when I see you again, and can greet our father Rhine. When that will be I cannot yet say. This much will I tell you, that you will only see me again when I am really great; not only greater as an artist, but as a man you shall find me better, more perfect; and if in our native land there are any signs of returning prosperity, I will only use my art for the benefit of the poor. O, happy moment, how fortunate I think myself in being able to get a fatherland created here!

You want to know something about my present state; well, at the present moment it's not so bad. Since last year, Lichnowsky, who, however incredible it may seem when I tell it you, was always my warmest friend, and has remained so (of course there have been slight misunderstandings between us, but these have only strengthened our friendship), has settled a fixed sum of 600 florins on me, and I can draw it so long as I fail to find a suitable post. My compositions are bringing in a goodly sum, and I may add, it is scarcely possible for me to execute the orders given. Also, for every work I have six, seven publishers, and if I choose, even more. They do not bargain with me; I demand and they pay. You see how pleasant it is. For example, I see a friend in distress, and if my purse does not allow of my helping him, I have only to sit down, and in a short time he is relieved. Also I am more economical than I was formerly. If I should settle here, I shall certainly contrive to get one day every year for concerts, of which I have given some.

Only my envious demon, my bad health, has thrown obstacles in my way. For instance, my hearing has become weaker during the last three years. Frank wished to restore me to health by means of strengthening medicines, and to cure my deafness by means of oil of almonds, but, *prosit!* nothing came of these remedies; my hearing became worse and worse. This continued until the autumn of last year, and ofttimes I was in despair. Then an Asinus of a doctor advised cold baths, a more skilful one, the usual tepid Danube baths. These worked wonders; but my deafness remained or became worse. This winter I was truly miserable; I had terrible attacks of colic, and I fell quite back into my former state. So I remained for about four weeks, and then went to Vering. He ordered tepid Danube baths, and whenever I took one, I had to pour into it a little bottle full of strengthening stuff. He gave me no medicine until about four days ago, when he ordered pills for the stomach, and an application of herbs for the ear. And through these I can say I feel stronger and better; only the humming in my ears continues day and night without ceasing. I may truly say that my life is a wretched one. For the last two years I have avoided all society, for it is impossible for me to say to people, "I am deaf." Were my profession any other, it would not so much matter, but in my profession it is a terrible thing; and my enemies, of whom there are not a few, what would they say to this? To give you an idea of this extraordinary deafness, I tell you that when at the theatre, I am obliged to lean forward close to the orchestra, in order to understand what is being said on the stage. When somewhat at a distance I cannot hear the high tones of instruments, voices. In speaking it is not surprising that there are people who have never noticed it, for as a rule I am absent-minded, and they account for it in that way. Often I can scarcely hear any one speaking to me; the tones yes, but not the actual words; yet as soon as any one shouts, it is unbearable. What will come of all this, heaven only knows! Vering says that there will *certainly be improvement, though perhaps not a perfect cure*. I have, indeed, often — — cursed my existence; Plutarch taught me resignation. If nothing else is possible I will defy my fate, although there will be moments in my life when I shall be God's most wretched creature. I beg you not to tell any one about this; don't say even a word to Lorchen. I only tell it you as a secret; I should be glad if you would open up correspondence with Vering on the subject. Should my present state continue, I would come next spring to you. You would take a house for me in some beautiful place in the country, and so I would rusticate for six months. By that means there might come a change. Resignation! what a miserable refuge, and yet it is the only one for me.

Pray forgive me for telling you of a friend's trouble, when you yourself are in sad circumstances. Steffen Breuning is now here, and we are together almost daily. It does me good to hark back to old times. He is really a good, noble young fellow, who knows a thing or two, and whose heart, as with all of us more or less, is sound. I have very fine rooms now, which look on to the bastion, and this for my health is of double value. I really think I can arrange for Breuning to come and live with me. You shall have your Antiochus, and a rare lot of my new compositions, unless you think it will cost you too much. Honestly speaking, your love for art gives me the highest pleasure. Only write to me how it is to be managed, and I will send you all my works, of which the number is now pretty large, and it is daily increasing. In place of the portrait of my grandfather, which I beg you to send as soon as possible by stage-coach, I send you that of his grandson, your ever good and affectionate Beethoven. It is coming out here at Artaria's, who, like other art firms, have often asked me for it. I will write shortly to Stoffel, and read him a bit of a lecture about his cross temper. He shall hear what I have to say about old friendship, he shall promise on his oath not to grieve you any more in your, apart from this, sad circumstances. I will also write to kind Lorchen. I have never forgotten a single one of you dear good people, although you never get any news from me; but writing, as you well know, was never a strong point with me—years, even, have passed without my best friends receiving anything. I only live in my music, and I have scarcely begun one thing when I start on another. As I am now working, I am often engaged on three or four things at the same time.

Write often to me now; I will see to it that I find time sometimes to write to you. Greetings to all, also to the good wife of the privy councillor, and tell her that I still, occasionally, have a "raptus." I am not surprised at the change in K.; fortune is fickle, and does not always favour the most worthy, the best. A word about Ries, to whom hearty greetings. As regards his son, about whom I will write shortly, although I am of opinion that to make his way in the world, Paris is better than Vienna. The latter city is over-crowded, and even persons of the highest merit find it hard to maintain themselves. By the autumn or the winter I will see what I can do for him, for then every one is returning.

Farewell, good, faithful Wegeler. Rest assured of the love and friendship of

Your
BEETHOVEN.

26. To Dr. FRIEDRICH Von MATTHISSON

August 4, 1800.

HIGHLY HONOURED SIR,

Herewith you receive a composition of mine which was published some years ago, and of which, to my shame, you as yet have no knowledge. To excuse myself and say why I dedicated something to you which came warm from my heart, yet without letting you know anything about it, that I am unable to do. Perhaps at first, it was because I did not know your address, also partly timidity, fearing that I had been over-hasty in dedicating something to you without knowing whether it met with your approval. Even now, indeed, I send you the *Adelaide* with diffidence. You yourself know what change a few years produce in an artist who is constantly advancing; the greater the progress he makes in art, the less do his old works satisfy him. My most ardent wish is gratified if the musical setting of your heavenly *Adelaide* does not altogether displease you, and if thereby you feel moved soon again to write another poem of similar kind, and, not finding my request too bold, at once to send it to me, I will then put forth my best powers to come near to your beautiful poetry. Look upon the dedication partly as a token of the pleasure which the setting of your *A.* afforded me, and partly as a token of gratitude and high esteem for the great pleasure your poetry generally has always given, and still will give me.

In playing over the *A.* think sometimes of your

sincere admirer,
BEETHOVEN.

VIENNA, *August* 4, 1800.

[Matthisson himself, in a note to his poem, says: "Several composers gave a musical soul to this lyrical phantasy; but no one, such is my inmost conviction, by his melody enhanced the poem so deeply as the gifted Ludwig van Beethoven at Vienna" (notes to his poems, Vienna, 1815, 1st Part). Beethoven must have seen this edition and been delighted.]

[In a letter written by the poet to Carl Sondershausen, he offers to his friend best congratulations on learning that a daughter, a "new earthly pilgrim," has been born. And he adds: "And now hearty thanks for the real joy you have prepared for me in deciding to dedicate to me your little maiden. This joy was materially heightened, when I perceived the name (i.e. Adelaide) which you intend to give her! How that would have gladdened the heart of the excellent *Beethoven*, to whom alone belongs the honour of causing that poem still to be held in remembrance."—TR.]

27. TO DR. FRANZ WEGELER, BONN

November 16 [1801?].

MY GOOD WEGELER!

I thank you for the fresh proof of your anxiety concerning myself, and all the more as I am so little deserving of it. You want to know how I am, what I am taking; and however unwillingly I may discuss the matter, I certainly like best to do it with you. For the last few months Vering has ordered blistering plasters to be constantly placed on both arms; and these, as you will know, are composed of a certain bark. This is a most unpleasant cure, as, until the bark has sufficiently drawn, I am deprived for a day or so of the free use of my arms, to say nothing of the pain. I cannot, it is true, deny that the humming, with which my deafness actually began, has become somewhat weaker, especially in the left ear. My hearing, however, has not in the least improved; I really am not quite sure whether it has not become worse. Especially after I have taken lukewarm baths a few times, I am fairly well for 8 or 10 days. I seldom take anything strengthening for the stomach; I am now applying herbs according to your advice. Vering won't hear of shower-baths, but I am really very dissatisfied with him; he shows so little care and forbearance for such a malady; if I did not actually go to him, and that costs me a great effort, I should never see him. What is your opinion of Schmidt? I do not like making a change, yet it seems to me that Vering is too much of a practitioner to be able to take in new ideas through books. Schmidt appears to me a very different kind of man, and perhaps would not be so remiss. Wonders are told about galvanism; what do you say about it? A doctor told me he had seen a deaf and dumb child in Berlin who had recovered his hearing, also a man who had been deaf for seven years. I have just heard that your Schmidt is making experiments with it.

My life is again somewhat pleasanter, for I mix in society. You can scarcely imagine what a dreary, sad life I have led during the past two years. My weak hearing seemed always to be haunting me, and I ran away from people, was forced to appear a misanthrope, though not at all in my character. This change has been brought about by an enchanting maiden, who loves me, and whom I love. Once again after two years I have had some happy moments, and for the first time I feel that marriage can bring happiness. Unfortunately she is not of my station in life, and now —for the moment I certainly could not marry—I must bravely bustle about. If it were not for my hearing, I should already long ago have travelled half over the world, and that I must do. For me there is no greater pleasure than that of practising and displaying my art. Do not believe that I should feel happy among you. What, indeed, could make me happier? Even your solicitude would pain me; at every moment I should read pity on your faces, and that would make me still more miserable. My beautiful native country, what was my lot when there? Nothing but hope of a better state, and, except for this evil, I should already have won it! O that I could be free from it and encompass the world! My youth, yes I feel it, is only now beginning; have I not always been sickly? My strength, both of body and mind, for some time has been on the increase. Every day I approach nearer to the goal; this I feel, though I can scarcely describe it. Only through this can your Beethoven live. Don't talk of rest! I know of no other than sleep, and sorry enough I am that I am compelled to give more time to it than formerly. If only half freed from my infirmity, then—as a thoroughly mature man—I will come to you and renew the old feelings of friendship. You will see me as happy as my lot can be here below, not unhappy. No, that I could not endure; I will seize fate by the throat; it shall certainly never wholly overcome me. Oh! life is so beautiful, would I could have a thousand lives! I feel I am no longer fit to lead a quiet life! Do write as soon as you can. See to it that Steffen makes up his mind to get an appointment in the Order of German Knights. For his health, life here is too fatiguing. And besides, he leads such a retired life, that I do not see how he can get on. You know how it is here; I do not mean to say that society would render him less languid; he can never be persuaded to go into it. Some time ago I had a musical party at my house; but our friend Steffen did not turn up. Do advise him to take more rest and to be more steady. I have done all I could; without he takes this advice, he can never become either happy or healthy. Now tell me in your next letter, whether it matters if I send you a great deal of my music. What you really don't want you can sell, and so you will have your postage—also my portrait. Best remembrances to Lorchen—also Mamma—and Christoph. You do really love me a little, do you not? Be as well assured of this (of my love), as of the friendship of your

BEETHOVEN.

[I follow Nohl in dating the letter 1800. The "enchanting maiden" whom Beethoven mentions, i.e. Giulietta Guicciardi, was, in any case, in his circle before 1801. To the famous physician, Professor J. A. Schmidt, Beethoven, in 1802, dedicated the arrangement of the Septet as Trio for pianoforte, clarinet (violin) and 'cello. Dr. S. attended the composer in his severe illness after the break with Giulietta. One outcome of that illness was the "Heiligenstadt Will." Stephan and Christoph (Stoffel) were the brothers of Eleonore (Lorchen) v. Breuning.]

28. TO CAPELLMEISTER HOFMEISTER, LEIPZIG

VIENNA, December 15 [1800].

DEAREST BROTHER,

I have often wished to answer your inquiries, but as a correspondent I am fearfully lazy, and so a long time passes before I write, instead of notes, dry letters [of the alphabet]; but at last I have forced myself to come up to the mark.

Pro primo, know that I am very sorry, my dear brother in art, that you did not let me know sooner, so that I could have offered you my quartets for sale, also many other things of which I have already disposed. However, if you, Mr. brother, are as conscientious as many other honourable engravers, who prick us poor composers to death, you will also know, when they are published, how to make profit out of them. I will now set down in brief what you can have of mine. (1) A Septet for *violin, viola, 'cello, contra basso, clarinet, corno, fagotto*—all obbligato (I cannot write anything non-obbligato, for I came into the world with an obbligato *Accompagnement*). This Septet has greatly pleased; for more frequent use a violin, viola and another 'cello could be indicated in place of the *fagotto, clarinetto and corno*. (2) A grand symphony for full orchestra. (3) A pianoforte Concerto, which I really do not give out for one of my best, and so of another which will be published here by Mollo (this as news for the Leipzig critics), because I still *keep the better for myself until I make a tour*; still it will not in any way disgrace you to print it. (4) A grand *solo Sonata*. That is all I can offer for the moment; a little later on you can have a Quintet for strings, and perhaps Quartets and other things which as yet are not ready. In your reply you might fix prices, and as you are neither *Jews nor Italians*, and I neither of the two, we shall no doubt come to an agreement. Farewell, dearest brother, and be assured of the esteem of

Your brother
L. V. BEETHOVEN.

December 15, 1880.

29. TO THE SAME

VIENNA, 15th (or something like it) January, 1801.

With great pleasure, my dearly beloved brother and friend, have I read your letter. I thank you right heartily for the good opinion you have expressed concerning me and my works, and hope I may prove myself really worthy of it. Please also convey my dutiful thanks to Herr K. for his courtesy and friendly feelings towards me.

Your undertakings likewise make me glad, and I hope, if works of art can procure gain, that it will fall to the lot of genuine true artists, rather than to mere shopkeepers. That you wish to publish the works of *Sebastian* Bach rejoices my heart, which beats in unison with the high art of this forefather of harmony, and I desire soon to see the scheme in full swing. I hope that here, so soon as golden peace has been proclaimed, I shall be able to be of great assistance in the matter, when you issue a subscription list. As regards our special business, since you wish it, I hope this may be to your liking: I now offer you the following: *Septet* (concerning which I have already written to you; by *arranging* it for pianoforte it would become better known and be more profitable) 20 ducats, *Symphony* 20 ducats, *Concerto* 10 ducats, Grand *Solo Sonata* (*allegro*, *adagio*, *Minuetto*, *Rondo*) 20 ducats. This *Sonata* is A1, dearest brother! Now for a word of explanation; you will perhaps be surprised that I here make no difference between *Sonata*, *Septet*, *Symphony*, because I find that there is not such a demand for a Septet or a *Symphony* as for a Sonata; that is why I do so, although a *Symphony* is undoubtedly of greater value (N.B., the Septet consists of a short introductory *Adagio*, then *Allegro*, *Adagio*, Minuetto, *Andante* with *Variations*, *Minuetto*, another short introductory *adagio*, and then *presto*). The *Concerto* I only value at 10 ducats, because, as I have already written, I do not give it out as one of my best. All things considered, I do not think you will find this excessive; anyhow I have tried to name prices for you as moderate as I possibly could. Concerning the money order, since you leave me the choice, you could make it payable at Geimüller's or Schüller's. The full amount would therefore be 70 ducats for all four works. I do not understand any other money than Viennese ducats; how many thalers and gulden that makes is no affair of mine, for I am a bad *business* man and reckoner.

There is an end of the troublesome business. So I name it, because I only wish it could be otherwise in the world. There ought to be an artistic *depôt* where the artist need only hand in his artwork in order to receive what he asks for. As things are, one must be half a business man, and how can one understand—good heavens! —that's what I really call *troublesome*. As for the Leipzig O. [?], let them just go on talking; *they* will never by their chatter confer immortality on any one, neither can they take it away from any one for whom Apollo has destined it. Now may heaven have *you and yours* in its keeping. For some time I have not been well; and so it is now somewhat difficult for me to write notes, still more so alphabet letters. I hope that we shall often have opportunity to assure ourselves that you are a great friend to me, and that I am

Your devoted
brother and friend,
L. v. BEETHOVEN.

Send an answer soon—adieu.

[The Sonata referred to as "A 1" is the B flat Sonata (Op. 22), first published by Hofmeister and Kühnel. The *Leipziger O.*, Leipzig oxen, or *Leipziger R.* as Schumann's paper has it, which probably stands for *Leipziger Rindfleische*, i.e. "Leipzig blockheads," were the Leipzig gentlemen of the press, who, at any rate in the early period, made sport of Beethoven's art-work.]

30. To the Same

VIENNA, *April* 22, 1801.

You have good cause to complain of me. My excuse⁻ is that I have been ill, and, in addition, have been very busy, so that it was scarcely possible for me even to think about what I had to send you; moreover my affairs are not always in the best order—perhaps the only mark of genius of which I can boast—and yet there is no one but myself who can help. For instance, in the score of my concerto, the piano part, according to my custom, was not written out, and I have only just done so; hence, to avoid delay, you will receive it in my own, not very legible, handwriting.

In order that the works may follow so far as possible in the proper order, I point out to you that there should be placed:

on the Solo Sonata	. .	opus 22.
on the Symphony	. .	opus 21.
on the Septet	. .	opus 20.
and on the Concerto	. .	opus 19.

The *titles* I will send shortly. Put me down as *subscriber* to Johann Sebastian Bach's works, also Prince Lichnowski. The quartet transcription of the *Mozart Sonata* will reflect honour on you, and certainly be also profitable. I wish that I myself could be of more help *on such occasions*, but I am not an orderly man, and in spite of the best goodwill, forget everything; yet I have spoken here and there about it, and find every one in its favour. If you, my good brother, in addition to publishing the Septet, would also arrange the same for flute, e.g. as a Quintet, you would do a good thing, for amateur flute players, who have already approached me on the subject, would swarm round it like insects and feed on it. To say something more about myself, I have written a Ballet in which, however, the ballet-master has not made the best of his part. Baron Lichtenstein has also bestowed on us a product which does not answer to the idea which the newspapers gave us of his *genius*; another specimen of newspaper criticism. The Baron seems to have taken Herr Müller at the *puppet-show* as his ideal, but without even coming up to that standard. These

are the fine prospects amid which we poor creatures germinate.
My dear brother, do make haste and give the world a sight of the
works, and write to me soon, so that I may know whether through
my dawdling, I have quite lost your further confidence. All pleasant
and kind wishes to your *associé* Kühnel. In future everything shall
be ready and sent off promptly. The Quartets may be published
in a few weeks, and now, farewell, and continue to love your friend
and brother,

BEETHOVEN.

[The herein-mentioned ballet is Op. 43: *Ballo serio : Die Geschöpfe des
Prometheus*, produced 28 March, 1801. The work was dedicated to Princess
Lichnowsky. Baron Carl August Liechtenstein (1767–1845), son of the minister
at Gotha, was active as opera-writer, and intendant at the Court Theatre at
Dessau. In 1800 he went to Vienna and became director of the Court Opera
and of the Ballet.]

31. TO THE MUSIC PUBLISHERS BREITKOPF AND HAERTEL, LEIPZIG

VIENNA, April 22, 1801.

P. P.

Forgive this late answer to your letter; for a long time I have
been continuously unwell, and overwhelmed with business matters;
moreover, as I am not the most diligent of correspondents, this may
serve as an extra excuse. With regard to your request for works
from me, I am very sorry to say that just now I cannot satisfy
you. But please be kind enough to let me know what kind of compositions you wish to have, symphony, quartet or sonata, etc., so
that I may act accordingly; and if I have anything of the kind
that you require, be able to place it at your service. At Mollo's,
if I am not mistaken, up to 8 works are coming out, likewise 4 at
Hofmeister's. I may just mention that Hofmeister is publishing
one of my first concertos, and Mollo, one actually composed later,
but neither *do I reckon among my best of the kind*. This is just a hint
for your *Musikalische Zeitung* with regard to the reviews of these
works, though they can be best judged if one can hear them well
performed. Musical policy necessitates the keeping to one's self
for a time the best concertos. Advise your critics to exercise more
care and good sense with regard to the productions of young authors,
for many a one may thereby become dispirited, who otherwise
might have risen to higher things; for myself, though I am indeed
far from considering myself to have attained such a degree of
perfection as to be beyond censure, the outcry at first of your

critics against me was so humiliating, that when I began to compare myself with others, I could scarcely blame them; I remained quite quiet, and thought they do not understand it. And I had all the more reason for being quite quiet when I saw how men were praised up to the skies who here are held of little account by the better musicians *in loco*, and who here are almost forgotten, however honest they may have been. But now *pax vobiscum*—peace with you and me—I would never have mentioned a syllable about it, had it not been done by you yourselves.

When I recently visited a good friend of mine, and he showed me *the amount which had been collected for the daughter of the immortal god of harmony*, I was astonished at the small sum which Germany, and especially *your Germany*, had thought sufficient for the person worthy to me of honour on account of her father. And that leads me to the idea, how would it be if I published something by subscription for this person's benefit, and publicly announced the amount and the yearly interest, so as to protect myself from any attack—you could help most in the matter. Answer quickly how this can best be brought about so that it may be done before this daughter of Bach dies, before *this brook* dries up, and we can no longer supply it with water. That you must publish this work is of course understood.

I am, with all esteem,
Your devoted,
Ludwig van Beethoven.

[Beethoven's depreciation of his first two pianoforte concertos in C and B flat need not cause surprise, for the far superior *third* one in C minor (Op. 37) had long lain in his desk; though finished in 1800 it only appeared in print in 1804. Finally we have in this letter new proof of Beethoven's admiration for the genius of Bach. In the same year, in a letter to Hofmeister, he had spoken of the great art of this progenitor of harmony. It was now a question of doing something for Regina Johanna, the youngest child of J. S. Bach, who was living alone and in poverty. F. Rochlitz, the editor of the *Allgemeine Mus. Ztg.*, therefore properly issued an appeal to the public in her favour. In it he says: "And this daughter, now aged—this daughter is *in want*; this last branch of so fruitful a stem ought not to be left to wither and die." This brought help. Bach's daughter passed the last days of her existence in ease and cheerfulness.] ["Bach" in German means "brook," so Beethoven does not lose the chance of a play upon the word.—Tr.]

32. To Capellmeister HOFMEISTER, Leipzig

Vienna, June, 1801.

I am really somewhat astonished at what you have said to me through the representative of your firm here; that you should think me capable of such a mean trick is enough to grieve me. It would be otherwise had I only disposed of my music to covetous dealers, and then, in an underhand way, made another good speculation; but *artist against artist*, it is rather hard lines to suspect me of such a thing. The whole affair seems to me to have been thoroughly thought out in order to test me, or to be mere conjecture. Anyhow I inform you, that, before you received the Septet, I sent it to London to Mr. Salomon (so that he might perform it at his concert, and this solely by way of friendship), but added that he must be careful not to let it get into other people's hands, as I intended to have it published in Germany. Concerning which, if you think it necessary, you can make inquiry of Salomon himself. But as further proof of my honesty, *I herewith give you my assurance in writing, that to you only, Herren Hofmeister and Kühnel, have I sold the Septet, the Concerto, the Symphony and the Sonata, and that you can consider them your property exclusively ; and for this I give you my word of honour.* Anyhow, you can make what use you please of this assurance—for the rest I think it just as unlikely that Salomon would be so base as to publish the Septet, as that I should have sold it to him. I am so conscientious, that I refused the piano arrangement of the Septet to *various publishers* who asked me for it, yet I do not even know whether you will publish anything of the kind. Here follow the long-promised titles of my works:

Concert pour le piano-forte avec deux violons, viola, basse et violoncelle, une flute, deux oboes, deux cors, deux fagots, composé et dedié à Monsieur Charles Nikl noble de Nikelsberg Conseiller aulique de sa Majesté Impériale et Royale par Louis van Beethoven. Œuvre 19.

Septette pour un violon, viole, violoncelle, contre basse, un cors, une clarinette, un fagot. Composé et dedié à sa Majesté l'imperatrice et Reine par louis van Beethoven. Œuvre 20.

---

grand symphonie avec deux violons, viole, violoncelle et contre basse, deux flûte, deux oboe, deux cors, deux fagots, deux clarines et tymbales. Composée et dediée à son altesse serenissime maximilien françois Prince Royal d'hongrie et de Boheme Electeur de Cologne, etc., par louis van Beethoven. Œuvre 21.

---

grande sonate pour le piano-forte composée et dediée à Monsieur
le comte de Browne Brigadier au service de S.M.J. de touttes les
Russies par louis van Beethoven.

Œuvre 22.

There will be many things to alter and improve in the titles,
that I leave to you. I shall expect a letter from you shortly, and
soon too the works which I wish to see engraved, as later ones
have been and will be published which are related to these [opus]
numbers. I have also written to Salomon, but as I look upon your
statement as mere report which you somewhat too easily accepted,
or as mere conjecture which—having heard in some way or other
that I sent it to S.—forced itself on you. To such credulous friends,
I can only, with a certain coldness, call myself,

Your friend,

L. v. BTHVN.

[Johann Peter Salomon, born about 1745, like Beethoven, was a native
of Bonn, and he was a distinguished violinist. After holding many posts in
Germany, he settled in London, where he zealously supported the cause of
German music. It was through his efforts that Haydn in 1790 made his
first triumphal journey to England. Owing to a fall from his horse he died
in 1815; and in what high esteem he was held is evident from the fact that he
was buried in Westminster Abbey. The dedication in this letter of the first
Symphony to the Elector, Maximilian Franz, is quite surprising. Beethoven,
then, still in the year 1801, must have been in communication with his former
Elector. The Symphony, however, which Hofmeister and Kühnel published
in the same year was dedicated to Baron Swieten; this change was probably
owing to the death of the Elector in July, a month after this letter was written.]

33. TO COUNTESS GIULIETTA GUICCIARDI

July [1801 ?].
On the 6th July in the morning.

MY ANGEL, MY ALL, MY VERY SELF,

Just a few words to-day, and only in pencil—(with thine)
only till to-morrow is my room definitely engaged, what an unworthy waste of time in such matters—why this deep sorrow where
necessity speaks. Can our love endure otherwise than through
sacrifices, through restraint in longing. Canst thou help not being
wholly mine, can I, not being wholly thine. Oh! gaze at nature in
all its beauty, and calmly accept the inevitable—love demands
everything, and rightly so. *Thus is it for me with thee, for thee with
me*, only thou so easily forgettest, that I must live for myself and
for thee—were we wholly united thou wouldst feel this painful

fact as little as I should—my journey was terrible. I arrived here only yesterday morning at four o'clock, and as they were short of horses, the mail-coach selected another route, but what an awful road; at the last stage but one I was warned against travelling by night; they frightened me with the wood, but that only spurred me on—and I was wrong, the coach must needs break down, the road being dreadful, a swamp, a mere country road; without the postilions I had with me, I should have stuck on the way. Esterhazi, by the ordinary road, met the same fate with eight horses as I with four—yet it gave me some pleasure, as successfully overcoming any difficulty always does. Now for a quick change from without to within: we shall probably soon see each other, besides, to-day I cannot tell thee what has been passing through my mind during the past few days concerning my life—were our hearts closely united, I should not do things of this kind. My heart is full of the many things I have to say to thee—ah!—there are moments in which I feel that speech is powerless—cheer up—remain my true, my only treasure, my all!!! as I to thee. The gods must send the rest, what for us must be and ought to be.

Thy faithful,
LUDWIG.

Monday evening, July 6.

Thou sufferest, thou my dearest love. I have just found out that the letters must be posted very early Mondays, Thursdays— the only days when the post goes from here to K. Thou sufferest— Ah! where I am, art thou also with me; I will arrange for myself and Thee. I will manage so that I can live with thee; and what a life!!!! But as it is!!!! without thee. Persecuted here and there by the kindness of men, which I little deserve, and as little care to deserve. Humility of man towards man—it pains me—and when I think of myself in connection with the universe, what am I and what is He who is named the Greatest; and still this again shows the divine in man. I weep when I think that probably thou wilt only get the first news from me on Saturday evening. However much thou lovest me, my love for thee is stronger, but never conceal thy thoughts from me. Good-night. As I am taking the baths I must go to bed [two words scratched through]. O God— so near! so far! Our love, is it not a true heavenly edifice, firm as heaven's vault.

Good morning on July 7.

While still in bed, my thoughts press to thee, my Beloved One, at moments with joy, and then again with sorrow, waiting to see

Beethoven at the age of thirty-one (1801)

whether fate will take pity on us. Either I must live wholly with thee or not at all. Yes, I have resolved to wander in distant lands, until I can fly to thy arms, and feel that with thee I have a real home; with thee encircling me about, I can send my soul into the kingdom of spirits. Yes, unfortunately, it must be so. Calm thyself, and all the more since thou knowest my faithfulness towards thee, never can another possess my heart, never—never—O God, why must one part from what one so loves, and yet my life in V. at present is a wretched life. Thy love has made me one of the happiest and, at the same time, one of the unhappiest of men—at my age I need a quiet, steady life—is that possible in our situation? My Angel, I have just heard that the post goes every day, and I must therefore stop, so that you may receive the letter without delay. Be calm, only by calm consideration of our existence can we attain our aim to live together—be calm—love me—to-day—yesterday—what tearful longing after thee—thee—thee—my life—my all—farewell —Oh, continue to love me—never misjudge the faithful heart

Of Thy Beloved

ever thine   L.
ever mine
ever each other's.

[According to the original manuscript in the Berlin Royal Library. It is, and will remain, the finest, most wonderful of all Beethoven's letters, which, so often as it is read, touches one to the quick with its glowing words of love and wisdom. It is also the most hotly debated of all Beethoven letters as regards the embodiment of the "Immortal Beloved One." Again and again has it been reprinted in Beethoven literature. The first to make it known— as early as in 1840—was Anton Schindler, who probably was present at the finding of the tripartite letter. He merely says: "Stephan von Breuning found it, after his friend's death, together with other important documents, in a secret little drawer of a cash box." Was it sent back after the rupture in 1803? Who can say? Dr. Gerhard von Breuning, in his book *Aus dem Schwarzspanierhause*, describes in detail the search for bonds left by Beethoven, adding: "The scene, according to father's later account, was becoming gradually more and more unbearable, when by chance Holz pulled out a nail projecting from a box, causing a parcel to fall out, and with it the bonds for which there had been such long search." To this was appended the footnote: "These bonds were not therefore, as stated in the *Grazer Tagespost*, found with the letters to the Countess Giulietta Guicciardi in the secret drawer of the writing-desk now in my possession." Stephan von Breuning, Carl Holz, and Schindler, who received the letters, and others, were present in the death-room when the letter to the "Immortal Beloved" was discovered. As, even after Schindler had published this tripartite love-letter, doubt was expressed as to the existence of an original document, he gave an excellent facsimile of the second part in pencil, with the date "Monday evening, July 6," in the third edition of his Beethoven Biography. Ludwig Nohl in his reproduction of these letters, "To the Countess Giulietta Guicciardi," boasts that "These letters to the Immortal Beloved to whom the C sharp minor Sonata is dedicated, are here for the first time reproduced with diplomatic [?!] fidelity from the original written in pencil on fine letter-paper." Now, if this is a question of diplomatic fidelity, words, orthography and punctuation, everything is of importance. And it will cause astonishment to learn that I was able to note more than seventy, let us say seventy, variations from the original. It is by no means easy to reproduce exactly a Beethoven letter. The attempt of A. W. Thayer, together with the writer, Mariam Tenger, to palm off the Countess Therese Brunswick as Beethoven's "Immortal Beloved" must now be regarded as having totally failed. The height of folly in this controversy has been reached by Dr. Th. Frimmel, who would have us regard the love-letter as addressed to Magdalene Willmann.

Documentary evidence shall now be brought forward to show that Beethoven, even after the rupture, took uninterrupted interest in Countess Guicciardi, afterwards Countess Gallenberg. First of all I shall briefly give events in chronological succession. In 1801 (?) (see p. 22) Beethoven writes to Wegeler about his "enchanting maiden." In the summer of 1801 the wonderful love-letter is written from a watering-place unknown to us. Circumstances render separation imperative, and by the year 1802 a complete rupture has taken place. This heartrending event was largely the cause of the young master's severe illness. Weariness of life, complete resignation, accordingly breathe forth from the well-known "Heiligenstadt Will." Yet in the following year there is an echo of this heart-sorrow, as may be clearly seen in a letter of Beethoven's (2 November, 1803) to his friend, the painter Macco. In it occur the following words: "For the rest I was sad at not being able to see more of you here, *but there are periods in one's life which have to be overcome.*" Nohl declares it to be both to the point and most interesting in that "it is a distinct echo of Beethoven's sad mood during the spring and summer of 1802, and thus helps to fix the point of time of the breaking-off of his love-connection with the Countess Giulietta Guicciardi." Nohl later on changed his opinion with regard to this matter. But at the present day there is scarcely any serious Beethoven investigator who accepts the Thayer-Tenger thesis. Sir George Grove in this matter overtrumps both Thayer and Mariam Tenger in that he most unintelligibly connects the fourth and even the fifth symphony with the love-letters.

It is beyond dispute that among all the women who had a place in Beethoven's heart, it was the Countess Gallenberg-Guicciardi alone in whom, even after the separation, he showed constant interest. That must be clear to every one from the conversations between Beethoven and Schindler, which took place in the year 1823—twenty years after the parting. These have been preserved, and must be given here exactly as they stand in the original manuscript. The conversations are in Book D., 10 February, 1823, at a time when Count Rob. Wenzel Gallenberg, Giulietta's husband, was in Vienna as co-administrator of the Italian Opera under Barbaja. Therein we read:

(Sheet 31 *b*. Schindler writes): "now what about Fidelio. What can I do to hurry on the matter?"

(Beethoven): "Steiner really has the score."

(Schindler): I am going to Count Gallenberg who will willingly lend you the score for a time."

(32*a*): "It would be best for you to have a copy made at your own expense."

[At this time there was much talk in Beethoven's circle of friends about a new opera. Then again Schindler:]

(33*a*): "I will go to-morrow morning to Gallenberg, and will also work diligently and swiftly at the Embassy, for I am fortunately free for some days."

[Further on we learn the result of Schindler's first visit to Gallenberg:]

(Sheet 39*a*): "Gallenberg presents his compliments and will send you the score, if they have two copies; should this not be the case, he will have the *score* copied for you. I am to go back to him in two days."

[What is written on Sheet 41 has no connection with the preceding on Sheet 40*b*. This offers further proof that detached sheets have been bound together. On 41*a* Schindler writes:]

"to-day he [Gallenberg] did not inspire me with any great respect *for him.*"

(Beethoven): "I was his invisible benefactor through others."

(Schindler): "He ought to know that, so as to show more respect for you than he appears to have."

[The subject is now dropped, but after a digression about food and press matters, it is resumed. Beethoven speaks (Sheet 42*a*):]

"So it seems you found G. none too well disposed towards me; this, however, does not matter to me, yet I should like to know how he expressed himself."

(Schindler, Sheet 43*b*): "He replied that he thought you yourself must have the *score*; but when I assured him that you really had not got it, he said that your unsteadiness and constant wandering about was the cause of your having lost it.

"What business is that of people?—still more, who will trouble about such men?"

(43*b*): "What then are you thinking of doing about the works at Steiner's? still keep silence? Dr. Bach [1] also recently asked me about this.

"I thought you wished to keep the score for yourself, because you had not got a copy."

"Also give away the five-part fugue for nothing?—my dear friend and teacher, that is far too generous for such men. You will only be laughed at."

[And now at last follow Beethoven's words concerning the queen of his heart, as Schindler, moreover, specially remarks: "the present Countess Gallenberg, *née* Countess Guicciardi."]

[1] Dr. Joh. Bach was Beethoven's lawyer and intimate friend.

(Beethoven, Sheet 44*b*): "j'étois bien aimé d'elle et plus que jamais son époux.

"il étoit pourtant (44*b*) plutot son amant que moi, mais par elle [many scratchings out and changes] j'en apprinois de son misère et je (45*a*) trouvais un homme de bien qui me donnait la somme de 500 fl. pour le soulager.

(45*b*) "il etoit toujours mon ennemi, et c'était justement la raison que je fusse tout le bien (46*a*) que possible."

(Schindler): "That is why he also said to me: 'he is an unbearable man,' out of pure gratitude probably. But, master, forgive them, for they know not what they do!!"

(46*b*): "Mad. la Comtesse?"
"était elle riche?"
"elle a une belle figure jusqu'ici."
"Mons. G.?"
"est ce qu'il y a longtemps, qu'elle est mariée avec Mons. de Gallenberg?"

(Beethoven):

> "elle est née
> Guicciardi.

(47*b*): "ell'était prise (?) qu'épousse de lui avant [son voyage: (Schindler)] de l'Italie—[arrivé a Vienne (Schindler)] elle cherchait moi pleure-ant, mais je la meprisois."

(47*b* Schindler): "Hercules at the parting of the ways!"

(Beethoven): "Had I chosen to give away my vital power with *my life*, what would have remained for that which is noble, better?"

[These conversations were carried on in a public place, not in Beethoven's house. The passages have been reproduced with the utmost care from the Conversation Books in the Berlin Royal Library.]

34. To Capellmeister HOFMEISTER, Leipzig

[re suggn from lady for a 'rev'y sonata] VIENNA, *April* 8, 1802.

Gentlemen, are you then all possessed of the devil, to propose to me *such a Sonata*? At the time of the Revolution fever that would have been all very well, but now, as everything is seeking to return to the beaten track—and the Concordat drawn up between Buonaparte and the Pope—a sonata of this kind? If only it were a *Missa pro Sancta Maria a tre voci*, or a *Vesper*, etc., then I would at once take pencil in hand, and with great pound notes [Pfund-

noten] write down a *Credo in unum,* but, good heavens, such a
Sonata in these newly commencing Christian times—hoho—leave
me out of it, nothing will come of it. Now, I will give you my
answer in most rapid *tempo.* The lady can have a Sonata from me,
and as regards *æsthetics,* I will in general follow her scheme—and
without following—the keys—the price, let us say 5 ducats. For
that, it will belong to her for one year, neither of us, however, to
be at liberty to publish it. At the expiration of this year the Sonata
is mine alone—i.e. I can and shall publish it, and she can, if she
thinks to gain any honour thereby, request me to dedicate it to her.
And now, gentlemen, God have you in His keeping.

My Sonata is beautifully printed, but it has taken a jolly long
time. Send my Septet into the world at a more rapid rate, because
the rabble is waiting for it, and you know the Empress has it,—
and there are scamps in the Imperial city as well as at the Imperial
court. But I won't vouch for it, so look sharp. Herr Mollo has again
recently published my Quartets, let us say full of faults and *errata,*
great and small; they swarm like fish in water, i.e. there's no end
to them. *Questo è un piacere per un autore.* That's what I call
printing; my skin is all over prickings and chaps from the beautiful
editions of my *quartets.* Now farewell, and remember me as I do
you. Until death, your faithful,

BEETHOVEN.

[The Sonata mentioned is the "great Sonata" in B flat (Op. 22). The
Quartets are the six of Op. 18. The letter was, as noted by the firm, received
on 16 April; in those days a letter sent from Vienna took a week to reach
Leipzig.]

35. To the Publishing House of BREITKOPF AND HAERTEL, Leipzig

(Fragment) *July* 13, 1802.

. . . With regard to arrangements, I am heartily glad that you
decline them. The *unnatural mania,* at the present day, to wish
to transfer *pieces for the pianoforte* to string instruments, which
in every way are so different, ought to be stopped. I firmly assert
that only Mozart himself could transfer his pianoforte music to
other instruments, and the same of Haidn; and without placing
myself on a level with these two great men, I make the same assertion with respect to *my pianoforte sonatas;* not only would whole
passages have to be omitted or entirely rewritten, but further
additions made—and herein lies the true *stumbling-block*—to

overcome which there must be *either the master himself*, or at least one possessing the same *skill* and *inventive power*. I changed just one sonata of my own into a quartet for strings, which I was pressed to do, and am sure that no other man could have accomplished the task as I have done.

[The question here arises: "Which sonata did Beethoven himself transform into a quartet?" It was probably the Sonata in E (Op. 14, No. 1), which was published in the key of F in 1802 under the following title, *Quatuor pour deux Violons, Alto et Violoncelle, d'après une Sonate composée et dédiée à Madame la Baronne de Braun par Louis van Beethoven arrangé par lui-même. A Vienne au Bureau d'Arts et d'Industrie*. Ries's positive statement that Beethoven himself only made *four* transcriptions, among which he does not name one of a sonata, must not be taken too literally. He adds: "Many other things were arranged by me and looked through by Beethoven, and then sold by his brother Caspar (Carl) under Beethoven's name."]

36. For my Brothers CARL and — BEETHOVEN

O ye men who regard or declare me to be malignant, stubborn or cynical, how unjust are ye towards me. You do not know the secret cause of my seeming so. From childhood onward, my heart and mind prompted me to be kind and tender, and I was ever inclined to accomplish great deeds. But only think that during the last six years, I have been in a wretched condition, rendered worse by unintelligent physicians. Deceived from year to year with hopes of improvement, and then finally forced to the prospect of *lasting infirmity* (which may last for years, or even be totally incurable). Born with a fiery, active temperament, even susceptive of the diversions of society, I had soon to retire from the world, to live a solitary life. At times, even, I endeavoured to forget all this, but how harshly was I driven back by the redoubled experience of my bad hearing. Yet it was not possible for me to say to men: Speak louder, shout, for I am deaf. Alas! how could I declare the weakness of a *sense* which in me *ought to be* more acute than in others —a sense which *formerly* I possessed in highest perfection, a perfection such as few in my profession enjoy, or ever have enjoyed; no I cannot do it. Forgive, therefore, if you see me withdraw, when I would willingly mix with you. My misfortune pains me doubly, in that I am certain to be misunderstood. For me there can be no recreation in the society of my fellow creatures, no refined conversations, no interchange of thought. Almost alone, and only mixing in society when absolutely necessary, I am compelled to live as an exile. If I approach near to people, a feeling of hot anxiety comes over me lest my condition should be noticed—for so it was during these past six months which I spent in the country. Ordered by my intelligent physician to spare my hearing as much as possible, he almost fell in with my present frame of mind, although many a time I was carried away by my sociable inclinations. But how humiliating was it, when some one standing close to me heard a distant flute, and I heard *nothing*, or a *shepherd singing*, and again I heard nothing. Such incidents almost drove me to despair; at times I was on the point of putting an end to my life—*art* alone restrained my hand. Oh! it seemed as if I could not quit this earth until I had produced all I felt within me, and so I continued this wretched life—wretched, indeed, with so sensitive a body that a somewhat sudden change can throw me from the best into the worst state. *Patience*, I am told, I must choose as my guide. I have done so—lasting, I hope, will be my resolution to bear up until it pleases the inexorable Parcae to break the thread. Forced already in my 28th year to become a philosopher, it is not easy; for an artist more difficult than for any one else. O Divine Being, Thou who lookest down into my inmost soul, Thou understandest; Thou knowest that love for mankind and a desire to do good dwell therein. Oh, my fellow men, when one day you read this, remember that you were unjust to me, and let the unfortunate one console himself if he can find one like himself, who in spite of all obstacles which nature has thrown in his way, has still done everything in his power to be received into the ranks of worthy artists and men. You, my brothers Carl and —, as soon as I am dead, beg Professor Schmidt, if he be still living, to describe my malady; and annex this written account to that of my illness, so that at least the world, so far as is possible, may become reconciled to me after my death. And now I declare you both heirs to my small fortune (if such it may be called). Divide it honourably and dwell in peace, and help each other. What you have done against me, has, as you know, long been forgiven. And you, brother Carl, I especially thank you for the attachment you have shown towards me of late. My prayer is that your life may be better, less troubled by cares, than mine. Recommend to your children *virtue*; it alone can bring happiness, not money. I speak from experience. It was virtue which bore me up in time of trouble; to her, next to my art, I owe thanks for my not having laid violent hands on myself. Farewell, and love one another. My thanks to all friends, especially *Prince Lichnowski and Professor Schmidt*. I should much like one of you to keep as an heirloom the instruments given to me by Prince L., but let no strife arise between you concerning them; if money should be of more service to you, just sell them. How happy I feel that even when lying in my grave, I may be useful to you.

So let it be. I joyfully hasten to meet death. If it come before I have had opportunity to develop all my artistic faculties, it will come, my hard fate notwithstanding, too soon, and I should probably wish it later—yet even then I shall be happy, for will it not deliver me from a state of endless suffering? Come when thou wilt, I shall face thee courageously—farewell, and when I am dead do not entirely forget me. This I deserve from you, for during my lifetime I often thought of you, and how to make you happy. Be ye so.

LUDWIG VAN BEETHOVEN.

HEIGLNSTADT, *the 6th of October,* 1802.

[Black seal]

[On the fourth side of the great Will sheet.]

"Heiglnstadt, October, 1802, thus I take my farewell of thee— and indeed sadly—yes, that fond hope which I entertained when I came here, of being at any rate healed up to a certain point, must be entirely abandoned. As the leaves of autumn fall and fade, so it has withered away for me; almost the same as when I came here do I go away—even the High courage which often in the beautiful summer days quickened me, that has vanished. O Providence, let me have just one pure day of *joy*; so long is it since true joy filled my heart. Oh when, oh when, oh Divine Being, shall I be able once again to feel it in the temple of nature and of men. Never— no—that would be too hard.

"For my brothers Carl and — to execute after my death."

[It first appeared in the Leipzig *Allgemeine Musikalische Zeitung* (17 Oct., 1827) about six months after Beethoven's death. In that paper it was stated that a copy had been sent to Moscheles in London, to be distributed among the worshippers of Beethoven in that city. Did Beethoven actually omit the name of his younger brother? Or was not rather the name "Johann" erased *after* Beethoven's death? Or, finally—did Beethoven himself, in whose keeping the Will remained from 1802 to 1827, in after years himself obliterate the name of the "pseudo brother"? To account for the suppression of the name "Johann" it has often been suggested that the composer could not overcome his dislike to name the brother whom he apparently so hated. It must, however, be remembered that at the time the Will was written, the unjust behaviour of the composer towards his brother John had not in any way made itself conspicuous.

The original document is now in the town library at Hamburg. The great folio sheet on which the *Pro memoria* was clearly written, was purchased at the sale of Beethoven's effects in 1827 by Artaria. A certificate on the fourth page states that J. Hotschewar, tutor to the nephew Carl, received it from Artaria and Co., 21 September, 1827. And underneath, the composer's surviving brother declares that he received it from Hotschewar. According to Schindler the autograph was for a long time in the autograph collection of

Franz Gräffer, until it was acquired by the violinist, Heinrich Ernst. The latter presented it, out of gratitude, to Otto and Jenny Lind-Goldschmidt, who in their turn presented it to the Hamburg library. Beethoven speaks of being in his twenty-eighth year, which would make 1774 the year of his birth; generally, however, he considered himself *two* years younger than was actually the case.

The instruments which Beethoven received from Prince Lichnowsky are now in the Beethoven House at Bonn. The first violin (a Guarnerius of 1718) and the viola (date 1690) were formerly in the possession of Carl Holz; the second violin, an Amati (date 1667) was purchased by Huber; while the 'cello (a Guarnerius of 1712) belonged to P. Wertheimber of Vienna.]

37. To the Music Firm of BREITKOPF AND HAERTEL, Leipzig

[Vienna, *October* 18, 1802.]

As my brother is writing to you, I add the following: I have composed two sets of *Variations*, one containing 8, the other 30—both are written *in an entirely new style*, each in *quite a different way*. I should very much like you to print them, under the *one condition that you pay me for both together about* 50 ducats. Do not let this proposal be made to you in vain, for I assure you that you will not regret taking these two works—each theme *is treated in a totally different manner*. I only hear what other people say when I have new ideas, for I never know it myself; but this time I must myself assure you, that the *style* of both works is on a totally *new plan of mine*. I cannot agree with what you once wrote to me *about the test of sale of my works*. It is surely a *great proof that they sell well*, if almost all *foreign publishers* are constantly writing to me for works, and even the re-printers,[1] of whom you justly complain, *are also of this number*, for Simrock *has already written to me several times for works to be his sole property*, and he will pay me as good terms as any other publisher. You may regard it as showing preference, that I make this proposal to you yourselves, for your business always deserves distinction. Yours,

L. van Beethoven.

[It is not easy to say definitely what the Variations mentioned were. The first set reckoned as 8 was probably those in F (Op. 34), which in fact were published by B. and H. in the following year. Still more difficult is it to determine the Variations which Beethoven reckons as 20. In regard to the recognition of genius this letter is specially noteworthy. An apt illustration to Beethoven's words is offered by Schiller, who says: "Genius always remains a secret to itself."]

[1] See Preface.

38. NOTICE

I think it due to the public, and also to myself, to announce publicly, that the two Quintets in C and E flat, the first of which (taken from a Symphony of mine) was published by Herr Mollo, of Vienna, and the other (taken from my Septet, Op. 20) by Herr Hofmeister, of Leipzig, are not original Quintets, but only transcriptions, prepared by the publishers. Transcription, indeed, is a thing against which nowadays (in this fruitful age of transcriptions) an author would strive in vain; one can, however, at least in justice, demand that the publishers should indicate it on the title-page, so that neither the honour of the author be disparaged nor the public deceived. This in order to prevent similar cases in future. I also make known that shortly a new original Quintet of my composition in C (Op. 29), will be issued by Breitkopf and Härtel at Leipzig.

LUDWIG V. BEETHOVEN.

[According to the *Intelligenzblatt zur Allg. Mus. Ztg.*, No. 4, November 1802. A similar notice appeared shortly before in the *Wiener Zeitung*. Beethoven must have suffered much at this time from the dishonesty of pirate publishers. Even the firm of Breitkopf and Härtel saw itself compelled to defend itself in the columns of its paper against such swindlers.]

39. TO THE MUSIC PUBLISHERS BREITKOPF AND HAERTEL, LEIPZIG

[VIENNA, *November* 13, 1802.]

I hasten to write to you only what is of prime importance. Know then, that the *arch swindler* Artaria, at a time when I was away in the country for the sake of my health, begged the Quintet from Count Fries to reprint, *under the pretext* that it was already printed, and was to be had here; their own was *faulty*, and actually some days ago they wished to delight *the public* with it. Good Count Fries, taken in, and not reflecting whether or no there was some dirty trick, gave it to them. He could not ask me—I was not there. Fortunately, however, I became aware of the matter in time; this was on *Tuesday of this week*. In my *zeal to save my honour, and to prevent, as speedily as possible, any loss to you*, I offered these contemptible fellows two new works if they would suppress the whole edition. But a cooler-headed friend, who was with me, asks me, Why ever do you want to *reward these rascals*? So the matter was settled under conditions; for they protested that *whatever was published by your firm would be reprinted by them.* So these *noble-minded* rascals decided for the term of 3 weeks after your copies had appeared here, then only to publish their copies (for they maintained that Count F. had made them a present of the copy). With this limit *the contract was to be drawn up,* and in return, I was to give them a work which I value at lowest at 40 ducats. Before, however, this contract was signed, my brother appears on the scene, as if sent from heaven. He hastens to Count Fries; the whole matter is the *greatest* swindle in the world. I will tell you in my next letter how cleverly they kept me away from Count F., and all the rest. I myself now go to F., and the enclosed *Revers* may serve as proof that I did everything to protect you from loss, and this account of the whole affair may likewise show you that for me *no sacrifice was too great* to save my honour and *protect you from loss.* From the *Revers* you will at the same time see what measures you have to take, I think you ought to send copies here as soon as possible, and if you can, at the same price *as that of the rascals.* Sonnleithner and I will, in addition, take all measures *which seem to us good, so that their whole edition may be destroyed.* Note well, Mollo and Artaria are really only *one firm,* i.e. *a whole family of rascals.* They have not forgotten the *dedication to* Fries, for my brother saw it on the title-page. The *Revers I myself copied,* for my *poor brother* was so busy and *yet did his very best* to save you and me. Besides, in the confusion he lost a faithful dog which he named his darling. He deserves a special letter of thanks from you: I have already done so for myself. Only think, from Tuesday *up to late yesterday evening* I have been solely occupied with this business, and the bare idea of this rascally trick may suffice to let you feel how unpleasant it was to have to deal with such wretched fellows.

L. V. BEETHOVEN.

Revers

The undersigned undertakes herewith under no pretext to issue, or to sell here or elsewhere, the Quintet by Lud. v. Beethoven received from Count Fries, until the *Original* edition has been in circulation *here*, in Vienna, for 14 days.

Artaria Comp.

VIENNA, *September* 12, 1802.

[This letter, full of angry passion, clearly shows the sad position of a composer, with regard to the publishing freebooters, at a time when there was no respect for *brain* property. The letter also specially illustrates the notices about to be communicated which Beethoven saw himself compelled to issue. The "cooler-headed friend" was certainly Sonnleithner who only lately had entered into closer relationship with Beethoven. He was secretary of the Court theatre, and it was he who arranged the *Fidelio* text from the French.]

40. To Baron ZMESKALL

[*Nov.* 1802.]

My dear Z.

For aught I care you can speak pretty strongly to Walter about my affair, for first of all, he deserves it, and ever since one has been under the impression that I am at loggerheads with Walter, the whole swarm of pianoforte makers is impatient to serve me—and in vain. Each of them wants to make me a pianoforte to my liking. Reicha, for instance, is earnestly entreated by his pianoforte maker to persuade me to let him make me a pianoforte, and he is really one of the *more honest* fellows where I have already seen good instruments. You, therefore, give him to understand that I will pay 30 ducats for it, though I can get one gratis anywhere else; but I will only give 30 ducats, on condition that it is made of mahogany, and, in addition with the *una corda* pedal. If he does not agree, give him to understand that I shall apply to one of the other makers, to whom I shall suggest this, and whom, in the meantime, I shall also take to Haydn, so that he may see his instrument. A Frenchman, unknown to me, is coming to-day about 12 o'clock.

[*volti subito.*

Then Herr R[eicha] and I will have the pleasure of my having to *display my art* on a Jockesch pianoforte—*ad notam*—if you will also come, we shall have a good time of it, because afterwards we, Reicha, our wretched Imperial-Baron also, and the Frenchman will dine together. You need not put on a *black coat*, as we are *amongst ourselves.*

Your

BEETH.

[We have here the first written evidence that Beethoven and Reicha, who had been on friendly terms at Bonn, were still on the same footing. From this letter we also learn, and in a surprising way, that Beethoven held intercourse with his former teacher, the old master, Joseph Haydn.]

41. To AMATEURS

[*January* 22, 1803.]

In informing the public that my long announced original Quintet in C major has appeared at Breitkopf and Härtel's, Leipzig, I at once declare that I have nothing to do with the edition of this

Quintet prepared at the same time by Messrs. Artaria and Mollo in Vienna. I am especially forced to make this declaration, in that this edition is most faulty, incorrect, and for the performer quite useless. On the other hand, Messrs. Breitkopf and Härtel, the rightful owners of this Quintet, have done everything in their power to bring out the finest edition possible.

Ludwig van Beethoven.

[This notice affords fresh illustration of the prevailing piracy of many publishers of that period. As regards Mollo, however, Beethoven found that he was mistaken, and publicly withdrew his accusation (1807).]

42. To FERDINAND RIES, Vienna

[*Spring* 1803.]

Be good enough to pick out the faults, and send at once a list of them to Simrock, adding that he must try and get it out soon. The day after to-morrow I will send him the sonata and the concerto.

Beethoven.

[This concerns the three pianoforte sonatas (Op. 31) in G, D minor, and E flat, the first two of which were printed by Nägeli, of Zurich, in a very faulty and arbitrary manner, so that, as Ries relates, Beethoven fell into a towering passion. Simrock, of Bonn, had to print the sonatas afresh and add "*Edition très correcte.*" The sonata mentioned at the end of this note was the "Kreutzer" Sonata (*Sonate concertante*), which was actually published by Simrock in 1805. The concerto can only have been the one in C minor, which, however, was not published by Simrock, but at the Industrie-Kontor, Vienna (1805).]

43. To the Same

[*Spring* 1803.]

That I am there, you will probably know. Go to Stein and learn whether he can send me an instrument here, for which I will pay. I do not like to have mine brought here. I am at Oberdöbling No. 4, the street on the *left*, where the hill goes down towards Heiligenstadt.

Beethoven.

[This note was written in *pencil*. The pianoforte maker, Andreas Stein, was a brother of Nanette Streicher, *née* Stein.]

44. To BREITKOPF AND HAERTEL, Leipzig

Vienna, *April* 8, 1803.

I have long been wanting to write to you, but my many business matters do not allow me to carry on even a short correspondence. With regard to the Variations, you are mistaken in thinking that there are not so many. They could not, however, be exactly indicated; for instance, in the great ones where the variations run into one another in the *adagio*; then the fugue certainly cannot count as a *variation*, and so with the introduction to these great variations, which, as you yourself have already seen, commences with the bass of the *theme*, then *a* 2, 3 and 4 parts. Finally the *theme* appears which again cannot be called a *variation*. If, however, all this is not clear to you, send me, as soon as a copy is printed, a proof for correction, together with the *manuscripts*, that I may be certain of no *confusion*. And you would show me a great kindness if from the great variations you would leave out the *dedication* to the Abbé Stadler, and put in its place this one: *A Monsieur le Comte Maurice Lichnowski*. He is the brother of Prince Lichnowski, and only recently has shown me unexpected kindness, and I have no other opportunity of doing anything nice for him. If you have already put the *dedication* to Abbé Stadler, I will willingly bear the costs of changing the title-page. You need not hesitate at all. Only write and say what it costs. I will willingly pay, and beg you earnestly to see to it, unless some have been sent away. The small Variations are to be, as arranged, dedicated to the Princess Odescalchi.

I thank you heartily for the beautiful things of Sebastian Bach, I will *keep and study them*. If any more follow, do please let me have them also. If you have a good text for a *Cantata*, or for any vocal piece, let me see it,

from one,
who holds you in high esteem,
BEETHOVEN.

[This letter is of special interest in that it reveals to us new information respecting Beethoven's relations to Abbé Maximilian Stadler. This priest and artist (1748–1833) was as glowing an admirer of Mozart as he was a despiser of Beethoven. Schindler names as the three chief men who were opposed to the composer's innovations: J. Preindl, Capellmeister Dionys Weber and Stadler. From this letter we learn that at this time Beethoven was so friendly with the artistic Abbé, that he seriously thought of dedicating to him the set of Variations in E flat (Op. 35). This artist, however, was never weary of running down Beethoven's music, and many of his remarks must have reached the composer's ears—consequently the dedication was withdrawn. Stadler's dislike for Beethoven's music increased. Schindler relates how "this Nestor never missed a performance of the 'Schuppanzigh' Quartet, but always left before the Beethoven work, which was always given after Haydn and Mozart." Beethoven, however, always respected the man, and when Stadler spoke out bravely in favour of the genuineness of Mozart's *Requiem*, Beethoven wrote and congratulated him in the well-known letter of February 1826. The Variations described by Beethoven as "small" were those of Op. 34.]

45. To Baron ALEXANDER V. WETZLAR

From my house, May 18, 1803.

Although we have never spoken to each other, I do not hesitate to recommend Mr. Brischdower, the bearer of this letter; he is very clever and a thorough master of his instrument. In addition to his concertos he plays excellently in quartets; I do hope that you will be able to increase his circle of acquaintances. He is already advantageously known to Lobkowitz and Fries, and to all other amateurs of note.

I think it would be a very good thing if you could take him one evening to the house of Therese Schönfeld which, so far as I know, is frequented by many foreigners, or have him at your house. I know that you yourself will thank me for this introduction.

[The violinist, George August Polgreen Bridgetower, a mulatto, was born in Biala, Poland, in 1779. From an Austrian passport from Vienna (27 July, 1803) his general appearance is thus given by Jahn: "George Bridgtower: character artist; born at Biala, Poland; 24 years old; middle height; smooth bronze complexion; dark brown hair; brown eyes; rather thick nose." During the years 1802 and 1803 he gave concerts at Dresden and Vienna. In May (22) he received permission to give concerts in the Augarten. "Lichnowski will introduce him to Beethoven," so it is stated in this passport. His father, of African birth, was well known under the name of the Abyssinian Prince. See interesting article, "George P. Bridgetower and the ' Kreutzer' Sonata," in the *Musical Times*, May 1908.—Tr.]

46. To the Violinist G. A. P. BRIDGETOWER

[*May* 1803.]

My dear B.,

Come to-day at twelve o'clock to Count Deym's, i.e., where we were together the day before yesterday. They perhaps wish to hear you play something or other, but that you'll find out. I cannot get there till about half-past one, and until then I rejoice at the mere thought of seeing you to-day.

Your friend,

Beethoven.

[Countess Josephine Deym was a sister of Giulietta Guicciardi.]

47. To the Same

[*May* 1803.]

Kindly look out for me at the Graben in Tarroni's coffee house about half-past one, and then we will go to Countess Guicciardi where you are invited to dinner.

Beethoven.

[From this we see that in the very year in which his "Giulietta" became Countess Gallenberg, Beethoven frequented the Guicciardi house. Beethoven played the "Kreutzer" Sonata with Bridgetower at a concert given by the latter in the Augarten (22 or 24 May). Ries relates that the music was far from ready, especially that of the pianoforte part, which was only written in here and there; also that "at eight o'clock in the morning" Bridgetower had to play the Variations from Beethoven's own manuscript, for "no time was left to copy it out." Yet in 1805, when the Sonata was published by Simrock in Bonn, it was not dedicated to Bridgetower, but to another great violinist, "to his friend," Rudolf Kreutzer. Bridgetower and Beethoven are said to have quarrelled about a girl. Hector Berlioz assures us that Kreutzer never played the Sonata at his concerts.]

48. To BREITKOPF AND HAERTEL, Leipzig

[Vienna, *June*, 1803.]

I shall probably always be a very irregular correspondent of yours, for, to begin with, I am by no means a diligent writer—but you must overlook it. I hope you will receive my brother's letter in which he begged you to give notice of the really unusually numerous and serious faults. In a few days, I myself will send you a list of them. However handsome the edition, it is a pity that it has been sent into the world with the utmost carelessness and inaccuracy. As you printed my *Variations* from my *manuscript*, I was always afraid many errors might have crept in, and much wished you had sent me a *proof* beforehand. It is a most unpleasant thing to see an otherwise beautifully printed work full of mistakes, and especially for the *author*. Then, again, in the grand *Variations* it was forgotten that the *Theme* was taken from an allegorical Ballet which I composed, viz., *Prometheus*, or in Italian, *Prometeo*, and this ought to have been stated on the title-page. If possible, I beg you still to see to it, i.e., if it has not yet been published; if the title-page has to be altered, let it be at my cost. Things of this kind are forgotten here in Vienna, and one scarcely gives a thought to them. The perpetual distraction and also the business bustle really cause so great disorder in such matters, so forgive me for mentioning it so late. I cannot yet have anything to do with a poem, but I very much wish that when the one you mentioned appears, you would inform me so that I may look out for it. Do not forget about the *Variations*, also about the corrections and about the title-page, if it is still possible to alter. If in any way I can be of service to you here, please at once have recourse to

Your

most devoted servant,

Ludwig van Beethoven.

[This letter makes it quite clear that the peaceful theme which appears in *four* of Beethoven's works was first used in the Prometheus Ballet. The Variations in E flat (Op. 35), dedicated to Count Moritz Lichnowsky, which were published by B. and H. in 1803, are based on it; it occurs also in No. 7 of 12 *Contretänze* for orchestra published by Mollo and Co. in 1802; and finally in the Finale of the *Eroica* (Op. 55).]

49. TO THE SAME

[*September* 1803.]

P. S.

I offer you the following works for 300 florins: (1) two sets of *Variations*, one on *God Save the King*, the other on *Rule Britannia*; (2) a Quail song of which the poem may be known to you; it consists of three stanzas, which, however, are set with each stanza to fresh music; (3) three four-hand Marches, easy, though not altogether unimportant; the last, indeed is so big that it may be called the March of the three Marches. Send an answer by *return of post*, as time presses.

The *Variations* of which you were good enough to send me some *copies*, were after all not so very correct. I should like anyhow to be able to see a *proof* of the others, for I am always afraid of more serious faults in the others. I will see about Bach's daughter at the beginning of the winter; for the present there are no persons of importance here, and without them nothing really good can be done.

Best thanks to the *editor* of the *Musikalische Zeitung* for his kindness in inserting so *flattering a notice* about my *oratorio*, in which *such big lies are told about the prices that I charged*, and in which I am treated so *infamously*. It probably shows impartiality—well, be it so—if that sort of thing does good to the *Musikalische Zeitung*.

A true artist is expected to be all that is noble-minded and this is not altogether a mistake; on the other hand, however, in what a mean way are critics allowed to pounce upon us.

Answer at once; next time about some other matter.

As always, yours very truly,

L. V. BEETHOVEN.

N.B.—All that I here offer you is quite new—unfortunately very many old things of mine have unfortunately been sold, also stolen.

[The *God Save the King* Variations were published (as number 25) not by B. and H., but at Vienna by the Industrie-Kontor, and the *Rule Britannia* at the Bureau d'Arts et d'Industrie. The three four-hand marches were also published by the Industrie-Kontor. The composer's remark about the last one is not quite clear, seeing that all three are about the same length. Or was this third March in D substituted for another and a greater one? With regard to Bach's youngest daughter, Beethoven wished to do something to benefit Regina Johanna Bach; but nothing seems to have come of it. With regard to the "*flattering notice* of my oratorio," the Vienna correspondent in his notice in the *A. M. Z.* of 25 May, 1803, says: "Beethoven also gave a cantata of his own composition: *The Mount of Olives*. No one on the following day could understand why for this concert Herr B. charged double price for the best places, treble for the orchestra-stalls, and for a box, instead of four florins, twelve ducats. One must not, however, forget that this was Herr Beethoven's first attempt of the kind. I honestly hope, however, that the next time the takings will be as good; but, as regards the composition, more characterisation, and a better thought-out plan."]

50. To GEORGE THOMSON, Edinburgh

VIENNE, *le* 5 8bre, 1803.

A Monsieur
George Thomson, Nr. 28 York Place.
Edinburgh. North Britain.

Monsieur!

J'ai reçu avec bien du plaisir votre lettre du 20 Juillet. Entrant volontiers dans vos propositions je dois vous déclarer que je suis prêt de composer pour vous Six Sonates telles que vous les desirez, y introduisant même les airs ecossais d'une manière laquelle la nation ecossaise trouvera la plus favorable et le plus d'accord avec le génie de ses chansons.

Quant au honoraire, je crois que trois cent ducats pour Six Sonates ne sera pas trop, vu qu'en Allemagne on me donne autant pour pareil nombre de Sonates, même sans accompagnement.

Je vous préviens en même tems que vous devez accélérer votre declaration, parce qu'on me propose tant d'engagements qu'apres quelque tems je ne saurois peut-être aussitôt satisfaire à vos demandes. Je vous prie de me pardonner, que cette reponse est si retardé, ce qui n'a été causée que par mon sejour à la campagne et plusieurs occupations tres pressantes. Aimant de préference les airs Ecossais je me plairai particulierement dans la composition de vos sonates, et j'ose avancer qui si vos interêts s'accorder sur le honoraire vous serez parfaitement contentes.

Agrées les assurances de mon estime distingué.

LOUIS VAN BEETHOVEN.

[Only the signature is in Beethoven's handwriting.]

51. WARNING

(October—November 1803.)

Herr Carl Zulehner, re-printer in Mayence, has announced an edition of my complete works for pianoforte and strings. I consider it my duty publicly to make known to all musical friends that I am in no way connected with this edition. I should never have agreed to assist in a collection of my works without first conferring with the publishers of the separate editions, and seeing that imperfect editions of various separate works were set right. Besides, I must state that the edition in question of my works, illegally undertaken, never can be complete, inasmuch as various new works will shortly appear at Paris, which Herr Zulehner, as a French subject, dare not reprint. With regard to a collection of my works under my own superintendence, and after strict revision, I will on another occasion explain myself in detail.

LUDWIG VAN BEETHOVEN.

[From the Intelligenzblatt of the *Allg. Mus. Ztg.*, Nov., No. iii. 1803. This warning was also inserted in the *Wiener Zeitung*, where it filled, in large type, a whole printed page; it appeared in this paper already on 22 October. This Zulehner was no ordinary "re-printer" (*Nachstecher*, see Preface). Born at Mayence in 1770, he studied composition with Eckart, Philidor and Sterkel, was conductor at Mayence, and a member there of the Academy of Arts and Sciences. He arranged more than a hundred operas and oratorios for pianoforte. N. Simrock printed not a few of Zulehner's original compositions: pianoforte concerto (Op. 5), second pianoforte quartet (Op. 13), etc.].

52. To FERDINAND RIES

Spring 1804.

DEAR RIES!

I beg you to show me the kindness of copying, even if only roughly, this Andante. I have to send it away to-morrow, and as heaven knows what may happen to it, I want a copy taken of it. But I must have it back to-morrow about one o'clock. The reason of my troubling you is that one copyist is already busy writing other important things, and the other is ill.

[The Andante mentioned in it is not the one in the "Kreutzer" Sonata (Op. 47), which had long been written, but the Andante in F originally intended for the "Waldstein" Sonata.]

53. To the Same

[*Beginning of July* 1804.]

DEAR RIES!

As Breuning did not scruple by his behaviour in your presence
and that of the landlord to represent me as a wretched beggarly,
mean man, I therefore select you first to give my answer by word
of mouth to Breuning; but only concerning one and the first point
in his letter, which I only answer, because this ought to vindicate
my character in your eyes. Tell him, therefore, that it never occurred
to me to reproach him for the delay in giving notice; further that
if Breuning were really at fault in this matter, to live in peace with
mankind is far too sacred a thing, far too much to my liking, for
me to injure one of my friends for a few hundreds, or even more.
You yourself know that quite in a joking way I accused you as the
cause of the notice being given too late. I am quite sure that you
will remember it; as for me I had quite forgotten the matter. Then,
at table, my brother began to say that he thought the fault was
Breuning's; I at once denied this, and said that you were the guilty
person. I mean, it was indeed clear enough, that I did not lay the
blame on Breuning. Thereupon Breuning sprang up, like a madman,
and said he would call up the landlord. This behaviour, of which
I had never seen the like amongst all the men with whom I am
constantly associating, made me lose self-command. I likewise
jumped up, knocked down my chair, went away, and never returned. Now this induced Breuning to give such a fine account of
me to you and to the landlord, and likewise to send me a letter which
indeed I only answered by silence. To Breuning I have nothing more
to say. His way of thinking and acting, as regards myself, shows
that there ought never to have been friendly relationship between
us, and also that there certainly never will be. Herewith I wish to
make known to you that your testimony has lowered my whole
way of thinking and acting. I know that if you had so understood
the matter, you certainly would not have acted thus, and with
that I am satisfied.

Now please, dear Ries! Immediately on receipt of this letter
go to my brother, the apothecary, and tell him that already in a
few days I am leaving Baden, and that he is to engage the rooms
at Döbling immediately after you have informed him of it.

I was almost inclined to come to-day; I am sick of this place,
tired of it. Do, for heaven's sake, get him to rent the rooms at once,
because I want at once to settle down in Döbling. Say and show
him nothing of what is written about B. on the other page. I want

in every way to show him that I am not so small-minded as he is, and only wrote to him after the letter mentioned, although my resolution to break off our friendship is and remains firm.

Your friend,
BEETHOVEN.

54. TO THE SAME

BADEN, *July* 24, 1804.

The affair with Breuning will probably have surprised you. But, dear friend! believe me; my flash of temper was only a final outburst after many unpleasant incidents connected with him in the past. I possess the power of concealing and suppressing my sensitiveness with regard to a number of things; but if I am once roused at a time when I am susceptible to anger, then I speak straight out, more so than any other person. Breuning certainly possesses excellent qualities, but he thinks himself altogether free from faults, yet those which he thinks to detect in others are for the most part the very ones which he himself has in the highest degree. He is small-minded, a quality which from childhood I have despised. My critical faculty almost warned me beforehand of what would happen with Breuning, for our ways of thinking, acting, feeling are utterly different; and yet I believed that even these difficulties could be overcome—experience has shown that I was mistaken. And now all friendship is at an end! I only found two friends in the world, with whom I never had a misunderstanding, but what men! One is dead, the other still living. Although, for the last six years, neither has had any news of the other, I know well that I hold the first place in his heart, as he does in mine. The foundation of true friendship demands kinship of human souls and hearts. I only wish you would read the letter I have written to Breuning, also his to me. No, nevermore will he occupy the place in my heart which he once held. A man who can attribute to his friend such base thoughts, and likewise act in such a base manner towards him, does not deserve my friendship. Do not forget about my rooms. Farewell; do not indulge in too much tailoring, and remember me to the fairest of the fair; send me half a dozen sewing-needles. I never could have believed myself capable of being as lazy as I am here. If a working fit is the result, I may turn out something really good.

Vale,
BEETHOVEN.

[The two friends mentioned were, first Lenz (Lorenz) von Breuning, who in 1794 travelled with Wegeler from Bonn to Vienna in order to study medicine there. He had the privilege of pianoforte lessons from Beethoven, but died at Bonn, in his twenty-second year, on 10 April, 1798. The second of these friends was probably Dr. Wegeler. The humorous passage, "Don't indulge in too much tailoring," etc., refers to Ries's living in the house of a tailor who had three handsome daughters.]

55. To BREITKOPF AND HAERTEL, LEIPZIG

VIENNA, *August* 26, 1804.

Highly honoured Herr Härtel, several reasons cause me to write to you. Perhaps you may have heard that I had bound myself by contract with a certain Viennese firm (to the exclusion of all other publishers) to let them publish all my works. Owing to the inquiries of several foreign publishers with regard to this, I tell you, unasked, that it is not true. You yourselves know that I could not, for that reason, accept—at any rate not for the present—a similar proposal from your firm. And here is another matter which I have at heart: several publishers are terribly long before they bring out my works, and one accounts for the delay in one way, another in another. I well remember your once writing me that you could deliver in a few weeks an immense number of *copies*. I have just now several works, and because I think of giving them to you, my wish to see them soon published will perhaps be satisfied all the sooner. I therefore tell you straight off what I can give you: my *oratorio*—a *new grand symphony*—a Concertante for violin, 'cello and pianoforte with full orchestra; three new Solo Sonatas, and if you should want one of these with accompaniment, I would agree to do it. Now if you are willing to take these things, you must kindly tell me exactly the time at which you would be able to deliver them. As I have a strong desire that at least the first three works should appear as soon as possible, we would fix the time by writing, or contract (according to your suggestion); and to this, I tell you quite frankly, I should hold you strictly. The *Oratorio* has not hitherto been published, because I have added to it an altogether new chorus and altered several things; for I wrote the whole oratorio in a few weeks, and afterwards I was not quite satisfied with it. These changes date only from the time when my brother wrote to you about the work. The Symphony is really entitled *Bonaparte*, and in addition to the usual instruments there are, specially, three obbligato horns. I believe it will interest the musical public. I should like you, instead of printing in parts, to publish it in *score*. About the other things I have nothing more to add, although a concertante with three such concerting parts is in fact something quite new. If, as I expect, you agree to the *conditions stated* for these works as regards their publication, I would give them to you for a fee of 2000 fl. I assure you on my honour, that with regard to certain works, such as, for instance, sonatas, I am a loser, since I get almost 60 ducats for a single *solo sonata*. Pray do not think that I boast—far be it from me to do anything of the sort—but in order the quicker to arrange for an edition of my works, I am ready to be a loser to some extent.

Please give me an immediate answer to this. I hope Herr Wiems will have received my letter; I took the liberty of *addressing* it to your care. In anticipation of a speedy answer, I am,

Yours very truly,
Ludwig van Beethoven.

[The works mentioned are the oratorio *The Mount of Olives*, the *Eroica*, and the triple concerto (Op. 56); the solo sonatas were probably those in C (Op. 53) and F (Op. 54). The title "Bonaparte" Symphony, first given by the composer to the *Eroica*, deserves note.]

56. To the Music Publisher, N. SIMROCK, Bonn

Vienna, October 4, 1804.

Dear, best Herr Simrock, I have been all the time waiting anxiously for my Sonata which I gave you—but in vain. Do please write and tell me the reason of the delay—whether you have taken it from me merely to give it as food to the moths? or do you wish to claim it by special imperial privilege? Well, I thought that might have happened long ago. This slow devil who was to beat out this sonata, where is he hiding? As a rule you are a quick devil, it is known that, like Faust, you are in league with the black one, and on that very account *so beloved* by your comrades. Once again— where is your devil—or what kind of a devil is it—who is sitting on my Sonata, and with whom you are at loggerheads? So hurry up and tell me when I shall see the Sonata brought to the light of day. If you will fix the time, I will at once send you a little note to Kreutzer, which be kind enough to enclose when you are sending a *copy* (as anyhow you will send copies to Paris, or will have them printed there). This Kreutzer is a good, amiable man, who, during his stay here, gave me much pleasure. His unaffectedness and natural manner are more to my taste than all the *Exterieur* or *inferieur* of most *virtuosi*. As the Sonata is written for a first-rate player, the dedication to him is all the more fitting. Although we are in correspondence with each other (i.e., I write once every year), I hope he will know nothing about it as yet. I constantly hear that your prosperity rests on a basis which is ever becoming more and more sound; I am heartily glad of this. Greetings to all your family, and to all whom you think will be pleased to receive a greeting from me. An answer soon, please.

BEETHOVEN.

[Beethoven's impatience about the Sonata is easy to understand. It was ready for printing in 1804, but was only published by Simrock in the following year. The Sonata in question was of course the one in A (Op. 47).]

57. To the Painter WILLIBRORD JOSEPH MAEHLER

[1804?]

Please let me have my portrait back as soon as you have made sufficient use of it—but if you still want it I beg you will at least hurry up with it. I have promised the portrait to a foreign lady who saw it at my house, to be placed in her room during her stay here of a few weeks. Who could refuse such charming requests? Of course I shall not forget to let you have a share of all the beautiful favours which thereby will be bestowed on me.

Yours truly,
BEETHOVEN.

[The contents relate to the excellent portrait which represents Beethoven, full figure, sitting. It was painted in 1804–5, and was for a long time in the possession of the widow of Carl von Beethoven. Willibrord Joseph Maehler, native of Rhineland, is mentioned in F. G. Boeckh's *Vienna's Living Authors, Artists and Amateurs*, as an amateur in portrait-painting (p. 267); he was formerly an official of the imperial and royal house, court, and State Chancery. He was also a poet and musician.]

58. To STEPHAN Von BREUNING, Vienna

[1804?]

MY GOOD DEAR STEPHAN,

Let what for a time passed *between us*, lie for ever hidden behind this picture. I know it, I have broken *your heart*. The emotion which you must certainly have noticed in me was sufficient punishment for it. It was not a feeling of *malice* against you; no, for then I should be no longer worthy of your friendship. It was passion

Beethoven at the age of thirty-four (1804–5)
From a portrait by W. J. Maehler

on *your* part and on *mine*—but mistrust of you arose in me. Men came *between us* who are not worthy either of you or of me. My portrait has long been intended for you. You know well that it was intended for some one, and on whom better could I, with warmest feeling, give it, than to you, faithful, good, and noble Stephan. Forgive me if I did hurt your feelings; I was not less a sufferer myself through not having you near me during such a long period; then only did I really feel how dear to my heart you are and ever will be.

Your [without signature].

Do fly to my arms again, as in former days.

59. To Princess JOSEPHINE LIECHTENSTEIN

[*November* 1805.]

[Without date, written a few days before the marching in of the French, 1805.]

Forgive me, most noble Princess! if through the bearer of this you perhaps experience astonishment of an unpleasant kind. Poor Ries, my pupil, is compelled to shoulder a musket in this calamitous war, and at once, as a foreigner, to leave this city in a few days. He has nothing, nothing at all, and must take a long journey. In these circumstances all opportunity for a concert is quite cut off. He must have recourse to benevolence. I commend him to your notice. I am sure you will forgive me for this step. Only in a case of extreme necessity can an honourable man have recourse to such means.

In this assurance I send the poor fellow to you, so that he may obtain some relief; he must have recourse to all who know him.

With greatest respect,
L. v. BEETHOVEN.

Pour Madame la Princesse Liechtenstein, etc.

[Princess Josephine Sophie von Liechtenstein was the wife of General Field-Marshal and reigning Prince von Liechtenstein, whom the Landgräfin von Fürstenberg married in 1776 when in her sixteenth year. She became the mother of thirteen children. Her acquaintance with Beethoven began at Lichnowsky's and, like so many other noble ladies, she became a pupil of the young master, who dedicated to her the Sonata in E flat (Op. 27, No. 1). Well known is her meeting with Napoleon at Schönbrunn in 1809, when the emperor in the most honourable manner avenged an insult offered to the princess at Hüttelsdorf by one of his majors. The lady died in February 1848, aged 72. This letter, by the way, was not delivered—and at this

Beethoven was extremely angry. Ries, however, preserved "the original written on a small, unevenly-cut quarto sheet, as proof of Beethoven's friendship and love" for him; and for this every one may be thankful.]

60. To the Opera Singer SEBASTIAN MAYER

[November 1805.]

DEAR MAYER,

The quartet in the third act is now all right; what is written with red pencil must be painted over with ink by the copyist, otherwise it will get obliterated. This afternoon I shall send again for the first and second acts, for I want to look through them myself. I cannot come, for I have been suffering since yesterday from diarrhœa, my usual complaint. Do not trouble about the *Ouverture* and the other numbers; if really pressing, everything could be ready by to-morrow morning. Owing to the present fatal crisis, I have so many other things to attend to, that everything that is not absolutely necessary I have to put off.

Your friend BEETHOVEN.

[Friedrich Seb. Mayer (or Meier), who lived from 1773 to 1835, was the brother-in-law of Mozart; his second wife was Frau Hofer, the eldest sister of Constance Mozart and Aloysia Lange. This note refers to the rehearsals for the production of *Fidelio*.]

60A. TESTIMONIAL FOR C. CZERNY

[December 7, 1805.]

We, the undersigned, cannot refuse to testify that the young man, Carl Czerny, has made extraordinary progress on the pianoforte, far beyond what his age, fourteen years, would lead one to expect; that in this respect, also with regard to his wonderful memory, he is deserving of all possible support, and all the more, seeing that his parents have spent their fortune on the training of their promising son.

LUDWIG VON BEETHOVEN.

61. To the Opera Singer SEBASTIAN MAYER

[April 1806.]

DEAR MAYER,

Baron Braun informs me that my opera is to be given on Thursdays; for this I will tell you the reason by word of mouth.

Now, I beg you most earnestly to see that the choruses are better rehearsed, for the last time they were an utter failure. Also on Thursday we must have a rehearsal with full orchestra at the theatre; the orchestra was really not bad, but on the stage were many slips. That, however, was to be expected, for the time was too short. I had, however, to risk the matter, for B. Braun threatened that if the opera was not given on Saturdays it would not be given at all. Your affection and friendship, which at any rate you formerly showed, lead me to expect that you will also now see to this opera. After that it will not require such rehearsals any more, and, if you like, you can conduct it. Here are two books; please give one to ——. Farewell, dear Mayer, and look well after this matter.

[This and the following letter concern the revival of *Fidelio*, now in two acts, March and April 1806. The management of the opera, in the year 1806, was still in the hands of Peter von Braun, a large manufacturer, who had been raised to the rank of a nobleman. The baron, and still more his wife, were distinguished for their musical gifts. To the baroness, Beethoven had dedicated the two Sonatas for piano in E and G (Op. 14), also the Horn Sonata in F (Op. 17).]

62. TO THE SAME
[*April* 1806].

Please request Herr v. Seyfried to conduct my opera to-day; I myself want to-day to see and hear it at a distance; by that means, at any rate, my patience will not be so severely tried, as when close by I hear my music murdered. I cannot help thinking that it is done purposely. I say nothing about the wind instruments, but that all *pp*, *crescendos*, all *decrescendos* and all *fortes ff* were struck out of my opera; no notice is taken of a single one. If that's what I have to hear, there is no inducement to write anything more! The day after to-morrow I will fetch you to dinner. To-day I am unwell again.

Your friend,
BEETHOVEN.

P.S.—If the opera should be given the day after to-morrow, there must be a rehearsal to-morrow in the room—otherwise it will get worse and worse every day!

[Ignaz Xaver Ritter von Seyfried was appointed conductor at the Theater an der Wien when twenty-one years old; he was an enthusiastic admirer of Beethoven. He died at Vienna in 1841.]

63. To Count FRANZ Von BRUNSWICK, Hungary

[*May* 1806]

May 11*th*, 1806. VIENNA *on a Mayday*.

P. S.

DEAR, DEAR B.!

I just tell you that I have concluded a good bargain with Clementi. I receive £200 sterling, and in addition I have the right to sell the same works in Germany and France. He has also commissioned me to write other works, so that I have reason to hope that while still in the prime of life I may win the dignity due to a true artist. Dear B., I want the *Quartets*; I have already begged your sister to write to you about them. It is too long to wait until you have copied them from my score; but do make haste and send them straight off by letter-post—you shall have them back at latest in 4 or 5 days. I earnestly request you to see to this, as otherwise I shall incur a great loss. If you can arrange for me to come to Hungary and give a few concerts, please do so—you could have me for 200 gold ducats; I can't get on with the princely theatre rabble. So often as *we* (several friends) drink of your wine, we drink you, i.e., your health. Farewell, make haste—haste—haste, and send me the quartets—otherwise you will greatly embarrass me. Schuppanzigh is married—it is said to some one *very like him*—what a family????
Kiss your sister Therese; tell her, I fear I shall have to become great, without any memorial from her contributing thereto. Send off at once the quartets to-morrow—quar—tets—t—e—t—s.

Your friend,

BEETHOVEN.

[The advantageous contract between the composer and the music dealer Muzio Clementi was agreed upon in the year 1807. The quartets mentioned are the *Rasumowsky* (Op. 59, in F, E minor and C). Anyhow they were already begun in the spring of 1806, yet only completed in the early months of the following year. Then again Beethoven writes in this merry letter: "I can't get on with the princely theatre rabble," i.e. Prince von Lobkowitz, Count von Palffi, etc., who succeeded Peter von Braun as managers of the theatre in the year 1807. The almost student-like greeting to the count's sister, Therese von Brunswick, has absurdly been put forward as a special proof of Beethoven's deep attachment to this countess. I have repeatedly shown such a conclusion to be untenable; I refer readers to my pamphlet, *Beethoven's "Immortal Beloved": Giulietta Guicciardi or Therese Brunswick*. Schuppanzigh, the "fat one," married a ponderous woman, a native of Bohemia, whose younger sister, Frl. Killitschky, took part in a Beethoven concert, at the very time Capellmeister Reichardt of Berlin was in Vienna.]

64. To BREITKOPF AND HAERTEL, Leipzig

VIENNA, *July* 5, 1806.

P. S.,

I inform you that my brother is travelling to Leipzig on business connected with his chancery, and he is taking with him a pianoforte score of the overture of my *opera*, my oratorio and a *new pianoforte concerto*. Also you can arrange with him about new *violin quartets*, of which I have already finished one; and now intend to devote myself almost exclusively to this kind of work. As soon as you have come to an agreement with my brother, I will send you the complete piano score of my *opera*—you could also have the full score of it. I hear that the symphony which I sent you last year, and which you returned to me, has been *severely criticised*; I have *not read the article*. If they think to harm me they are mistaken— all the more as I have made no secret of the fact that you had returned to me this symphony with other compositions. Remember me kindly to v. Rochlitz. I hope his bad temper towards me has somewhat toned down. Tell him that I am not so ignorant of foreign literature as not to know that von Rochlitz has written some very fine things, and if I should ever come to Leipzig, I am convinced that we should certainly become very good friends, his criticism notwithstanding, and without prejudice; also remembrances to Cantor Müller, whom I highly esteem. Farewell.

With respect, your sincere,

LUDWIG VAN BEETHOVEN.

(Besides, if something comes of the bargain with my brother, I should like to receive from you the published scores of Haydn and Mozart.)

[The pianoforte concerto was the fourth in G (Op. 58); begun long ago, it was completed in the following year, and appeared, dedicated to the Archduke Rudolf, in August 1808, at Vienna and Pesth (Kunst und Industrie-Kontor). Delightful are the words concerning the *Eroica*, rejected by the Leipzig firm and then mercilessly run down in their newspaper. Rochlitz's "bad temper" against the composer of this symphony really became visibly milder. Like his organ, the *Allg. Mus. Ztg.*, so did he become more and more enthusiastic for Beethoven. The "Cantor Müller" mentioned in the letter was August Eberhard Müller, the excellent pianist and composer. At the time it was written he was already cantor at the Thomas School, Leipzig, and musical director at both the principal churches of that city. In the year 1810 he was called to Weimar as court conductor, and died there in 1817 at the age of fifty.]

65. To GEORGE THOMSON, EDINBURGH

[*October* 1, 1806.]

SIR,

A short excursion which I have made to Silesia is the cause of my having delayed up to now answering your letter of the 1st July. Having now returned to Vienna, I hasten to send you my remarks and decisions concerning the offer you kindly made me. And in doing so I shall be frank and exact, qualities which I like in business matters, and which alone can prevent any complaint on the one side or the other. I now proceed, honoured Sir, to give the following explanations:

(1) I am not disinclined, considering the matter generally, to accept your proposals.

(2) I will endeavour to make the compositions easy and pleasant, so far as I am able, and so far as it is in agreement with that sublimity and originality of style, which, according to your own statement, characterise my works and to their advantage, which standard I shall ever seek to maintain.

(3) I cannot make up my mind to write for the flute, as this instrument is too limited and imperfect.

(4) In order to give more variety to the compositions which you will publish, and in order that I may have fuller play, though the task of making them easy would always bother me, I will only promise you three trios for violin, viola and violoncello and three quintets for two violins, two violas and a violoncello. In place of the other three trios and three quintets I will let you have three quartets, and, finally, two sonatas for pianoforte with accompaniment, and a quintet for two violins and flute. In a word, I would beg you, with regard to the second set of compositions desired by you, to trust entirely to my judgment and loyalty, and I am sure you will be perfectly satisfied. Lastly, if this change is not at all to your liking, I will not obstinately insist on it.

(5) I should be very glad to see the second edition of the compositions published six months after the first.

(6) I want a clearer explanation about a statement in your letter, to the effect that no copy printed under my authority shall be introduced into Great Britain; for if you are agreed that these compositions can be published also in Germany and indeed in France, I cannot well see how I can prevent copies being introduced into your country.

(7) Finally, as regards the honorarium, I expect you to offer me £100 sterling, or 200 Vienna ducats in gold, and not in Vienna

bank-notes, which under present circumstances entail too great a loss; for the sum would, if paid in these notes, be as little commensurable with the work which I should let you have as with the fees which I receive for all my other compositions. Even a sum of 200 ducats in gold is by no means excessive payment for all that has to be done to satisfy your wishes. Finally, the best arrangement will be for you to send me by post a bill of the value of 100 ducats in gold, when I send you the first and again when I send the second set; it must be drawn on a business house at Hamburg, or you must commission some one in Vienna to return me each time such a bill, while the same will receive from me the first and the second set.

You will name to me at the same time the day on which each set will be published by you, so that I can bind the publishers who issue these same compositions in Germany and France, to be guided thereby.

I hope that you will find my explanations just, and of such a kind as will probably enable us to come to a definite understanding. In this case it will be well for us to draw up a proper contract, of which you might be kind enough to have a duplicate copy made, which I would send you back with my signature.

I only await your answer to set to work, and remain with highest esteem,

Sir,
Your obedient servant,
Louis van Beethoven.

P.S.—I will also fulfil your wish to provide short Scottish songs harmonised, and with regard to this await a more exact proposal, as I know well that Mr. Haydn was paid £1 sterling for each song.

[This letter was originally written in French, and only signed by Beethoven. Concerning the relations between Beethoven and George Thomson of Edinburgh, cf. Letter 50, 5 October, 1803, and especially the explanations there given. Only one of the proposals made by Beethoven in this letter was accepted, viz., the harmonisation of Scottish songs.]

66. To Messrs. BREITKOPF AND HAERTEL, Leipzig

[November 18, 1806.]

P. S.

Partly my distractions in Silesia, partly the events in your country were to blame for my not as yet having answered your last letter. If circumstances prevent you arranging with me, then you are not bound to anything, only I beg you to send me an answer by next post, so that in case you won't come to terms with me, I need not leave my works on the shelf. With regard to a contract for three years I would settle at once with you, if you would agree to my selling several works to England or Scotland or France. *It is understood that the works which you receive from me, or which I sold to you, also belong to you alone, viz., are entirely your property and have nothing in common with those sold to France or England or Scotland—only I must reserve to myself the liberty of selling other works of mine to the above-named countries.* In Germany, however, you would be *the sole owners of my works*, to the exclusion of all other publishers. I would willingly renounce the sale of my works in those countries, but, for instance, from Scotland I have important offers, and *terms* such as I could never ask from you; besides a connection abroad is of importance for the reputation of an artist, and in case he travels. As I, for instance, in the offers from Scotland, am still free to sell the same works in Germany and in France, so you, for instance, could readily obtain them from me for Germany and France, so that for your sale only London, and perhaps *Edinburgh* (in Scotland), would be closed to you. In this way I would willingly enter into a contract with you for three years; you would always get sufficient stuff from me—the orders from those countries are frequently for something to please individual taste, which we do not want in Germany. For the rest, however, I am of opinion that there is no need to draw up a contract and that you ought to rely entirely on *my word of honour*. I undertake to give you the preference in Germany over all other publishers, it being understood that neither France nor Holland can have any share in these works— you are the sole owners. Do as you like in the matter, only drawing up a contract gives a lot of trouble; I would name to you the *fee* for each work—and the lowest possible. For the present I offer you three quartets and a pianoforte concerto—I cannot yet send you the promised *symphony*, for a gentleman of quality has taken it from me, on the understanding that after six months I am at liberty to publish it. [About two lines scratched through.] I ask from you 600 fl. for three quartets and 300 for the concerto. *Both sums in convention-Gulden*, according to the twenty-Gulden scale. The best would be for you to give notice that the money was at your place, or else at some well-known banker's, whereupon I would draw a bill from here on Leipzig. If this does not suit, you could send me a bill for the sum reckoned in 20 fl. Gulden according to the exchange.

It might be possible for me to be able to have the *symphony* printed sooner than I expected; in that case you could soon have it. Only send me a speedy answer—so that I may not be kept waiting. For the rest be assured that I prefer your firm to all others, and shall continue to do so,

With esteem,

Your most devoted servant,

L. v. BTHVN.

VIENNA, *November* 18, 1806.

[The question of a contract between Beethoven and this firm fell through; even the compositions mentioned in this letter were not published by B. and H., but by the Vienna Industrie-Kontor. The "gentleman of quality" was either Count Fries, or Count Moritz von Oppersdorf, to whom the 4th Symphony in B flat was dedicated.]

67. AGREEMENT BETWEEN BEETHOVEN AND MUZIO CLEMENTI

[*April* 1807.]

"La convention suivante a été faite entre Monsieur M. Clementi et Monsieur Louis v. Beethoven.

1. Monsieur Louis v. Beethoven cède à Monsieur M. Clementi les manuscrits de ses œuvres ci-après ensuivis, avec le droit de les publier dans les royaumes unis britanniques, en se réservant la liberté de faire publier ou de vendre pour faire publier ces mêmes ouvrages hors des dits royaumes:

a. trois quatuors.

b. une symphonie

N.B. la quatrième qu'il a composé(e).

c. une Ouverture de Coriolan

tragédie de Mr. Collin.

d. un concert pour le piano

N.B. le quatrième qu'il a composé.

e. un concert pour le violon

N.B. le premier qu'il a composé.

.f. ce dernier concert arrangé pour le piano avec des notes additionnelles.

2. Monsieur M. Clementi fera payer pour ces six ouvrages à M. L. v. Beethoven la valeur de deux cents Liv. Sterl. au cours de Vienne par Mess. Schuller et Comp. aussitôt qu'on aura à Vienne la nouvelle de l'arrivé de ces ouvrages à Londres.

3. Si Monsieur L. v. Beethoven ne pouvait livrer ensemble ces six ouvrages, il ne seroit payé par Mess. Schuller et Comp.

qu'à proportion des pièces livrées, p. ex. en livrant la moitié, il recevra la moitié, en livrant le tiers il recevra le tiers de la somme convenue.

Monsieur L. van Beethoven promet de ne vendre ces ouvrages soit en allemagne, soit en france, soit ailleurs, qu'avec la condition de ne les publier que quatre Mois après leur depart respectif pour l'angleterre: pour le concert pour le violon et pour la Symphonie et l'Ouverture, qui viennent de partir pour l'angleterre, Mons. L. v. Beethoven promet de les vendre qu'à condition de ne les publier avant le 1 Sept. 1807.

5. On est convenu de plus, que Mons. L. v. Beethoven compose aux memes [*sic*] conditions dans un temps non déterminé et à son aise trois Sonates ou deux Sonates et une Fantaisie pour le piano avec ou sans accompagnement comme il voudra, et que Mons. M. Clementi lui fera payer de la meme [*sic*] manière soixante livres Sterl.

6. Mons. M. Clementi donnera à Mons. L. v. Beethoven deux exemplaires de chacun de ses ouvrages.

fait en double et signé à Vienne le zo [*sic*] Avril 1807.

MUZIO CLEMENTI. LOUIS VAN BEETHOVEN.

comme témoin

J. Gleichenstein."

[The three quartets (Op. 59) were, according to a change in Beethoven's own hand, to be dedicated "à Son Altesse le Prince Charles de Lichnowsky"; in the arrangement of the violin Concerto the name "Frau von Breuning" was scratched through. The pianoforte Concerto in G was dedicated to the Archduke Rudolf, but in its place was chosen a French title with "Dedié à son ami Gleichenstein." The original titles, however, were restored. The agreement refused by Pleyel was concluded with Clementi in a brilliant manner for Beethoven. Clementi often came to Germany; his musical contest with Mozart in 1781 will be remembered. Ries, in the Biographical Notices, explains at length the reason of the time it took before Beethoven and Clementi made each other's acquaintance.

An account is given in an article entitled "Clementi Correspondence," signed J. S. S., in the *Monthly Musical Record* for August 1902, in which is given a portion of a letter from Clementi to Collard, his business partner in London, in which he describes his meeting Beethoven "by chance one day in the street," and how he "made a compleat conquest of that *haughty beauty*." Clementi then describes the agreement made with him as in the above document. From other letters of Clementi in this article, we learn that Beethoven had not been paid *two years and a half* after the signing of the agreement.—TR.]

68. To BARON GLEICHENSTEIN

[1807.]

As Frau M. told me yesterday that she really wanted to select *another piano* at Schanz's to-day, I wish she would give me full liberty to select one. It shall not cost more than 500 fl. but will be worth a great deal more. You know that although the firms offer me a certain sum, I never accept it. But as by this means I can buy an expensive instrument at a very cheap price, I would willingly, on this occasion, make the first exception to my fixed practice in such matters, as soon as you let me know whether my proposal is accepted. Farewell, dear good Gleichenstein. We shall see each other to-morrow and you can give me the answer.

Your BEETHOVEN.

[Outside in an unknown hand.]

"Gigaud's pretty collar [?]
Secretary key belonging to F. v. Malfatti.
4, Greetings from all of us to Gigaud, not
5, *forgetting* B.; I earnestly beg this of you."

[From this letter we hear of Beethoven's praiseworthy custom with regard to commissions on pianos. Another exception to his hard and fast practice will be found in Letter 184. In the present and later instance, the instrument was to be selected from the pianoforte manufactory of Schanz; otherwise Beethoven favoured the Streicher-Stein and the Graf instruments. The addition in an unknown hand refers to Gigons, the pet dog of Baroness Malfatti. A small adventure with this little dog will be found in the next letter.]

69. TO THE SAME

[1807.]

Here is the S. which I promised Therese. As I cannot see her to-day, give it to her. Remember me to them all, I am so happy in their company; it is as if the wounds, which bad people have inflicted on my soul, might through them be healed. I thank you, good G., for having introduced me to them. Here are another 50 fl. for the neckcloths; if you want more, let me know. You are mistaken, if you believe that Gigons only follows you. No, even I have had the pleasure of seeing him keep close to me. He sat beside me at dinner in the evening, he followed me home; in short, he procured very good entertainment for me—at any rate I never could get right to the top, but fairly low down—farewell, love me.

Yours,
BEETHOVEN.

[The Sonata (S.) sent to Therese was perhaps the *Appassionata*. The little dog Gigons had, so it seems, attached itself to Beethoven, of whose fondness for dogs nothing has been as yet heard.
For concluding sentence, see Preface, *re* play upon words.—TR.]

70. To the Same

[1807.]

The Countess invites you to dinner to-day. Write to Fezburg [Pressburg?] and ask the highest price they will give for the purchase of a piano. Do not forget about the Hamburg quills.

[This was the period when there was much music-making with his dear Countess Erdödy, to whom he dedicated the two Trios (Op. 70) composed in 1808.]

71. To THERESE Von MALFATTI

[1807.]

You receive herewith, honoured Therese, what I promised, and had it not been for urgent hindrances, you would have received more, in order to show you that I always *offer more to my friends than I actually promise*. I hope and have every reason to believe that you are nicely occupied and as pleasingly entertained—but I hope not too much, so that you may also think of us. It would probably be expecting too much of you, or overrating my own importance, if I ascribed to you "people are not only together when they are together; even he who is far away, who has departed, is still in our thoughts." Who would ascribe anything of the kind to the lively T. who takes life so easily?

Pray do not forget the pianoforte among your occupations, or, indeed, music generally. You have such fine talent for it. Why not devote yourself· entirely to it? you who have such feeling for all that is beautiful and good. Why will you not make use of this, in order that you may recognise in so beautiful an art the higher perfection which sheds its rays even on us. I am very solitary and quiet, although lights [1] now and again might awaken me; but since you all went away from here, I feel in me a void which cannot be filled; my art, even, otherwise so faithful to me, has not been able to gain any triumph. Your piano is ordered and you will soon receive it. What a difference you will have found between the treatment of the theme I improvised one evening, and the way in which I recently wrote it down for you. Explain that to yourself, but don't take too much punch to help you. How lucky you are, to be able to go so soon to the country; I cannot enjoy that happiness until the 8th. I am happy as a child at the thought of wandering among clusters of bushes, in the woods, among trees, herbs, rocks.

[1] *Lichter* (lights) or, according to some, the word is *Dichter* (poets).—Tr.

No man loves the country more than I; for do not forests, trees, rocks re-echo that for which mankind longs.

[Here follow four lines struck through, which refer to a composition.]

Soon you will receive other compositions of mine, in which you will not have to complain much about difficulties. Have you read Goethe's *Wilhelm Meister, the Schlegel translation of Shakespeare*; one has much leisure in the country, and it will perhaps be agreeable to you if I send you these works. I happen to have an acquaintance in your neighbourhood, so perhaps I shall come early one morning and spend half an hour at your house, and be off again; notice that I shall inflict on you the shortest *ennui*.

Commend me to the good wishes of your father, your mother, although I can claim no right for so doing—and the same, likewise, to cousin Mm. [?]. Farewell, honoured T. I wish you all that is good and beautiful in life. Keep me, and willingly, in remembrance —forget my wild behaviour. Be convinced that no one more than myself can desire to know that your life is joyous, prosperous, even though you take no interest in

Your most devoted servant and friend,

BEETHOVEN.

N.B.—It would really be very nice on your part to send me a few lines to say in what way I can be of service here?

72. To Baron GLEICHENSTEIN

BADEN, *June* 13, 1807.

DEAR GLEICHENSTEIN,

The night before last I had a dream. It seemed to me as if you were in *a stable*, so absorbed in gazing at two magnificent horses, that you were oblivious to all that was going on round about you.

Your hat purchase has turned out badly. Early this morning as I came here it got *slit*; as it costs too much money to be duped in this dreadful manner, you must try and get them to take it back and give you another. Meanwhile you can inform these bad shopkeepers that I am sending it back to you—it is really too irritating.

Yesterday and to-day I have been very ill; I have suffered fearfully from headache. May heaven rid me of it—one infirmity is enough for me. If you can, send me Bahrd's translation of Tacitus.

More another time; I feel so ill that I can only write a few lines—
farewell—think of my dream and of myself.

Your faithful
BEETHOVEN.

[This is a postscript though not so marked.]

From Simrock's letter I gather that we may expect a favourable
answer from Paris. Tell my brother to write whether you think so,
in order that everything may be copied again quickly. Send me the
number of your house.

Pour Mr. de Gleichenstein.

Send me an answer about the hat.

73. TO PRINCE ESTERHAZY

BADEN, [26th July, 1807.]

MOST SERENE, MOST GRACIOUS PRINCE,

As I am told that you, my prince, have inquired about the Mass
which you commissioned me to write for you, I take the liberty
to anounce to you, most serene prince, that you will receive it at
latest by the 20th of August—so that there will be sufficient time
to arrange a performance for the name-day of the most serene
princess. Exceptionally advantageous offers which were made to
me from London just as I had the misfortune to be disappointed
of my benefit day at the theatre, and which *necessity* forced me
gladly to accept, delayed the completion of the Mass, however
much I indeed wished to appear with it in your presence, most serene
prince. In addition I suffered later on with my head, which at
first, and afterwards, prevented me from working, and even now
I cannot do much. Now as everything is so readily explained to
my disadvantage, I herewith enclose, most serene prince, one of
the letters from my physician. May I add that with much fear I
shall hand to you the Mass, since you, most serene prince, are
accustomed to hear the inimitable masterpieces of the great Haydn.

Most serene, most gracious prince! with high esteem,

Your most devoted servant,
LUDWIG VAN BEETHOVEN.

[A copy of the score, with many corrections in Beethoven's hand, bore
the following autograph:

Missa composta e dedicata al Ser^{mo} Eccell^{mo}
Principe
Nicolo Esterhazy de Galantha, etc., etc.
di Luigi v. Beethoven.

The exact date of the first performance was 13 September, 1807. Beethoven, in his reference to Haydn's masterpieces, seems to have been in earnest. The prince's taste was spoilt by Haydn's style; that of Beethoven did not appeal to him. It was the custom at Eisenstadt for the native and foreign musical notabilities to assemble in the prince's drawing-room, after service, and exchange opinions with him concerning the music which had been performed. When Beethoven entered, the prince greeted him with the puzzling question: "But, my dear Beethoven, what have you been doing now?" while Joh. Nep. Hummel, the new Capellmeister, standing next to the prince, is said to have laughed. The work, after all, was not dedicated to the prince, but to Prince Kynsky. Three movements from the Mass were performed at Beethoven's benefit concert in 1808, but the complete work only in 1816. It was published by B. and H. in 1812.]

74. To Frau MARIE BIGOT, née KIENÉ

[*Summer* 1808.]

MY DEAR, HONOURED MARIE!

The weather is so divinely beautiful—and who knows whether it will be so to-morrow? I therefore propose to come and fetch you to-day about 12 noon for a drive. As Bigot is probably already out, we cannot of course take him with us—but to give it up entirely on that account, even Bigot himself would not make such a demand. Only the forenoons are now best. Why not seize the moment which passes away so quickly. It would be quite unlike Marie, who is so enlightened and well-bred, if for the sake of mere scruples she would wish to deprive me of the very great pleasure. Oh! whatever reasons you might assign for not *accepting* my proposal, I should ascribe it entirely to the little confidence which you place in my character—and should never believe that you entertain true friendship for me. Wrap up Caroline in swaddling-clothes from head to foot, so that nothing may happen to her. Answer me, my dear M., whether you can. I do not ask whether you are willing—for the latter would only bring a declaration to my detriment—so only answer in [one of] two words, yes or no. Farewell, and arrange that the selfish pleasure may be granted to me of sharing with two persons in whom I take so great interest, the cheerful enjoyment of bright beautiful nature.

Your friend and admirer,
L. VON BEETHOVEN.

[Bigot, who had been in Berlin, became in 1808 librarian to Prince Rasumowsky, in whose palace Beethoven was a frequent guest. The next letter shows clearly that Marie Bigot did not accept Beethoven's invitation to take her and little Caroline, about three years old, for a drive.]

75. To the Married Couple BIGOT

[*Probably Summer* 1808.]

Dear Marie, dear Bigot,

Only with the deepest regret am I forced to perceive that the purest, most innocent, feelings can often be misconstrued. As you have received me so kindly, it never occurred to me to explain it otherwise than that you bestow on me your friendship. You must think me very vain or small-minded, if you suppose that the civility itself of such excellent persons as you are, could lead me to believe that—I had at once won your affection. Besides, it is one of my first principles never to stand in other than friendly relationship with the wife of another man. Never by such a relationship [as you suggest] would I fill my breast with distrust against her who may one day share my fate with me—and so taint for myself the most beautiful, the purest life.

It is perhaps possible that sometimes I have not joked with Bigot in a sufficiently refined way; I have indeed told both of you that occasionally I am very free in speech. I am perfectly natural with all my friends, and hate all restraint. I now also count Bigot among them, and if anything I do displeases him, friendship demands from him and you to tell me so—and I will certainly take care not to offend him again—but how can good Marie put such bad meaning on my actions.

With regard to my invitation to take a drive with you and Caroline, it was natural that, as Bigot, the day before, was opposed to your going out alone with me, I was forced to conclude that you both probably found it unbecoming or objectionable—and when I wrote to you, I only wished to make you understand that I saw no harm in it. And so when I further declared, that I attached great value on your not declining, this was only that I might induce you to enjoy the splendid, beautiful day; I was thinking more of your and Caroline's pleasure than of mine, and I thought, *if I declared that mistrust on your part or a refusal would be a real offence to me,* by this means almost to compel you to yield to my wish. The matter really deserves careful reflection on your part, how you can make amends for having spoilt this day so bright for me, owing as much to my frame of mind as to the cheerful weather. When I said that you misunderstand me, your present judgment of me shows that I was quite right, not to speak of what you thought to yourself about it. When I said that something bad would come of it, if I came to you, this was more as a joke. The object was to show you how much everything connected with you attracts me; so that

I have no greater wish than to be able always to live with you; and that is the truth. Even supposing there was a hidden meaning in it, the most holy friendship can often have secrets, but—on that account to misinterpret the secret of a friend because one cannot at once fathom it—that you ought not to do. Dear Bigot, dear Marie, never, never will you find me ignoble. From childhood onwards I learnt to love virtue—and all that is beautiful and good —you have deeply pained me; but it shall only serve to render our friendship ever firmer. To-day I am really not well, and it would be difficult for me to see you. Since yesterday after the quartets, my sensitiveness and my imagination pictured to me the thought that I had caused you suffering. I went at night to the ball for distraction, but in vain. Everywhere the picture of you all pursued me; it kept saying to me, they are so good and perhaps through you they are suffering. Thoroughly depressed I hastened away—write to me a few lines.

Your true friend Beethoven embraces you all.

[Marie Bigot, *née* Kiené, was born at Colmar in 1786. She married in 1804 and came to Vienna. Soon after 1809 she and her husband went to Paris, where Marie Bigot soon became much sought after as a teacher of the pianoforte. Her physical strength, however, soon declined, and she died in September 1820, in her thirty-fourth year.]

76. Pour Monsieur De BIGOT

[1808.]

My dear good Bigot,

I wished to come to you yesterday, in order to settle my little debt, but was prevented. As to-day again I may not be able to come, I do so by writing. Please thank Madame Moreau once again for the pleasure which she afforded me; even though she was not exactly willing, still I was enabled to spend a most pleasant evening with you all. Farewell, and do not kiss your wife too often.

Wholly yours,
BEETHOVEN.

[Madame Moreau was probably the lady often mentioned by J. F. Reichardt in his *Vertraute Briefe*, as the very musical wife of the architect Moreau. In one letter (26 January, 1809) he writes about a select party at the house of Madame Bigot de Morogues. It had been arranged in honour of Reichardt, so that he might hear performances of Beethoven's new grand sonatas and chamber-works. On this evening she played no fewer than five grand sonatas. There was also a Madame Julie Moreau, a court actress and singer, who may have belonged to Beethoven's circle of friends.]

77. To Messrs. BREITKOPF AND HAERTEL, Leipzig

VIENNA, *8th June* [1808].

SIRS,

This letter is the fault of the *private tutor of young Count* Schönfeld, for he assured me that you again wished to have some works from me—although after so many breakings off I felt almost convinced that this renewal also would again prove fruitless. At the present moment I only offer you the following works—2 Symphonies, one Mass, and a Sonata for pianoforte and 'cello. N.B.: for the lot I ask 900 florins; [1] this sum of 900 florins, however, must be paid according to *Vienna currency, in convention-coin,* and this must be expressly stated on the draft. For several reasons I must make the condition with regard to the 2 Symphonies, that, reckoning from June 1st, they must not be published before six months. I shall probably make a tour as winter approaches, and at any rate I do not wish them to become known during the summer. I could, if I chose, let the Industrie-Kontor here have them, for last year they accepted 7 important works of mine, almost all of which are now in print. And though, indeed, they would willingly accept all I offer, yet, as I have often told you, I prefer your firm to all others. If you only decide to treat with me, I am convinced that both you and myself will gain thereby. In many things you will find me by no means greedy after money, but, on the contrary, ready to meet you, and waive all question of profit; and through such a connection something really good might result not for me alone, but also for art. Let me know your decision as soon as possible, so that I may still be in good time to arrange with the Industrie-Kontor. Try and manage for us to come together and remain together—on my side I will certainly do my best. You will always find me frank, without any reserve even in *this* connection —in short, everything may show you how willingly I enter into connection with you.

Your most devoted,

L. VON BEETHOVEN.

[The works here offered by Beethoven are the C minor and Pastoral Symphonies. Both were produced at the Theater an der Wien under Beethoven's direction on 22 December, 1808, and were published by Breitkopf and Haertel in the following year; also the proffered Mass in C (Op. 86), which was issued by the same firm in November 1812, and, finally, the Sonata for piano and 'cello in A (Op. 69), which appeared in 1809. Beethoven's

[1] Hurry is my excuse for the blot.

statement that his Mass was given "with much applause" at Eisenstadt, deserves note. It is generally supposed that the prince's comment on the work: "But, my dear Beethoven, what have you been doing now?" really indicated that the composer had not given satisfaction.]

78. To the Same

[16*th July*, 1808.]

SIRS,

Here is my decision in answer to your letter—and from it you will certainly perceive my readiness to meet your wishes so far as is possible. First of all the scheme, and then the why and the wherefore. I give you the Mass, together with the 2 Symphonies and the 'cello and piano Sonata, and in addition, two other Sonatas for the piano, or instead of these, perhaps another Symphony, all for 700 florins (seven hundred florins in convention-coin). You see that I give more and take less—but that is the lowest figure. You must take the Mass, otherwise I cannot give you the other works— for I am considering what brings honour, and not only what is profitable. You say "there is no demand for church music." You are quite right when it is composed by mere thorough-bassists; but only arrange for a performance of the Mass at Leipzig, and see whether you will not at once find amateurs who want to have it; give it for my sake in pianoforte score with German text. I will guarantee that each time and always there will be success.

Perhaps even by *subscription*; I am sure from here I could procure for you a dozen or two dozen *subscribers*—but that is certainly unnecessary. As soon as you have accepted, as I fully expect, my proposal, you will receive the 2 Symphonies, the Sonata with 'cello, the Mass, the two other pianoforte Sonatas or perhaps instead of them a Symphony, at latest four weeks after that. But I beg you at once on receipt of the first 4 works to let me have the *honorarium*. I will also enter in the schedule the Symphony, or in its place the 2 Sonatas which you are to receive from me; and in writing, so that you may have no misgiving, bind myself to send you within 4 weeks the Sonatas or the Symphony. I beg you to send me the 700 florins in a draft specifying 700 florins convention-coin, or order it to be payable in bank-notes according to the exchange on the day of receipt in Vienna. For the rest, I undertake after a time to present you with an Offertory and Gradual for the Mass; for the moment, however, they are not ready—but please let me know your decision as quickly as possible. I cannot consent to any modifications. It is the lowest I can manage, and I am convinced that you will not repent the bargain. With high esteem.

Yours faithfully,

LUDWIG VON BEETHOVEN.

[According to the original manuscript in the possession of the B. and H. firm; *unpublished*.]

79. TO THE SAME

[Written after the 16th July, 1808.]

SIRS,

With regard to your repeated proposal through Wagener, I answer that I am also ready fully to release you from what concerns the Mass—so I make you a present of it, even the costs of copying you will not have to pay; for I am firmly persuaded that if you only give a performance of it at your winter concerts in Leipzig, you will certainly publish it, and with a German text. Happen what may, it belongs to you; as soon as we have come to an agreement, I will send you the score of it together with the other works, and will also enter it in the schedule as if you had paid for it. The reason why I particularly wanted to get you to publish this Mass was, first of all because, in spite of all coldness at the present day towards such works, I have it especially at heart; secondly, because I thought that by means of your type notes for printed notes it would be easier for you than for other German publishers, who for the most part know nothing about scores.

Now for the rest: as the Mass is not included, you will now receive two Symphonies, a Sonata with obbligato 'cello, two Trios for piano, violin and 'cello (of which there is a scarcity), or, instead of the last-named two T., a Symphony, for 600 florins in convention-coin according to the exchange, as I arranged in my first two letters to you. As soon as you accept, and of this I entertain no doubt, you could pay in two instalments, viz.: as soon as I hand over to your representative here in Vienna the two Symphonies and the Sonata with 'cello obbligato, I receive a draft for 400 florins; a few weeks later I will hand over the two Trios, or at your pleasure the Symphony, and then you could let me have the remaining 200 florins by draft—so everything is free from doubt. The score of the Mass, as soon as I get an answer, will be copied and sent to you without fail in the second parcel. I must be greatly mistaken if you still hesitate; you must surely see that I have done everything in my power to come to terms with you. For the rest, you may rest assured that for my compositions I receive here quite as much and even more; it is, however, a fatal circumstance that a publisher here does not pay at once, but very slowly. Here you have the explanation of the matter, but I hope you are honourable enough not to misuse my frankness. I see for the rest that you are entering into an engagement with me of unusual importance, and you will certainly often perceive that I am disinterested. I have too great love for my art to be guided entirely by interest; but for the last two years I have suffered many misfortunes, and here in V.—but no more of this. Do answer at once, for I have waited all the time for your sake. If you are under the impression that I could not get the same terms here, you are mistaken; there is no other reason than the one given to you.

With high esteem,
Yours faithfully,
LUDWIG VON BEETHOVEN.

[It is well-nigh incredible to read of the almost insuperable difficulties Beethoven had to overcome, even in the year 1808, when he already enjoyed world-wide fame, in order to dispose of a grand sacred work. From a letter which will be given later on, it appears that B. and H. not only published the Mass in C (Op. 86) but also—notwithstanding that Beethoven wished to make them a present of it—paid him an honorarium for it. The Mass first appeared in 1812—after which Beethoven could see, to his great joy, that the firm was really entering into important engagements with him, for among other great works there appeared the Symphonies in C minor and F, the *Egmont* music and *Fidelio*, etc.]

80. To BARON GLEICHENSTEIN

[Autumn 1808?]

DEAR GOOD GLEICHENSTEIN!

I really cannot help telling you of my anxiety with regard to Breuning's spasmodic, feverish state, and at the same time entreat you to do your very best to keep in closer touch with him, or rather to get him to attach himself more to you. *My circumstances* only allow me to fulfil in small degree the high duties of friendship. I therefore beg, entreat you in the name of the good, noble feeling which you certainly possess, to relieve me of this anxiety which to me is a real torture. It will be especially good if you can persuade him to go out with you here or there (however much he may incite you to diligence), and try to restrain him from his excessive, and, to my thinking, not always necessary work. You can scarcely believe in what an overwrought state I have already found him—you will have heard of his yesterday's worry—all caused by his terrible excitability, which, if he cannot prevent it, will surely be the ruin of him.

I therefore lay on you, my dear Gleichenstein, this charge concerning one of my best, most trustworthy friends, and all the more, seeing that your occupations will establish a kind of tie between both of you; and you will be able to strengthen this by often making him perceive how anxious you are for his welfare; and this will be all the easier as he really likes you. But your noble heart, so well known to me, needs no directions in this matter— so act for me and for your good Breuning. With hearty greetings,

BEETHOVEN.

[The great quarrel between Beethoven and Stephan von Breuning had long been settled (see Letter 58), yet small misunderstandings were not unfrequent. Stephan, for instance, writes to Dr. Wegeler, his brother-in-law, under date 10 January, 1809: "I have not seen Beethoven for over three months, and although he writes me in a friendly tone, for some reason unknown to me, he no longer comes to see me."]

81. To BREITKOPF AND HAERTEL, Leipzig

VIENNA, 7th January, 1809.

You will say it is this and that, and that and this—it is true there cannot be a stranger letter-writer—but you have received the terzets. One was already finished, when you went away, but I wished only to send it with the second; this latter has also been ready for the last few months without my even thinking of sending it to you—finally, the C[opyist] bothered me about it. You will show me a very great kindness, and I earnestly beg you to do so, if you do not publish before Easter all the things you have of mine, for I certainly shall be with you during Lent. Also, until then, let none of the new symphonies be heard, for I am coming to Leipzig, so it will be a real festival to perform these with the, to me, well-known honesty and good-will of the musicians at Leipzig —and when there I will at once see to the correcting.

Finally, I am compelled through intrigues, cabals, and low tricks of all kinds to leave the only German Vaterland. I am going at the invitation of his Majesty the King of Westphalia as his Capellmeister with a yearly pay of 600 ducats in gold. I have sent off by post my acceptance, and I am now awaiting my decree so as to make preparations for the journey, when I shall pass through Leipzig. In order that the journey may be the more brilliant for me, I beg you, if not too disadvantageous to you, not to make known any of my compositions before Easter. With regard to the Sonata dedicated to Baron Gleichenstein, please leave out the

Imperial Royal draughtsman, for he does not like anything of that sort. There will probably be some abusive articles in the *Musikalische Zeitung* with regard to my last concert. I certainly do not wish everything that is against me to be suppressed, but people should know that no one has more personal enemies here than myself; and this is all the easier to understand, seeing that the state of music here is ever becoming worse. We have conductors who understand as little about conducting as about conducting themselves— at the Wieden it is really at its worst—I had to give my concert there, and on all sides difficulties were placed in my way. There was a horrid trick played in connection with the Widows' concert, out of hatred to me, for Herr Salieri threatened to expel any musician belonging to their company who played for me; but in spite of several faults which I could not prevent, the public received everything most enthusiastically. Nevertheless, scribblers will not fail to write wretched stuff against me in the *Musikalische Zeitung*. The musicians were specially in a rage that through carelessness mistakes arose in the simplest, plainest piece. I suddenly bade them stop, and called out in a loud voice, *Begin again*. Such a thing had never happened there before; the public testified its pleasure. Things become worse every day. The day before my concert, the orchestra in the theatre in the town got into such a muddle in that easy little opera, *Milton*, that conductor and director and orchestra came to grief—for the conductor, instead of giving the beat beforehand, gave it afterwards, and then only the director appears on the scene. Answer at once, my good friend,

With esteem,

Your most devoted servant,

BEETHOVEN.

[On the reverse side of the cover.]

I beg you to say nothing definite in public about my appointment at Westphalia until I write to you that I have received my decree. Farewell and write to me soon. At Leipzig we will talk about my works. Some hints might be given in the *Musikalische Zeitung* about my going away from here—also a few stabs, since no one here has been really willing to help me.

(Address.) To Breitkopf and Härtel, Leipzig.

[In this letter we have from Beethoven himself a most lively account of the concert in which, to a partly enthusiastic, partly puzzled world, the Symphony in C minor was produced, together with other great works. We shall have more to say about this concert, but the best, after all, will remain what we here gather from the composer's own mouth. For the rest, the letter shows the composer's proud satisfaction concerning his call to the Westphalian

Court. Now only did independent friends of the composer become truly alive to the might and importance of his genius, and proper steps were being taken to keep him. Also the description which Beethoven gives of the Vienna orchestras, especially the one at the "An der Wien," is not exaggerated. Contemporary writers have expressed themselves in the same way; what, however, is new, is the declaration that Salieri pursued Beethoven with his hatred. The new Trios are here curiously named terzets, a term generally used only for vocal compositions.]

82. To Baron ZMESKALL-DOMANOVECZ

[about *January* 1809.]

Cursedly invited Domanowetz—not a musical Count, but an eating Count, dinner Count, supper Count, etc. To-day, at half-past 10 or 10 o'clock, will the quartet be rehearsed at the house of Lobkowitz; His Serene Highness, usually absent-minded, is not yet there—you come too, if you can escape from the prison ward at the Chancery. To-day, Herzog, who is to be my servant, will come to you. Settle with him and his obbligato wife, for 30 florins—wood, light, small livery. I must have some one to cook; so long as I have such bad food I shall always be ill. I am dining at home to-day for the sake of the better wine; if you will order what you wish to have, I shall be glad if you will also come to me. You will have the wine gratis, and far better than at the rascally Swan.

Your small BEETHOVEN.

83. To Baron GLEICHENSTEIN

[Sketch of a Musical Constitution]

[*1st quarter*, 1809.]

First, the offer from the King of Westphalia is to be written out.

B. cannot be tied down to any conditions concerning this salary, since the principal aim of his art, namely, the writing of new works, would suffer by it. This pay must be assured to B. so long as the same of his own free will does not renounce it. The Imperial title also, if possible, to alternate with Salieri and Eibeler—the promise of the Court to let me enter as soon as possible into actual service of the Court—or adjunction, if it is worth the trouble. Contract with the theatres, likewise with the title of a member of the committee of the theatre direction—a fixed day every year for a concert, even though the management change, in the theatre; Beethoven, on the other hand, to bind himself to write a new work every year for a concert for the poor whenever it may be most profitable—or to conduct two of them—a place at a money-changer's or something of the kind, where Beethoven can receive the stipulated salary. The salary must be binding on the heirs.

[Antonio Salieri had held the title and rank of Court Capellmeister since 1788. He was Beethoven's teacher in dramatic composition, and his pupil dedicated to him the three violin sonatas, Op. 12. The church composer, Joseph von Eybler (1765–1846) was an intimate friend of Mozart's; in 1804 he became Court Vice-Capellmeister, and after Salieri's death in 1825, principal Court Capellmeister. Beethoven never succeeded in becoming Court Capellmeister—fortunately for him he had not the necessary qualifications.]

84. TO THE SAME

[*1st quarter*, 1809.]

My dear fellow, your friend Frech let Breuning last year have some *wood* which is cheaper. Be kind enough and speak to his *Boldness* [1] in my name and ask him kindly to let me have some cords. Countess E. is very ill, otherwise I would have invited you.

85. TO THE SAME

[*1st quarter*, 1809.]

Rake of a Baron—in vain I waited for you yesterday—do please let me know whether the wood is coming to me through his *Boldness*, or not. I have received a fine offer to be Capellmeister to the King of Westphalia—I shall get good pay—I have only to say *how many ducats* I want, &c. I would like to talk the matter over with you. Cannot you come this afternoon about half-past three—this morning I must go out?

86. TO THE SAME

[*1st quarter*, 1809.]

Countess Erdödy thinks that you ought to sketch out a plan with her according to which you can act, if you, as she thinks certain, are approached in the matter,

Your friend,

LUDWIG BEETHOVEN.

P.S.—If you have the time this afternoon, the Countess will be pleased to see you.

[His faithful friend, Countess Erdödy, is also anxious to help in preventing Beethoven from leaving Vienna.]

---

[1] *Frechheit* (boldness) has as first syllable the friend's name. One of Beethoven's many plays upon words.—TR.

87. To the Same

[*March* 1809.]

You see, my dear Gleichenstein, from the enclosed, how honourable my remaining here has become for me. The title of Imperial Capellmeister will follow, &c. Write to me as soon as you can, and say whether you think that I could travel in the present warlike circumstances, and whether you are still firmly resolved to travel with me. Many dissuade me from it, but I will follow you entirely in the matter; so that you and I may come to some arrangement —write quickly. Now you can help me to look out for a wife. If you find a beautiful one in F. who perhaps may bestow a sigh on my harmonies, but it must be no Elise Bürger, at once tackle her—but she must be beautiful, for I cannot love anything that is not beautiful—otherwise I should love myself. Farewell, and write soon. Remember me to your parents, to your brother,

I heartily embrace you, and am,
Your true friend,
BEETHOVEN.

[The warlike circumstances are clear. Napoleon was marching towards Vienna. Beethoven did not want to have a wife like Elise Bürger, the third wife of the poet, who offered her hand to him. She was born at Stuttgart in 1769 and died at Frankfort in 1833. She was twenty years old when she proposed to the poet in a poem. After a long correspondence, Bürger actually married his "Swabian maiden" in the autumn of 1790. It was an unhappy marriage; there was a legal separation after two years.]

88. To the Countess MARIE Von ERDÖDY

[*Spring* 1809.]

My dear Countess, I have erred, I confess it, forgive me; it was certainly not intentional badness on my part, if I have caused you pain. Only since yesterday evening do I really know what happened, and I am extremely sorry that I acted thus. Read your note calmly, and judge yourself whether I have deserved it, and whether you have not punished me sixfold, for I offended you without meaning to do so. Send me back my note to-day, and write just one word that you are again good friends. It will cause me no end of pain, if you will not do this; I can do nothing, if things are to continue thus. I await your forgiveness.

[The relationship between Countess Erdödy, *née* Countess Niszky, and Beethoven is so important in the history of the composer's life, that a few words about the fate of these letters appear imperative. Jahn took copies of ten letters to the countess, and seven notes to her music-teacher and Magister Brauchle. L. Nohl learnt at Munich, where the countess died in 1837, that she bequeathed a number of letters from Beethoven to herself to Brauchle's widow, the latter informing Nohl that she had burnt them. O. Jahn, however, and long before, had taken copies of these letters, with exception of one which she presented to Ignaz Lachner in Frankfort-on-Main. All the other letters of the group were given by Jahn to the young scholar, Dr. Alfred Schöne, for publication, and on the occasion of the silver wedding of Dr. Moritz Hauptmann, in 1867, they were actually published by B. and H. . . . Countess Anna Maria von Niszky, born about 1779, married at an early age (about 1795), Count Peter von Erdödy (at Monyorókerék). After the rupture with Giulietta Guicciardi, Beethoven sought and found consolation in the society of the countess. Reichardt gives a fascinating account of her and of her devotion to music. He writes: "I received a very friendly, warm-hearted note from Beethoven, whom I had missed seeing, inviting me to another pleasant dinner at Countess Erdödy's, a Hungarian lady. Intense excitement almost spoilt the joy I felt. Imagine a very handsome, small, refined person five-and-twenty years old, who was married in her fifteenth year. Immediately after her first confinement she contracted an incurable malady, so that for ten years, with exception of two or perhaps three months, she had been bedridden. Yet she gave birth to three dear, healthy children, who clung to her like creepers. Music is her sole enjoyment; she plays Beethoven's compositions extremely well, and with swollen feet limps from one pianoforte to another, but, for all that, cheerful and friendly—frequently I felt melancholy during an otherwise right joyous meal in company of six or eight kind, musical souls."]

89. To BREITKOPF AND HAERTEL, Leipzig

March 28, 1809.

HIGHLY HONOURED SIR,

Herewith you receive the pianoforte improvements in the *symphonies*. Have the plates corrected at once. The title of the *Symphony in F* is: Pastoral Symphony, or Reminiscence of Country Life, expression of feeling rather than painting. Notice besides, that in the Andante of the same symp. there must still be marked in the bass part, right at the beginning: due Violoncelli Solo I^{mo} e 2do con Sordino ma gli Violoncelli tutti coi Bassi.

You said you had found another mistake in the third movement of the *Symphony in C minor*—I do not remember of what kind—the best is always to send me the score back with the proofs; in a few days everything would be sent back. With the Trios and Cello Sonata I should like the same thing to be done. If the title of the Cello Sonata is not printed it can still stand to my friend the Baron, &c. So far as I know I have only sent two *trios*. There must be some mistake here. Has Wagner, perhaps, been playing some joke, and added a third *of his own invention or of some one else's*?

In order to avoid any mistake, I here set down the themes of the movements.

In my next I will answer the other points in your letter. With kindest regards.

In haste,
Yours truly,
BEETHOVEN.

[The letter concerns corrections for the 5th and 6th Symphonies. Later on, reference will be made to an error in the Scherzo of the C minor Symphony, which has acquired amazing importance in the history of that work.]

90. To the Same

VIENNA, *April* 5, '09.

HIGH HONOURED SIR,

I was pleased to receive your letter. I thank you for the article in the *M.Z.*, and only hope that when an opportunity presents itself, you will correct what concerns R. I was not in any way engaged by him; on the contrary, Count Truchsess-Waldburg, chief chamberlain to His Majesty the King of Westphalia, made me the offer of becoming Chief Capellmeister to his M. of Westphalia, even before Reichardt was in Vienna. The latter himself was surprised, so he said, that nothing of all this had come to his ears. R. did his very best to *dissuade me from going there.* As, indeed, I have very good grounds to call in question the character of Herr R., and he himself may have communicated something to you for various political reasons, I therefore think that in any case I am more deserving of credit, also that at the very next opportunity, and that is easily found—there is no need for any pompous revocation, yet truth must be brought to light—the actual fact should be inserted for truth's sake. *For my honour this is of importance.* By next post I send you all three works—the *oratorio, opera,* Mass— and all I ask for them is 250 fl., convention-coin. I do not think that you will complain of this amount. I cannot for the moment find the letter in which Simrock also was willing to give me for the Mass 100 fl. in convention-money; and even here I could have got even higher terms from the Chemical Printing Works. I am not in any way boasting, that you know. I, however, send you all three works, because I am convinced that you will not let me be a loser thereby. Make out the titles to your liking in French. Next time you will again receive a few lines about the other matter—to-day it is not possible.

Your most devoted friend and servant.

Please do not forget to address me as Chief Capellmeister. I laugh at such things, but there are *Miserabiles*, who know how, after the manner of cooks, to serve up such things.

[This letter gives further information about the proceedings with regard to Westphalia. Whether Reichardt, for political reasons, mixed himself up in the matter, cannot be said; anyhow, he often was engaged in politics; and in such matters the two brothers in Apollo were fairly well akin. The Leipzig *Allg. Mus. Ztg.*, actually inserted in their number of 3 March, 1809, the following: "Beethoven received the call to Cassel through Count Truchsess-Waldburg, royal Westphalian chief chamberlain, as *Chief Capellmeister.*"]

91. To Baron ZMESKALL

[*Spring* 1809.]

It does not suit me to see the woman again, and although she *may* be somewhat better than he is, I wish to know as little about her as about him. Hence I send to you the required 24 fl., kindly add to it the 30 kr., take my stamped paper of 15 kr. and make the *servant* write on the same *that he has received these 24 fl., 30 kr., for boot and livery money.* I will tell you more by word of mouth, how abominably she recently lied to you. I wish, meanwhile, that you would show the respect which, as a friend of mine, you owe to yourself. Tell them *that you have only induced me still to give this*; for the rest, do not trouble unnecessarily about them, for neither of them is worthy of your intercession. I did not wish to take her husband back again, but partly circumstances necessitated it; I wanted a servant, and a housekeeper and man-servant cost too much. Besides, I found her several times with her husband below at the clockmaker's in my house, she even wanted to go out with him; but as I wanted her, I let him come back, since, for the sake of the rooms I was forced to keep her; had I not taken him I should only have been the more swindled. That is how the matter stands, *both are good-for-nothing creatures.*

Farewell,
I'll see you soon,
Your friend,
BEETHOVEN.

92. To Count FRANZ Von BRUNSWICK

[*Spring* 1809?]

DEAR FRIEND! BROTHER!

I ought to have written to you before now, in my heart I have already done so a thousand times. You ought to have received the T. and the S. much sooner; I cannot understand how R. kept these back so long. So far as I can remember, I certainly told you that I would send to you both *Sonata* and *Trio.* Do as you like, keep the Sonata or send it to Forray. The Quartet was really intended for you long ago, only my disorder was the cause that you only just receive it on this occasion—and speaking of disorder, I must unfortunately confess to you that it haunts me everywhere. Nothing has been decided about my affairs; the unfortunate war will probably cause a further delay of the final end, or my affairs may get into a worse plight. I first resolve upon this, then upon that; unfortunately, I must remain hereabouts, until this matter is settled. Oh, unfortunate decree, seductive as a Siren; I ought, like Ulysses, to have stopped my ears with wax, resolved not to sign anything. If the waves of war should roll nearer, I will come to Hungary, perhaps, if I have nothing beyond my own miserable self to care for; I shall probably fight my way through; it will be all up with nobler plans! Endless our striving; vulgarity, in the long run, puts an end to everything! Farewell, dear Brother, be one to me; I have no one whom I could thus name; do as much good around you as the bad times permit. In future, put the following on the cover of your letters to me: To Herr B. v. Pasqualati. The rascal Oliva (no noble rascal, however) comes to Hungary; do not have much to do with him; I am glad that this connection, which was only formed through necessity, will hereby be entirely broken off. More by word of mouth. I am now in Baden, now here—in Baden I must be inquired for at the Sauerhof. Farewell, let me soon have news of you.

Your friend,
BEETHOVEN.

[Forray was the husband of a cousin of Count Franz, Countess Julie von Brunswick; he was an able pianist. We shall often come across complaints about the siren-like decree. Beethoven lived frequently in the Pasqualati house on the Mölker Bastion. As regards the "rascal" Oliva, thereby hangs a tale. Franz Oliva was a man of letters and a musician. He was for a long time an official in the Bank of Ofenheim and Herz. During the years 1810 and 1811 Beethoven held much intercourse with him; in 1811 he was, indeed, the bearer of a letter to Goethe. The variations in D (Op. 76) composed in the year 1809 were dedicated to him; the original edition expressly says: "composées et dediées à son ami Oliva." Anyhow, there was ebb and flow in the friendly relationship. Even the Conversation Books of the years 1819 and 1820 rarely speak of Oliva. After 1820 his name is no longer heard of in connection with Beethoven.]

93. To BREITKOPF AND HAERTEL, LEIPZIG

VIENNA, 20th [June?] 1809.

MOST HONOURED SIR!

The fatal period now approaching only allows me to write you a few lines in haste. First of all, the uncertainty of the post prevents me sending you anything—for the moment, only what still occurs to me about the Trios. First of all, if the title is not ready, I should like the dedication to be made at once to the Archduke Rudolph; you could take it from the Concerto in G, which has been printed *here by the Industrie-Kontor*. I have noticed now and again that if I dedicate something to another person, and he happens to like the work, he feels a slight regret; he has become very fond of these Trios; it would, therefore, probably again cause him pain if they were dedicated to any one else; if, however, it has been done, there is no help for it.

With regard to the *Trio* in *E flat*, I would ask you to see whether in the last *Allegro* after the 102nd bar in the second part, this passage stands so for the 'cello and violin.

If this passage is written in the score as at No. 1, it must be changed, and put as in No. 2. I found this passage so in the written-out parts, and that led me to suppose that perhaps the copyist had made the same mistake in the score—if not, all the better. If there are *ritardandos* in several places *in this same movement, strike them all out*. Wherever they may be, they have no place in the whole of this movement. It will not be bad in the following passages in this same piece to mark the fingering thus:

You will easily be able to find these passages without my indicating how many bars from some starting-point.

The constant distraction amidst which I have been living for some time did not permit me to point this out to you at once. However, I shall soon be *myself* again—and a thing of that sort will not occur any more. Heaven only grant that I may not be again disturbed by any terrible event of some other kind. But who can feel concerned about the similar fate of so many millions? Farewell, write to me soon, by then, at least, the letter post ought to be still open.

In haste,
BEETHOVEN.

[From this letter we learn two interesting things. First, the surprisingly delicate reference to the musical likings of the Archduke Rudolph—and that already in the year 1809. Secondly, the letter gives fresh opportunity for studying Beethoven's system of fingering. The composer rarely indicated fingering in his pianoforte pieces. The score of the Trio in E flat, in its final movement, actually gives this fingering for the left hand, but—and that is still more extraordinary—with certain differences. Anyhow, we have again to express our astonishment at the extraordinary care the master took in the correction of his works.]

94. TO THE SAME

VIENNA, [26th July, 1809].

DEAR SIR,

You make a great mistake in thinking that I was so prosperous. We have passed through a great deal of misery. When I tell you that since the 4th May I have brought into the world little that is connected, only here and there a fragment. The whole course of events has affected me body and soul; nor can I have the enjoyment of country life, so indispensable to me—my *position*, only lately assured, rests on a loose foundation. Even during this short period I have not had all the *promises made to me* actually fulfilled. From Prince Kynsky, one of the persons concerned, I have not received a farthing, and that just at the time when it is most needed. Heaven only knows how things will go on; I shall now probably have to change my residence. Contributions begin from *to-day*. What a disturbing, wild life all around me, nothing but drums, cannons, men, misery of all sorts. My present position forces me again to bargain with you; hence I believe that you could probably send me 250 fl. in convention coin for the three great works. I really do not think that it is at all an out-of-the-way sum, and I now need it—for on all that is promised me in my decree I cannot at this moment count. Write to me whether you accept this proposal; for the Mass alone I could get an honorarium of 100 fl. in convention coin; you know that in such matters I always speak frankly to you.—Here's a fair lot of faults, which have been pointed out to me in the 'cello part by a good friend, for I have never in my lifetime troubled about what I have already written. I will have a list written or printed, and announced in the paper, so that all who have bought the work can get it. This brings me back to the confirmation of the experience which I have made, that it is best to have things printed from my own manuscript—probably there are also many faults in the copy which you have; but in *looking over* the music the composer actually *overlooks* the faults. You will shortly receive the song *Ich denke dein*, which was to have been included in the *unfortunate Prometheus*, and which, without your reminding me of it, I should have quite forgotten. Accept it as a small present. I *only now* thank you for the really beautiful translation of the tragedies of Euripides; I have marked something out of *Kallirhöe* among pieces of poetry which I have decided to set to music instrumental or *vocal*—only I should like to know the name of the *author or translator of these tragedies*. I have got from Traeg the *Messiah* as a *privilege*, which you already granted to me with some eagerness when here; in fact I have taken further advantage of it, for I had commenced to have vocal music at my house every week, but the unhappy war put a stop to all that. For this purpose I should be pleased if you would let me have by degrees the scores of the masters which you have, as for example, Mozart's Requiem, etc., Haydn's Masses, especially everything of the scores of, for instance, Haydn, Mozart, Bach, *Johann Sebastian Bach, Emanuel*, etc. Of *Emanuel* Bach's pianoforte works I have only a few things, yet a few by that true artist serve not only for high enjoyment but also for study; and it gives me the greatest pleasure to play over to a few genuinely artistic friends works which I have *never* or *only seldom* seen. I will arrange to compensate you in a way which ought to satisfy you. I hear that the *first Trio is in Vienna*; I have received no *copy* and therefore beg you, I should indeed very much like it, if you would still send to me the other works, which have to be published, for correction. You will in future receive all scores in my own handwriting; I may possibly send you the written-out parts used at performances. If I change my place of residence, I will at once let you know, but if you write at once, your answer will safely find me here. I hope Heaven will grant that I may not have entirely to give up Vienna as my settled abode. Farewell, all kind wishes to you so far as our wild period permits, bear in remembrance,

Your most devoted servant and friend,

BEETHOVEN.

[This long letter gives a picture of the general miserable state of the Austrian people and especially of Beethoven. It was in July, a few weeks after the fearful battle of Wagram, and after the brief interval of sunshine for Austria at Aspern, that humiliation ensued. After Napoleon had accepted the crown, Beethoven became a bitter enemy of the Corsican. Here stood one powerful world spirit opposed to another. Already, in July of this year, Beethoven's position was "on a loose foundation," although the contract had been only signed on the 1st March. So Beethoven was hesitating whether or not he should quit Vienna for good; however, in his secret heart he hoped Heaven would prevent his having to go away. We here learn that the song *Ich denke dein* was originally intended to be included in the *Prometheus* Ballet. The song was published in 1810. In spite of the terrible events, Beethoven shows his fondness for ancient literature and for *modern* literature connected with it. *Kallirhöe* was a tragedy by Johann August Apel, which appeared in 1807. This poet and writer was born at Leipzig in 1771, and died there in August 1816. In this letter we also learn that Beethoven had arranged a small gathering at his house for the performance of vocal music, from which it is a pleasure to know that the master's deafness at that period cannot have been very severe. The fact also serves to show that the reproach levelled against Beethoven of showing indifference towards other composers is not justified. He asks for Haydn, Mozart, Bach (father and son); his high appreciation of the pianoforte works of Philip Emanuel Bach deserves special note. The first Trio here mentioned, that is the first of the Erdödy Trios, D major (Op. 70), was published.]

95. TO THE SAME

VIENNA, *August* 8, 1809.

I have handed over to Kind [1] and Co. a *sextet* for 2 *clarinets*, 2 *bassoons*, 2 horns, and 2 German *Lieder* or songs, so that they may

---

[1] Or "Kunz."

reach you as soon as possible—they are presents to you in return for all those things which I asked you for *as presents*—the *Musik Zeitung* I had also forgotten, I remind you in a friendly way about it. Perhaps you could let me have editions of Goethe's and of Schiller's complete works—from their literary abundance some-thing *comes in to you*, and I then send to you many things, i.e., *something which goes out into all the world*. Those two poets are my favourite poets, also Ossian, Homer, the latter of whom I can, unfortunately, only read in translation. So these (Goethe and Schiller) you have only to shoot out from your literary store-house, and if you send them to me soon you will make me perfectly happy, and all the more so, seeing that I hope to pass the remainder of the summer in some cosy country corner. The *sextet* is one of my early things, and, moreover, was written in one night—the best one can say of it is that it was composed by an author who, at any rate, has produced better works—and yet for many, such works are the best.

Farewell, and send very soon news

To your

most devoted,

BEETHOVEN.

Of the 'cello Sonata I
should like to have a *few* copies;
I would indeed beg you
always to send me half a
dozen *copies*—I never sell
any—there are, however,
here and there poor *Musici*,
to whom one cannot refuse
a thing of that sort.

[The Sextet was published by B. and H., January 1810, without opus number. The *Lieder* are the already mentioned *Lied aus der Ferne*, by Reissig, and *Andenken*, by Matthisson. The 'cello Sonata in A (Op. 69) was completed this summer; on the copy which he gave to his friend, v. Gleichenstein, he wrote the melancholy words, "Inter Lacrymas et Luctum."]

96. TO THE SAME

VIENNA, 19*th Wine month*, 1809.

HONOURED SIR,

In answer to your letter of the 21st of August I declare that I am thoroughly satisfied if you pay me some items in Vienna *currency* (but not much)—the 3 works are already sent off, but I really wish that you would send me the *honorarium* for these 3 works before they arrive in Leipzig; if you would make it payable immediately to me here I should be very glad—we are here in want of money, for it costs us twice as much as formerly—cursed war—please put *tempo Allegretto* to the song in D—otherwise it will be taken too slowly—please write to me what the editions of Schiller, Goethe cost in convention coin, also the small-size edition of Wieland —if I buy them, I would rather have them from you, for all the editions here are bungled and dear—Next time about the quartets which I am writing—I do not care to have to do with pianoforte solo Sonatas, *yet* I promise you some—*do you know that I have already become a member of the Society of Fine Arts and Sciences?* —so I have got a title—ha ha! I cannot help laughing.

Farewell, I have only time to say that I call myself your most devoted

BEETHOVEN.

Do not forget my request about the money.

[The "song in D" can surely only be the *Andenken* by Matthisson. It actually came out in May 1810. This song is marked *Andante con moto*, a *tempo* which, though not quite the same as *Allegretto*, is something very like it. With regard to Beethoven's confession respecting pianoforte sonatas, it may be noted that after the *Appassionata*, composed between 1804 and 1805, the only important sonatas up to 1809 were those in F sharp (Op. 78) and the *Adieux* Sonata (Op. 81a).]

97. TO GEORGE THOMSON, EDINBURGH

VIENNE, le 23 Novembre, 1809.

MONSIEUR!

Je composerai des Ritornelles pour les 43 petits Airs, mais je demande encore 10 livres sterling ou 20 ducats de Vienne en especes plus, que vous m'avez offert ainsi au lieu de cinquante livres sterling ou cent ducats de Vienne en especes, je demande 60 livres sterling ou 120 ducats de Vienne en especes—Cette [*sic*] travail est outre cela une chose, qui ne fait pas grand plaisir à l'artiste, mais pourtant je serai toujours pres de vous en consentir, sachant qu'il y a quelque chose utile pour le comerce.—Quant à les Quintuors et les trois Sonates, je trouve l'honorar trop petit pour moi—je vous en demande la some de 120 c'est à dire cent vingt livres sterling ou deux cents quarante ducats de Vienne en especes, vous m'avez offert 60 livres sterling et c'est impossible pour moi de vous satisfaire pour un tel honorar—nous vivons ici dans un tems ou tous les choses s'exigent à un terrible haut prix, presque on paye ici trois fois si cher come avant—mais si vous consentiez la some que je demande, je vous servirai avec plaisir—Je crois quant à la publication de ces œuvres ici en Allemagne, je me voulais engager de ne les publier pas plutot, qu'apres sept ou huit mois, quand vous trouverez ce tems suffisant pour vous.—Quant a contre Basse ou Basson je voudrais que vous me laissez libre, peut-etre que je trouverai encore quelque chose plus agreable pour vous—aussi on pouvait choisir avec la flute un Basson ou quelques autres instrumens à vents, et faire seulement le 3me Quintuor pour deux Violons, deux Viola, Violoncelle, come le genre sera par cela plus pur— Enfin soyez assures Monsieur que vous traitez avec un vrai Artiste qui aime d'etre honorablement payé mais qui pourtant aime encore plus sa gloire et aussi la gloire de l'art—et qui n'est jamais content de soi meme et je tache d'aller toujours plus loin et de faire de progres encore plus grands dans son art.

Quant aux chansons je les ai deja commencé et je donnera envers huit jours à Fries—donnes moi donc bientot une Reponse, Monsieur, et recevez ici la consideration particuliere

de

votre

serviteur

LOUIS VAN BEETHOVEN.

une autre fois je vous prie
aussi de m'envoyer les paroles
des Chansons, come il est bien
necessaire de les avoir pour donner
la vrai expression.

[According to the original manuscript in the British Museum.—TR.]—[Towards the end of September 1809, Thomson sent forty-three Welsh and Irish melodies to Beethoven with the request that he would compose, and very quickly, *ritornelli* and accompaniments for pianoforte or pedal-harp—in addition for violin and 'cello.]

98. To BREITKOPF AND HAERTEL, LEIPZIG

VIENNA, *the 4th February*, 1810.

I hope you will already have received back the draft for 500 florins which you sent to me, and I beg you to let me know. My health is not quite restored, but there is an improvement—with the next letter you will receive the books of the *opera* and of the *oratorio*—ought you not to have a German text for the Mass, though without leaving out the *Latin*? I specially send you the organ part. If you have not already printed it, I want it to appear in quite a different way, but if it has already been printed there is nothing to be done.—Here of new works: a Fantasia for pianoforte alone—likewise for piano with full orchestra and choruses. N.B.—Likewise those about which you wrote. 3 pianoforte *solo* Sonatas.—N.B. the 3rd consisting of 3 movements, *Abschied, Abwesenheit, das Wiedersehn,* to be published separately.

Variations for pianoforte alone.

12 songs with pianoforte accompaniment, partly with German, partly Italian text, nearly all through-composed.

Concerto for pianoforte with full orchestra.

Quartet for 2 violins, viola, violoncello.

As I shall probably be able to send these works to London, you can send them to any other place but England; your edition, however, for the reason just stated, must not appear sooner than the 1st September of this year 1810—I do not think that I am asking extravagant terms. *I want 1450 florins* in convention coin in the same way as the *honorarium* was paid to me for the *oratorio, opera,* and Mass. You could forward this sum in two halves, the first could be assigned to me after you had received the first half of the works, and likewise the other half after the second half of the works.

With regard to the *oratorio* I beg you to see whether the 3 trombones, drums and trumpets are in my score sent to you, at the places here indicated.

Alto *Tenor* } Trombones Bass		in the Aria No. 2, "o heil euch" with chorus, where all 3 must come in at the *alla breve* time *allo molto*
Trumpets Drums		also come in at ₵ *allo molto* of No. 2 and are in E flat; the drums only at the 48th bar, *Allo molto* ₵ and they are in A—
Alto Tenor } Trombones Bass		in Recit: No. 3 "Verkundet Seraph"

Drum in C in the chorus in C "wir haben ihn gesehen"—

Trumpets in D in the chorus in D "hier ist er der Verbannte"
Drums

Alto
Tenor } Trombones *last chorus* in C "Welten singen"
Bass
Trumpets
Drums

If any of the said parts are wanting I will have them written out in small notes and sent to you.

The *Gesang in der ferne* which my brother recently sent you, was, as you may have noticed, by an amateur, as indeed you must have seen, who begged me, to set it to music, but also takes the liberty of giving the Aria to Artaria to print. I have therefore thought, as proof of my friendly feeling towards you, to inform you of this. As soon as you receive it, put it into the hands of the printers. You can then send it here or anywhere else; if you make haste the Aria will arrive here before it comes out here; I know for certain that Artaria will publish it. I only wrote the A. *as a favour*, and in like manner I *also* give it *to you*. I, however, beg for myself the following book, Bechstein's *Naturgeschichte der Vögel* in two stout volumes with coloured engravings. In presenting it to a good friend of mine, I shall give him great pleasure. Of the permission to ask for scores which you have at Traig's and at the Industrie I have as yet made no use. Please send me something in writing that I can show them. I have received your bill, which I have already cashed. I am sorry if I perhaps made a mistake, but I don't understand anything about such matters. My health is not yet very sound—we get poor food and have to pay an incredible price for it. The matter of my post is not yet in order, from Kinsky I have not received anything. I fear, or I almost hope, that I shall have to run away, even perhaps on account of my health. It will be long ere the present state of things improves; of a return of the former there is no hope.

Your most devoted,

BEETHOVEN.

[The works offered in this letter were all published by B. and H. The Fantasia in G minor for pianoforte (Op. 77) appeared in December 1810; the C minor Fantasia for pianoforte, chorus and orchestra, dedicated to King Joseph of Bavaria, in 1811. The three pianoforte sonatas were Op. 78, dedicated to Countess Therese of Brunswick, which appeared in December 1810; Op. 79, which likewise appeared at the same time; and the great characteristic Sonata in E flat, (Op. 81a), which appeared in July 1811. The pianoforte variations, those in D, dedicated to his friend Oliva, appeared December 1810. Of the twelve songs, six appeared, as Op. 75, dedicated to Princess Kynsky; and to these probably belonged the four Ariettas and a Duet (Op. 82), which appeared in 1811; finally, also, one or other of those in Op. 83. The pianoforte Concerto was the one in E flat, dedicated to the Archduke Rudolph, and the Quartet the one in E flat (Op. 74), dedicated to Prince Lobkowitz.]

99. To Baron ZMESKALL

[*18th April*, 1810.]

Dear Zmeskall, please send me for a few hours, the looking-glass which hangs next to your window, mine is broken. Also be good enough to buy me one to-day like it; if so, you will please me greatly, you shall be paid at once what you lay out—please forgive dear Z. my importunity. I hope soon to see you.

Your BEETHOVEN.

[Beethoven's desire for a looking-glass will be easier to understand if one remembers that he was now living within the enchanted circle of the Sibyl of romantic literature. Bettina Brentano, afterwards von Arnim, was now in Vienna and was much in the society of the composer. His marriage plans for this year probably concerned the gifted Bettina.]

100. To the Same

[1810; *April?*]

Dear Z, do not be angry about my little note—do you not remember the situation in which I am, as once Hercules with Queen Omphale??? I asked you to buy me a looking-glass like yours, and I beg you as soon as you can do without yours which I am now sending you, to send it back to me to-day, for mine is broken. Farewell do not speak any more of me as "the great man," for I have never felt the power or the weakness of human nature as I do now—do not forget me.

[Everything points to the high-flown intercourse with the enchanting maiden Bettina.]

101. To Dr. F. G. WEGELER

VIENNA, *2nd May*, 1810.

Good old friend—I can well imagine that my lines will surprise you—and yet, although you have had no proof in writing, I always keep you in lively remembrance.—Among my manuscripts there has been for a long time one which was intended for you, and which you will certainly receive before the end of this summer. A few years ago, quiet peaceful life came to an end for me. I have been powerfully drawn into public life; as yet I have formed no decision in its favour, perhaps rather against it—for who can escape the storms from without? But I should be fortunate, perhaps one of the most fortunate of mortals, had not the demon taken up his abode in my ears. Had I not read somewhere that a man ought not of his own free-will to take away his life, so long as he could still perform a good action, I should long ago have been dead—and, indeed, by my own hand. Oh how beautiful life is, but for me it is for ever poisoned.

I am sure you will not refuse me a friendly request, if I beg you to see to my certificate of baptism. Whatever expenses you incur, as Steffen Breuning has a running account with you, you can at once pay yourself, and I can settle everything here with Steffen. If you yourself think it worth the trouble to hunt up the matter, and care to make the journey from Coblenz to Bonn, put everything down to my account; but there is one thing that you must bear in mind, namely, that a brother *was born before me* who was also called Ludwig, only with the additional name *Maria*, but he died. In order to fix my exact age, this must therefore be first found, for I already know that through others, a mistake has been made in the matter, and that I have been regarded as older than I actually am. Unfortunately I have lived a long time without even knowing my age. I had a family book, but it has gone astray, Heaven knows how! So do not be angry, if I commend this matter very warmly to you, viz., to find out about the Ludwig Maria and the present Ludwig who came after him. The sooner you send the certificate the greater will be my obligation. I am told that you sing a song of mine in your Freemasons' Lodge, probably the one in E, of which I have no copy; send it to me and I promise to compensate you three and fourfold in another way. Think of me however little I may seem to deserve it. Embrace, kiss your worthy wife, your children, all that is dear to you, in the name of your friend,

BEETHOVEN.

[Dr. Wegeler received no dedication from his friend, but with praiseworthy resignation he remarks: "My fate in this respect was the same as that of his pupil, Ries: the dedication remained in the letters. But is not such a one of higher value?" From the above letter we see that Beethoven did not know his exact age; as, however, he had thoughts of marrying, he had to get his baptismal certificate. In a short article from the pen of Dr. Knichenberg, director of the Beethoven House, Bonn, in the *Frankfurter Zeitung* of 16 October, 1906, we read that: "Beethoven himself, likewise many of his friends, was firmly convinced that he was born at Bonn in 1772. Alfred Kalischer, in the critical edition of the letters which has recently appeared, in connection with the first letter, which, if not actually composed, was transcribed by Beethoven, once again discusses, exhaustively, this strange error. . . . It concerned the dedication of the first three Sonatas in E flat, F minor, and D, composed by Beethoven, *eleven years of age*. Thus runs the title; as a matter of fact, the young composer was then thirteen. But it is generally known that the official entry in the church book of St. Remigius at Bonn gives 17 December, 1770, as the day of baptism. Kalischer thus considers, and rightly, that the day of birth was 15 December; for, according to canonic rule, the exact observance of which by the servants of the Archbishop may be taken for granted, the baptism had to take place within three days after birth. How the error, both of the master and of his friends, probably arose, is made clear by a simple, yet interesting document which lately came into the possession of the Bonn Beethoven House. It consists of a scanty little concert bill of a performance at Cologne in 1778, in which Johann van Beethoven, tenor singer at the Electoral Court, and father of Ludwig, announces as follows:

" ' NOTICE

' " This day, 26 *Martii*, 1778, Beethoven, tenor singer to the Elector of Cologne, at the Academy Hall in the Sternengass, will have the honour of producing two of his pupils, viz., Mlle. Averdonc, court alto singer, and his little son, aged 6. The former with various fine arias, the latter with various pianoforte concertos, will have the honour of waiting on the audience. He flatters himself that he is offering to all gentry great pleasure, all the more as both were graciously allowed to perform before the whole court, and to its complete satisfaction,' etc.

" It was, therefore, Beethoven's father who made his son two years younger than he actually was; thus, as it is easy to understand, the error in the year of birth gradually took firm root in the minds of his son and his son's friends. Even in those days infant prodigies grew up more slowly than ordinary mortals.—Kg."

The marriage-scheme was probably with Therese v. Malfatti, as, indeed, the master, as her relatives asserted, actually made a proposal of marriage. But, as I already wrote in 1906, if it be supposed that an offer of marriage had been made by Beethoven in 1809, Bettina Brentano may be regarded as the lady in question.]

102. To BREITKOPF AND HAERTEL in Leipzig

VIENNA, *6th June* [1810].

Much to do, also some recreation, very busy all at once, and at times not being able to avoid being idle, all this is the cause of my only answering you to-day—you can still have all that I offered you, Nb.[1] I now give you in addition the *music to Goethe's Egmont* which consists of 10 numbers: Overture, Entr'actes, &c., and I want for it the sum of *fourteen hundred gulden in silver money*, or convention scale, same standard as with the oratorio, &c., the 250 fl.:—I cannot accept anything else without being a loser, I have kept back *on your account*, although you do not deserve it from me, for your conduct is often so unexpected that one must have as good an opinion of you as I have, to continue to transact business with you—I myself would like in a certain way to continue business relationship with you—but I cannot afford to lose—I therefore beg you when you write to me, to send once more the list

[1] Nb. Among the songs which I offer you are several by Goethe, also " Kennst du das Land?" which greatly impresses people—these you could publish at once.

of works which I have offered to you, so that no mistake may occur —but answer at once, so that I may not be kept waiting any longer, all the more, as *Egmont* will be performed in a few days, and I shall be approached concerning the music—besides the cost of everything here has so much increased, that it is terrible to think of what one wants here, and in fact, as generally, the honorarium is certainly not put at too high a figure.

My 4000 fl. with which I cannot well manage, and in addition Kynsky has not paid a farthing, although it is safe—do not even amount to a thousand fl. in convention coin—to-morrow more— make haste and answer.

Yours,
LUDWIG VAN BEETHOVEN.

[The relationship of Beethoven with the Leipzig firm, in spite of many differences, was really very friendly at this time. B. and H. purchased the whole of the *Egmont* music. The work was performed for the first time on 24 May, 1810; the overture appeared in February 1811, but the other numbers only in April 1812.]

103. To GEORGE THOMSON, EDINBURGH

VIENNE *le* 17 *Juillet* 1810.

MONSIEUR!

Voilà, Monsieur, les airs écossais dont j'ai composé la plus grande partie *con amore*, voulant donner une marque de mon estime à la nation Ecossaise et Anglaise en cultivant leurs chants nationaux.—Pour ce qui regarde les répétitions dans les airs que j'ai composés à deux parties, vous n'avez qu'à les omettre à votre gré, et à faire les airs *senza replica*.—Come j'ignorais, si l'un ou l'autre de ces airs avait plusieurs couplets ou non, il m'a fallu les composer de manière qu'on pût les répeter au besoin; ainsi c'est à vous, d'arranger la chose, et de laisser les repetitions dans les airs qui out plusieurs couplets ou de les omettre dans les airs qui n'en ont qu'un seul.—Je voudrais bien avoir les paroles ·de ces airs écossais pour en faire usage en allemagne dès que vous les aurez publiés en Ecosse—Vous pourriez même me les faire parvenir dès à présent; je les ferai traduire, et j'attendrais la nouvelle de la publication faite en Ecosse.

Je vous prirois de m'envoyer les paroles notées sur la simple mélodie.

Quant aux trois quintors et trois sonates, j'accepte votre proposition, et j'espère qu'ils seront à entière satisfaction. Vous pourrez me faire payer les cent vingt livres sterling ou les deux cent quarante ducats en espèce en deux termes; moité, lorsque je delivrerai les 3 sonates aut vice versa.

A l'égard des airs avec paroles anglaises, je les ferai à très bas prix, pour vous temoigner, que je suis porté a vous servir, c'est pourquoi je ne demande que vingt livres sterling, ou quarante ducats en espèce pour ces airs—je ne pourrois les composer à moindre prix sans perdre, car on me donne ici d'avantage pour douze airs avec paroles allemandes, qui ne me font point de difficulté par la langue, au lieu qu'il me faut faire traduire les paroles angloises, faire des observations sur la prononciation, et qu'avec tout cela je suis toujours géné.

Par ce qui regarde enfin le terme après lequel je pourrais disposer de ces ouvrages en allemagne, je crois que six mois pour les quintors et les sonates, et trois mois pour les airs à compter du jour ou vous les aurez eu publiés en Ecosse, suffiraient.

Je vous prie cependant, de m'écrire là dessus.

Agréez, Monsieur, les assurances de la plus parfaite considératien avec laquelle j'ai l'honneur d'être,

> Monsieur
> Votre très-obéissant
> > serviteur
> > LOUIS VAN BEETHOVEN.

P.S. Je ne veux pas manquer de vous avertir que je viens de toucher la somͫe de cent cinquante ducats pour cinquante trois airs Ecossais che le banquier Fries.

Plusieurs de mes simphonies sont arrangées en quatuors ou quintuors; si ces piéces arrangées vous conviennent, je m'empresserais de vous les envoyer— — —

NB. quand on prend *l'ultima volta* dans les airs Ecossais, on laisse

1 2 3 etc. *voltà* c'est à dire on ne sonne pas toute la mesure de

1 2 3 etc. *volta*, si ce n'est pas assez clair pour notre pays, il faut que vous faites à un autre manière.

[According to autograph in the British Museum. Of the melodies sent by Thomson to the master, more were Irish than Scotch, but as Thayer remarks, "For Beethoven everything was Scotch."]

104. To BETTINA BRENTANO

VIENNA, 11th August, 1810.

DEAREST BETTINA [FRIEND!]

No finer spring than the present one, I say that and also feel it, because I have made your acquaintance. You yourself have probably seen that in society I am like a frog [fish] on the sand, which turns round and round, and cannot get away until a benevolent Galatea puts him again into the mighty sea. Yes, I was quite out of my element, dearest Bettina, I was surprised by you at a moment when ill-humour was quite master of me, but it actually disappeared at sight of you. I at once perceived that you belonged to a different world from this absurd one, to which with the best will one cannot open one's ears. I myself am a wretched man and yet complain of others!—You will surely forgive me, with your good heart, which is seen in your eyes, and with your intelligence, which lies in your ears:—at least your ears know how to flatter when they listen. My ears, unfortunately, are a barrier wall through which I cannot easily hold friendly communication with men. Else!—perhaps!—I should have had more confidence in you. So I could only understand the great, intelligent look of your eyes, which so impressed me that I can never forget it. Dear Bettina [friend], beloved maiden!—art!—Who understands it, with whom can one speak concerning this great goddess!—How dear to me were the few days when we gossiped or rather corresponded together; I have kept all the little notes on which stand your clever, dear, very dear answers. So I have at any rate to thank my bad hearing that the best part of these fleeting conversations has been noted down. Since you went away I have had vexatious hours, hours of darkness, in which one can do nothing; after your departure I roamed about for full three hours in the Schönbrunner Alley, also on the ramparts; but no angel met me who could take such hold on me as you, angel—forgive, dearest Bettina [friend], this digression from the key; I must have such intervals in order to give vent to my feelings. Then you have written, have you not, to Goethe about me?—I would willingly hide my head in a sack, so as to hear and see nothing of what is going on in the world, because you, dearest angel, will not meet me. But I shall surely receive a letter from you?—Hope nourishes me, it nourishes indeed half the world, and I have had it as my neighbour all my life; what otherwise would have become of me?—I here send written with my own hand *Kennst du das Land* in remembrance of the hour in which

I made your acquaintance. I also send the other which I have composed since I parted from you dear, dearest heart!—

> Herz mein Herz was soll das geben,
> Was bedränget dich so sehr;
> Welch ein fremdes, neues Leben
> Ich erkenne dich nicht mehr.

Yes, dearest Bettina [friend], send me an answer, write to me what will happen to me since my heart has become such a rebel. Write to your most faithful friend,

BEETHOVEN.

[Bettina von Arnim herself published the three much disputed letters of Beethoven to her in her wonderful book, *Ilius Pamphilius und die Ambrosia* (1848 and 1857). The slight differences of text in the second edition are noted above in square brackets. These important utterances of Beethoven's genius have been reproduced hundreds of times and have produced whole volumes of literature. Are they genuine or otherwise? That, to a certain extent, is still a question under discussion. Since, however, the second of these letters belonging to the year 1811 has appeared in facsimile, the genuineness of at least *one* of the letters can no longer be in dispute. I shall have more to say about all of them when I come to the *third*, belonging to the year 1812. Already, in my article, *Beethoven und die Sibylle der romantischen Literatur*, I remarked, "that these letters, taken as a whole, were probably written by Beethoven, but that possibly the genial authoress is responsible for a few interpolations." The passion of Beethoven for Bettina in the year 1810 is evident, so that no one can seriously believe that just in this very year Beethoven could still be occupied with plans of marriage with the "immortal beloved one."]

105. To BREITKOPF AND HAERTEL, Leipzig

BADEN, *on 21st Summer-month [June] of* 1810.

The enclosed letter is written to you by one of my friends, and I add to it my comments—with Paris or France I have not entered into any agreement with regard to all these works, as indeed the receipt will make clear to you, as soon as you have received everything from me and I from you—There can be no question of a *copy* on the Continent, I scarcely believe it at all likely that these works have already arrived in London, for the blockade is now stricter than ever, and the English have to pay very heavily even for letters to Germany, and much dearer for heavy parcels—in short I am convinced that still in September not a note of the works sent to you will have appeared in print—for the rest set out what you would give me for a concerto, a quartet, &c., and then you will certainly be able to see that 250 ducats is a small fee. At a time when banknotes were almost equal in value to silver or gold, I received 100 ducats for three Sonatas. N.B.—You yourself have given me for a quintet 50 ducats—am I to go backwards instead of forwards, for I really hope that that reproach will not be made about my art-work. However many guldens a ducat may be worth with us, there is no gain, for we now pay 30 fl. for a pair of boots, 160[1] or even 70 fl. for a coat, &c., the deuce take economy in music. My 4000 fl. last year, before the French came, were something, this year they are not even worth 1000 fl. in convention coin—I do not intend, as you think, to become a musical usurer, who only writes to become rich. Certainly not, yet I love an independent life, and I cannot have this without a small fortune; and then the honorarium itself must bring some honour to the artist, as indeed to all that he undertakes. I would not dare to tell anyone that Breitkopf and Härtel gave me 200 ducats for these works—you as a more humane being, and a more cultured head than all the other publishers of music, ought not to pay poor terms to the artist, but rather help him on the road to accomplish undisturbed what is in him, and what one expects from him. It is no boast, if I tell you, that I give you the preference before all others. I have often been approached from Leipzig, and here also by others who from there had full authority, and lately, personally, by one who offered me what I chose to ask. I have, however, refused all offers in order to show you that I would rather, owing to your cleverness (of your heart I know nothing), deal with you, and would even rather lose something so as to preserve this connection. But I cannot take anything less from you than 250 ducats, I should lose too much, and this you cannot surely desire—so you have my last word. Now as regards the works to be published. It was impossible for me to write to you about the dedications, viz., the violin quartet to Prince Lobkowitz—from another work you can see what his unmusical titles are—the Sonata in F sharp À Madame la Comtesse Thérèse Brunswick; the Fantasia for pianoforte only A mon ami Monsieur le Comte François de Brunswick, and the six Ariettas to Princess Kynsky, *née* Countess Kerpen. As regards the two Sonatas, publish them separately, or if you wish to publish them together, then put the dedication on the first in G major, *Sonate facile* or *Sonatine*, which you can also do in case you publish them together. With regard to the violin quartet, I remind you that the turning over should be comfortable; then still add to the superscription of the second piece: *adagio ma non troppo*—and $\frac{3}{4}$ measure to the third piece in C minor after the major *più presto quasi prestissimo*, where the minor key again comes in. The first time the first part is to be repeated as indicated; *on the*

[1] Beethoven probably meant to write 60.

*other hand, the repeat marks given to the second part must be taken
away, so that the second part will only be played once.*

In the Song of the Flea from *Faust*, if my remarks are not clear
to you, you have only to look it up in Goethe's *Faust*, or send me
only the melody so that I can look through it. The last number of the
last works which *you are publishing* may serve to you as a guide
how to *number* these works properly—the *quartet* is earlier than the
others—the concerto is still earlier than the *quartet*, if you wish to
number them chronologically, but as both belong to the same year
it is not really necessary—and please take note that in the quartet,
in the third movement in C minor where the *più presto quasi prestissimo* begins, an N.B. has still to be marked, thus: *N.B. Si
ha s'immaginar la battuta di 6/8*—for the rest, as I know that
however correct the *manuscript* may be, there are sure to be misunderstandings, I really wish to see the *proofs* beforehand so that
your beautiful editions may profit thereby. At the same time I
want four *copies* of each work for myself. I give you my word of
honour that I will never sell any of them, but here and there there
is a poor musician to whom I would willingly offer one; they are
meant for that. When are the Mass, the *Oratorio*, the *Opera* to be
brought to light?—please write to me the titles of the songs which
you have received, for I do not remember which I have already
sent you; you may receive some which will not be published in
London—You will now soon have received all that belongs to the
second lot with exception of three songs; for these I am waiting
until you have sent me the titles of those which you already have
—in a few days everything belonging to the third lot will be sent
off, but I am still waiting for an answer from you—the concerto
is to be dedicated to the Archduke R. and has merely the title
"Grand Concerto dedicated to His Imperial Highness the Archduke
Rudolph of, etc." *Egmont* also to *him*; as soon as you have received
the score you will at once see what use to make of it, and how to
draw the attention of the public to it—I wrote it simply out of love
for the poet, and in order to show this, I took nothing for it from
the theatre managers, which you also agreed to; and as a reward,
as always . . . they treated my music *very carelessly.*

There is nothing smaller than our great folk, but I make an exception of the Archdukes—Tell me your opinion with regard to a complete edition of my works; the great difficulty seems to me this,
that I should suffer as regards the disposing of the quite new works
which I am constantly producing. My friend writes, with regard
to Paris, about a *copy* in the National Library, and this is how the
matter stands: a French publisher himself wrote to me that the

lawsuit with Pleyel, etc., arose because he had forgotten to send a *copy* to the National Library: but now everything is all right and clear.

For Vienna you would probably have to adopt another course; perhaps I may manage so that my works which are printed abroad can never be reprinted here *in loco*.

In *Egmont* indicate everywhere in the violin part where other instruments come in, as for example in the funeral music after

Clara's death, where the kettledrum comes in, etc.  etc.

This is necessary in a century in which we have no longer any conservatoires, hence no more directors; there is no training whatever, but everything is left to chance. We have, however, money for a *castrato*, whereby art gains nothing, but it tickles the taste of our *blasé* folk, our so-called nobility. For the Fantasia with chorus you could perhaps also include the vocal parts in the piano score. You may wish to print another text, as the text like the music was written very quickly so that I could not even write out a *score*. Still with another set of words I want the word *kraft* to be kept or one very similar to it in its place—*satis est*. You have received a good portion, keep what you want of it, for I am glad that everything is there, as I do not care to write about such things—I hope very soon to receive from you one of your intelligently written letters—and remain with esteem,

Your most faithful friend and servant,

BEETHOVEN.

Letters to me, as usual, to Vienna.

[The Song of the Flea, with its drastico-comic tone-painting, appeared as No. 3 of the *Six Songs* (Op. 75). Beethoven writes that he composed *Egmont* out of love for the poet, and took nothing from the theatre management for it, and the same thing is to be found in the second letter to Bettina Brentano of 10 February 1811. In the present letter there is a passage which gives a key to the mysterious tone of devotion in which Beethoven referred to the Archduke Rudolph. The enclosed letter from a friend speaks about a complete edition of the works of Beethoven, and the master is informed that in France a work can be protected against reprint if a copy be sent to the National Library. The composer's verdict against *castrati* deserves all praise. At the Italian Opera—not only in Italy, but also in Vienna, Berlin, Dresden, etc., they exercised great influence in Beethoven's time and still later; one need only recall Salimbeni, Cassarelli, and Crescentini, who indeed, in Beethoven's time, in 1803, was singing master to the Imperial family. The words to the Choral Fantasia, which, according to the master's assurance, were written in a very short time, were by Christopher Kuffner. The poet is not named here, neither in the printed edition of the score by B. and H. The word "Kraft," as Beethoven specially wished, was actually retained; it is treated in grand style in the music.]

106. To the Same

[*21st August*, 1810.]

P. S.

Finding your letter written a fairly long time ago, I notice a passage in which you say, "To the other numbers of the *oratorio* there are trombones, to the chorus they are however wanting, also the trumpets and drums," but you do not say which chorus. I should be very glad if you could at once give me an answer about this; if the parts are not to be found, I must look up the matter for publication—but do please write and tell me which of the three works you intend to publish first—I wished formerly to send you another organ part, meanwhile I was pressed in so many directions, that it was impossible for me; if there is still time I would send it to you—I have still found the following faults in the Symphony in C minor, namely, in the third movement in ¾ time, where after the major the minor again comes in. It stands thus, I give the bass part, namely:

The two bars above which is marked the ✕ [1] are redundant, and must be struck out, and of course in all the other parts which are silent.

[Mendelssohn first drew attention to the mistake in the Scherzo of the C minor Symphony here noted. This happened in the year 1846 at the Lower Rhenish Musical Festival at Aix-la-Chapelle, when he appealed to a letter of Beethoven sent to the publishers B. and H., in which the master himself drew attention to the two superfluous bars in the Scherzo. The firm then inserted in their *Allgemeine Musikalische Zeitung* of July 1846, a correction as follows: "In comparing our edition with the original manuscript of the score of Beethoven's Symphony in C minor, doubt arose about a passage in the third movement, namely about the second and third bars of page 108 of the printed score. Hence we felt induced to look through Beethoven's letters sent to us, and amongst them we found one of the 21st August, 1810, with full explanation of this matter. We therefore gave in facsimile the portion of it belonging to this matter."

The publishers remark: "The matter itself needs no explanation, but the fault in printing arose from the fact, according to the original MS., that Beethoven had the intention, as in many other Symphonies, to repeat the minor three times and the major twice. Hence in the MS., the bars struck out in the letter are marked with 1, and the two following with 2. This, as well as the mark written above in red pencil, 'Si replica con Trio allora' was overlooked in printing."]

[1] This cross is not in the manuscript over the two bars to be struck out; but the lines are drawn through both bars.

FACSIMILE OF THE PORTION OF LETTER RELATING TO THE TWO REDUNDANT BARS IN THE SCHERZO OF THE C MINOR SYMPHONY

107. To the Same

VIENNA *the 15th Autumn-month [September,* 1810].

My dear Sir!

Here is the explanation of the delay with the quartet. You see that it is only just this, that while the minor for the first time after the major is to be repeated, the first part of the minor twice ; the second part, however, is only to be played once, that is, without repetition. As to the song from *Faust,* I cannot oblige you, for I have not got a copy of it—the first thing is that all the stanzas must be written out, not in abbreviated form as I have done: the safest way would be for you to send me the upper stave of the pianoforte part on a little sheet of paper with the vocal part as you print it, and I shall at once see if it is right.

In the 2nd *adagio* of the quartet I made some remark about the tempo, but that has been attended to—Take heed, and yield to my oft-expressed wish that you should send a proof, and also the *manuscript.* Complaints are being made about the printing errors, and I have noticed that even the clearest writing can be misinterpreted—we recently went through the 4-part songs and other things of Haiden which you have published, and found incredible faults, and many of them—Has what I said about the two redundant bars in the symphony, been seen to? I have a faint remembrance that you asked me something about this, but perhaps I forgot to answer you at once, and so they were not cut out.

The reason I want the manuscripts with the *proof copies,* is that I have scarcely any; for here and there some good friend asks for one, as, for instance, the archduke for the score of concerto, and they are never returned. Although convinced, that this time the manuscripts are as correct as, humanly speaking, possible, yet I do beg you not to risk anything with the *terzets* and other things. Besides, it is unpleasant for an author to know that there are mistakes in his work.—N.B. If *Sieges Simphonie* is not written over the last number in *Egmont,* see that it is put there. Hurry on with it, and please let me know when you have quite done with the *original* score, because I will then ask you to send it, from Leipzig, to Goethe, to whom I have already written about its coming. I hope you will have no objection to this, since you are probably as great an admirer of him as I myself am. I would have sent him a copy from here, but as I have no trained copyist on whom I can quite rely, and only the torture of looking over the copy is certain, I thought it the better course, and a saving of time for me. Here is the heading for the variations: Veränderungen Seinem Freunde

Oliva gewidmet von, etc. In a few days you will receive the organ part of the Mass and the trombones for the *oratorio*. It ought to be possible to get a German text for the Mass which agrees better with the music. The opera *lenore*, dedicated to my friend Stefan von Breuning, Imperial Court Secretary and Military Councillor, by the composer Ludwig, etc. The Mass to Herr von *Zmeskall*, nb., here must follow some additions which I do not remember for the moment. The *lieder* to Ihrer Durchlaucht der Frau Fürstin *Kynsky*, gebohrne Frejin von Kerpen—you must add *Ich denke dein* to this collection. I have seen it printed separately, and even here a *wrong mordent* introduced somewhere; as I have not a copy, I cannot remember in which bar. One other thing; you must at once publish the *Gesang aus der Ferne*, which I once sent to you, if you have not already done so. The poetry is by that rascal Reissig. Formerly it had not appeared in print; and it was not until nearly six months later, that this rascal declared, that "only for his friends" had he given it to Artaria to print. I sent it to you by letter-post, but received no thanks for it. The 50 ducats may have arrived, but I had not then returned, and the postman would not deliver them to any one else. I will at once make inquiry. By next post go off all the other compositions which I have to send you. So you can forward me the remaining 100 ducats, plus 30 thalers in convention-coin, seeing that in your first letter you at once offered me scores to the amount of 80 thalers, and yourselves reduced it, according to the notice to Traeg, to only 50. I will certainly take scores to the amount of 50 thalers, but I beg you to send an order for the 30 in gold to me here. Also, as I have already given you many trifles gratis, for which you formerly offered to send me the *Musik Zeitung* and some scores, you might at least let me have the *Musik Zeitung* which according to your letters has been more than once on the way. Then I would like to have all the works of Karl Philip Emanuel Bach, all of which you actually publish, also a Mass by J. Sebastian Bach in which there is the following *Crucifixus* with a *Basso ostinato*, very like yourselves, viz.,

Then you must have the best copy of Bach's *Tempered Clavier*, and

this I also beg you to send me. Here you have the *ultimatum*, to which I adhere. I will then give the document concerning owner-ship—nevertheless I shall never venture to disclose what I receive. As regards the edition of all my works, this must be carefully con-sidered, and then I will explain myself in detail—*Satis est*, I hope. Pay attention to all I have set out in writing. Farewell, and let me have a speedy answer,

your

most devoted

servant and friend,

BEETHOVEN.

[One of Beethoven's longest letters. The passage in which Beethoven again pleads for the striking out of the two bars in the symphony deserves special notice. Cf. this letter with 106 and the explanations. The dedications named were altered. To Stefan von Breuning had been dedicated Op. 61; now in recognition of his friendly services in obtaining the certificate of baptism, and of his enthusiasm over *Fidelio*, Beethoven wanted to dedicate this opera to him; nothing, however, came of it. Neither was the Mass dedi-cated to Zmeskall, but to Prince Kynsky. Beethoven by "very like your-selves" illustrates musically the obstinacy of the firm in sticking to their terms.]

108. To BETTINA BRENTANO

VIENNA, *February* 10, 1811.

DEAR, DEAR BETTINE!

I have already two letters from you, and from your letter to Toni I perceive that you still keep me in remembrance, also that your opinion of me is far too favourable—I carried your first letter about with me the whole summer, and it was often a source of happi-ness. If I do not write to you frequently, still I write to you 1000, 1000 times a thousand letters in my thoughts. Even if I had not read about you, I could easily imagine to myself how you feel in the rotten society in Berlin: talking, chattering about art without deeds!!!! The best description of it is to be found in Schiller's poem *Die Flüsse*, in which the Spree speaks. Dear Bettina, you are going to be, or are already married, and I have not been able to see you once beforehand. May all good wishes wherewith marriage blesses married folk attend you and your husband. What then shall I say for myself: "Pity my fate," I exclaim with Johanna; if I live still a few years, also for this and for all other weal and woe, will I thank the Highest who encompasses all things. When you write to Goethe about me, select all words which will express to him my inmost reverence and admiration. I am just on the point of writing to him about *Egmont*, to which I have written the music, and indeed purely out of love for his poems which cause me happiness. Who can be sufficiently thankful for a great poet, the richest jewel of a nation? And now, no more, dear good B.; I only came back from a bacchanalian festival at four o'clock this morning, at which, indeed, I was forced to laugh a great deal, with the result that I have to weep almost as much to-day. Noisy joy often drives me powerfully back into myself. Many thanks to Clemens for his kindness. As regards the cantata, the matter is not of sufficient importance for us here—it is different, however, in Berlin. In the matter of affection, the sister has such a large share of it, that there is not much left for the brother; don't you think that is sufficient for him? Now, farewell, dear, dear B.; I kiss you [here follows something thickly scratched out] on your forehead, imprinting on it, as with a seal, all my thoughts for you. Write soon, soon, frequently to your   Friend,

BEETHOVEN.

[*On the address side.*] Beethoven lives on the Mölker Bastion in Pascolati's house

[*Address in a foreign hand*] from Vienna

To
Fräulein Bettina Brentano,
Visconti Laroche,
in

Care of H. v. Savigny,   Berlin.
Monbijou-Platz, No. 1.

[The lines from Schiller's poem which Beethoven had in his mind are the following, in which the "Spree" says:
"Sprache gab mir einst Ramler und Stoff mein Cäsar; da nahm ich meinen Mund etwas voll, aber ich schweige seitdem."
"Toni" is Antonie Brentano, wife of Franz Brentano; both great, truly noble-hearted benefactors of Beethoven.
The quotation in the letter from Schiller's *Jungfrau von Orleans* is not quite correctly given by Beethoven. He was probably thinking of what Johanna says to Agnes Sorel: "Beklage mich! Beweine mein Geschick" (Act IV. Sc. ii.), i.e. "Pity me, feel compassion for my fate."]

109. TO THE COUNTESS VON ERDÖDY

[*March* 1811.]

MY DEAR WORTHY COUNTESS!

With much pleasure have I received your last lines; for the moment I cannot however answer your dear letter fully — as regards the Trio you have only to let me know whether you wish to see to its *being copied at your house or whether I shall undertake it?* either will suit me, and what is most convenient to you will be most agreeable to me. Herr Linke, who has something *good* for his concert to-morrow, is in a hurry. Hence only all kind messages to you and your children. I will seize the very next opportunity to be with you all; till then farewell, dear worthy Countess.

Your true
friend,
BEETHOVEN.

[The letter refers to Beethoven's last Trio in B flat (Op. 97), dedicated to the Archduke.]

110. TO THE ARCHDUKE RUDOLPH

[March 1811.]

YOUR IMPERIAL HIGHNESS!

Please be kind enough to let me have the *Trio* in *B flat* with the parts, also the Violin *Sonata* in G, both parts, for I want to have them quickly copied for myself, as I cannot at once find them amongst my many other scores—I hope that the bad weather will not have bad influence on the health of Y.I.H.; it always throws me a little out of my reckoning—at latest in three or four days I shall have the honour of returning you both works.

Your Imperial Highness's most obedient
LUDWIG VAN BEETHOVEN.

Do the musical pauses still continue?

111. TO BREITKOPF AND HAERTEL, LEIPZIG

P. P., VIENNA, *the* 12th (?) *April*, 1811.

My friend Oliva brings these lines, I hope you will let him participate in our friendly relationship, and enjoy pleasant intercourse with you. For the moment I have only commissioned my friend to offer you my new *Trio* for *Piano, Violin* and *'Cello.* He has full power to discuss and settle with you.

Yesterday I received your parcel; our post, like everything else, has become still dearer; the bank-notes, however, are of less value than formerly; what do you say to our finance directors???? A *deus ex machina* must come—otherwise, there's no hope.

In haste,
Yours,
BEETHOVEN.

The three songs, also the Italian, to the Princess Kinsky—the *Lebewohl* and *Wiedersehen* can only be dedicated to the Archduke Rudolph.

[Concerning friend Oliva, to whom the Variations in D major (Op. 66) were dedicated, mention has already been made. From 1811 to 1813 he was one of Beethoven's foremost friends. The Trio in B flat (Op. 97) which Oliva was to show to B. and H., found no favour in their sight; it was first published in 1816 by Steiner at Vienna. In this letter we hear the first complaint of the composer about the ever-decreasing value of bank-notes. Anton Schindler introduces this financial misery in the following words: "The next year, 1811, introduced the calamitous finance patent, by means of which the nominal value of the gulden was reduced to one-fifth." Hence Beethoven's annuity of 4000 gulden appeared reduced to 800 gulden, paper money. The matter, however, was not quite so bad as it looks. His patrons were gradually persuaded to pay him the stipulated sums in full in redemption bonds. The first who set this noble example was the master's friend, the Archduke Rudolph.]

112. TO HERR VON GOETHE EXCELLENZ

VIENNA, *April* 12, 1811.

YOUR EXCELLENCY

The pressing opportunity of a friend of mine, one of your great admirers (as I also am), who is leaving here in a great hurry, gives me only a moment to offer my thanks for the long time I have known you (for I know you from the days of my childhood)—that is very little for so much. Bettine Brentano has assured me that you would receive me in a kindly, yes, indeed, friendly spirit. But how could I think of such a reception, seeing that I am only in a position to approach you with the deepest reverence. with an inexpressibly deep feeling for your noble creations. You will shortly receive from Leipzig through Breitkopf and Härtel the music to *Egmont*, this Glorious *Egmont*, with which I, with the same warmth with which I read it, was again through you impressed by it, and set it to music. I should much like to know your opinion of it; even blame will be profitable for me and for my art, and will be as willingly received as the greatest praise.

Your Excellency's
great admirer,
LUDWIG VAN BEETHOVEN.

[According to the original manuscript in the Goethe and Schiller archives at Weimar; first printed by Th. Frimmel (*Neue Beethoveniana*, 1890). Subjoined is Goethe's answer to Beethoven's letter:]

"CARLSBAD, *June* 25, 1811.

"Your friendly letter, highly esteemed Sir, I received to my great pleasure, through Herr von Oliva. I am most thankful to you for the opinions expressed therein, and I assure you that I can honestly reciprocate them, for I have never heard one of your great works performed by skilful artists and amateurs without wishing that I could for once admire you at the pianoforte, and take delight in your extraordinary talent. The good Bettina Brentano really deserves the sympathy you have shown her. She speaks of you with rapture and the liveliest affection, and counts the hours she spent with you as the happiest of her life. The *Egmont* music I shall probably find when I return home, and I thank you in advance—for I have already heard it spoken of in high terms by several persons, and think I shall be able to give it this winter at our theatre, accompanied by the music in question; by this means I hope to provide great enjoyment both for myself and for your numerous admirers in our parts. What, however, I most wish, is to have properly understood Herr Oliva, who held out the hope that in the course of a journey you propose to take, you might visit Weimar. May it take place at a time when the court and the whole music-loving public is here. You would certainly meet with a reception in keeping with your merits and sentiments. But no one would take greater interest in it than I myself. I wish you farewell, beg you to keep me in kind remembrance, and offer you hearty thanks for the pleasure which through you I have often received."

[This letter was printed in the twenty-second volume of Goethe's Letters (No. 615) in the great Weimar edition, published by order of the Grand-Duchess Sophie of Saxony. The two great men made each other's acquaintance in the following year (1812) at Teplitz, when Goethe had ample opportunity of gratifying his wish to hear Beethoven play. In the poet's diary under 21 July, 1812, we find "Spent the evening at Beethoven's house. He plays most delightfully." The diaries also show that Beethoven was often with Goethe at Carlsbad.]

113. To BREITKOPF AND HAERTEL, Leipzig

VIENNA, *the 6th May* [1811].

P. P. Faults—faults—you yourself are an unparalleled fault—I shall have to send my copyist, I shall have to come myself, if I do not want my works to be mere faults—the Music Tribunal in Leipzig, so it appears to me, cannot produce a single proper proof-reader; and then you always send the works before you have received the corrected proof—at any rate in important works with other parts, the bars should be counted, but in the Fantasia, etc., one can see what happens—in the pianoforte edition of the *Egmont* Overture a whole bar is missing. Here is the list of faults.

My warmest thanks for setting in motion a matter so interesting for me. Farewell, I hope for improvement—the Fantasia is already gone, and the Sonata goes off to-morrow. Commit as many faults as you like, leave out as much as you like—you are still highly esteemed by me; that is the way with men, they are esteemed because they have not committed still greater faults.

Your most devoted servant,

BEETHOVEN.

N.B. Notice that in my correction of the (violin) concerto, the first violin part in the first Allegro page 5, line 6, bar 1

the *piano* is to be placed above these

notes , but not under the violin notes.

[According to Thayer (iii. 166), "communicated by Jahn."]

114. TO THE SAME

VIENNA, *the 20th May.*

I express my warmest sympathy at your just grief concerning the death of your wife; it seems to me that this parting which happens to almost every husband must restrain people from entering into wedlock. Your Sonata is also on the road with the Fantasia. Make out the title, as I wrote it out, in French and German, not in French alone—and so with the other titles. See to better proof-reading, complaints are also being made about the uncomfortable turns—the misfortune of reprinting here in Vienna ought at any rate to be got rid of, for I shall sue for a *privilegium* forbidding my works being reprinted in Austria. So long as the present exchange lasts, you must agree to a lower price—as regards other countries, or other places, I cannot give any advice—the corrections which you lately sent off shall be attended to as soon as I get them—as regards the *Trio*, there is still time—what you say about an *opera* is greatly to be desired, also the management would pay well for it; certainly circumstances are now unfavourable, but if you write to me, I will see about getting a poet. I have written to Paris for books, for successful melodramas, comedies, etc. (for I cannot trust any poet here to write an original opera), to serve as a libretto —O poverty of intellect—of purse—

Yours,

BEETHOVEN.

[With regard to the title of the Characteristic Sonata (Op. 81*a*) no atten-tion appears to have been paid to Beethoven's wish, for the title of the original edition which appeared in July 1811, runs: "Les Adieux, l'Absence et le Retour. Sonate pour le Pianoforte composée et dediée à Son Altesse Impériale l'Archiduc Rodolphe d'Autriche, par L. van Beethoven. Chez Breitkopf & Härtel à Leipsic. Œuvre 81." So only in French. Whether the composer, as he states in the above letter, had really tried to get a privilege against reprinting of his works in Austria, we cannot say. The Trio mentioned (Op. 97 in B flat) was not published by this firm. Finally, we perceive here that Beethoven was seriously thinking of new operas; the intellectual poverty of the Viennese poets frightened him, so that he had to turn to "books from Paris."]

115. To Baron ZMESKALL-DOMANOVECZ

[*May* 1811.]

DEAR ZMESKALL,

Send me at once your servant, mine is going away to-day, and I do not yet know whether and when the other comes—in any case I must have him here for an hour.

Yours in haste,

BEETHOVEN.

Address : POUR MONSIEUR DE ZMESKALL.

[Of the ever-ready friend of the composer, Baron von Zmeskall, mention has already been made in these letters. After the year 1813 his services to the master were overshadowed by those of Nanette Streicher.]

116. To the Theatre Poet, FRIEDRICH TREITSCHKE

[*6th June*, 1811.]

Have you, my worthy Treitschke, read the book, and may I venture to hope that you feel inclined to work at it?—Please answer me about this matter, I am prevented coming myself to you. If you have already read the book, please send it me back, so that I may once more look through it before you begin to work at it— I especially beg you, if it is your intention to let me rise aloft on the pinions of your poetry, to bring this about as soon as possible.

Your most devoted servant,

LUDWIG VAN BEETHOVEN.

[Georg Friedrich Treitschke, the dramatic writer, *régisseur* and entomologist, was born in 1776 at Leipzig, and died at Vienna in 1842; he was one of the friends and admirers of Beethoven. His connection with the composer first became of importance in the year 1814, when *Fidelio* was revised. But as early as this, determined efforts were being made to induce Beethoven to write a new work for the stage, for we find him in correspondence with various poets of Vienna—especially with his friend, Treitschke. Beethoven had only recently delivered his flattering verdict on the Viennese poets to B. and H.: "I cannot trust any poet here to write an original opera" (Letter 114). There were, however, to be, as we shall perceive, many attempts with such poets.]

117. To GEORGE THOMSON, EDINBURGH

VIENNE, *le* 20 *Juillet*, 1811.

MONSIEUR,

Comme les trois exemplaires de ces cinquante-trois chansons ecossaises que j'ai vous envoyé il-y-a longtemps, se sont perdu et avec eux la composition originale de ma propre main, j'etois forcé de completter mes premièrs idees qui me restoient encore dans un manuscrit, et de faire pour ainsi dire la meme composition deux fois. L'etat de nos finances a influencé sur tous les artistes et ils manquaient pour quelque temps tous les moyens de les contenter; mais à present ou l'ancien ordre est rétabli, j'ai trouvé un copiste raisonnable et invariable et je suis en état de pouvoir servir plus promptement.

A l'égard de ces cinquante trois chansons Ecossaises il est à observer, que j'ai donné dans ma composition à peu près à chaque chanson deux parties croyant que chaque chanson consistoit en deux parties; mais il dependera de vous, de vous en servir ou non; il est *ad libitum*.

Il sera superflu de dous parler de ¼ d.s.; mais ou vous trouverez prima et alors seconda Volta vous pouvez rayer la mésure de prima Volta et commencer de suite avec la mesure de seconda Volta. Dans le cas ou on trouve 1, 2, 3, Volta et l'ultima volta ou il fine on est obligé d'executer seulement la mesure ou plusieurs mesures de 1, 2, 3, Volta, quand on retourne à dal segno, ou quand ou veut commencer de nouveau. En cas contraire si on veut continuer sans commencer de nouveau on peut se dispenser de la mesure 1, 2, 3, Volta et on prend d'abord la mesure de l'ultima Volta ou noté il fine. J'èspere que ces détails suffiront pour Vous éclairer de ma composition et que vous l'accueillerez.

Je vous prie d'ajouter dans l'avenir toujours le texte, sans cela on est hors d'etat de satisfaire aux pretentions des connaisseurs et de composer un accompagnement digne d'une bonne poesie.

Vous avez tort de m'exprimer votre mefiance; et je sais de respecter mon parole d'honneur et je Vous assure, que je ne confierai pas à personne une de mes compositions jusqu'a que le temps convenu sera échu.

Je reviens encore une fois sur vôtre lettre du 17 Sept., 1811, malgré que la réponse en est partie tout suite après sa recette. A l'égard de l'offre de cent ducats en or pour les trois sonates je Vous declare que je les accepterai pour Vous plaire et je suis aussi prête de Vous composer trois quintettes pour cent Ducats en or; mais quant aux douze chansons avec le texte en anglois le prix fixe en est de 60 Ducats en or.[1] Pour le cantate sur la pataille dans la mer baltique je demande 50 Ducats; mais à condition que le texte original n'est pas invective contre les Danois; dans le cas contraire je ne puis pas m'en occuper.

---

[1] Pour quatre chansons le prix est de 25 Ducats.

Pour l'avenir il me sera agreable de travailler pour Vous; mais à l'égard de la crise malheureuse dans laquelle nous vivons et à l'égard des grandes pertes que j'ai déja souffert par ma confiance envers vos concitoyens il est une condition essentielle, qu'il Vous plaira de donner ordre à la maison de Fries et Compagnie d'accepter mes compositions pour Vous contre payement contant; sans cela il me sera impossible de satisfaire à Vos Commissions.

J'attends de Vous que Vous fixéréz l'epoque à laquelle Vous il plaira de publier mes compositions et que Vous m'en avertirez pour que je puisse après le terme echu les faire imprimer et ainsi rendre compte au public du Continent de mes occupations dans la partie dont je m'occupe.

Je me manquerai pas de Vous communiquer sous peu mes Simphonies arrangées, et je m'occuperai avec plaisir d'une composition d'un oratoire, si le texte en sera noble et distingué, et si l'honoraire de 600 Ducats en or Vous conviendra. Les derniers cinq chansons écossaises Vous recevrez sous peu par la maison de Fries.

En attendant Votre réponse je Vous prie d'être assuré de ma plus haute considération avec laquelle j'ai l'honneur d'être

Votre très humble et très obéissant
Serviteur,
Louis van Beethoven.

[Adresse:]

Messieurs Thomas Coutts et Co. pour Mr. G. Thomson d'Edinbourg

Strand   Londres.

[This letter, only signed by Beethoven, is in the British Museum.—Tr.]— [It is to be regretted that Campbell's *The Battle of the Baltic* is not among the copies of poems preserved among the Schindler-Beethoven documents in the Berlin Library. The poet paid several visits to Germany—Hamburg, Munich. On his return to England in 1801 he saw the preparations for the battle of Copenhagen. Campbell was held in high esteem by Goethe and Freiligrath; the latter imitated his *The Last Man*.—Beethoven's objection to set *The Battle of the Baltic*, if it contained anything abusive concerning the Danes, shows that he entertained friendly feelings towards that nation. It is extraordinary, however, to find him writing thus to a Britisher; moreover he was sympathetically disposed towards the English nation.]

118. To BREITKOPF AND HAERTEL, Leipzig

P. P.,   [*July* 1811?]

That you are already sending away the Concerto to the Industrie-Kontor, and goodness knows where else, before you have received the corrections, does not please me. Why will you not publish a single work of mine without *faults*; already the day before yesterday the corrections of the Concerto went off (if now the Industrie-Kontor receives the Concerto, must I the faults. . . .

Next Saturday the corrections in the Fantasia, together with my score, will also be sent off; the latter, however, I ask you to send me back at once.

[On the margin.]

nb. There are a jolly lot of faults in the Concerto.

[The contents concern the E flat Concerto and the Choral Fantasia. Both works were published this year, the former in May, the latter in July. It is therefore extraordinary that this burst of anger with regard to the many faults in the Concerto should only occur now.]

119. To the Same

Teplitz, *the 23rd August*, 1811.

While here for the last three weeks seeking health, I receive your letter of the 2nd of August? It may have been lying in Vienna for a time; I had just undertaken the *revising* of the *oratorio* and the songs, and in a few days you will receive both—here and there the *text* must remain as it was at first. I know that the *text* is a very bad one, but when once one has thought out a whole, even from a bad text, it is difficult to prevent disturbing this whole by single changes; so if there is a single word to which sometimes special meaning is attached, it must be kept; and an author must be a [wretched] one who does not know how, or try to get as much good as he can out of even a bad text; and if this be the case, changes will not improve the whole—I have left some, as they really are improvements.

Farewell, and let me soon have news of you; Oliva is here and intends to write to you. The good reception given to Mozart's *Don Juan* gives me as much pleasure as if it were my own work. Although I know plenty of unprejudiced Italians who render justice to the German—that the nation itself is inferior is probably the cause of the backwardness and easy-going methods of Italian musicians—yet I have learned to know many Italian amateurs who prefer our music to their Paisiello—I render more justice to him even than his own countrymen have done.

Your most devoted servant,

Ludwig van Beethoven.

SKETCH FOR FIRST MOVEMENT OF THE E FLAT CONCERTO (OP. 73)

[Beethoven's remarks about the treatment of the text refer to the oratorio *The Mount of Olives* (Op. 85). The changes were most probably made by Dr. Schreiber. Beethoven's enthusiastic delight in Mozart's master-work, *Don Juan*, is most refreshing. In his later years he spoke, it is true, in a very different tone about it to Rellstab. Also he is reported to have said: *"Don Juan* is still quite in the Italian style, and, besides, holy art should never degrade itself by becoming a foil to so scandalous a subject."]

120. TO BARON ZMESKALL

[*September* 10, 1811?]

DEAR Z.,

Don't do anything yet about the rehearsal; I must go again to the doctor's; of his bungling I am at last quite weary. Thanks for your time-measurer—we will see whether we can be measured thereby for all eternity; nothing ought to stand in the way of yours, as regards *lightness* and *intelligibility*. Meanwhile we will hold a conference on the subject. Although, naturally, with clock-work one gets more mathematical exactness, yet in former small experiments you have made in my presence with your time-measurer, I have found much that is profitable, and I hope that we shall *arrange it quite to our satisfaction.* I shall soon see you.

Your friend,

BEETHOVEN.

[The contents concern the invention of a metronome; but whether of Maelzel's invention cannot be said with certainty; anyhow, in the following year, Maelzel became acquainted with Beethoven.]

121. TO BREITKOPF AND HAERTEL, LEIPZIG

VIENNA, *the 9th October*, 1811.

A thousand excuses and a thousand thanks from here for your pleasant invitation to Leipzig, I am very sorry that I cannot follow my own inclination and go there to the places round about, but just now there has been such a lot to do. The Hungarian Diet is sitting; there is already a talk of making the Archduke *Primate* of Hungary, and of his resigning the Bishopric at Olmütz. I have proposed to H.I.H., who as Primate of Hungary will have an income of not less than three millions, to squander away a million on me every year (of course you understand the good musical spirits which by that means I shall set in motion). In Teplitz I received no further news, because they knew nothing of my plan to go further; I think also for the journey which I have in view, considering my attachment, that I shall have unwillingly to yield to him, and all the more as I shall be wanted at the festivities. So after having selected the *pro*, I am off to Vienna, and the first thunder-word which I hear is that our gracious lord has entirely given up being, or acting as a priest; and so nothing will come of the whole matter.

It is said he is to become a general, a thing, as you know, easy to understand, and I, quartermaster-general in the battle, which, however, I am determined not to lose—what do you say to that? Another event was caused by the Hungarians, for as I was stepping into my carriage to go to Teplitz, I received a parcel from Buda-Pesth with the request to write something for the opening of the new theatre. After I had spent three weeks in Teplitz, and was pretty well, I set to work, in spite of the order of my doctor, to help these mustachioed men, who are well inclined towards me. I send my parcel there on the 13th of September, thinking that the opening would be between the 1st and 8th October; meanwhile the whole affair is put off for a whole month; and the letter in which this was announced to me, I only received here through some misunderstanding; and yet this theatre matter also decided me to go back to Vienna.—Meanwhile, what is postponed is not lost. I have enjoyed the journey, and it has done me good; now I should like to be off from here again—I have just received *Das Lebewohl*, etc., I see that you really have other copies with French title. But why? *Lebewohl* is something very different from *Les Adieux*; the first is said in a hearty manner to a single person, the other to a whole assembly, to whole towns. As you allow me to be *reviewed* in so shameful a manner, you must also suffer for it; besides, you should have used fewer plates, and the difficult turning over would thereby have been made easier; enough upon this subject—How in Heaven's name did my Fantasia with orchestra come to be dedicated to the King of Bavaria? give me an answer about this at once; if thereby you wished to offer me an honourable gift, I will thank you for it, otherwise it does not please me. Did you perhaps draw up this dedication yourself, what is the meaning of it? One cannot dedicate anything to kings with impunity—then the *Lebewohl* was not dedicated to the Archduke, why were not the year, the day and *datum*, as I wrote them, printed. In future please keep to the titles unchanged as I have sent them. You may have the oratorio, and indeed everything reviewed by whom you like. It annoys me to have written a word to you about the wretched review. Who troubles about such critics when one sees how the most wretched scribblers are praised up by such critics, and how they speak in the harshest way of works of art, and are indeed forced to do so, because they have not, as the cobbler has his last, the proper standard. If there is anything to notice about my *oratorio*, it is that it was my first and early work of the kind; it was written in fourteen days amidst all possible *tumult* and other unpleasant, anxious events (my brother was dying). If I mistake not, Rochlitz, already before it was given to you to print, spoke not favourably about the chorus of the disciples, "Wir haben ihn gesehen"; he called it comic, a feeling which at any rate was not experienced by any one of the public here, and among my friends there are also critics. That I should now write quite a different kind of *oratorio* is certain. And now *criticise* as long as you like, I wish you much pleasure; it may give one a little prick like the sting of a gnat, and then it becomes quite a nice little joke. *Not for ever ; that you cannot do.* And so good-bye. In the *oratorio* there was a passage in which the horn ought to have been written in the printed copy on two staves, namely, the second horn has the bass clef, but the first the treble; your proof-reader will easily find the place. Every man must have more than one key, even if he opens nothing. I will send you a letter addressed to Kotzebue, and beg that you will see that it is sent to his address. Also somebody will send his own letters to you from Berlin. I wish to save him the postage, so be kind enough to send them on to me. You won't think badly of me; with regard to postage, each time you give me notice, I will repay at once. Now Heaven preserve you; I hope soon to see you and have a talk; you see by that my firm intention to travel—all kind messages to the Saxon, and especially to the Leipzig amateurs for their good feeling towards me, of which I have heard much; also many thanks to the artists of whose zeal for me I have also heard.

Yours,
LUDWIG VAN BEETHOVEN.

When will the Mass appear?—*Egmont ?* Do send the whole score copied for my sake, and at my cost, to Goethe; how can a first-rate German publisher be so impolite, so impudent towards the German poet? So send the score quickly to Weimar. Concerning the Mass, the dedication could be changed; the lady is now married, and as the name would have to be changed, leave out the dedication. Only write to me when you are going to publish it, and then we will find a saint for this work.

[Beethoven wrote music to Kotzebue's *Nachspiel, The Ruins of Athens*, for the opening of the Pesth theatre, and so quickly that it was already forwarded on 13 September, 1811; also to the poet's *Vorspiel, König Stephan*, or

Ungarns erster Wohltäter (Op. 117). Both works were performed at the opening of the theatre on 9 February, 1812. Very extraordinary are Beethoven's remark concerning the title of the E flat Sonata (Op. 81*a*), *Das Lebewohl*. In his letter of 2 July, 1810, he describes it as a "Charakteristische Sonate, *der Abschied*, Abwesenheit, das Wiedersehen." In a former letter to the firm, Beethoven expressly asks them to give "the title as I wrote it out, in French and German, not in French alone" (Letter 114). No attention was paid to the request, and this led to ill-humour on both sides. Whether Beethoven's subtle distinction between "Lebewohl" and "Adieux" is to the point, may be left to specialists in romanesque philology; anyhow, his digression is striking. In stating that the *Lebewohl* was not dedicated to the Archduke, Beethoven makes a mistake, for he had expressly stated in a former post-script (No. 111, of April 1811) that "*Das Lebewohl, das Wiedersehen* can only be dedicated to the Archduke Rudolph." A word may be said about the composer's philippic against critics. He was evidently deeply annoyed at the criticism of his E flat quartet (Op. 74), in the Leipzig *Allgemeine Musikalische Zeitung* of 2 May, 1811. Yet the review was not as a whole appreciative, but Beethoven's original style was condemned. Among other things, the writer said: "In quartet writing the aim should surely not be to commemorate the dead, or to express the feelings of one in despair, but by soft, pleasing play of the imagination to refresh and gladden one's heart!" From the above letter we see that Beethoven had nothing to do with the dedication of one of his works to the King of Bavaria! The first intention was, apparently, to dedicate the first Mass to Bettina von Arnim, who was married in this same year.]

122. To Baron ZMESKALL

[1811?]

Most worthy councillor and owner of mines, also Burgundian and Buda tyrant! please tell me how this matter stands, and this afternoon at latest I want to make use of the answer to your [my?] question. If I give a fortnight's notice to the servant from to-day —he receives his monthly money, as always, from me at the end of the month—must I then, when at the end of fourteen days he goes away, pay him a whole half-month?—we have been terribly taken in with this fellow, and it is only owing to my patience that I put up with him. As he was a valet de chambre, nothing is right for him, and every day he makes increased demands in order to do less; so I must put an end to the matter; he has given me notice after a fashion for the second time, although this time only in order to get more money, but I will not listen any more to anything he says—I therefore beg you to give me an answer to-day, so that this very day I may give him notice for good—this time I must have recourse to the police about a servant, for with all that I have had in this way, I have not been successful. I am very busy and will come to see you to-morrow or the next day. As always,

Yours,

L. v. BEETHOVEN.

[At the side].

Perhaps you could do something among your countrymen for your friend and countryman.

To Herr von Zmeskall.

[Zmeskall was an officer in the Royal Hungarian Chancellery, and he possessed estates in the territory of Buda-Pesth. The secretary's "countrymen" were the Hungarians, but as a citizen of Vienna he was also Beethoven's countryman.]

123. To the Poet AUGUSTUS Von KOTZEBUE

VIENNA, 28th January, 1812.

HIGHLY ESTEEMED, HIGHLY HONOURED SIR!

As I wrote music to your Prologue and Epilogue for the Hungarians, I could not refrain from the ardent desire to possess an opera from your unique dramatic genius, whether romantic or quite serious; heroic, comic, sentimental, in short whatever pleases you I will accept with pleasure. Certainly I should most like a big historical subject, and especially from the Dark Ages, for example about Attila, etc. However I will accept with thankfulness whatever be the subject, anything that comes from you, from your poetic soul, which I will transfer to my musical soul. . . .

[Beethoven, out of love to the "mustachioed," had set to music Kotzebue's *Ruins of Athens*, and the prelude to *King Stephen*. The first performance and the dedication of the Pesth German theatre took place on 9 February, 1812. The master about this time was more than ever drawn towards dramatic music. He lacked the right poet, and hoped finally to have discovered him in Kotzebue; he was even ready to compose a comic opera if Kotzebue would grant his wish. However, nothing more came of the matter between the two.]

124. To BREITKOPF AND HAERTEL

VIENNA, the 28th January, 1812.

P. P.,

As a punishment for your total silence, I order you to see at once that these two letters are delivered to the persons addressed. A Livonian swaggerer promised to see that a letter was given to K., but probably, as in general Russians and Livonians are swaggerers and big boasters, he did nothing at all, although he gave himself out as a good friend of his—I also beg you, although I ought properly to inflict it on you as a punishment for the many faulty editions, false titles, negligences, etc., and other human weaknesses, to attend to this matter, so I beg you most humbly to see that these letters are properly delivered—And then, send the letter to Goethe together with the *Egmont* score, but not in your usual style, with perhaps here and there a number missing, etc.; not so, but everything in perfect order. I have given my word, and hold to it all the more if I can compel another person such as you to the carrying out of it—ha, ha, ha. It is your fault that I can use this language to a sinner like you, who, if I wished, would have to wander about in penitential garment made of hair for all the wicked things that he has done to my works. In the chorus in the *oratorio* "Wir haben, ihn gesehen," in spite of my *nota* for the old text, the unfortunate change has remained. Good heavens! do they really believe in Saxony that the word constitutes the music? If an unsuitable word can ruin music, which it certainly can, one ought to be glad when one finds that music and word are one; and although the word-expression may be a vulgar one, they should not try to improve it—*dixi*—I have taken very little of the fifty thalers' worth of music, for with Herr Traeg everything is slow [*traeg*]; send me also Mozart's Requiem, *Clemenza di Tito*, *Cosi fan tutte*, *Don Juan*—the small meetings at my house are beginning again, so I want these things sent by post as cheaply as possible, for I am a poor Austrian musician. The C. P. Emanuel Bach things you could really make me a present of, they are spoiling at your place—If the three songs of Goethe are not yet printed, hurry up with them, I want to give them to Princess Kynsky, one of the prettiest, plumpest ladies in Vienna; and the *Egmont* songs, why are they not published? why is not the whole edition out, out, out—if here and there you want a coda stuck on to the entr'actes, I can manage it, or else let a Leipzig proof-reader of the *Musik-Zeitung* see to it; they understand such matters about as well as a brick-wall—Kindly debit me with the postage for the letters—It seems to me, it has been whispered that you are again going to be married, and to that I ascribe all your previous muddles. I hope that, like the holy Grecian Socrates, you may meet with a Xantippe, so that for once I may see a German publisher, and that is saying a great deal, yes see him in downright perplexity—I hope soon to be honoured with a few lines from you,

Your friend,

BEETHOVEN.

[The letter to be "given to K," was probably the one written the same day (No. 123) to Kotzebue, who at this time was living on his estate in

Esthonia. Beethoven earnestly begs the firm to send the score of *Egmont*, together with a letter, to Goethe; the composer himself, in the previous year, had sent, through his friend Oliva, a letter to the poet, in which he assured him that *Egmont* should be forwarded. The letter of 1812, mentioned above, to be sent with the score, has not yet been found.]

125. To Baron ZMESKALL

2nd February, 1812.

Not extraordinary, but very orderly, ordinary quill - cutter, whose virtuosity in this matter has already decreased, these need repairing—when will you cast away your fetters? when? you know a fine lot about me; life here in this Austrian Barbary is a cursed thing—I now go mostly to the Swan, as I cannot get away from importunate folk at other inns.

Farewell, as well as I can wish you without me,

Your friend,

BEETHOVEN.

Most extraordinary one, we beg for your servant to find some one to clean out the rooms; as he knows the parish, he can at once fix the price.

But soon—carnival ragamuffin ! ! ! ! ! ! ! ! ! ! ! ! ! to Herr von Zmeskall.

The enclosed letter is at least
eight days old.

126. To the Same

[*February* 8, 1812.]

Wonderful, chief soaring man in the world, and that without help of lever ! ! ! ! We are greatly indebted to you for having bestowed on us a portion of your buoyancy. We desire personally to thank you for it, and therefore invite you to come to-morrow to the Swan Inn, which by its name shows that it is the very place to talk of such a matter.

Yours truly,

BEETHOVEN.

[*Re* play upon words, see Preface.—Tr.]

127. To Baron ZMESKALL

[February 1812.]

Damned, dear little ex-music Count, what the devil do you mean—will you come to-day to the Swan? no? yes. From the enclosed you see all that I have done for the Hungarians. It is something quite different when a German, without giving his word, undertakes something, as, for instance, a Hungarian Count B., who allowed me, for some paltry trifle or other, to travel all alone, and in addition kept me waiting without my expecting anything—

best ex-music Count
I am your best real
dear little BEETHOVEN.

Send back the enclosed at once, for we want to blame the Count for something else.

[Beethoven here points his sarcastic humour at his friend, the Hungarian Count Brunswick, who the year before let him travel with Oliva, instead of being the much-desired travelling companion, although the composer had done so much for the Hungarians; in this letter he had in mind his compositions for the inauguration of the new Pesth theatre.]

128. To GEORGE THOMSON, EDINBURGH

VIENNE, *le 29 Févr.*, 1812.

MONSIEUR!

En m'assurant que vous ne me refuserez pas de me faire payer ches Messieurs Fries et Comp. au liu de 3 ducats en or 4 ducats en or pour chaque chanson, j'ai rendu les 9 chansons a susdites Messieurs, j'aurais ainsi encore 9 ducats en or a recevoir.

Haydn même m'assure qu'il a aussi reçu pour chaque chanson 4 ducats en or et pourtant il n'ecrivit que pour le clavecin et un violon tout seul sans ritournelles et violoncelle. Quant à Monsieur Kozeluch, qui vous livre chaque chanson avec accompagnement pour 2 ducats je vous félicite beaucoup et aussi aux éditeurs anglois et ecossis quand ils en goûtent. Moi je m'estime encore une fois plus supérieur en ce genre que Monsieur Kozeluch (: Miserabilis:) et j'espère crogant que vous possedez quelque distinction, laquelle vous mette en état de me rendre justice.

Je n'ai pas encore reçu la réponse à ma lettre dernière, et je souhaite de savoir a quoi que je suis avec vous. Vous auriez déjà longtemps les 3 Sonates pour 100 ducats en or et les 3 Quintettes pour la même somme, mais je ne peux rien risquer en cette affaire et il faut que je recoive les sommes fixées de Messrs. Fries en presentant les exemplaires.

A ce qui regard les 12 chansons, avec le texte angloise le honoraire est 70 ducats en or. Pour la Cantate contenant la bataille dans la mer Baltique 60 ducats en or, pour l'Oratoire je demande 600 ducats en or, mais il est nécessaire, que le texte soit singulièrement bien fait. Je vous prie instamment d'adjoindre toujours le texte aux chansons ecossaises. Je ne comprends pas comme vous qui êtes connaisseur ne pouvez comprendre, que je produirais des compositions tout à fait autre, si j'aurai le texte à la main, et les chansons ne peuvent jamais devenir des products parfaits, si vous ne m'envoyez pas le texte et vous m'obligerez à la fin de refuser vos ordres ultérieurs.

Puis je voudrois savoir si je peux faire la violine et le violoncelle obligé, de sorte que les deux instruments ne peuvent jamais être omis, ou de manière presente, que le Clavecin fait un ensemble pour soi-même; alors notez-moi à chaque chanson s'il y a plusieurs versettes et combien? S'il y a des répétitions ⫴ qui sont quelquefois très mal noté par ces deux ‖ lignes.

Je vous prie de répondre bientôt car je retiens plusieurs compositions à cause de vous. Je souhaite aussi de recevoir les 9 ducats en or, pour les chansons ecossaises, nous avons besoin d'or ici, car notre empire n'est rien qu'une source de papier à présent, et moi sur tout, car je quitterai peut-être ce pays ici et je me rendrai en Angleterre et puis à Edinbourg en Ecosse, ou je me réjouis de faire votre connaissance en personne. Je suis avec l'estime le plus parfait.

Monsieur,

Votre très humble serviteur,

Louis van Beethoven.

[That the commonplace composer, Kozeluch, should have been cast in Beethoven's teeth was bound to produce fierce scorn. Kozeluch (1748–1818) was Mozart's successor as Court Composer and Imperial Capellmeister, who in the early stage of Beethoven's career was held up to him, by the critics, as a model. If Kozeluch is here somewhat maliciously treated, his only daughter Katharina, viz., Katharina Cibbini, who was a brilliant pianist, was held in high esteem by Beethoven. Mr. Cuthbert Hadden states that Beethoven only received this February letter in December; meanwhile Thomson had written twice to the composer (5 August and 30 October).]

129. To BREITKOPF AND HAERTEL, Leipzig

[*May* 1812.]

P. P.,

Herewith I send the Mass; and please do not play tricks with me, and magnanimously present it to the public adorned with great faults. If it is coming out so late, the dedication ought to be altered, viz., to Prince Kynsky, and for this you will receive the further *Titularium*. So must it be. In the chaos amid which we poor Germans live, who can say whether you will see me in the North—Farewell; I am writing 3 new *Symphonies*, one of which is now completed. I have also written something for the Hungarian Theatre—but in the slough in which I find myself, all that is as good as lost—I only hope I shall not entirely lose myself.

Fare right well; be glad that you are more fortunate than other poor mortals.

Yours very truly,

BEETHOVEN.

[The dedication of the Mass in C, which was probably intended for Bettina von Arnim, was, "the lady being now married," definitely assigned to Prince Kynsky, and so it appeared in November 1812. Beethoven here communicates the information that he is writing three symphonies: the first was the divine one in A, the second the humorous one in F (Op. 93). And the third? The composer was probably already thinking of his Symphony in D minor, which only assumed definite shape a decade later.]

130. To THE SAME

TEPLITZ, 17*th July*, 1812.

We only say to you that we are here since the 5th July, how? —Concerning that there is not much to say; in all there are not so many interesting folk as last year, and fewer; the crowd appears less than few.—My rooms are not exactly what I should like, but I hope soon to get better ones. You will have received the corrections for the Mass—At the beginning of the *gloria* I have written, instead of common, *alla breve* time and change of *tempo*. It was written so at first; a bad performance, at which the tempo was taken too quickly, led me to it. As I had not seen the Mass for a long time it struck me at once, and I saw that one has, unfortunately, to leave such things sometimes to chance.—In the *Sanctus* it might be indicated somewhere that at the enharmonic change the flats might be taken away and sharps substituted for them thus:

instead of *flats*, the sharps to be kept here
(Nb.! at B on the same line)

I could never hear this passage sung in tune by our choirs unless the organist quietly gave the chord of the 7th. Perhaps with you they are better—it will at least be well to indicate somewhere that one could take the *sharp* in this passage instead of a *flat*, as here indicated. (Of course it will be added in print as here.) Goethe is here—farewell and let me soon know something about your doings—

Your most devoted,
Ludwig van Beethvn.

Nb. II. *Please add all you have printed of separate songs of mine.*

Nb. I. As the 50 thalers are not quite paid up, and even if they were, it does not need very strong imagination to consider the same as not yet paid; we beg you, therefore, either in return for the actual or imagined 50 thalers, to send the following works in my name to a most amiable lady at Berlin; namely, first the score of the *Mount of Olives*; secondly and thirdly, both books of Goethe's songs, namely, the one with 6, the other with 3 songs. The address is: "Amalie Sebald, Bauhof No. 1, Berlin"; she is a pupil of Zelter, and we are well disposed towards her.

Nb. II. You can also send me here some copies of the last of the works; one often wants such a thing for musicians, when one sees that they are not likely to buy—I hope that with your amiability you will carry out punctually my amiable liberality with regard to A. S.

[This letter belongs to the small number in which the composer employs technical musical terms. "Goethe is here," is written in the above letter. In this year these two intellectual giants approached each other; becoming, however, conscious that they were totally opposed in character, they soon separated. The letters A. S. refer to Amalie Sebald. On the very same day Beethoven wrote a letter to a girl pianist aged from eight to ten, as follows:]

131. To EMILIE M. at H.

TEPLITZ, 17th July, 1812.

MY DEAR GOOD EMILIE, MY DEAR FRIEND!

I am sending a late answer to your letter; a mass of business, constant illness must be my excuse. That I am here for the restoration of my health proves the truth of my excuse. Do not snatch the laurel wreaths from Händel, Haydn, Mozart; they are entitled to them; as yet I am not.

Your pocket-book shall be preserved among other tokens of the esteem of many people, which I do not deserve.

Continue, do not only practise art, but get at the very heart of it; this it deserves, for only art and science raise men to the God-head. If, my dear Emilie, you at any time wish to know something, write without hesitation to me. The true artist is not proud, he unfortunately sees that art has no limits; he feels darkly how far he is from the goal; and though he may be admired by others, he is sad not to have reached that point to which his better genius only appears as a distant, guiding sun. I would, perhaps, rather come to you and your people, than to many rich folk who display inward poverty. If one day I should come to H., I will come to you, to your house; I know no other excellences in man than those which causes him to rank among better men; where I find this, there is my home.

If you wish, dear Emilie, to write to me, only address straight here where I shall still be for the next four weeks, or to Vienna; it is all one. Look upon me as your friend, and as the friend of your family.

LUDWIG V. BEETHOVEN.

[Thayer relates that Emilie M., at H., was a little girl of eight or ten years old, who raved about Beethoven. This dear child wrote under the guidance of her governess to the composer, and added to the letter a piece of handiwork—a pocket-book which she begged the master to accept. And thereupon followed the letter, a veritable cabinet-piece of artistic wisdom, in childlike language.]

132. To BREITKOPF AND HAERTEL, Leipzig

FRANTZENS BRUNN, near EGER,
9th August, 1812.[1]

Only what is most necessary; you have not got the title of the Mass, and I have many things too much, taking baths, doing nothing and etc., also other unavoidable things. I am tired of chance things, surprises—you see and think I am now here, but my doctor drives me from one place to another in search of health, from Teplitz to Carlsbad, from there back here. In C. I played to the Saxons and Prussians some music for the benefit of those who had suffered from the fire at Baden; it was, so to speak, a poor concert for the *poor*—Signore Polledrone helped me, and after he had once got rid, as usual, of his nervousness, played well—"Seine Durchlaucht dem Hochgebohrnen Fürsten Kynsky," something of that sort for the title—and now I must refrain from writing any more; instead of that, I have to go again and dabble about in water; scarcely have I filled my inside with a good *quantity* of the same, than I have then to bathe myself all over—very shortly will I answer the other points in your letter—Court air suits Goethe more than becomes a poet. One cannot laugh much at the ridiculous things that *virtuosi* do, when poets, who ought to be looked upon as the principal teachers of the nation, forget everything else amidst this glitter.

Yours,
BEETHOVEN.

[On a scrap of paper attached to the first page:]

I have just written for the full title of Prince Kynsky, you will receive it however in good time, as I presume the Mass will not come out before the autumn—

[Concerning the concert with the great violinist Polledro, something more will be said after the next letter to the Archduke Rudolph. Let us notice carefully the words which here refer to Goethe: for they give us the key to the fact that already in Teplitz an estrangement between these two geniuses had taken place.]

[1] The climate here is such that one might date the letter November 9. [Beethoven's own words.]

133. To BETTINA Von ARNIM

TEPLITZ, [15th?] *August, 1812.*

DEAREST, GOOD BETTINA!

Kings and princes can certainly create professors, privy councillors and titles, and hang on ribbons of various orders, but they cannot create great men, master-minds which tower above the rabble; this is beyond them. Such men must therefore be held in respect. When two such as I and Goethe meet together, these grand gentlemen are forced to note what greatness, in such as we are, means. Yesterday on the way home we met the whole Imperial family. We saw them from afar approaching, and Goethe slipped away from me, and stood on one side. Say what I would, I could not induce him to advance another step, so I pushed my hat on my head, buttoned up my overcoat, and went, arms folded, into the thickest of the crowd—Princes and sycophants drew up in a line; Duke Rudolph took off my hat, after the Empress had first greeted me. Persons of rank *know* me. To my great amusement I saw the procession defile past Goethe. Hat in hand, he stood at the side, deeply bowing. Then I mercilessly reprimanded him, cast his sins in his teeth, especially those of which he was guilty towards you, dearest Bettina, of whom we had just been speaking. Good heavens! had I been in your company, as he has, I should have produced works of greater, far greater importance. A musician is also a poet, and the magic of a pair of eyes can suddenly cause him to feel transported into a more beautiful world, where great spirits make sport of him, and set him mighty tasks. I cannot tell what ideas came into my head when I made your acquaintance. In the little observatory during the splendid May rain, that was a fertile moment for me: the most beautiful themes then glided from your eyes into my heart, which one day will enchant the world when Beethoven has ceased to conduct. If God grant me yet a few years, then I must see you again, dear, dear Bettina; so calls the voice within me which never errs. Even minds can love one another. I shall always court yours; your approval is dearer to me than anything in the whole world. I gave my opinion to Goethe, that approval affects such men as ourselves, and that we wish to be listened to with the intellect by those who are our equals. Emotion is only for women (excuse this); the flame of music must burst forth from the mind of a man. Ah! my dearest child, we have now for a long time been in perfect agreement about everything! ! ! The only good thing is a beautiful, good soul, which is recognised in everything, and in presence of which there need be no concealment. *One must be*

somebody if one wishes to appear so. The world is bound to recognise one; it is not always unjust. To me, however, that is a matter of
no importance: for I have a higher aim. I hope when I get back to
Vienna to receive a letter from you. Write soon, soon, and a very
long one; in 8 days from now I shall be there; and the court goes
to-morrow; there will be one more performance to-day. The Empress
rehearsed her part with him. His duke and he both wish me to play
some of my music, but to both I made refusal. They are mad on
Chinese porcelain, hence there is need for indulgence; for intellect
has lost the whip-hand. I will not play to these silly folk, who
never get over that mania, nor write at public cost any stupid stuff
for princes. Adieu, adieu, dearest; your last letter lay on my heart
for a whole night, and comforted me. *Everything* is allowed to
musicians. Great Heavens, how I love you!

Your sincerest friend and deaf brother,

BEETHOVEN.

[This is the third and most problematical of the three letters of Beethoven
to Bettina. There is no doubt that it was inspired by Beethoven. The question
has become more difficult since Bettina's great letter to Prince Pückler-
Muskau, which contains not only many things similar to *Goethes Brief-
wechsel mit einem Kinde* concerning Bettina's personal intercourse with
Beethoven, but also important passages of the letter in question.

Among other things it is told how Beethoven gave Goethe "a good talking
to," "that one ought not to associate in dandy fashion with princes and
princesses, as Goethe does." "I," said Beethoven, "have treated them
differently. When I had to give lessons to Duke Raimer, he kept me waiting
in the ante-room, in return for which I twisted his fingers about without
mercy. When he asked me why I was so impatient, I told him he had made
me lose my time in the ante-room, and that now I could not get patient
again. After that he never kept me waiting; yes, and I had also shown him
that this was just an occasion to expose their brutishness."

This long epistle concludes with the following words:

"Then Beethoven came running towards us, and told us everything, and
was as pleased as a child at having teased Goethe.—What he said is word for
word true, nothing essential has been added. Beethoven *related it several
times in this way*, and in more than one respect it seemed to me of high
importance. I told it to the Duke of Weimar, who was in Teplitz, and quite
teased him, without telling him where I got it from. Isn't it a good story!—
Can you make use of it? Shall I write down another one to-morrow?"]

134. TO AMALIE SEBALD, TEPLITZ

16th September, 1812.

I a tyrant?! Your tyrant! Only misunderstanding can allow
you to say this, as if even this your verdict indicates no sympathy
with me. I do not blame you on that account; it is rather a piece of

good fortune for you.—Since yesterday I have not been quite well, since this morning I am worse; the cause is something indigestible which I have taken. Irascible nature in me seizes hold, so it appears, of the bad as well as the good; do not apply this, however, to my moral nature. People say nothing, they are only people; they see mostly in others what they are themselves, and that is nothing at all; no more of this, the good, the beautiful needs no people. Without any assistance it is there, and that appears to be the ground of our agreeing together.—Farewell, dear Amalie. If the moon shines this evening as brightly as the sun in daytime, you will see the smallest of small beings at your house.

Your friend,
BEETHOVEN.

[Amalie Sebald belonged to the Tiedge–Elise von der Recke circle.]

135. TO THE SAME

[September 1812.]

Dear good Amalie. Since I left you yesterday, I have become worse, and since yesterday evening up to now I have not been able to leave my bed. I wanted to let you have news to-day, and then I thought that I should make myself appear too important, and so did nothing.—What are you thinking about in saying that you can be nothing to me? we will talk over that, dear Amalie, together. I have always wished that my presence might give you rest and peace, and that you would show yourself trustful towards me. I hope to be better to-morrow and that there will still be a few hours for us to spend and to enjoy together amid the beauties of nature.—Good-night, dear Amalie, many thanks for the proof of your kind intentions for your friend

BEETHOVEN.

I will look through Tiedge.

136. TO THE SAME

[September 1812.]

I only announce to you that the tyrant is chained like a *slave* to his bed—so it is! I shall be very glad if I get through with only the loss of this one day. My walk yesterday at break of day in the woods, where it was very misty, has increased my indisposition, and perhaps made my getting better more difficult. Bustle about meanwhile with Russians, Laplanders, Samoyedes, etc., and do not sing the song, "Es lebe hoch" too much.

Your friend,

BEETHOVEN.

["Russians, Laplanders, Samoyedes," is a humorous reference to the Russian ladies and gentlemen of the Tiedge-Recke circle.]

137. TO THE SAME
[*September* 1812.]

I am already better. If you think it *becoming* to pay me a visit alone, I should be delighted; but if you find it *unbecoming*, you know how I honour the freedom of all men; and however you may act in this or any other case, according to your principles or your caprice, you will always find me well-disposed and your friend.

BEETHOVEN.

138. TO THE SAME
[*September* 1812.]

My illness does not seem to increase, but rather to crawl on, so no standstill yet! that is all I can tell you about it.—I must give up the idea of seeing you at your house; perhaps your Samoyedes will let you off your journey to polar regions, so come to

BEETHOVEN.

139. TO THE SAME
[*September* 1812.]

[In Amalie Sebald's handwriting:]

My tyrant orders a bill—here it is:

A fowl—1 fl. Vienna value.

The soup 9 kr.

I truly hope this may be to your liking.

[In Beethoven's hand:]

Tyrants do not pay, but the bill must be receipted, and that can be best done if you will come yourself NB. with the bill to your humbled tyrant.

[With that the Amalie episode in Beethoven's life is for the present at an end. Amalie returned to Berlin and there married Councillor Krause (about 1815). She, however, continued to blossom in Beethoven's remembrance. She was born in the year 1787, and was therefore about twenty-five years old when she enraptured the suffering composer by her bewitching charms. It is generally thought that Beethoven bore love for Amalie silently in his heart for a number of years. It is possible that his impassioned composition *Liederkreis an die ferne Geliebte* of the year 1816 had reference to the beautiful Teplitz period. In the same year Beethoven writes to his former friend and pupil Ferdinand Ries: "All kind messages to your wife, unfortunately I have none; I found one who probably will never be mine; nevertheless I am not on that account a woman-hater." In the same year he spoke to the Giannatasio del Rio family in a similar strain: "He was unfortunate in love! Five years ago he had made the acquaintance of some one, union with whom would have been the highest happiness he could have in life. There was no longer any thought of it, almost an impossibility, a mere chimera, yet he felt as on the first day. This harmony he had not yet found. Yet it did not get as far as a proposal; he, however, could not get it out of his thoughts." Beethoven remembered her for many a long year. In 1823 her name appears in the master's Conversation Books.]

140. To the Archduke RUDOLPH

[*December* 1812.]

Your Imperial Highness

To-morrow very very early will the copyist be able to commence the last number. As I myself, meanwhile, am writing several other works, I have not hastened very much with the last movement for the sake of mere punctuality; and all the more, as in writing it I must take into consideration Rode's style of playing. We are fond of rushing passages in our *finales*, yet that does not suit Rode, and—it really troubles me somewhat.—For the rest all will go right on Tuesday. I beg to take the liberty of doubting whether I can appear on that evening before Y.I.H., in spite of my earnest desire to serve. Instead of that I will, however, come to-morrow morning or to-morrow afternoon, so as quite to satisfy the wishes of my noble pupil.

Your Imperial Highness's most obedient,

Ludwig van Beethoven.

[Pierre Rode, the celebrated violinist and composer for his instrument, was born at Bordeaux in 1774, and in the course of a tour through Austria came to Vienna in 1812 and gave concerts there in January 1813. Before his public appearance, a private concert was first given in the palace of Prince Lobkowitz, at which the Archduke, together with Rode, performed Beethoven's last violin Sonata (Op. 96), which was dedicated to him. The last three movements of this work had been only just written down ready for printing, and—as we learn from this letter—many things in it were contrived to suit the taste and style of playing of Rode.]

141. To GEORGE THOMSON, Edinburgh

VIENNE, *le* 19 *Février*, 1813.

Monsieur George Thomson a Edinbourg,

J'ai reçu vos trois cheres lettres du 5 Aout, 30 Oct. et 21 Dec.
a: p:; j'ai remarqué avec bien du plaisir que les 62 airs, que j'ai
composé pour vous vous sont enfin parvenus, et que vous en etes
satisfait, à l'exception de 9 que vous me marquez et dont vous
voulez que je change les Ritournelles et les accompagnements. Je
suis faché de ne pas y pouvoir vous complaire. Je ne suis pas accou-
tumé de retoucher mes composition; je ne l'ai jamais fait, pénétré de
la vérité, que tout changement partiel altere le Caractère de la
Composition. Il me fait de la peine que vous y perdez, mais vous
ne sauriez m'en imputer la faute, puis que c'etoit à vous de me
faire mieux connoître le gout de votre pays et le peu de facilité de
vos executeurs. Maintenant muni de vos renseignements je les ai
composér tout le nouveau, et comme j'espere de sorte qu'ils répon-
dront à votre attente. Croyez-moi, que c'est avec grande repugnance,
que je me suis resolu de mettre à gene mes Idees et que je ne m'y
serais jamais preté si je n'avais reflechi que comme Vous ne voulez
admettre dans Votre Collection que de mes compositions, mon refus
y pourait causer une manque et fruster par consequence le beaucoup de paine et de dépenses que vous avéz employé pour obtenir
un œuvre complet. J'ai donc remis ces 9 Airs à Mess. Fries et Cie.,
avec les autres 21, et j'en ai touché le montant de 90 $[1] à raison
de 3 $ par pièce.

J'ai fait faire trois Exemplaires que Mess. Fries et Cie. expé-
dieront aux adresses prescrits; l'exemplaire que vous recevréz
par la voie de Paris est celui que je trouve le plus correct et le
propre à etre imprimé, parceque dans cet exemplaire les notes sont
le plus exactement rangées.

La plus part des abreviatures n'est pas applicable dans l'im-
primerie, il faudroit donc mettre au lieu de 𝄞 , 𝄞 au lieu
de 𝄞 , 𝄞 , etc. etc., au lieu de *simile*, il faut
toujours mettre les notes.

Le trio en 𝄞 No. 9, des derniers 10 Airs peut être chanté
avec la Basse ou Baritons, mais en ce cas la taillebasse ne chante
pas.—J'y ai ajoute encore un Basse pour qu'il puisse être chanté

---

[1] $ = ducats, not dollars.

en quatuor. La taillebasse doit être imprimé dans la clef de Taille comme vous apprendrez par la feuille y jointe. J'ai composé deux fois le No. 10, des derniers 10 Airs. Vous pouvez inserer dans votre collection le quel de deux vous plaira le plus.—

Les deux derniers Airs dans votre lettre du 21 Dec. m'ont beaucoup plut. C'est pourquoi je les ai composé con amore surtout

l'autre de ces deux. Vous l'avez ecrit en , mais comme ce

ton m'a paru peu naturel et si peu analogue à l'inscription *Amoroso*, qu'au contraire il le changerait en Barbaresio [? Barbaresco], je l'ai traite dans le ton lui convenant.

Si à l'avenir entre les airs que vous serez dans le cas de m'envoyer pour être composér il y avoit des *Andantinos* je vous prierais de me notifier si cet *Andantino*, est entendu plus lent, ou plus vite que l'*Andante*, puis que ce terme comme beaucoup d'autres dans la musique est d'une signification si incertaine, que mainte fois *Andantino* s'approche du *Allegro* et mainte autre est joué presque comme *Adagio*.

Pour les reste j'approuve fort votre inttention de faire adopter les Poésies aux airs, puisque le Poete peut appuyer par le rythme des Vers sur quelques endroits que j'ai élevé dans les ritornelles, p: e: dans l'une des derniers, ou j'ai employe les notes de la Mélodie

au ritornel.

Le Prix que vous dites avoir payé à Haidn est tres modéré; mais observ que Haydn n'a composés ni ritournelles, ni cadences à l'ouverture, ni Duos, et Trios, ni accompagnements de violoncelle; On ne peut don quant au travail pas du tout paralelliser ses airs aux miens. Pour montrer cependant combien j'aime à composer pour Vous, je veux harmoniser les 40 airs mentionés dans votre lettre à 140 $ en bloc. Si cela vous convient, il vous plaira de remettre les mélodies à Mrs. Fries et Co. le plus tot possible. Aussi je suis prêt à composer les 12 Canzonettes et ne vous en demande que 50 $. Pour 3 Sonates avec accompagnement de Violon vous me payerés seulement 100 $. J'y prendrais seulement pour chaque de ces 3 Sonates un thème caracteristique national, ou Autrichien, ou Ecosse ou Hongrois; ou si vous souhaitiéz d'autres, celui qu'il vous plaira de me notifier.

Le Cours des Postes étant tout à fait ouvert maintenant, de sorte que les lettres de Londres arrivent ici en 30 jours, vous pouvez me repondre bientôt sur-tous ces objets, en quelle attente je suis avec bien d'estime, Monsieur!

Votre très obeis. Serviteur,

LOUIS VAN BEETHOVEN.

[Cuthbert Hadden's opinion that certain passages in this letter concerning retouching of his compositions display "abruptness and hauteur" must certainly be rejected. Beethoven speaks here solely with the well-justified self-consciousness of the artist. Thomson, indeed, seems to have taken them in good part. The letter contains an interesting contribution to the problem of key characteristics. Beethoven, as is known, stoutly defended the theory that each key had its specific quality; hence he was opposed to any transposition. His unfavourable opinion of the key of A flat, is, however, in contradiction to his own works. Is there anything barbaric in the theme of the A flat Sonata (Op. 26)? or in the *Andante* of the C minor symphony? The words of Beethoven with regard to another problem of æsthetics are freer from prejudice—viz., concerning the tempo character of *Andantino*. It is still under discussion as to whether it is to be taken faster, as fast, or less lively than *Andante*. The matter is uncertain; hence a composer must in each case exactly state the rate he wishes for his *Andantino* (this is now done by means of the metronome); for, as Beethoven says, "Sometimes *Andantino* is very nearly an *Allegro*; on the other hand, it is often to be played as *Adagio*."]

142. TO THE ATTORNEY OF THE EXCHEQUER VARENA, GRAZ

VIENNA, 8th April, 1813.

MY WORTHY V.!

I receive with much pleasure your letter, but again much displeased with the 100 fl. which our poor convent ladies intended for me. I keep them meanwhile, and shall employ them for the *copying*; what remains over will be sent back to the noble convent ladies with the statement of the costs of *copying*; I never take anything in this respect. I thought perhaps the third person whom you mentioned might be the former *King of Holland*, and that from him, who perhaps took many things from the Dutch not altogether in a lawful way, I need have no scruples, considering my present position, in receiving something; but now I beg you most kindly to say no more of the matter—write to me whether perhaps if I came myself to Graz I could give a *concert*, and what you think I should probably make by it, for unfortunately Vienna can no longer be my place of residence; perhaps it is now already too late; an explanation about this from you will always be welcome. The works will be copied, and you will have them as soon as possible; with the *oratorio* do whatever you please; if it is any use to you, it will best answer my intention.

With respect,

Your most devoted,

L. v BTHVEN.

Kind messages to our worthy
Ursulines; being again
able to be of use to them affords me great
joy.

143. TO THE SAME

BADEN, *4th July*, 1813.

MY DEAR SIR!

Forgive my late answer, the cause is always the same, my troubles, contending for my rights, and everything proceeds very slowly. I have indeed to do with a rascal of a prince, Prince Lobkowitz. Another noble Prince, quite a different man, died, and as neither he nor myself thought of his dying, he left nothing in writing about me; this matter must now be fought out in the law courts of Prague. What a business for an artist to whom nothing is so dear as his art; and into all this perplexity I have been brought through His Imperial Highness, the Archduke Rudolph. Regarding the works which you have received from me, I beg you to send me back the following as soon as possible, for they do not belong to me, namely: the Symphony in C minor, the Symphony in B flat, the March—you can keep by you the other pieces if you like; I only beg of you not to give them into other hands, as nothing has yet been published. Anyhow the expenses will be deducted from the 100 fl. which I have received from the venerable ladies, and which I have to send back to you—as regards the Oratorio, there is no hurry, as I do not want it—so only the three works named above. My best thanks for the 150 fl. from the Society for the Preservation of the Woods. My best respects to this esteemed Society; I am however ashamed about it; why should the small kindnesses that I have shown to the honourable women be valued so highly? I hope that my troubles will soon be at an end, and that I shall come into the full possession of what belongs to me by right. As soon as this is the case I will come in the autumn to Graz, and the 150 fl. shall at once be taken into account. I will then give a concert, a great one, for the benefit of the good Ursulines, or for any other institution which may be proposed to me as the most needy and the most useful—my respects to his Excellency the Governor, Count Bissingen. Tell him that it will always be with me a most pleasant duty to do for Graz anything in my power.

Thanks for your picture! why all this trouble? I see you wish to really make me greatly your debtor, hence I name myself your debtor and friend,

BEETHOVEN.

All kind messages to the venerable ladies and especially to the Superior.

N.B.—I am better in health and probably shall feel quite well as soon as the moral causes which influence me have passed away. As I am still in Baden I beg you to send the music to Vienna to the same address as that of your former letter.

[We here perceive Beethoven in the middle of his troubles of the year 1813, struggles, law-suits with his patrons. His anger about his beloved honoured archduke is to be set down to the punishment account of the "rascal" Prince Lobkowitz, to whom the archduke did not, as he promised, administer a sound rebuke. Scarcely had the composer brought his law-suit to a successful close, when there began the endless worry of a new law-suit with regard to the guardianship of his nephew.—Dr. Josef Ignaz, Edler von Varena, lawyer in the higher courts, barrister in Styria, barrister for the provinces, sworn public notary, etc.; he died in 1839. Count Bissingen was privy-councillor and chamberlain, Governor of Styria-Carinthia.]

144. TO THE ARCHDUKE RUDOLPH

VIENNA, 24th July, 1813.

YOUR IMPERIAL HIGHNESS!

From day to day I thought I should be able to return to Baden. Meanwhile these dissonances detaining me here will probably drag on until the end of next week—for me to be kept in the city during the summer is a torture, and when I reflect that thereby I am hindered from waiting on your Imperial Highness, the torture is the greater and still more annoying to me. Meanwhile it is really the affairs of Lobkowitz and Kynsky which are keeping me here; instead of thinking about a number of bars, I have to make notes about a number of calls which I must pay; without this I should scarcely live to see the end there. You will have heard of the misfortune to Lubkowitz. He is to be pitied, for to be so wealthy is no happiness! Count Fries is said to have paid to Duport alone 1900 ducats in gold, for which the old Lubkowitz house served as a guarantee. The details are beyond all belief—Count Rasoumowsky, I hear, will come to Baden and bring with him his Quartet; and this would be delightful, since your Imperial Highness would thereby have good entertainment; I know no greater enjoyment in the country than quartet music. May your Imperial Highness graciously accept my most heartfelt wishes for your health, also my regret at having to remain here under such vexatious conditions. Meanwhile I will endeavour in Baden doubly to make up for all that you are thereby losing.

Your Imperial Highness's most
obedient and faithful servant,
LUDWIG VAN BEETHOVEN.

VIENNA, *the 24th July*, 1813.

[The annuity disputes lasted up to 1815 and still longer, until they were finally settled to Beethoven's satisfaction. Duport was ballet-master and dancer at the Court Opera; he was afterwards one of the lessees of the Royal Theatre, and in that capacity entered into relationship with the composer concerning a new opera. The famous Rasumowsky Quartet probably consisted at this time of: Schuppanzigh (1st violin), Sina?? (2nd violin), Weiss (viola), and Linke (violoncello). So says Schindler. Other authorities make no mention of Sina, but state that Count Rasumowsky himself generally took the 2nd violin, being sometimes represented by Mayseder.]

145. TO BARON ZMESKALL

The 21st September, 1813.

If your servant is honest and knows of an honest one for me, you would show me a great kindness in letting your *honest* servant find an honest one for me—I wish in any case for a married man; not that I expect greater honesty from him, but probably more order. At the end of this month my present beast of a servant is going away, the new servant can therefore come in at the beginning of next month—since yesterday I have had to keep in on account of my cold, and shall probably have to do so for several days —if you wish to come and see me, let me know at what time. As I give no livery, with exception of a cloak, my servant gets 25 fl. per month. Forgive, dear Zmeskall,

Your friend,
BEETHOVEN.

146. TO THE SAME

[*September* 1813?]

Highest born! Clarissime amice! my former quill-cutter is probably praying above for me that I may soon be able to write without pens—read this about the chronometric *tempo* indication—it appears to me the best I have seen on the subject—we will shortly speak about it—please do not lose it.

In haste your

BEETHOVEN.

[Matters concerning the metronome caused lively discussions at that time; Beethoven himself took great interest in them.]

147. To NEPOMUK HUMMEL

[Between the 8th and 12th December, 1813.]

Dearly beloved Hummel! Please conduct this time the drum-heads and the cannonades with your excellent conducting Field-Marshal staff—please do this; and if one day you may want me to praise you, I am at your service body and soul.

[This letter shows us that the friendship between Beethoven and Hummel had long been restored.]

148. LETTER OF THANKS

[December 1813.]

I consider it my duty to thank all the worthy members who took part in the concerts given on the 8th and 12th of December for the benefit of the Imperial Austrian, and Royal Bavarian warriors wounded at the battle of Hainau, for the zeal displayed by them in so worthy a cause. (It was a rare union of distinguished artists, in which each and all, fired with the thought of being able to be of some service to the fatherland, without any order of precedence, and even in subordinate places, worked together, and with excellent results.) Herr Schuppanzigh stood at the head of the first violins, and by his fiery, expressive playing carried with him the whole orchestra; also the Chief Capellmeister, Herr Salieri, did not hesitate to beat time for the drums and cannonades, while Herr Spohr and Herr Mayseder, each through his art worthy of the highest leadership, sat at the second and third desks. Herren Siboni and Giuliani also occupied subordinate places. (The conductorship of the whole fell to me because I had composed the music; had it been by some one else, I would as willingly, as Herr Hummel, have taken charge of the bass-drum, for we were all animated by pure feelings of love for our country, and joyfully devoted our powers for those who had sacrificed so much for us.) (Herr Maelzel indeed deserves special thanks, in that he, as organiser, first conceived the idea of this *concert*, while to him afterwards fell the most trying part, viz., making the necessary preliminary arrangements and attending to all details.) And I must also specially thank him, for through this concert he gave me the opportunity [to produce] this *composition* solely composed for this public benefit, and works handed over to him and to see fulfilled—the ardent wish long entertained by me, in the present circumstances, to be able to place an important work of mine (it is well known that the idea of the work on Wellington was my own idea) on the altar of the Vaterland. As, however, a list will shortly be printed of all who co-operated on this occasion, and of what parts they undertook, the public will see for itself with what noble self-denial a number of great artists worked together for one great aim.

The coming together of the chief M. [Masters] was through my encouragement.

[Of the two concerts (8 and 12 December, 1813) Schindler says: "We stand before one of the most important moments in the life of the composer, in which all hitherto dissentient voices, with exception of a few professionals, united in proclaiming him worthy of the laurel." From this concert dates Beethoven's popularity in Vienna. The letter of thanks here given was not published by Beethoven, probably because of the disagreement with Maelzel, of which the letters of the following year will make mention.]

149. To Dr. Von BEYER, Prague

VIENNA, *18th December*, 1813.

My worthy Friend!

Thus I name you, and so I will embrace you one day. Already several times have I cursed this unhappy decree, since through it I have fallen into endless trouble. Oliva is no longer here, and it is unbearable to me to lose so much valuable time on such matters; I rob my art, for nothing is done—I have now sent fresh legal opinion to Wolf. He intends beginning the law-suit, but I think it best, as I have indeed written to Wolf, that a petition should be handed in to the Law Court—do yourself help in the matter, and do not let me come to grief, surrounded here by numerous enemies; in everything which I do, I feel almost in despair.

My brother whom I loaded with benefits, for whose sake I am now for the most part in misery, has become—my greatest enemy! Embrace Koschak in my name, and tell him that my experiences and my sorrows would fill a book—I would willingly have taken the whole business from Wolf and handed it over to you, but we should only have made new enemies—only attend to your part— more about this shortly—and send me your street and the number where you live, also the same for Koschak, for I always have to send you my letters through other people. Please acknowledge receipt of this at once.

Yours,

BEETHOVEN.

[In this letter to Dr. Beyer at Prague there appears a hitherto unknown personage in the history of Beethoven. It is the period of the law-suit with the heirs of Kynsky regarding the annuity. For Beethoven, the lawyers of Bohemia, especially at Prague, were for a long time the most sought-after inhabitants of the world, and this Dr. Beyer is now one of great importance. Every new Prague lawyer appears to the master seeking for help, as a new star dropped down from Heaven. We know already of one lawyer at this time to whom Beethoven entrusted his business, and this was Dr. Wolf, about whom Beethoven indulged in grim jokes in his letters to the better lawyer, Dr. Kanka. The third is Dr. Beyer, to whom this letter is addressed; while through him Beethoven sends greeting to a fourth lawyer, Dr. Koschak, a name which is of deep importance in the history of Beethoven. Weighty is the complaint about his brother; he can only mean Carl, of whom, formerly, he was so fond.]

150. To the Archduke RUDOLPH

[1813.]

YOUR IMPERIAL HIGHNESS!

Not presumption, not as if I ought to venture to plead for any one, neither can I boast of being in special favour with your Imperial Highness, nothing of the kind causes me to put before you a matter of great simplicity. Yesterday evening old Kraft was at my house; he wondered whether it would be possible for rooms to be given him in your palace; in return he would be at the service of your Imperial Highness as often as he was wanted. He had been for twenty years in the house of Prince Lobkowitz, and for a long time without receiving any salary; now he is obliged to give up his rooms without receiving any compensation. The situation of the poor worthy old man is a hard one, and I should certainly become guilty of hardness myself if I did not venture to put the matter before you. Trojer will request an answer from your Imperial Highness. As the matter concerns the easing of the position of a human being, your Imperial Highness will, of course, excuse your faithful and obedient servant,

LUDWIG VAN BEETHOVEN.

["Old Kraft," for whom Beethoven here intercedes, was the 'cello player, Anton Kraft, born 1751. In the year 1795 he left the chapel of Prince Grassalkowitz, and entered the service of Prince Lobkowitz, wherein he remained up to his death in 1820. Beethoven highly esteemed old Kraft. In a letter he says: "I do not deny that his playing gives us all the highest pleasure."

Here, and often afterwards, occurs the name of Count Troyer. Who he was cannot be exactly determined. The Troyers were an old Luxemburg noble family.]

151. FROM THE "WIENER ZEITUNG." NOTICE

[*Dec.* 31, 1813.]

MUSICAL ACADEMY

The wish expressed by many amateurs, whom I hold in high respect, once again to hear my great instrumental composition on Wellington's Victory at Vittoria, renders it my pleasant duty to announce herewith to the worthy public, that on Sunday, January 2, I shall have the honour, with the assistance of the most excellent artists of Vienna, of performing the said composition together with new vocal pieces and choruses, in the great Imperial Redoutensaal.

Tickets can be obtained daily at the Kohlmarkt, in the house of Baron Haggenmüller in the court on the right, ground floor, in Baron Pasqualati's office. For the pit 2, and for the gallery 3 gulden.

LUDWIG VAN BEETHOVEN.

152. TO BARON ZMESKALL

New Year 1814.

DEAR WORTHY FRIEND!

All would be well if there were a curtain, without this, the aria will be a *failure*; I only heard of this to-day from S., and it grieves me; let it be only a curtain, even though it be a bed-curtain, or some kind of *screen* that can be moved in a moment, or some gauze, etc. There must be something, the aria is written for the theatre in too *dramatic* a style to produce any effect in a concert; *without curtain, or something similar to it, all meaning will be lost!* —*lost!*—*lost!*—*everything will go to the devil!* The court will probably come. Baron Schweiger earnestly begged me to go there, Archduke Charles gave me audience and promised to come.—*The Empress did not promise, neither, on the other hand, did she refuse—— Curtain!!!!* or the aria and I will be hung to-morrow morning. A happy new year to you, I press you to my heart as much as in days gone by. *With curtain* or *without curtain.*

Your

BEETHON.

[The person indicated by S. was either v. Seyfried or Schuppanzigh. In a notice of the concert in the Viennese *Dramaturgischer Beobachter*, it is related, concerning the aria from the *Ruins of Athens*, sung by Weinmüller, that "the letting down of a curtain suddenly disclosed the portrait of our adored monarch, and all present shouted with joy."]

153. To Count FRANZ Von BRUNSWICK

The 13th February, 1814.

DEAR FRIEND AND BROTHER!

You lately wrote to me, I am writing to you now—you probably rejoice at all conquests—also at mine. On the 27th of this month I give a second concert in the great Redoutensaal—come to it— you know now. Thus I am gradually rescuing myself from my misery, for I have not yet received a farthing of my annuity. Schuppanzigh wrote to Michalcowicz to ask whether it would really be worth while to come to Buda, what do you think? Something would have to be performed in the theatre. My opera will also be given on the stage, but I am making many changes. I hope you are living happily, which is not a small thing. So far as I am concerned, yes, indeed often, my kingdom is in the air; as often the wind, so my tones whirl, so is it within my soul. I embrace you.

Your friend,

BEETHOVEN.

[(Outside:) A Monsieur le Comte François Brunswick à Bude en Hongrie. (In a strange hand:) Herr Von Beethoven at the Bartenstein House on the Mölker Bastion, No. 94 on the first floor.

The contents make known to us the master's great new plans for this year 1814; first, the great concert in February and then the work connected with the revival of *Fidelio*.]

154. To the Singer ANNA MILDER

[February 1814.]

MY WORTHY M.!

To-day I wished to come to you, but it is not possible, you yourself will understand how many things one has to see to in connection with a concert—*only this much*, Maelzel had no order whatever to ask you to sing. The matter was talked about, and you were the first person that I thought of to embellish my concert; I myself would have agreed to your singing an Aria by another master, but those who were managing the concert for me were *weak* enough to decide that the Aria must be my own composition; but I have not time to write a new one; the one out of *my opera*, owing to its *situation*, is not suitable for such a great hall as the Redoute.

So is it, my dear honoured M. M. had not the slightest *order*, because I myself did not yet know what I should do and what I could do, since I have to follow the opinion of those who are managing my concert—if I had a *new* Aria at my disposal, I would have placed myself at your feet, so that you might listen to my request —for the rest, receive my best thanks for your good-natured intentions towards me. It is to be hoped my circumstances will soon improve (for you probably know that I have lost almost everything), and then my first business will be to write an opera for our *unique* Milder, and I will put forth all my strength to show myself worthy of you.

With kind regards,
Your friend,
BEETHOVEN.

(I enclose some tickets for my concert which you will probably not despise.)

[It is not quite clear whether Beethoven really wrote something new or not for this concert. At the noteworthy concert of 22 February of this year was brought forward as a great novelty, the Symphony in F (Op. 93), and as a further novelty a " new Terzet for soprano, tenor and bass" (" Tremate, empi, tremate "), performed by Milder-Hauptmann, Siboni and Weinmüller. Was this the "new" air that Beethoven had to write for Milder? But the sketches for this Terzet dated back to the year 1801. Schindler merely says: "New Terzet for soprano." What is a novelty at a concert? The term is always taken to imply a first public performance.]

155. To FRIEDRICH TREITSCHKE

DEAR WORTHY TR——! [*February* 1814.]

I have not yet thought about your song! but I will at once see about it; perhaps I shall pay a visit this afternoon and give you my ideas on the subject.

Whether a rehearsal can be held on Monday I cannot say positively, but probably it will take place a day later. You have not the slightest conception of the work which such a *concert* entails, only necessity forces me to give it, to undergo all the trouble connected with it!

In haste,
Your friend,
BEETHOVEN.

[This small letter also concerns the concert which took place on 27 February of this year. A lively correspondence ensued with the theatre poet and *régisseur* Treitschke, for this was the man who revised the libretto when it was seriously thought of reviving *Fidelio*. Through the revision of the text by Treitschke, the composer, as he himself expressed it, was induced to "restore the crumbling ruins of an old castle." The work mentioned in this note may possibly have been Treitschke's *Der Ruf vom Berge*. This poem, however, was not set by Beethoven until later on.]

156. To the Same

[February—March 1814.]

Here, dear, worthy T., is your song! With great pleasure have I read your improvements in the opera; it determines me all the more to restore the crumbling ruins of an old castle.

Your friend,

Beethoven.

157. To the Same

[Spring 1814.]

My worthy Tr.—

According to advice I went to the Public Works office, and the matter has already been settled on most advantageous terms for me; it is far better to have to deal with *artists* than with so-called *grand folks* (small-minded)! You will receive your song at a moment's notice whenever you ask for it—I hasten to thank you for what you have done for my opera. If an opportunity occur, you might give *Egmont* at the Wieden Theatre. The arrival of the Spaniards, which is only indicated in the play, not made evident, at the opening of that *big barn*, the Wieden Theatre, can be made useful, also many other things as a *spectacle for the public*. The music, too, would not be quite lost, for that purpose; I would indeed, if *new* stuff were required, write it.

Worthy friend! Farewell! To-day I spoke with the principal bass singer of the Austrian Empire, full of enthusiasm for a new opera by Girowitz. I inwardly smiled at the new artistic path which this work will open to us.

Yours ever,

Beethoven.

[The contempt of our composer for the new opera of Adalbert Gyrowetz, just now when he was occupied with the revision of his one opera, was more than justified. A. Gyrowetz (1763–1850), one of the most prolific German composers, wrote twenty-four operas and operettas, but none of them survived him.]

158. To the Same

[Spring 1814.]

Dear worthy Tr.—

The cursed concert—which I am compelled to give, partly owing to my bad circumstances—has put me all behindhand with regard to the *opera*. The *Cantata* which I wished to give, robbed me of 5 or 6 days; now, indeed, something must be done suddenly, and I

"LEONORE" OVERTURE

SIXTH AND THREE FOLLOWING BARS
BEFORE TRUMPET SIGNAL

would write something *new* quicker, as I am accustomed to write, than now the *new* to the *old*. Also in my instrumental music I always have the *whole* in my mind; here, however, that whole is to a certain extent divided, and I have afresh to think myself into my music! To give the opera in 14 days is probably impossible, but I think it could be managed in four weeks.

Meanwhile the first act will be finished in a few days, but there is a great deal still to do to the second act; also a new Overture, which indeed is the easiest thing, as it will be quite new. For my *Akademie* I have only sketched out here and there, both in the first and second acts; only a few days ago was I able to set to work.

The score of the opera was the most frightful writing that I have ever seen, I had to look at it note by note (it was probably stolen).

In short! I assure you dear Tr.— the opera is gaining for me a *martyr's crown*. Had you not taken so much trouble, and so improved everything, for which I am eternally thankful to you, I could scarcely have forced myself to it! You have thereby also saved something from a stranded ship! Meanwhile, if you think that the delay with the opera will be too great for you, put it off to a later period. I am now going away until all is ended, also quite changed by you, and for the better; and of this at every moment I become more and more aware. Still it does not go as quickly as if I were writing something new; and in 14 days that is impossible! Act as you think best, but also quite as a friend of mine! there is no lack of zeal on my part.

Yours,
BEETHOVEN.

[These sighs about Beethoven's martyrdom over the new *Fidelio* show us in the clearest manner that the recasting of the opera was to a great extent due to the poet Treitschke. The latter was never tired of encouraging the master to crown his work, for in May of this year the revival of *Fidelio* was to take place. Treitschke also wanted to know what use was to be made of his "Germania" chorus. The following note refers to the matter.]

159. To THE SAME

[*Spring* 1814.]

Dear Tr.! I am delighted at your satisfaction with the chorus— I thought that you would have used all the pieces *to your advantage*, *and also to mine*; but if you do not want this, I should like it to be sold solely for the *benefit of the poor*. Your copyists came to me about it, also Wranitzky; I said that you, worthy Tr., were absolute master in the matter, hence I am only waiting for your opinion.

Your copyist is—an ass! but he has not the well-known magnificent ass's skin [1]—hence my copyist has undertaken the matter, and it will be nearly finished by Tuesday, and my copyist will bring everything to the rehearsal. For the rest, the whole matter concerning the opera is the most troublesome in the world, for I am dissatisfied with most things, and there is scarcely a number to which I have not been compelled here and there to tack on *some satisfaction* to my present *dissatisfaction*. There is a very great difference between free reflection and giving oneself up to one's inspiration.

Yours ever,

BEETHOVEN.

[Beethoven's remark about the revision of his *Fidelio* being "the most troublesome thing in the world," is especially well known. This sentence was given by Treitschke in his long, detailed, excellent account about the whole matter in *Orpheus*. His concluding words are as follows: "According to his [Beethoven's] request I offered our work to various theatres. Several accepted it, while others declined, as they were already in possession of Paer's opera. Many preferred a cheaper plan, viz., to procure it by means of crafty copyists, who, as was then the custom, stole both text and music. *Fidelio* was translated into several languages and a lot of money was made by it, but this brought us little good and small thanks."]

160. TO BARON ZMESKALL

[*Spring* 1814.]

Dear Z., I am not going to travel, at least I will not in any way tie myself down—the matter must be carefully thought over. Meanwhile the work has been forwarded to the Prince Regent. *If people want me they can have me,* and then I am *free* to say *yes* or *no.* Freedom! ! ! What more can one want? ? ?

I should very much like to speak with you as to how I am to arrange about my rooms.

[Thayer, with regard to the new rooms of the composer, remarks: "This new dwelling-place for which Beethoven was now leaving the Pasqualati house, lay on the first floor of the Bartenstein house, likewise on the Mölker Bastion (No. 94). He therefore was close to his friends, Princess Christian Lichnowsky and Countess Erdödy. Prince Lichnowsky, Beethoven's great patron, died on 15 April of this year. We read about a journey of Beethoven's. It appears that now for the first time he had planned a journey to England, a project of which we shall often hear, but of which nothing ever came. The work for the Prince Regent shows us clearly that it concerned the Battle Symphony which was to be forwarded to the Prince Regent of England. In a letter to Ferdinand Ries on 22 November, 1815, Beethoven writes:

---

[1] Thayer gives the delightful explanation: "On March 10, Hummel's *Die Eselhaut* was performed at the Theater an der Wien."

"*Wellington's Victory at the Battle of Vittoria* must have reached Th. Coutts and Co. long ago." The master frequently complained, and laughed in derision about his never having received any recognition from the Regent for what he sent, or for the dedication. In a letter to Ries of 8 March, 1816, we read: "So also with the Prince Regent" (who was afterwards King George IV.), "from whom I have not even received the copying costs of my Battle which I sent—no, not even thanks either by writing or by word of mouth." Still, after a number of years, namely, in December 1822, Beethoven speaks sarcastically about King George IV. of England to Ries thus: "Our amiable friend Potter ought to see whether he cannot at least obtain a butcher's knife [1] or a tortoise; of course, the printed copy of the Battle was likewise given to the king."]

161. MUSICAL NOTICE

VIENNA, *the 28th June*, 1814.

The undersigned, at the request of Herren Artaria and Co. herewith declares that he has handed over to the said art firm the score of his opera *Fidelio*, for the purpose of publishing the same under his direction in a complete pianoforte edition, as quartets, or arranged for wind band. The present musical version is thoroughly different from the former one, as nearly every number has been changed, and more than the half of the opera newly composed. Unauthorised copies of the score, together with the book in MS., can be obtained from me or from the librettist, Herr F. Treitschke, theatre poet. Other illegal copies will be dealt with by law.

LUDWIG VAN BEETHOVEN.

[This notice was given in the *Wiener Zeitung* of 1 July, 1814.]

162. TO HERR VON HUBER

[*Summer* 1814.]

Here, my dear Huber, you receive my promised engraved portrait; as you yourself thought it worth while to ask me for it, there is no fear of my being accused of vanity.

Farewell, and think sometimes of your sincere friend,

LUDWIG VAN BEETHOVEN.

[Who this Huber was—certainly not the poet of the *Mount of Olives* text, who died in 1809—cannot be determined. The engraving mentioned was one of the best which we possess of Beethoven—that by Blasius Höfel, after the drawing by Letronne.]

[1] The work was entitled *Schlacht Symphonie*, etc., and butcher's knife in German is *Schlachtmesser*, one of Beethoven's many plays upon words.—TR.

163. To the Archduke RUDOLPH

[July 1814.]

Your Imperial Highness!

For to-day it is not possible for me, as I wish, to wait upon you. I am attending to the work, *Wellington's Victory*, for London; such things have to be done within a fixed period, so that they cannot be put off without everything being put off. I hope to-morrow to be able to wait on your Imperial Highness.

Your Imperial Highness's
most true and obedient,
Ludwig van Beethoven.

164. To HERR Von ADLERSBURG

[July 1814.]

Of my own accord I wrote, and *gratis*, a S.S. [Schlacht-Symphonie] for M.'s Panharmonica. After having it for a time, he brought me the score, from which he had begun to print, and wished it to be arranged for full orchestra. Already before that, I had the idea in my mind of a Battle, which, however, could not be applied to his P. We came to an agreement to give this work and also other compositions of mine for the benefit of the wounded. In the meantime I found myself in the most terrible money perplexity. Abandoned here in Vienna by the whole world, in expectation of a draft, &c., M. offered me 50 ducats. I accepted them and told him that I would either return them to him here, or, if I did not travel *myself* with him, would give him the work to take to London, where I would refer him to an English publisher who would pay him this. The score, as arranged for his P., I received back from him. Now while preparations were being made for the concerts, Herr M.'s scheme and character began to reveal themselves. Without my consent, he put on the bill that the work was his own *property*; thereupon in a rage I compelled him to take it down. Then he added, that out of friendship I had allowed him this for his journey to London, while I thought I was still free to name the conditions under which I would let him have the work.[1] I was still writing the work, and, wholly absorbed in the heat of inspiration, scarcely thought of the matter. Meanwhile, immediately after the first University concert, I was told from many quarters,

---

[1] "I remember during the printing of the bill to have had a hot dispute, but the time was too short." [This unfinished sentence was written as an afterthought by Beethoven.—Tr.]

and by trustworthy men, that M. had everywhere announced that he had paid me 400 ducats in gold. Thereupon I sent the following to the newspaper, but it was not inserted—as M. is on good terms with every one. Immediately after the first concert I returned M. his 50 ducats, and declared to him that as I had here learnt to know his character, I would never dream of travelling with him; that I was justly incensed at his having drawn up the bill without consulting me; that all the arrangements for the concerts were bad; that by the following expressions he was himself showing his *unpatriotic character*: (I spit at V., only think what London will say at 10 florins being charged, why, that I did this not for the wounded, but for ——); and that I had given him the work to take to London, only *under certain conditions* which I was to make to him. Now he asserts that it was a friendly gift, had this put into the newspaper after the second concert, without making the least inquiry of me. As M. is a coarse fellow, without education, without culture, it can easily be understood how he behaved towards me at that time, and therefore roused my anger more and more. And who would think, under compulsion, of making a friendly present to such a man? Then an opportunity occurred to send the work to the Prince Regent. It was therefore now quite impossible *to give him this work without conditions.* He now came to you and made propositions. *He was told on what day to appear so as to receive the answer—but he never turned up, left Vienna, gave the work in Munich.* How did he get hold of it? It was impossible for him to *steal* it—Herr Maelzel had some parts for a few days at home—and from these he got some low fellow to botch it up, and now he goes hawking it the world over. Herr Maelzel promised me some ear trumpets. In order to encourage him, I arranged the *Victory Symphony* for his Panharmonica. Finally he completed his instruments, but they were of no practical use to me. For this small trouble Herr M. pretended that I ought, after I had arranged the *Victory Symphony* for grand orchestra, *also to compose the Battle, and make him sole proprietor of the work.* Now even supposing that with regard to the ear-trumpets I ought to have felt to a certain extent under obligation to him, this was discharged, in that by the Battle which he had *stolen from me, or put together in mutilated form*, he made at least 500 florins, convention coin—and thus he paid himself. He had even the audacity to say here that he possessed the Battle; and even showed it in manuscript to several persons; I however did not believe it, and was so far right, as the whole was not mine, but put together by some other hand. Also the honour which he attributes to himself alone ought indeed to be a sufficient reward. *The military council made no mention whatever of me*, and yet everything in the two concerts was mine. If Herr M., as he hinted, delayed his journey to London on account of this Battle, this was merely a hoax. Herr M. remained until he had completed his patch-work, the first attempts not having succeeded.

BEETHOVEN.

165. EXPLANATION AND APPEAL TO THE ARTISTS IN LONDON

VIENNA, *July* 25, 1814.

Herr Maelzel, who is at present in London, on his way thither performed my *Siegessinfonie und Wellingtons Schlacht bei Vittoria* in Munich, and, according to report, will also give it at concerts in London, just as he had intended doing in Frankfort. This induces me openly to declare: That I did not ever in any way give or surrender the works named to Herr Maelzel; that nobody possesses copies of them, and that the only one given away by me, I sent to his Royal Highness, Prince Regent of England.

The performance of these works by Herr Maelzel is therefore an imposition on the public, since he, according to the explanation here given, does not possess them, or if he does, has injured me, seeing that he has got possession of them illegally.

But even in the latter case, the public will be deceived, for what Herr Maelzel offers to it under the title: *Wellingtons Schlacht bei Vittoria und Siegessinfonie*, must evidently be a spurious or a mutilated work, for of these works, with exception of a single part for a few days, he has never received anything from me.

This suspicion becomes a certainty if I add the assurance of composers here, whose names, in case of necessity, I am empowered to publicly mention, that Herr Maelzel on his departure from Vienna told them that he had *these works in his possession*; also that he showed them some parts, which, as I have already shown, can only be mutilated or spurious. Whether Herr Maelzel is capable of doing me such an injury?—is answered by the fact that he announced in the public papers, without any mention of my name, that he *alone* undertook the concerts which I gave in Vienna for the *benefit of those who were wounded in the war*, at which only my works were performed.

I therefore call upon artists in London, as their art colleague, not to suffer such injury to be done to me, by the intended performance of the *Schlacht bei Vittoria und Siegessinfonie* arranged

by Herr M., and to prevent the London public being deceived by
him in the aforementioned way.

[The original of this explanation is not in Beethoven's handwriting; it
was first printed by Nohl. But among the Beethoven papers bequeathed by
Schindler to the Berlin Library, there is a special vindication of Beethoven.
The following is an exact copy:]

We the undersigned testify for the sake of truth, and are ready
if necessary to swear, that several meetings took place here at the
house of Dr. Adlersburg between Herr Louis van Beethoven and
the court mechanician Herr Maelzel, concerning the *Battle of
Vittoria*, and the journey to England. Several propositions were
made by Herr Maelzel to Herr van Beethoven in reference to the
above-named work, or at least acquiring the right of first performance. As however Herr Maelzel did not appear at the last appointed
meeting, nothing was settled about the matter, as he had not
accepted the first proposals made to him.

In proof of which
    my own hand
    Vienna, October 20, 1814
    Joh. Freih. v. Pasqualati,
    privileged wholesale merchant,
    Carl Edler von Adlersburg,
    Court barrister and notary.

166. To Dr. JOHANN KANKA, Lawyer, Prague

[*Midsummer* 1814.]

A THOUSAND THANKS, MY HONOURED K.,

I once again meet with a *lawyer* and a man who can write and
think without making use of empty formulæ. You can scarcely
imagine how I sigh for an end to this business, as in everything
which concerns my household economy I am unsettled—not to
speak of other damage. You yourself know that the creative spirit
ought not to be fettered by wretched wants, and through them I
am deprived of many things calculated to brighten my life. Even
to my longing, and to the duty which I have undertaken, viz., to
work by means of my art for needy humanity, I have been compelled and am still compelled to set limits. Of our monarchs, etc.,
monarchies, etc., I write nothing to you, the papers will tell you
everything—for me the spiritual kingdom is dearest, it is above

Beethoven at the age of forty-four (1814)
From an engraving by Hoefél after the drawing by Louis Letronne

all intellectual and worldly monarchies—only do write what you really want *for yourself* from me, from my weak musical powers, so that I may be able, so far as is possible, to write something for *your* own musical intelligence or feeling. Do you not want all the papers which refer to the Kynsky matter? In this case I would send them to you, as amongst them is important testimony which I think you read over at my house—think of me, and consider that you are representing an unselfish artist against an haggling family. How readily men take away from a poor artist *what in another way they bestow on him*—and Jupiter no longer exists, so that one could invite oneself to a feast of ambrosia—give wings, dear friend, to the slow steps of justice. When I find myself in high spirits, when I have happy moments in the sphere of my art, then earthly spirits drag me down again, and to these also belong the 2 law-suits. You, too, have unpleasantness, although I should not have thought it considering your usual intelligence and capabilities, specially in your profession, so I must refer you to myself. I have emptied the cup of bitter sorrow, and through my dear art-disciples and art-companions I have won martyrdom in art—I beg you to think every day of me as if I were a whole world; otherwise it would be expecting too much of you to think of such a small individual as myself.

With the most sincere respect and friendship,

Yours truly,

LUDWIG VAN BEETHOVEN.

[This letter to the Prague lawyer, Dr. Johann Kanka, gives a striking picture of the bitter sorrows which were the lot of the composer during his law-suit with the Kynsky heirs. Also from the letter we see that the great lawyer had already discussed the whole matter with the composer during this year, and had seen all the necessary papers. Beethoven, amidst these worries, quotes his Schiller. That he cannot invite himself to an ambrosial feast with Father Jupiter is a reminiscence from Schiller's *Teilung der Erde*, where Zeus consoles all disinherited poets thus:

> Willst du in meinem Himmel mit mir leben,
> So oft du kommst, er soll dir offen sein.

> (If thou wilt live with me in my heaven,
> Whenever thou comest, it shall be open to thee.—TR.)]

167. TO THE ROYAL NATIONAL THEATRE IN BERLIN

VIENNA, *June* 23, 1814.

The undersigned have the honour of offering herewith to the Royal National Theatre the text and score of their opera *Fidelio* in the exact and only legal copy, for a fee of 20 ducats in gold, for the use of that theatre, without authority, however, to produce it elsewhere either as a whole, or any parts of it.

The said opera appeared a few weeks back at the Court Opera here, and had the good fortune to be unusually successful, and it always drew full houses. The *text and music* are *not to be mistaken for the opera of the same name* which several years ago was performed at the Theater an der Wien, some copies of the score of which were stolen. The whole has been thoroughly revised and in its changed form is much more effective on the stage, and more than half written afresh.

All means have been taken to safeguard this properly; in any case the National Theatre is requested not to place confidence in any other offers, but kindly to inform the undersigned.

A reply concerning to the National Theatre is to be addressed to the co-signatory, F. Treitschke.

LUDWIG VAN BEETHOVEN.
Fr. Treitschke
Court Theatre Poet.

168. To S. A. STEINER & CO.

[*Summer* 1814.]

Worthy friend! At last my wish is granted, and I go the day after to-morrow for an excursion of a few days. I therefore beg you to say to Herr Mathias A., that I will certainly not force him to take my pianoforte score. I therefore send you the one by Halm, so that as soon as you have received back my pianoforte score you can hand the Halm to M. A.—but if Herr A. will keep my pianoforte score for the fixed sum of 12 ducats in gold, I only ask that this should be stated by himself in writing, or that he hand over to you the fee—and for this purpose I enclose the receipt—I cannot in any way be burdened with the pianoforte score as a debt. You know my situation!

Yours as ever,
BEETHOVEN.

[Anton Halm, born 1789, at Altenmarkt in Styria, from an officer became a musician. He was on a very friendly footing with Beethoven. According to Schindler it was generally considered that the arrangement as a pianoforte duet of the great Quartet Fugue in B flat (Op. 139) was the work of Halm. According to Nottebohm, Halm arranged it about 1826; his work, though also known to Beethoven, was never printed. Schindler, on the other hand, states that the arrangement of the fugue bore a special opus number. He also states that "Beethoven trusted him (H.) with one of the most difficult arrangements, namely, of the fugue from the great Quartet in B flat for pianoforte, and was perfectly satisfied with the way in which he accomplished it." Halm died at an advanced age, in the year 1872, at Vienna.]

169. To the Same

[*Summer* 1814.]

My dear Steiner, as soon as you send me the *opera* which I want for reasons I have told you, you can have the parts of the Symphony at once—this is not done according to contract but out of kindness. I never answer insults.

All else, how or why I have done it, I am ready to explain at any moment.

Your most devoted,

LUDWIG VAN BEETHOVEN.

[At this period begins constant intercourse with the music firm of S. A. Steiner and Co., and this gave Beethoven opportunity to show in a variety of ways the humorous side of his genius. The connection of Beethoven with this firm in the Paternostergässchen, which has become celebrated, may have been the cause of the connection with B. and H. finally coming to an end in the year 1815. In order to understand the many humorous letters addressed to the gentlemen in the Paternostergasse it may be mentioned that the firm itself, the directorship, is abbreviated into Gllt, G—l l—t, or G. L., meaning the head of the firm, Herr S. A. Steiner, the General Lieutenant; G. or G—s, the composer himself as Generalissimus. The assistant in the firm, Herr Tobias Haslinger, who later on became the chief of the whole business, is named Adjutant, abbreviated into Ad—rl (=Adjutanterl) the suffix "erl" giving the meaning "little adjutant," as a term of endearment.—TR.]

170. To Count MORITZ Von LICHNOWSKY

BADEN, *21st September,* 1814.

WORTHY HONOURED COUNT AND FRIEND,

I unfortunately only received your letter yesterday. Hearty thanks for thinking about me, likewise kind messages to the Princess Christiane worthy of all respect. I took a beautiful walk yesterday with a friend in the Brühl, and amid the friendly talk we specially mentioned you, and see, yesterday evening on my arrival I find your kind letter. I see that you always load me with kindnesses; and as I should not like you to think that the *step* which I have taken was prompted *through a new interest* or, indeed, anything of that kind, I tell you that soon a Sonata of mine will be published, which I have *dedicated to you*. I wished to surprise you, for the dedication to you had long been intended, but your letter of yesterday forces me to disclose it to you. No other inducement was needed in order to publicly show you my feeling with regard to your friendship and welfare; but if you were to give me anything in the shape of a present it would pain me, for then you would entirely misconstrue my intention; all things of that sort I could only refuse.

I kiss the hands of the Princess for her thought and good wishes for me; I have *never forgotten how much I am indebted to all of you,* although an unfortunate event brought about conditions which prevented me showing it as I wished.

As to what you say to me with regard to Lord Castlereagh, I find that the matter has begun in the best manner. If I may have an opinion of my own, I believe it best for Lord Castlereagh not to write about the Wellington work until the Lord has heard it here. I shall soon come into the town when we can discuss all matters with regard to a great concert. Nothing can be done with the Court; I have offered myself, but

but silence ! ! !

A thousand hand-kisses to the honoured Princess C. Farewell, my honoured friend, and consider me ever worthy of your good-will.

Yours,

BEETHOVEN.

[Such a fine letter ought to be facsimiled.[1] The dedication concerns the pianoforte Sonata in E minor (Op. 90), which was composed in the summer of 1819; it appeared with this dedication at Steiner's in June 1815. Schindler has given an interesting clue to the contents of this Sonata. The composer is said to have told the count that he wished to set to music the love-story with his wife (formerly a dancer). As superscriptions the count was to put "First movement: struggle between heart and head," and over the second movement: "Intercourse with the beloved." The Lord Castlereagh referred to was the statesman, Robert Stewart, Viscount Castlereagh, Marquis of Londonderry, who lived from 1769-1822. He was very active during the fall of Napoleon and the following hundred days, also during the Congress. With the help of Count Lichnowsky, Beethoven tried to induce him to see the Prince Regent of England respecting the Battle Symphony.—TR.]

171. TO THE ARCHDUKE RUDOLPH

[*November* 1814.]

I notice that your Imperial Highness wishes to make an experiment on horses by means of my music It is to see, so I perceive, whether the riders thereby can make some clever somersaults.

---

[1] The autograph belongs to the Donaldson Museum at the R.C.M., London. The date is clearly 1814, *not* as Marx prints it, 1841.—TR.

Ha ha, I must really laugh at your Imperial Highness thinking of me in this matter; for that I shall be to the end of my life

Your most willing servant,

LUDWIG VAN BEETHOVEN.

N.B.—The desired horse-music will reach your Imperial Highness at full gallop.

[On the 23rd November, 1819, there was a kind of tournament in the Imperial Riding School. It is possible that Beethoven was asked by the Archduke to compose something for it, but no such music is known.]

172. TO THE LAW COURT

[*End of* 1814.]

TO THE WORSHIPFUL LAW COURT.

Quite ignorant of legal matters, and thinking that all claims on an estate must be liquidated, I sent to my legal friend at Prague the agreement concluded with H.I.H. Archduke Rudolph, with His Highness, Prince Lobkowitz and with His Highness Prince Kynsky, by means of which these noblemen agreed to pay me yearly 4000 florins. My constant endeavour to make him take the matter to heart, even, I must confess it, the reproaches which I made to him as if he had not properly opened proceedings, seeing that the steps which he had taken concerning the guardianship had remained fruitless, may have induced him to go to law.

However much this step was against my feelings to appear as plaintiff against my benefactor, only he can judge who knows of my high esteem for the late Prince Kynsky.

In these circumstances I chose the shorter way, being convinced that the princely guardians will be as inclined to value art as they are to uphold the acts of the late Prince Kynsky.

According to the enclosed contract, *sub* A., H.I.H., the Archduke Rudolph, likewise their serene Highnesses, Prince Lobkowitz and Prince Kynsky, undertook to give me 4000 fl., until I had obtained a post of equal value; yes, indeed, in case through misfortune or old age I was prevented from exercising my art, these high contracting parties promised me this sum for life, while I, on the other hand, undertook not to quit Vienna.

Great was the promise, great the fulfilment of it; for I had never a single hitch, and was quiet in the enjoyment of the annuity until the Imperial *finance-patent* appeared. This change of value made no difference as regards H.I.H. the Archduke Rudolph, for I received his share in redemption bonds, as formerly in bank-notes, without any reckoning of the *scale*; and so also His Highness, the late Prince Kynsky, promised to pay his contribution of 1800 fl. in redemption bonds.

But as he neglected to give the order to his treasurer, difficulties arose for me. Although my circumstances are not brilliant, still I would not venture to present this claim to the princely guardians, had it not been that honest men had themselves gathered this assurance from the mouth of the late Prince, namely, to pay me the share, as well for the past as for the future, in Vienna value, as the enclosures B. C. D. of this suit show. In these circumstances I leave it to the princely guardians to judge whether rather than offend *delicatesse* I had not cause to rest satisfied with the prince's promise; hence the objection of the *curator* to the witnesses owing to their not being present at the time, was highly mortifying to me. In order therefore to extricate myself from this truly un-pleasant position I venture to promise the princely guardians, and to assure them that I, for the past and the future, am willing to accept 1800 fl. Vienna value, and I flatter myself that they will graciously take into consideration that I, on my side, have sacrificed not a little, since, owing to my high esteem for these noble princes, I elected to make Vienna my settled residence, and that at a time when most advantageous offers were being made to me from abroad. I therefore beg the worshipful Court to present this petition to the Kynsky guardians and kindly to inform me of the result.

L. v. B.

VIENNA.

[The manuscript further states that the Prague Law Court gave consent whereby the guardians, instead of the 1800 fl. assured by writing, were ordered to pay to the composer a sum of 1200 fl. Vienna value from 3 November, 1812, under conditions named. The decision of the Court is dated from Prague, 18 January, 1815.]

173. To FRAU ANTONIE BRENTANO, FRANKFORT-ON-MAIN

[1814?]

My worthy friend, all my affairs, which now seem on the point of improvement, enable me to accept without scruple the bill of exchange sent from Franz and yourself—I received the same from a stranger, who, so it seems to me, had not the matter very much at heart, for after not finding me at home at his first visit, he only returned a week later, handed me the bill without even wishing to come into my room. Now when I came to Pacher, they had themselves, the day before yesterday, not received any advice, also, so they say, they do not know the drawer. I therefore thought it wise to let you know at once about it and I await your decision I should already have sent you back the bill, but, as you know, I do not understand things of this kind, and therefore could easily make a mistake. In haste, yours respectfully,

BEETHOVEN.

[As from this time we shall have other letters to the Brentanos, and as these letters are documents of special importance in the history of Beethoven, we may here say something generally about this collection. For many years it was known that the Brentano family in Frankfort possessed a considerable number of important letters written by Beethoven to Franz and Antonie Brentano. This family was always most unselfishly ready to help in Beethoven's affairs. The wife of the former senator, Franz Brentano, the Antonie (die Toni) known to all the intellectual aristocracy, a daughter of Melchior von Birkenstock, came from Vienna. In the Birkenstock house Beethoven had made the acquaintance, somewhere about 1810, also of Bettina von Arnim, née Brentano. After their marriage, the Brentanos spent several years in Vienna settling affairs connected with their inheritance, and then the long intercourse with Beethoven developed into an intimate and never-to-be-disturbed friendship. Later on there was an exchange of letters between the composer and his noble, faithful friends at Frankfort, of which some between the years 1814 and 1823 are to hand. In the year 1867 the Beethoven biographer, L. Nohl, made the acquaintance of Antonie, then eighty-seven years old, and learned from her much that was new concerning her intercourse with Beethoven; and he also gained an insight into the correspondence between the Brentanos and Beethoven. The heirs of this family obstinately stood out for a long time against letting these letters be published, nor would they part with these precious family treasures. At last they came into the market, about fourteen in number, in the year 1890. The Beethoven House at Bonn received nine letters of Beethoven from this family.]

174. To Herr S. A. STEINER

VIENNA, 1st February, 1815.

HONOURABLE GENERAL LIEUTENANT!

I have to-day received your letter to my brother, and am satisfied with it, yet I must beg you to bear in addition the *costs of the pianoforte scores*, as I first have to pay for everything, and one thing *dearer than another*, so it would fall very heavily on me; besides I do not think that you can complain of the honorarium of 250 ducats. However, I do not care to complain, hence see to the scores yourself, but everything must be looked over by me, and, if necessary, improved; I hope that you are satisfied with this. Also you might give to my brother the *collections of Clementi's, Mozart's, Haidn's pianoforte works ;* he wants them for *his little son.* My very dear Steiner, do this, and do not be like a stone, however stony your name may be. Farewell most excellent General Lieutenant, I am always,

Your most devoted Superior General,

LUDWIG VAN BEETHOVEN.

[The pianoforte editions are those of the 7th and 8th Symphonies (Op. 92 and Op. 93), which were published by this firm in the year 1816. Here also is mention made of the nephew Carl, who after the death of the father in 1815 became a factor of great importance in the history of the composer. ("Stein," German for stone, makes clear the play upon the name "Steiner." —TR.)]

175. To Mr. GEORGE THOMSON, MERCHANT IN THE MUSICAL LINE, EDINBOURGH, SCOTTLAND

VIENNA, *Feb.* 7, 1815.

SIR!

Many concerns have prevented my answers by your favors, to which I reply only in part. All your songs with the exception of a few are ready to be forwarded, I mean those to which I was to write the accompagnements; for with respect to the 6 Canzonettes, which I am to compose. I own that the honorary you offered is totally inadequate. Circonstances here are much altered and taxes have been so much reised after the English fashion that my share for 1814 was near 60 £; besides an original good air—and what you also wish—an Overture, are perhaps the most difficult undertakings in musical compositions. I therefore beg to state that my honorary for 6 songs or airs must be 35 £ or seventy imp^l Ducats and for un Overture 20 £ or 50 imp^l Ducats. You will please to assigne the payment here as usual, and you may depend that I shall do you justice. No artiste of talent and merit will find my pretensions extravagent.

Concerning the overture you will please to indicate in your reply whether you wish to have it composed for an easy or more difficult execution. I expect your immediate answer having several orders to attend, and I shall in a little time write more copiously in reply of your favors already received. I beg you to thank the author for the very ingenious and flattering verses, which obtained to be means. Allow me to subscribe myself,

Sir,

your very obed^t, humble serv^t,

LUDWIG VAN BEETHOVEN.

[The letter was only signed by Beethoven. The high fees exasperated Thomson, who, according to Hadden, wrote: "Two years ago you asked 25 ducats for 6 original melodies, now you ask three times as much." T. offers 35 ducats, adding: "If you will not accept 35 ducats, I must ask you to have the goodness to put all the verses I have sent you on the fire." We learn from Hadden that in 1816 Beethoven arranged German, Polish, Russian, Tyrolese, Venetian and Spanish folk melodies; and not only that they were sent to Thomson, but that they were most favourably received. What has become of them?]

176. To Countess MARIE Von ERDÖDY

28th(?) February, 1815.

I have read, worthy Countess, your letter with great pleasure, and the renewing of your friendship has been equally gratifying. It has long been my wish once again to see you, and also your dear children, for although I have suffered much, I have not yet lost my earlier feelings for childhood, for beautiful nature and for friendship. The trio, and everything which as yet is not published, stands, dear Countess, at your service; as soon as it is written, you shall receive it. Not without sympathy and interest have I often inquired after your state of health, but now I am coming in person to you, and glad to show my interest in all that concerns you. My brother has written to you, you must be a little indulgent with him, he is really an *unfortunate, suffering man.* I hope that the approaching spring will have the best influence on your health and perhaps make you quite well again. Farewell dear, worthy Countess, my best remembrances to your dear children, whom in spirit I embrace. I hope soon to see you.

Your true friend,

LUDWIG VAN BEETHOVEN.

[Address:]

To the Countess Erdödy
née Countess Niszky.

[The trio here named is the one in B flat (Op. 97), which was published in the following year (1816) by Steiner. Brother Carl was now seriously ill; he died in November of the same year.]

177. Corrections of Misprints to BREITKOPF AND HAERTEL

[1815.]

Faults in the pianoforte part of the first *Allegro*, bar 7

the E marked with a *

must be C, namely, 𝄞 [music notation] Two shakes are omitted in the 11th

bar, on B, [music notation] A ♯ is wanting to the

second A in bar 12, namely, [music notation] , in the 22nd bar

of the second part of the first *Allegro*, there must be *ffmo* (*fortissimo*)
on the first note; in the 151st bar in the bass, instead of

[music notation] there must be [music notation]

Second movement *Allegro molto*, in the 1st bar the *ff* must be

struck out—from there, after the signature [music notation] has been changed

to [music notation] is a similar case, and must, instead of *ff*, have a *p*

placed on the first note. The second time when the signature [music notation]

is changed into [music notation] the *ff* is again to be left out, and a *p* put

at once in the first bar.

Adagio cantabile. In the pianoforte part in the 17th bar, instead

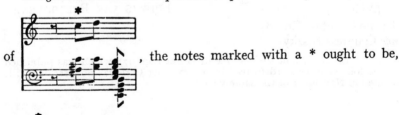

of [music notation] , the notes marked with a * ought to be,

[music notation] namely, the ⌣ slur between the two E's must be

taken away and placed above in the soprano, and below in the bass as indicated here. In the 18th bar of the same movement the arpeggio

sign is left out, and it ought to be there, namely, so

In the *Allegro vivace* in the pianoforte part (Nb.), in the third

bar there are two ties

Faults in the 'cello part—first *Allegro* at the 27th bar there is a dot after the minim A which must be taken away—in the 69th

bar a sharp has been left out, thus 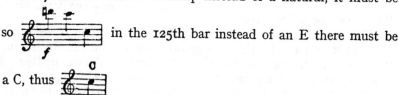 before

the D. Between the 77th and 78th bars there must be a tie, which

has been left out, namely, it is here

indicated by a *.

(Nb) in the second part—
in the 72nd bar there is a sharp instead of a natural, it must be

so in the 125th bar instead of an E there must be

a C, thus

In the *Adagio cantabile* in the 5th bar the slur is to be left out

over the two *staccato* signs, ``, namely, where here

the * is marked; in the 17th bar in the turn there is a note, namely,

D, here marked with a *, which is left out , in

the *Allegro Vivace* in the 4th bar there must be a slur over the five

notes from where the * is marked, 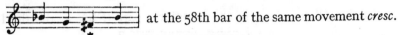—in

the 56th bar *dolce* is left out, and it must be added—in the second part of the same movement at the 9th bar, instead of F sharp there must be G sharp, as here, where the * is marked,

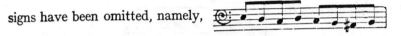 at the 58th bar of the same movement *cresc.*

has been forgotten—at the 116th bar the slur ⌣ and the ''staccato

signs have been omitted, namely,

[On the fourth empty page of these corrections of faults the firm has written: "After these corrections have been made I want the paper with the list of faults returned. H."

On a sheet containing corrections (not in Beethoven's hand) of the *Egmont* Overture and the Ariettas the master has written:

"The 3 German Ariettas are to be again dedicated to the Princess Kynsky." And so it appeared as Opus 83.

All the above corrections of Beethoven belong to the sonata for pianoforte and 'cello (Op. 69), published in April 1809. All players of this famous sonata will do well to enter in their copies the corrections according to this letter.]

178. To CARL AMENDA, Talsen

VIENNA, 12*th April*, 1815.

MY DEAR GOOD AMENDA!

The bearer of this letter, Count Keyserling your friend, paid me a visit and awoke the remembrance of you in me, by saying that you are living happily, that you have children, neither of which I can say of myself. It would be too great a digression to say more about this, another time when you again write to me on the subject. I think 1000 times of you and of your patriarchal simplicity, and how often have I wished that I could have such men as yourself about me—but fate, for my good or for that of others, has not granted me my desire. I may say that I live almost *alone* in this greatest city of Germany, and am forced to live apart from all the men whom I love, whom I could love. On what sort of a footing is music at your place? Have you yet heard any of my great works there? I say great—in comparison with the

Almighty everything is small.[1] Farewell my dear good A., and think sometimes of your friend,

LUDWIG VAN BEETHOVEN.

When you write to me, you need only put my name.

[Count Keyserling who, according to this letter, was personally acquainted with Beethoven, is not mentioned in any of the biographies of the composer. This man was probably the father of the well-known traveller, Count Alexander Keyserling. This letter takes no notice of one written by Amenda to Beethoven from Talsen, 20 March, 1815, which is contained in Schindler's Beethoven Papers, in the Berlin Royal Library. The letters, therefore, must have crossed. The very interesting Talsen letter begins with these words: "My Beethoven! After long guilty silence, I approach your noble Muse with an offering, so that you may be reconciled with me, and may once again think of Amenda, who has almost become a stranger. Oh, those unforgettable days, when I was so near to your heart, when this loving heart and the enchantment of your great talent continually bound me to you! They still stand in their most beautiful light before my soul. They are, in my inmost feeling, a jewel of which time can never rob me." Amenda proceeds to give a long account of the opera poem which he was sending: "*Bacchus*, grand lyrical opera in three acts, by Rudolph von Berge." Although Amenda asserts of the poem that "its equal does not exist. Therefore only you and no other should set it to music," Beethoven paid as little attention to this *Bacchus* as to all the other poems which were placed before him after *Fidelio*. Another reason for his not doing so was that he had taken a fancy to Treitschke's Romulus poem, and had seriously begun to set it to music. We have, however, neither a Romulus nor a Bacchus opera. Of the relations between Beethoven and Amenda nothing more is known. Provost Carl Amenda died at Talsen in 1836, about nine years after the death of his great friend.]

179. TO JOHANN PETER SALOMON, LONDON

VIENNA, 1st June, 1815.

MY HONOURED COUNTRYMAN!

I always hoped to see my wish fulfilled of speaking to you one day in London, but many hindrances have always prevented me carrying out this wish; and just because I am not in a position to do so, yet I hope that you will not refuse my request which consists in this, that you would be kind enough to speak with a publisher there and offer him the following works of mine: a grand Terzett for pianoforte, violin and 'cello, 80 ducats; Sonata for pianoforte with a violin, 60 ducats; Grand Symphony in A (one of my best); a small Symphony in F; Quartet for 2 violins, viola and 'cello in F minor; a grand Opera in score, 30 ducats; Cantata with chorus

---

[1] This should be compared with a passage in a letter written by Beethoven to Schott in the summer of 1824: "What is all this in comparison with the Great Composer above—above—above—and rightly the Highest of all? Here below it is a mere mockery. The tiny dwarf—the Almighty."

and soli; score of the *Battle of Vittoria and Wellington's Victory*, 80 ducats; also the pianoforte score if, as I am assured here, it has not already been published. I have, by the way, added to several works the fee which I think will be right for England; I however leave these and the others to you to do what you think best about them. I hear indeed that Cramer is also a publisher, but my pupil Riess lately wrote to me that he had already declared himself opposed to my compositions; but I hope for no other reason than to benefit art, and so I have nothing to say against it. If, however, Cramer wishes to have some of these pernicious works of art, he is as acceptable to me as any other publisher—I only reserve to myself the right of giving them to a publisher here, so that these works can really only come out in London and Vienna, and indeed at the same time. Perhaps it will be possible for you to show me how I can at least get from the Prince Regent the costs of copying the Battle Symphony on Wellington's Victory in the battle of Vittoria, for I have long given up the thought of getting money from any other quarter. I have not even been honoured with an answer as to whether I may dedicate this work to the Prince Regent; while I am publishing it I hear indeed that the work has already appeared in London in pianoforte score—what a misfortune for an author! While the English and German newspapers are full of the success of this work which has been performed at Drury Lane Theatre, while the theatre itself had two good receipts, the author himself cannot point to a single friendly line about the matter, not even compensation for the cost of copying; yes, and further, the loss of all chance of profit; for if it is true that the pianoforte score is published, no German publisher will take it. It is probable that the pianoforte edition will soon be reprinted by some London publisher or other, and I shall lose honour and fee. Your well-known noble character gives me reason to hope that you will show some sympathy, and be active on my behalf. The bad paper money of our State has already been reduced to a fifth part of its value, and I was paid according to that scale; after many struggles I however received the full value together with the named loss. We are now at a moment when paper money has already risen far above the fifth part, but my annuity seems about to become nothing for the second time, without any hope of compensation. My only means are my compositions. If I could count upon the sale of them in England that would be most advantageous for me. I shall be most grateful to you and hope for an answer very soon.

Your admirer and friend,
LUDWIG VAN BEETHOVEN.

[With regard to Salomon, see Letter 32. In this very year (1815), he had a fall from his horse and died soon after, and was buried in Westminster Abbey. In February of this year the Battle Symphony was performed for the first time in London at Drury Lane Theatre, and achieved exceptional success. The work was performed during several seasons, and Smart gained from it a clear profit of £1000, and the composer nothing.]

180. To COUNTESS MARIE Von ERDÖDY

[*Summer* 1815.]

Dear, dear, dear, dear, dear Countess, I am taking baths which only end to-morrow, so that I shall not see you and all your dear ones to-day. I hope you are enjoying better health. It is no consolation to better men to say to them that others also suffer; yet one must always institute comparison, and then it will be found that we all suffer or err only in a different way. Take the better edition of the quartet and give the bad one, with a gentle shake of the hand, to the 'Cello; as soon as I come to you, my care will be to put him into a quandary. Farewell, embrace your dear children in my name, although it occurs to me I ought no longer to kiss the daughters, as they are now grown up; in this matter I do not know what to do; act according to your wisdom, dear Countess.

Your true friend and admirer,

BEETHOVEN.

To the Countess Marie Erdödy.

[Now commences a charming intercourse between Beethoven and his "father confessor," Marie Erdödy; the tutors of her children, Magister Brauchle, the 'cellist Linke, and the bailiff Sperl, help to give to the pleasant joyous life on the Jedlersee estate of the countess the necessary relief; thus the letters to the countess and to Magister Brauchle are connected. The quartet was very probably the one in F minor dedicated to Zmeskall (Op. 95), which was ready in manuscript in 1810, although it only appeared in print in the following year. The "better edition of the quartet" was probably a better copy.]

181. To THE SAME

[*Summer* 1815.]

MY DEAR WORTHY COUNTESS!

You again make me a present, and that is not right, you thus deprive me of all small services which I would render you. It is uncertain whether I can come to you to-morrow morning, however much I should like to do so—but certainly in a few days, even should it be only in the afternoon. My position is very entangled, more about it by word of mouth. Greet in my name, and press to your heart all your children so dear to me. Give a gentle box on the ear to the Magister, a stately nod to the Chief Bailiff; the 'Cello is to betake himself to the left bank of the Danube and to play until every one is drawn over from the right bank, in this manner your population will soon increase. For the rest as before, I calmly take my way, over the Danube; with *courage*, when it is of the *right kind*, one wins in every direction. I kiss your hands many times, remember

Your friend,

So do not send any carriage,   BEETHOVEN.
rather dare! than a carriage!
   The promised music will be sent from town.

[This original letter of Beethoven's to his "father confessor" is probably the only one which has been preserved; the others as already related, were burned after O. Jahn had, with his notorious cunning, taken a copy of them. The Chief Bailiff is Sperl, who belonged to the household of the countess. (The postscript has a play upon the word "Wagen," which, as substantive, means "carriage"; as verb, "to dare.")]

182. To the Archduke RUDOLPH

[Summer 1815.]

YOUR IMPERIAL HIGHNESS!
   Please let me have the Sonata in E minor; I want it for correcting—on Monday I shall wait on your Imperial Highness; *new events* are the cause that many works, which are to be printed, have to be hastened on as quickly as possible, and I myself am only half well. I beg your Imperial Highness to be kind enough to let me have a few words about your state of health; I always hope to get better news, yes, soon the very best news about it.

Your Imperial Highness's most
obedient and faithful servant,
LUDWIG VAN BEETHOVEN.

[The pianoforte Sonata in E minor appeared in the summer of 1815.]

183. To Countess MARIE Von ERDÖDY

[Summer 1815.]

   Worthy Countess, forgive my having kept back your music so long, I only wished to have a copy taken of it, but the copyist kept me waiting for ever so long. I hope I shall see you soon again and for longer than yesterday; I press your dear children in my thoughts to my heart, and beg you to mention me to the others who take interest in me. I rejoice heartily at the progress of your health, and even at the increased fortunate circumstances (which you, dear Countess, so well deserve), although I do not wish that you should ever count me amongst those who hope to profit by them. A very hearty farewell.

From your friend,
BEETHOVEN.

To the Countess Erdödy, *née* Countess Niszky.

[In order to give a proof of the exceptional idolising of her great friend by the countess, we will give a poetical invitation which was sent to the master:

> Apollo's chief son
> Greatest of great spirits,
> The first master in composition
> Now known to Europe,
> To whom even Apollo yields,
> And from the throne of the Muses
> Rewards with his crown.
> Hear our request,
> Remain to-day in our midst—
> Thou great man, Beethoven,
> Give fiat to our hopes.

> The old Marie
> The young Marie
> The unique Fritzi
> August ditto
> Magister ipse
> The cursed 'cello
> The old Baron of the Empire
> The Chief Bailiff.

184. To the Archduke RUDOLPH

VIENNA, *the 23rd July*, 1815.

YOUR IMPERIAL HIGHNESS!

When you were lately in the city, this chorus again came into my head. I hastened home to write it down, but I was longer about it than I at first thought I should be, and so to my great sorrow I missed Y.I.H. The bad habit which I have had from childhood of always having to write down my first ideas, without their often succeeding, has also harmed me here.—I therefore sent to your Imperial Highness my accusation and excuse, and hope to find grace with you. Probably I shall soon be able to visit your Imperial Highness and make inquiry about the health so dear to us all.

Your Imperial Highness's faithful
and most obedient,
LUDWIG VAN BEETHOVEN.

[The chorus mentioned is probably "Es ist vollbracht," the chorus in Treitschke's operetta, *Die Ehrenpforten*. Highly worthy of notice is the composer's own admission as to his manner of composing.]

185. To VARENA, ATTORNEY OF THE EXCHEQUER, GRAZ

VIENNA, 23*rd July*, 1815.

You will, my dear Varena, receive the piano at latest in a fortnight.

It was not possible for me to get it sooner for you; besides, in all that concerns carrying out anything, discharging commissions, &c., I am an extremely unskilful person.

It costs 400 fl. with packing; any other person would have had to pay 600 fl. Schuster will at once pay here the 400 fl.; if you want decorations, please add 50 fl. and write at once to me.

The instrument is by Schanz, from whom I also have one.

Yours in haste,
BEETHOVEN.

Remember me to your family.

[Schanz was considered at that time one of the best pianoforte manufacturers in Vienna. It is not unimportant to remember Beethoven's custom with regard to commissions on pianos. (See Letter 68.)]

186. To TOBIAS HASLINGER

[1815; *June*?]

BEST OF FRIENDS!

Be good enough to send me the *Rochlitzian writing* about B.'s *writing*; we will send it back to you at once by the flying, driving, rising, or going post.—

Wholly yours,
B—N.

[Address:]

Herr Tobias von Haslinger.

[In the months of May and June in 1815 there were long and original articles about *Fidelio* in the Leipzig *Allgemeine Musikzeitung*, and these are what Beethoven refers to as "Rochlitzian writing." The articles were written by Professor Amadeus Wendt. These articles, in which Beethoven was first described as the "musical Shakespeare," attracted the special notice of the composer.]

187. To STEINER

[1815?]

I send herewith to my best G—l l—t the corrected pianoforte score, the improvements of Czerny are to be adopted; for the rest the Gllt has again to look at the Adjutant's many mistakes in the pianoforte score. In conformity with this, the same *punishment* as yesterday is to be applied to his other ear. Should he however be found *quite innocent*, the *punishment* must still be carried out, so that he may be struck with fear and terror of all crimes in the future. Meanwhile a report has to be drawn up of yesterday's and to-day's *punishment*. I embrace my best Gllt, while sending the pianoforte score of the *Symphony* in F which is very difficult to *perform*.

The——

L. v. B.

[Here the pianoforte score is either only of the 7th Symphony or of the 7th and 8th. It is known that the pianoforte edition of the A Symphony was looked through by Beethoven himself, improved, and dedicated to the Empress of Russia. From this letter we learn, with certainty, that Carl Czerny improved the pianoforte score; his improvements met with the highest approval. Haslinger, who is here found fault with, arranged the pianoforte score of the Symphony in F, which was only improved by Beethoven. Both symphonies were published by the Steiner firm in 1816.]

188. To MR. BIRCHALL, LONDON

[Autumn 1815.

Mr. Beethoven send word to Mr. Birchall that it is severall days past that he has sent for London Wellington's Battel *Simphonie* and that Mr. B[irchall] may send for it at Thomas Coutts. Mr. Beethoven wish Mr. Bl. would make ingrave the sayd *Simphonie* so soon as possible and send him word in time the day it will be Published that he may prevent in time the Publisher at Vienna.

In regard the 3. Sonata which Mr. Birchall receive afterwerths there is not wanted such a g^t hurry and Mr. B. will take the liberty to fixe the day when they are to be Published.

Mr. B[irchall] sayd that Mr. Salomon has a good many tings to say concerning the Symphonie in G [? A].

Mr. B[eethoven] wish for an answer so soons as possible concerning the days of the Publication.

[Birchall was proprietor of a music business, which after his death passed into the hands of C. Lonsdale, who for a long time was Birchall's agent. "All the letters here published," says Chrysander, "are in the possession of

Robert Lonsdale (son of C. Lonsdale), and were kindly placed by him at my disposal." We also learn that "The French letters were written by Beethoven himself, the others were only signed by him." With the above undated note begins the classic English from Vienna.]

189. To the Archduke RUDOLPH

Autumn 1815 (?)

Your Imperial Highness!

You must almost believe that my illness is a pretence. But it is not so, I am compelled to get home early of an evening; for the first time that your Imperial Highness was gracious enough to send for me, I afterwards returned straight home; but as from that time I seemed to be better, I made my first attempt the evening before last to stay out a little longer. Unless your Imperial Highness sends any order to the contrary, I shall have the honour of waiting on you this evening about 5 o'clock. I shall bring with me the new Sonata, but only for to-day; as it is going to be printed at once, it is not really worth while having it copied out.

Your Imperial Highness's most
obedient and faithful servant,

L. v. Beethoven.

[Beethoven's excuses were certainly not pretence; the master was unfortunately only too often ill; and nearly always after 1815. The sonata referred to can only be the one in A (Op.101) which was played in public in February 1816, but not published by Steiner until 1817.]

190. To the Countess MARIE ERDÖDY

Vienna, 19*th October*, 1815.

My dear honoured Countess!

As I am bound to see, my anxiety is aroused for you with regard to your journey, and your occasional troubles when travelling, but the aim appears really to have been achieved by you, and so I consoled myself, and also speak words of consolation to you; we mortals with immortal minds are only born for *sorrows and joys*, and one might almost say that the most excellent only receive their *joys through sorrows*. I hope soon to receive news of you, your children must be a consolation to you, and their honest love and endeavours to do all that is good for their dear mother, are already a great reward for your sorrows. Then there is the honourable Magister, your true squire—then many other rascals, among whom

Violoncello, master of the guild, sober justice in the High Bailiff—
that is a following which would satisfy many a king. Nothing about
myself—that means *nothing about nothing.* God give you further
strength to arrive at your *Temple of Isis,* where the refining fire
will consume all your evil, and you will arise a new phœnix.

[The deep ethical thoughts contained in this letter, especially the one
about the most distinguished men receiving joy through sorrow, recall the
words of Isaiah xlviii. 10: "I have refined thee, but not with silver; I have
chosen thee in the furnace of affliction." Here reference is made to the Isis
Temple of the countess. Probably Beethoven is referring to the temple which
the countess erected to the master. Anton Schindler, in the first edition of
his biography of Beethoven, states that Countess Erdödy erected to her
teacher and friend in the park of one of her castles in Hungary, a beautiful
temple, over the entrance of which was an inscription which expressed homage
to the great artist. The 'Cello, master of the guild, is Linke, the master's
"cursed 'cello," who, together with the other persons connected with the house,
has already been mentioned in the letter of invitation given on p. 177.]

191. To ROBERT BIRCHALL, London

VIENNA, 28*th October,* 1815.

DEAR SIR,

I announce to you that the pianoforte score of the *Battle
Symphony of Wellington's Victory* has already been sent to
London several days ago, and, in fact, to the house of Thomas
Coutts in London, whence you can fetch the same. I beg you to
hurry up as much as possible in printing this, and to *fix for me the
day* on which you wish to publish it, so that I may announce this
in time to the publishers here. With the three works which follow,
such great haste is not necessary; these you will very soon receive,
when I shall *take the liberty* of fixing myself the day—Mr. Salomon
will be kind enough to explain to you why there is more haste with
the Battle and Victory Symphony.

I await your answer, which I hope will soon come, with regard
to the fixing of the *day of publication* of the works now received.

[The correspondence of Beethoven with Birchall and Stumpff is contained,
as already mentioned, in the *Jahrbüchern für Musikwissenschaft,* vol. i.,
1863. The above letter, however, forms an exception; it was communicated
to Thayer for his Biography by Herr A. Ganz. With regard to the first so-called
letter to Birchall in wonderful English (see No. 188), Thayer gives the right
explanation that it is merely an attempt of some German living in England
to reproduce in English the contents of the following letter of Beethoven.]

192. To the Same, London

Enclosed you will receive the pianoforte edition of the Symphony in A. The pianoforte edition of the *Symphony of Wellington's Victory at the Battle of Vittoria* was sent off four weeks ago through the agent, Herr Neumann, to Messrs. Coutts and Co. there; so they must have been in your hands a long time since.

In a fortnight you will still receive the Trio and the Sonata, in exchange for which please pay to Thomas Coutts and Co. the sum of 130 gold ducats. I beg you to hasten with the publishing of this composition, and to inform me of the day of publication of the Wellington Symphony, so that I may take my measures here.

With respect, I remain,

Yours faithfully,

LUDWIG VAN BEETHOVEN.

Mp.

193. To FERDINAND RIES, London

VIENNA, *Wednesday, the 22nd November*, 1815.

Dear Ries! I hasten to write to you that I have sent off by post to-day the pianoforte edition of the Symphony in A, addressed to the firm of Thomas Coutts and Co. As the Court is not here, there are no couriers, or very few; besides, this is really the safest way. The Symphony must be published about March, I will fix the day. Things have already been too much delayed for me to be able to fix a shorter term. For the Trio and the Sonata for violin there is more time, and both will be in London in a few weeks. I beg you earnestly, dear Ries, to look after this matter, so that I may receive the money; sending the things is expensive; I want it.

I have lost 600 fl. of my yearly pension; at the time of the bank-notes it did not matter; then came the redemption bonds, and thus I lost 600 fl. After several years' vexation, with entire loss of the annuity—and now we have arrived at the point, that the redemption bonds are worse than ever the bank-notes were; I pay 1000 fl. house rent, you can form an idea of the misery which the paper money causes. My poor unfortunate brother (Carl) is just dead. He had a bad wife; I may say he had consumption for several years, and in order to make life easier for him, I reckon that I gave him 10,000 fl. in Vienna coin. For an Englishman that is nothing, but for a poor German or rather Austrian it is a lot. The poor fellow had much changed during the last years, and I can say I pitied him from my heart; and it now comforts me to be able to say to myself, that with regard to maintaining him I have nothing to reproach myself with. Tell Mr. Birchall to make good to Mr. Salomon and to you the cost of postage of your letters to me and mine to you; he can deduct it from the sum which he has to pay me; I want those who work for me to suffer as little as possible.

Wellington's Victory at the Battle of Vittoria must have reached Th. Coutts and Co. long ago. Mr. Birchall need not pay the money until he has all the works. Make haste and let me know the day when Mr. Birchall publishes the pianoforte score. For to-day I only beg you to show warmest zeal in this matter; I am, whatever it may be, at your service. Farewell from my heart, dear Ries! Also the title on the pianoforte score.

Your friend,

BEETHOVEN.

[We know already that the German violinist, J. P. Salomon, together with Ries, Neate and others, was very active in the cause of Beethoven's music; we also know that Salomon fell from his horse in August 1815, and died 25 November of the same year.]

194. To CHARLES NEATE

VIENNA, *December* 1815.

MY DEAR MR. NEATE,

I have received a letter from Mr. Ries, as amanuensis to Salomon (who has had the misfortune to break his right shoulder in a fall from his horse), and he tells me on the 29th of September, that the three Overtures which you took of me for the Philharmonic Society four months ago, had not then reached London. This being the second remembrancer which Mr. Salomon sends me on the subject, I thought I had better let you know. Should you not have sent them off, I should like to revise the Overture in C major, as it may be somewhat incorrect. With regard to any written agreement you may like to have about these things for England, that is very much at your service at a moment's notice. I would not have them suppose that I could ever act otherwise than as a *man of honour*. There are dispositions so fickle that they think *one way* to-day and *another way* to-morrow, and fancy others as ready to change their mind; and with such tempers one cannot be positive and mistrustful enough. So fare you well, my dear Mr. Neate.

Yours truly,

LUDWIG VAN BEETHOVEN.

[Charles Neate, an enthusiastic admirer of the works of Beethoven, made the acquaintance of the composer during this year, became his personal friend, and later on was of great service to him. Neate was born at London in 1784, became one of the directors of the Philharmonic Society, and died at the ripe age of ninety-three.]

195. To Frau ANNA MILDER-HAUPTMANN, Berlin
VIENNA, *January* 6, 1816.

MY HIGHLY PRIZED UNIQUE MILDER, MY DEAR FRIEND!

My letter to you is a much belated one. How I should have liked to have taken part in the enthusiasm of the Berliners which you excited in *Fidelio*! I thank you a thousand times for having remained faithful to my *Fidelio*. If you would beg Baron de la Motte Fouqué in my name to think of a good opera subject which at the same time would be suitable for you, this would be rendering a great service to me, and also to the German stage. And I should like to write such a work exclusively for *the Berlin Theatre*, for with the niggardly direction here I shall never be able to succeed with a new opera. Send an answer soon, as soon as possible, very quickly, as quickly as possible, with utmost haste—and say whether the thing is practicable. Capellmeister V. [or W.?] has praised you up to the skies, and he is right. Happy may that man esteem himself whose fate depends on your muse, your genius, your noble qualities and excellences—and such a one am I. However it may be, every one around you may only call himself a secondary personage. I alone legitimately bear the honourable title of leading man [*Hauptmann*], and only quite quietly, between ourselves.

Your true friend and admirer,
BEETHOVEN.

(My poor unfortunate brother is dead—this the cause of my long silence.)

As soon as you have sent an answer, I will also write to Baron de la Motte Fouqué. Your influence in Berlin will surely make it easy to arrange for me to write a whole opera for the Berlin Theatre, with a *rôle* specially written for you, and on acceptable conditions —*only answer soon*, so that I may arrange about my other scribblings.

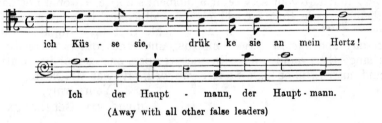

ich Küs - se sie,   drük - ke sie an mein Hertz!

Ich   der Haupt - mann, der Haupt - mann.

(Away with all other false leaders)

[The musical joke at the end of the letter was published by Thayer in his *Thematic Catalogue of the Works of Beethoven,* but incorrectly reproduced. The first transcriber of the letter took the notes on both staves to be written in the tenor clef. Moreover, the specially humorous division of the word before a pause (see bar 2 of second stave) was not indicated. Thayer, both in his *Thematic Catalogue,* also in his *Beethoven Biographie,* gives the joke in F major, and all in the bass clef. *Fidelio* was given for the first tin.e at Berlin with Frau Schultze, *née* v. Killitschky, the sister-in-law of Schuppanzigh, the "Bohemian lady with the fine contralto voice," on 11 October, 1815; then, on 14 and 17 October, followed the epoch-making *Fidelio* performances with Milder-Hauptmann as Fidelio, and to these reference is made in the above letter. The Vienna theatre management is probably dubbed "niggardly" in remembrance of the story connected with the *Romulus* opera on a poem by Fr. Treitschke. Nothing came of the proposition *re* de la Motte-Fouqué. Friedrich, Baron de la Motte-Fouqué (1777–1843), was the author of *Undine.*]

196. To Baron ZMESKALL

January 1816.

With terror I see only to-day that I have not answered the proposal with regard to writing an *Oratorio* for the Gesellschaft der Musikfreunde of the Austrian Imperial States.

The death of my brother two months ago whereby the guardianship of my nephew fell to me, together with many other unpleasant things and events, is the cause of my late answer. Meanwhile the poem of Herr v. Seyfried is already begun, and I shall soon set it to music. I need not say that I regard the proposal as highly honourable for me; that is evident, and in so far as my weak powers permit, I will endeavour to prove myself worthy of it! *With regard to the artistic means* for the performance, I certainly will keep them in mind; I hope, however, that I shall not have to keep strictly to the already established custom in this matter. I hope I have expressed myself intelligibly. As they will, of course, want to know what fee I shall expect, I ask myself whether the society will consider 400 ducats in gold at least a suitable sum for such a work. I once again beg the society to excuse my late answer; meanwhile you, at any rate, dear friend, have already by word of mouth declared my willingness to write this work, and that to some extent sets me at ease.

My worthy Z.,
Your B.

[Zmeskall had been instructed to call the attention of the gifted composer, who troubled little about the difficulty of performing such works, to the fact that he must of necessity take into consideration the size of the orchestra, which at the great concerts ran up to seventy persons.

"As the Society only stipulated for the exclusive use for a year, and not for the ownership, and in addition had undertaken to pay the special fee for the poem, and must therefore consider what money they had at disposal, they replied to the composer that they were ready, for use agreed upon, to pay 200 ducats in gold. B., without raising any objection, was satisfied, and according to his wish received an advance, the receipt of which he acknowledged. B., however, would not work on the first poem selected, and expressed the wish for another. The Society left him perfectly free choice. Herr Bernard undertook to deliver a new one. B. arranged with him about the subject, but Herr B., busy about other matters, could only deliver it bit by bit. B. would not begin until he had the whole before him. Meanwhile he wrote a grand symphony and a small cantata for England, which in 1819 he offered to the Society for performance, if they would grant him a second performance for his benefit, which offer, however, owing to various hindrances, could not be accepted.

"The many works which he had to attend to to maintain himself and to educate his nephew, to whom he sacrificed everything, proved a special hindrance to his fulfilling his promise. Even in November 1819 he told Prince Odescalchi, at that time deputy for H. Praeses, that delivery of the work was uppermost in his thoughts. Bernard at length completed the work; B., however, whose health had greatly suffered, was dissatisfied with everything: he kept on wanting the text to be altered. As late as October 1824 the Society made a serious attempt to induce him to accept the work, but finally abandoned hope of one of their dearest wishes ever being fulfilled." I have herewith given the whole passage from Fischoff, so that in all future references in the letters to this oratorio question, the information from this excellent source may serve as guide. Carl Bernard's *Sieg des Kreuzes* (*Victory of the Cross*) was not set to music.]

197. To FERD. RIES, London

VIENNA, *January* 20, 1816.

My dear Ries! — — — The Symphony will be dedicated to the Empress of Russia. The pianoforte arrangement of the Symphony in A must not, however, appear till the month of June; the publisher here cannot do so earlier. Dear, good Ries, let Mr. Birchall know this at once. The Sonata with violin, which will be sent off from here by next post, can likewise be published in London in the month of May. But the Trio later (that, too, will be sent by next post). The time I will fix myself.

And now my hearty thanks, dear Ries, for all the kindnesses you have shown me, and especially as regards the proof-reading. Heaven bless you, and cause you to make continual progress, in which I take genuine interest. Kind remembrances to your wife.

As always,
Your sincere friend
LUDWIG VAN BEETHOVEN.

[The pianoforte transcription of the Symphony in A was not made by Beethoven, but only improved by him. The violin sonata here mentioned was the one in G (Op. 96), completed in 1812, and published together with the Trio in B flat (Op. 97) by Steiner and Co. in 1816.]

198. To S. A. STEINER & CO.

January 1816.

If the corrected *copy of the Sonata* which I handed over to the *Adjutant* of the G. l., Tobias Haslinger, together with another free from all faults, | : *so that it may be seen that the faults in the copperplates have been corrected*: | , i.e., the one *corrected* (by me) together with another *Free-from-faults*, is not in my hands by to-morrow evening *between* 6 *and* 7 *o'clock*, we determine as follows: The G. L. will for a time be *suspended*; its Adjutant T. H. fettered crosswise. Our provost-general *diabolus diabelli* will be entrusted with the execution of the same. Only the strictest carrying out of our above-named command can preserve them from the already mentioned and just punishment.

THE G—S (IN THUNDER AND LIGHTNING).

199. FOR THE PHILHARMONIC SOCIETY, LONDON

VIENNA, *February 5, 1816.*

Mr. Neate has taken of me in July 1815 three Overtures for the Philharmonic Society of London, and has paid me for them the sum of 75 guineas, for which sum I engage not to have these said Overtures printed elsewhere, either in parts or score, always reserving for myself the right to have the said works performed wherever I please, and to publish them in pianoforte arrangement so soon as Mr. Neate shall write me word that they have been performed in London; besides which Mr. Neate assures me that he obligingly takes upon himself, after the lapse of one or two years, to obtain the consent of the Society to my publishing these three Overtures in parts as well as in score, their consent to that effect being indispensable. Thus I respectfully salute the Philharmonic Society.

LUDWIG VAN BEETHOVEN

[A "Manuscript Agreement as drawn up by Beethoven for the Philharmonic Society of London," concerning the above-named three manuscript overtures. These were the overtures to *The Ruins of Athens*, to *König Stephan*, and *zur Namensfeier*, all declined by the Philharmonic Society as "unworthy" of Beethoven. On the title-page of the third overture, published by Steiner in 1825, it is said to have been "gedichtet" (i.e. poetised) for orchestra, etc., the only work in which the composer used that word in place of the usual one "composed."]

200. Mons. BIRCHALL, Londres

VIENNE, *le* 3 *Févr.*, 1816.

Vous receues vi (ci-) joint,

Le Grand Trios p. PF. V. & V^{llo} Sonata pour PF. & Violin— qui form le reste de ce qu il vous à plus a me comettre. Je vous prie de vouloir payer le some de 130 Ducats d'Holland come le poste lettre a Mr. Th. Coutts & Co. de votre Ville et de me croire avec toute l'estime et consideration,

Votre tres humble
Serviteur,
Louis van Beethoven.

201. To FERDINAND RIES, London

VIENNA, *February* 10, 1816.

Highly honoured Friend!

No doubt you have received my letter of [?Jan. 20th]; for the present I only point out to you, that I now under date the third of this [3rd of February?] have sent the *grand Trio and the Sonata* to Mr. Birchall through Messrs. Coutts and Co., for which he has to pay to the latter the stipulated sum of 130 Dutch *ducats*. But in addition the expenses for copying and carriage concern him; the music was sent by letter post merely for his sake, that he might get it quickly. The account for these matters you will find at the end of this letter. I earnestly beg you to use your influence, so that Mr. Birchall pays to Messrs. Coutts and Co., the said sum for costs in 10 Dutch *ducats*; the loss of this sum would consume a great part of my whole fee. I hope soon to find opportunity to oblige Mr. Birchall in some other way.

I look forward to a speedy answer, and remain with friendly feelings of respect,

Your sincere friend,
Ludwig van Beethoven.

[Thayer states that Birchall sent Beethoven a document to the effect that the latter had received 130 Dutch ducats in gold for the Symphony, Trio and Sonata, and this document, as he was forwarding the money at the same time, he expected to receive back signed. But, adds Thayer, "In place of this document indispensable for his security, the publisher received a new demand from Beethoven! in fact, one for five pounds in the form of an account." Beethoven claimed "130 Ducats d'Holland" on 3 February, 1816, and sent the receipt required, but the date of that letter, "March 1816," is queried. Beethoven appears, as Thayer remarks, to have made a "new demand." What further correspondence *re* this demand took place one cannot say—the enclosed note mentioned above, for instance, is not forthcoming —anyhow, Mr. Birchall did finally pay the five pounds (see Letter 217).—Tr.]

202. To Baroness DOROTHEA Von ERTMANN

VIENNA, *February 23*, 1816 (?).

MY DEAR WORTHY DOROTHEA-CÄCILIA!

You must often have misjudged me, seeing that I must have appeared opposed to you; circumstances, especially formerly, when my behaviour was less understood than at present, will largely account for it. You know all about the teachings of the uncalled apostles who help themselves along by any other means than the Gospel; among such I have not wished to be counted. Now please accept what was often intended for you, and what may offer proof of my admiration for your talent as an artist, and of my attachment to you personally. That recently I could not hear you play at Czerny's must be set down to my illness, but now I am fairly on the road to convalescence.

I hope to hear from you, how matters stand at St. Pölten with ——, and whether you still hold in some esteem

Your admirer and friend,

L. VAN BEETHOVEN.

Best regards to your worthy husband.

[The A major sonata (Op. 101) was composed in 1815; in 1816 it was performed in public as new, and it was published by S. A. Steiner, in February 1817, as a sonata "für das Hammer-Klavier," and dedicated to Dorothea von Ertmann, *née* Graumann.—At Czerny's there were for a long time Sunday performances of music, at which Beethoven was frequently present. —General von Ertmann's regiment was formerly quartered at St. Pölten.]

203. To FERDINAND RIES, LONDON

VIENNA, *February 28*, 1816.

. . . For some time I have not been well; my brother's death has affected my spirits and my compositions. I am much pained at the news of Salomon's death, as he was a noble man whom I remember from my childhood. You have become executor to the will, and at the same time I have become the guardian of my poor dead brother's child. It is hardly possible that you will have had as much trouble as I have had through this death. Yet I have the sweet consolation of having saved a poor innocent child from the hands of an unworthy mother.

Farewell, dear Ries! If I can be of any service to you here, look upon me as your most faithful friend,

BEETHOVEN.

204. To Mr. BIRCHALL, London

March 1816 (?).

"Received March 1816, of Mr. Robert Birchall—Music-seller, 133 New Bond Street, London—the sum of One Hundred and thirty Gold Dutch Ducats, value in English Currency Sixty-Five Pounds for all my Copyright and Interest, present and future, vested or contingent, or otherwise within the United kingdom of Great Britain and Ireland in the four following Compositions or Pieces of Music composed or arranged by me, viz.,

1st. A Grand Battle Sinfonia, descriptive of the Battle and Victory at Vittoria, adapted for the Pianoforte and dedicated to his Royal Highness the Prince Regent—40 Ducats.

2nd. A Grand Symphony in the key of A, adapted to the Pianoforte and dedicated to

3rd. A Grand Trio for the Pianoforte, Violon and Violoncello in the key of B.

4th. A Sonata for the Pianoforte with an Accompaniment for the Violin in the key of G, dedicated to

And, in consideration of such payment I hereby for myself, my Executors and Administrators promise and engage to execute a proper Assignment thereof to him, his Executors and Administrators or Assignees at his or their Request and Costs, as he or they shall direct. And I likewise promise and engage as above, that none of the above shall be published in any foreign Country, before the time and day fixed and agreed on for such Publication between R. Birchall and myself shall arrive.

L. VAN BEETHOVEN."

205. To FERDINAND RIES, London

VIENNA, 3rd *April*, 1816.

Dear Riese, Herr V. has probably received by this time the Trio and Sonata; in the former letters I asked an extra 10 Ducats for copying and carriage; probably you will be able to procure these 10 ducats for me. I always feel anxious, because you must have laid out a considerable sum for postage. I should be very glad if you would kindly take in all my letters to you, and then I would reimburse you by sending from Friess here to the Coutts house in London. If the publisher V. should not find any difficulty, which he is requested to let me know about at once by post, the *Sonata* with violin *will come out here on the* 15th *June, the Trio on the*

15th July; I will let Herr V. know about the pianoforte score of the *Symphony, when it is to come out.* Neate is probably in London; I have given him several of my compositions; and he has promised to use his best interest for me. Greetings to him from me. The Archduke Rudolph also *plays* your music with me, dear Ries! *Il sogno* especially pleases me. Farewell, kind regards to your dear wife, also to all pretty young English ladies who will be glad to hear of me.

Your true friend,
BEETHOVEN.

[It is not clear who the publisher V. was; possibly instead of V. there should be a B., and then the name of the publisher would be Birchall. We shall soon learn that Beethoven was anything but satisfied with Neate's attempts to dispose of his compositions.]

206. To NEPOMUK HUMMEL

4th April, 1816.

A pleasant journey, dear Hummel, think sometimes of
Your friend,

LUDWIG VAN BEETHOVEN.

[Only when Beethoven was on his death-bed did the two friends see each other again. On these same words, Beethoven nine years later wrote a Canon for Sir George Smart.]

207. To CARL CZERNY

April (?) 1816.

DEAR CZ.,

Kindly give this to your parents for the recent dinner, which I certainly cannot accept gratis. Neither do I wish to accept your *lessons* gratis, even those already given shall be reckoned and settled for. Only for the moment I beg you will be patient, for there is nothing to be *got from* the widow, and I had and still have heavy expenses; but it is only borrowed for the moment. The little fellow will come to you to-day, and I later.

Your friend,

BEETHOVEN.

[Beethoven's nephew Carl began to take lessons from Carl Czerny soon after the death of Beethoven's brother.]

208. TO THE SAME

April (?) 1816.

DEAR CZERNY!

I cannot see you to-day, I will come to you to-morrow and have a talk with you. I burst out yesterday without thinking, but was sorry the moment afterwards. But you must forgive an author who would rather hear his works as written, however finely, for the rest, you played. I will however say something at the performance of the 'cello Sonata to make it all right.

Be convinced that I entertain the highest good-will for you as an artist, and I shall always strive to show it.

Your true friend,

BEETHOVEN

[Jahn states that this scene occurred when Czerny took many liberties in the rendering of a Beethoven work in 1812. According to Nohl it was probably in February 1816, but Thayer's April is the more likely date. The work which caused this scene was the Quintet in E flat for pianoforte and wind (Op. 16), in which Czerny played the pianoforte part.]

209. To FERDINAND RIES, LONDON

VIENNA, *8th May*, 1816.

My answer to your letter comes somewhat late; but I was ill and had much to do, so that it was impossible to answer sooner; now only what is most necessary. Of the 10 ducats I have not as yet received a single penny, and I already begin to believe that Englishmen are only generous when on the Continent; so also with the Prince Regent, from whom I have not even received the copying costs for the Battle which I sent to him, not even thanks by writing or by word of mouth. Fries deducted 6 fl., convention coin, from the money sent by Birchall, in addition to 15 fl. convention coin for carriage. Tell this to B.—and take care you get the money order for the 10 ducats, otherwise it will be like the first time. What you tell me about the undertaking of Neate *would be welcome to me,*

I *want* it—my annuity amounts to 3400 fl. in paper, I pay 1100 for house rent, and my servant and his wife cost 900 fl.; so reckon up and see what remains over. In addition I have to look entirely after my little nephew; up to now he is in the Institution; this comes to 1100 fl., and at that is not good, so that I shall have to set up proper housekeeping so as to have him with me. What a lot one has to earn in order to live here; and yet there is no end to it, for —for—for—you know what I mean.

Some orders, in addition to a concert, would be very welcome to me. Concerning the *dedication* to the Philharmonic Society, another time; I hope also soon to have news of Neate, *urge him on*; be assured of our sympathy in your good fortune, and do urge Neate on to *act* and to *write*.

For the rest, my dear pupil Ries ought to sit down and dedicate something really good to me, whereupon the master will answer and return like for like. How shall I send you my portrait? . . . Kindest regards to your wife; unfortunately I have none; I found only one who will probably never be mine; yet on that account I am not a woman-hater.

Your true friend,
Beethoven.

210. To Countess ERDÖDY, Padua

Vienna, May 13, 1816.

My worthy dear Friend!

You might perhaps be justified in thinking that I had quite forgotten you, but this is so only in appearance. The death of my brother was a cause of great grief to me, and the effort to save my dear nephew from his depraved mother was a heavy strain. I succeeded, but so far the best thing I could do for him was to put him in a school, and hence beyond my supervision. And what is a school in comparison with the direct sympathy and care of a father for his child, for such I now consider myself; and I am turning over in my mind one plan after another, as to how I can manage to have this dear jewel closer to me, so that my influence over him may be more rapid and advantageous—but to accomplish this is no easy matter. During the last six weeks my health has been very shaky, so that I often think of death, but without fear; only for my poor Carl would my death come too soon. I perceive from your last letter to me that you, my dear friend, have also been a great sufferer. It is the fate of mortals, but *even here one's power should become manifest, i.e., to endure unconsciously and to feel one's nothing-ness, and so attain to that perfection,* of which the Almighty through such means will deem us worthy.

Linke is probably already with you, and I hope that with his cat-gut he will awaken joy in your heart. Brauchle will not be disinclined to be made use of, so you can, as usual, make constant use of him. As to Vogel, I hear you are not satisfied with him, but why I do not know. I hear you are looking out for another private tutor, but do not decide on one in a hurry, and let me know your opinions and intentions; I may be able to give you some good information. Perhaps you are not quite fair to the sparrow in the cage? I embrace your children, and express in a Terzet the hope that they may make daily progress towards perfection. Let me know soon, very soon, how you are *on the little spot of earth* on which you live for the present. And if I do not always show it at once outwardly, I certainly am in full sympathy with your sorrows and also your joys. How long will you remain where you are, and where will you live in future? There will be a change in the dedi-cation of the violoncello-sonatas, but this will cause no change either in you or me.

Dear worthy Countess, in haste,

Your friend,

BEETHOVEN.

[It appears that the countess had travelled to Padua, without her children. The only son, Fritzi, died suddenly, as already related, at a castle belonging to the countess in Croatia. The persons named in this letter are: Linke, the 'cellist; Brauchle, *Magister*; the "bird" to be dismissed is the well-known Chief Bailiff, "Sperl." Beethoven speaks of a "Terzet," and the question is whether in the spring of 1816, he wrote for the family a vocal Terzet, or a new Trio? Nottebohm, in his *Ein Skizzenbuch aus dem Jahre 1815 und 1816*," speaks of "sketches for the first and third movements of an unfinished Trio in F minor for pianoforte, violin, and 'cello." From former letters we already know that Beethoven used the term "Terzet" for "Trio," so that the refer-ence may be to this F minor Trio, which he also mentions in a later letter to Birchall (October 1816).]

211. TO THE SAME

VIENNA, 15th May, 1816.

This letter [1] was already written, when to-day I meet Linke, and hear of your melancholy fate in the loss of your dear son. What consolation can I offer, nothing is more painful than the sudden departure of those who are dear to us; I too, cannot forget my

[1] i.e. the one of 13 May.

poor brother's death; the only consolation that one can think of, is that those who quickly depart suffer less—but I feel the deepest sympathy in your irreparable loss. Perhaps I have not yet told you that I likewise have not felt well for a long time; another cause of my silence is my anxiety about my Carl, whom in my mind I have often wished to be a friend of your dear son. I feel sad both for your sake and for mine, for I loved your son. Heaven watches over you, and will not wish to increase your already great sorrows, even though your health may be uncertain. Imagine that your son had been compelled to go into battle and there, like millions, had found his death; besides, you are still *mother* of two dear hopeful children. I hope soon to have news of you, I weep with you. For the rest pay no attention to all the gossip about my not having written to you; not even to Linke, who certainly is devoted to you, *but is inclined to gossip*—and I think that between you, my dear Countess, and myself, no go-between is wanted. In haste, with respect,

Your friend,
BEETHOVEN.

[This letter of consolation refers to the death of the only son of the countess. At the family estate in Croatia he was taken ill one morning, complained of his head, and with a cry of grief fell dead at his sister's feet.]

212. To CHARLES NEATE, London

VIENNA, May 18, 1816.

MY DEAR NEATE,

By a letter of Mr. Ries I am acquainted with your happy arrival in London. I am very well pleased with it, but still better I should be pleased if I had learned it by yourself.

Concerning our business, I know well enough that for the performance of the greater works, as the Symphony, the Cantate, the Chorus, and the Opera, you want the help of the Philharmonic Society, and I hope your endeavour to my advantage will be successful.

Mr. Ries gave me notice of your intention to give a concert to my benefit. For this triumph of my art at London I would be indebted to you alone; but an influence still wholesomer on my almost indigent life, would be to have the profit proceeding from this enterprise. You know that in a way I am now father to the lovely lad you saw with me; hardly can I live alone three months upon my annual salary of 3400 florins in paper, and now the additional burden of maintaining a poor orphan—you conceive how welcome lawful means to improve my circumstances must be to me. As for the Quatuor in F minor, you may sell it without delay to a publisher, and signify me the day of its publication, as I should wish it to appear here and abroad on the very day. Be pleased to do the same with the two Sonatas Op. 102 for pianoforte and violoncello; though with the latter there is no hurry.

I leave entirely to your judgment to fix the terms for both works, to wit, the Quatuor and the Sonatas, the more the better.

Be so kind to write to me immediately for two reasons; 1st that I may not be obliged to shrug my shoulders when they ask me if I got letters from you; and 2dly, that I may know how you do, and if I am in favour with you. Answer me in English if you have happy news to give me (for example, about giving a concert to my benefit), in French if the news is bad.

Perhaps you find some lover of music to whom the Trio and the Sonata with violin, Mr. Ries had sold to Mr. Birchall, or the Symphony arranged for the pianoforte, might be dedicated, and from whom a present might be expected. In expectation of your speedy answer, my dear friend and countryman, I am yours truly,

LUDWIG VAN BEETHOVEN.

[The following letter from Moscheles' *Life of Beethoven*, vol. ii. p. 240, will be read with interest.—TR.]

MR. NEATE TO BEETHOVEN

LONDON, *October* 29, 1816.

MY DEAR BEETHOVEN,

Nothing has ever given me more pain than your letter to Sir George Smart. I confess that I deserve your censure, that I am greatly in fault; but must say also that I think you have judged too hastily and too harshly of my conduct. The letter I sent you some time since, was written at a moment when I was in *such* a state of mind and spirits that I am sure, had you seen me or known my sufferings, you would have excused every unsatisfactory passage in it.

Thank God! it is now all over, and I was just on the point of writing to you, when Sir George Smart called with your letter. I do not know how to begin an answer to it; I have never been called upon to justify myself, because it is the first time I ever stood accused of dishonour; and what makes it the more painful is "that I should stand accused by the man who, of all in the world, I most admire and esteem, and one also whom I have never ceased to think of, and wish for his welfare, since I made his acquaintance." But as the appearance of my conduct has been so unfavourable in your eyes, I must tell you again of the situation I was in, previous to my marriage.

I remain in my profession, and with no abatement of my love of Beethoven! During this period I could not myself do anything publicly, consequently all your music remained in my drawer unseen and unheard. I, however, did make a very considerable attempt with the Philharmonic, to acquire for you what I thought you fully entitled to.

I offered all your music to them on condition that they made you a very handsome present; this they said they could not afford, but proposed to see and hear your music, and then offer a price for it; I objected and replied: "That I should be ashamed that your music should be put up by auction and bid for!—that your name and reputation were too dear to me"; and I quitted the meeting with a determination to give a concert and take all the trouble myself, rather than that your feelings should be wounded by the chance of their disapproval of your works. I was the more apprehensive of this, from the unfortunate circumstance of your Overtures not being well received; they said they had no more to hope for from your other works. I was not a director last season, but I am for the next, and then I shall have a voice which I shall take care to exert. I have offered your Sonatas to several publishers, but they thought them too difficult, and said they would not be saleable, and consequently made offers such as I could not accept, but when I shall have played them to a few professors, their reputation will naturally be increased by their merits, and I hope to have better offers. The Symphony you read of in the *Morning Chronicle* I believe to be the one in C minor; it certainly was not the one in A, for it has not been played at a concert. I shall insist upon its being played next season, and most probably the first night. I am exceedingly glad that you have chosen Sir George Smart to make your complaints of me to, as he is a man of honour, and very much your friend; had it been to any one else, your complaint might have been listened to, and I injured all the rest of my life. But I trust I am too respectable to be thought unfavourably of, by those who know me.

I am, however, quite willing to give up every sheet I have of yours, if you again desire it. Sir George will write by the next post, and will confirm this. I am sorry you say that I did not even acknowledge my obligation to you, because I talked of nothing else at Vienna, as every one there who knows me can testify. I even offered my purse, which you generously always declined. Pray, my dear friend, believe me to remain,

Ever yours, most sincerely,

C. Neate.

213. To FERDINAND RIES, London

Vienna, 11*th June*, 1816.

My dear R.!—I am sorry that you have had to pay postage money again for me; however willingly I help and serve all men, it pains me to be compelled to have to encroach upon other people's kindness. Of the 10 ducats *up to now* nothing has come, and I therefore conclude that in England, as with us here, there are braggarts and men who do not keep their word. In this I do not accuse you, nevertheless I must beg you once again to see Mr. Bishall about the 10 ducats, and to get them given to you. I assure you on my honour that I have paid for costs 21 fl. in convention coin, without counting the copyist and several postal expenses. The money was not even notified to me in ducats, although you yourself wrote to me that I should receive it in Dutch ducats. So there are in England such unconscientious men to whom keeping their word *is of no moment*!!! Concerning the Trio, *the publisher here* has approached me, so I beg you kindly to speak to Mr. B. so that this may appear in London by the *end* of August. He can get ready with the piano-forte score of the Symphony in A, since as soon as the publisher here fixes the day, I will at once inform you or B. As I have not received a syllable from Neate since his arrival in London, I now beg you to tell him to give you an answer whether he has already disposed of the Quartet in F minor, for I should like to bring it out here at once, also ask what I have to expect with regard to the 'cello Sonatas. Of all the other works which I gave to him I am almost ashamed to speak, and indeed for my own sake without any conditions, as I trusted entirely to him as a friend. The notice in the *Morning Chronicle* concerning the performance of the Symphony has been given me to read. Probably the same fate awaits this and all the other works which Neate took with him; as with the Battle, so with the latter, I shall probably not receive anything more than a notice in the papers about the performances. The pianoforte edition of the Symphony in A was quickly copied, and after careful revision I made certain changes which I will send to you. Kind regards to your wife.

In haste your true friend,
BEETHOVEN.

214. To Mr. BIRCHALL, London

MONSIEUR,   VIENNE, 22 *Juilliet*, 1816.

 J'ai reçu la déclaration de proprité des mes Œuvres entierement cedé a Vous pour y adjoindre ma Signature. Je suis tout a fait disposer a seconder vos vœux si tôt, que cette affaire sera entiere-ment en ordre, en egard de la petite somme de 10 louis d'or le quelle me vient encore pour le fieux de la Copieture de poste de lettre comme j'avois l'honneur de vous expliquier dans une note detaillé sur ses objectes. Je vous invite donc Monsieur de bien vouloir me remettre ces petits object, pour me mettre dans l'état de pouvoir Vous envoyer le Document susdit. Agrées Monsieur l'assurance de l'estime la plus parfait avec la quelle j'ai l'honneur de me dire

LOUIS VAN BEETHOVEN.

Copying	£1 10s. 0d.
Postage to Amsterdam	£1 0s. 0d.
Trio	£2 10s. 0d.
	£5 0s. 0d.

215. To his Nephew, CARL Von BEETHOVEN

September 1816.

My dear C.,

According to the orders of v. Smettana, you must take some baths before the operation. To-day the weather is favourable, and it is exactly the right time. I shall be waiting for you at the Stubenthor.

Of course you will first ask Herr v. G.'s permission. Put on drawers, or take them with you so that you can put them on when you come out of the bath, in case the weather should again become cooler. *If the tailor has not yet been to you,* when he comes let him also take your measure for linen drawers. You need them. If Frau v. G. knows where he lives, my servant can tell him to go to you. My [son] farewell; I am, and indeed through you,

Your breeches button,

L. v. BEETHOVEN.

[In September 1816 nephew Carl was successfully operated on by Dr. Smettana in the institution of H. Giannatasio. Most touching is Beethoven's motherly care for the tender, beloved son. This is probably the first letter we possess from the master to his nephew. Characteristic is the term he applies to himself: "Breeches button" was a nickname he gave to his youthful friend, Gerhard v. Breuning.]

216. To Dr. FRANZ WEGELER

VIENNA, 29th September, 1816.

I seize the opportunity, through J. Simrock, to remind you of myself. I hope you have received my engraved portrait [1] and also the Bohemian glass. When I again wander through Bohemia, you will again receive something of the same kind. Farewell, you are a man, a father; I also, though without a wife. Greet all yours— ours. Your friend L. v. Beethoven.

217. To Mr. BIRCHALL, Music-seller, London

VIENNA, 1 Oct., 1816.

My dear Sir,

I have duly received the £5 and thought previously you would not increase the number of Englishmen neglecting their word and honour, as I had the misfortune of meeting with two of this sort. In reply to the other topics of your favor, I have no objection to write variations according to your plan, and I hope you will not

[1] Drawn by Letronne, engraved by Höfel, 1814.

find £30 too much. The Accompaniment will be a Flute or Violon or a Violoncello; you'll either decide it when you send me the approbation of the price, or you'll leave it to me. I expect to receive the songs or poetry—the sooner the better, and you'll favour me also with the probable number of Works of Variations you are inclined to receive of me. The Sonata in G with the accompan^t of a Violin is dedicated to his Imperial Highness Archduke Rudolph of Austria—it is Op^a 96. The Trio in B flat is dedicated to the same and is Op. 97. The Piano arrangement of the Symphony in A is dedicated to the Empress of the Russians—meaning the wife of the Emp^r Alexander—Op. 98.

Concerning the expenses of copying and packing it is not possible to fix him before hand, they are at any rate not considerable, and you'll please to consider that you have to deal with a man of honour, who will not charge one 6d. more than he is charged for himself. Messrs. Fries and Co. will account with Messrs. Coutts and Co. The postage may be lessened as I have been told. I offer you of my Works the following new ones. A Grand Sonata for the Pianoforte alone £40. A Trio for the Piano with accomp^t of Violin and Violoncell for £50. It is possible that somebody will offer you other works of mine to purchase, for ex. the score of the Grand Symphony in A. With regard to the arrangement of this Symphony for the Piano I beg you not to forget that you are not to publish it until I have appointed the day of its publication here in Vienna. This cannot be otherwise without making myself guilty of a dishonourable act—but the Sonate with the Violin and the Trio in B flat may be published without any delay.

With all the new works, which you will have of me or which I offer you, it rests with you to name the day of their publication at your own choice: I entreat you to honor me as soon as possible with an answer having many orders for compositions and that you may not be delayed. My address or direction is

Monsieur Louis van Beethoven,

No. 1055 & 1056 Sailerstette 3d. Stock. Vienna.

You may send your letter, if you please, direct to your
most humble servant,
LUDWIG VAN BEETHOVEN.

(Mr. Birchall
Music Seller
No. 133 New
Bond Street,
London.)

[Harmony appears to be restored between Birchall and the composer.

The opus number 98 for the pianoforte score of the A major symphony is extraordinary. The new Trio offered for fifty pounds recalls the sketches of the years 1815-1816 (see note to Letter 210), among which there are sketches of a Trio in F minor.]

218. TO THE SAME

1055, SAILERSTETTE,
VIENNA, 14 *December*, 1816.

DEAR SIR,

I give you my word of honor that I have signed and delivered the receipt to the home Fries and Co. some day last August, who as they say have transmitted it to Messrs. Coutts and Co. where you'll have the goodness to apply. Some error might have taken place that instead of Messrs. C. sending it to you they have been directed to keep it till fetched. Excuse this irregularity, but it is not my fault, nor had I ever the idea of witholding it from the circumstance of the £5 not being included. Should the receipt not come forth at Messrs. C. I am ready to sign any other, and you shall have it directly with return of post.

If you find Variations—in my style—too dear at £30, I will abate for the sake of your friendship one third—and you have the offer of such Variations as fixed in our former lettres for £20 each Air.

Please to publish the Symphony in A immediately—as well as the Sonata—and the Trio they being ready here. The Grand Opera *Fidelio* is my work. The arrangement for the Pianoforte has been published here under my care, but the score of the Opera itself is not yet published. I have given a copy of the score to Mr. Neate under the seal of friendship and whom I shall direct to treat for my account in case an offer should present.

I anxiously hope your health is improving, give me leave to subscribe myself,

Deaɪ Sir,
your very obedient Servt.,
LUDWIG VAN BEETHOVEN.

[Owing to Birchall's illness, negotiations came to a standstill.]

219 TO BARON ZMESKALL

16th December, 1816.

HERE, DEAR Z.,

Accept my friendly dedication as I wish, namely, as an affectionate remembrance of our long-standing friendship, and as a proof of my esteem, and not as the end of a long-spun-out thread (for you were one of my earliest friends in Vienna). Farewell, keep from the rotten fortresses; an attack does more harm to them than to well-kept ones.

As always,
Your friend,
BEETHOVEN.

N.B. If you have a moment to spare, I beg you to tell me the highest one ought to reckon now for a livery (without cloak), washing, together with hat and boot money. Wonderful changes have taken place at my house. The man, thank God, has gone to the devil, and the woman seems on that account more determined to stick here.

[The Quartet in F minor (Op. 91), dedicated to his trusty friend Zmeskall, appeared in December 1816 at Steiner's. The friendship remained firm to the end of Beethoven's life, a praiseworthy testimonial for both.]

220. To Sir GEORGE SMART, London

Vienna, *December* 16, 1816,
1055, Sailerstätte, 3rd floor.

My worthy Sir,

You favour me with so much praise and so many marks of honour that you make me blush; I confess, however, that these are in the highest degree flattering to me, and I heartily thank you for the interest you have taken in my business affairs. These got somewhat in arrears through the strange situation in which our lost but fortunately found again Mr. Neate became involved. Your friendly letter of October 31 explains many things, and in a certain way to my satisfaction. I take the liberty of enclosing an answer to Mr. Neate, from whom I likewise received a letter, and beg of you kindly to support him in all the steps he has taken in my favour.

You say that the *cantata* will be useful with regard to your plan concerning the oratorios; I therefore ask you, whether you find £50 too high a price for the same? Up to now it has not brought me any profit; nevertheless, I should not like to ask a price which would result to you in a loss. Let us therefore say £40, and if it should prove an important success, then I hope you will have no objection to add the £10, so as to complete the first-mentioned sum. You will have the *right of publication*, and I will only stipulate that I may publish it *here* at a time which you will be kind enough to fix yourself, and not before. I have communicated to Mr. Häring your friendly opinions, and he unites with me in expressions of the highest esteem in which he has always held you.

Mr. Neate can have the various works with exception of the Cantata, when you have received them. And I hope that with your help it will be in his power to do something for me, which, considering my illness and the state of Austrian finance, would be most welcome.

Allow me to sign myself,

With the highest esteem and warmest friendship,

LUDWIG VAN BEETHOVEN.

[Among the documents in Schindler's *Beethovennachlass*, there is one from Neate which will make clear what Beethoven meant. This letter exists only in a German version: it is dated London, 29 October, 1816, and commences with Neate's confession of guilt. He recognises that he is to blame, but when he wrote the first letter he was troubled in mind—he finds himself accused by the man whom he most admires and esteems, to whom he is deeply indebted, and whose happiness he will never cease to promote to the best of his powers. "Until the question was decided whether my wife (whom I married on the 2nd of October) should be maintained by her family, I did not venture to appear as an artist. Now I remain a musician. Also, I would not allow any one else to act for you out of fear lest things should not turn out as they ought. *I acknowledge that I have not kept good faith with you, and in that I have acted wrongly*, but I have neglected every one—everything, and even myself. All your music remained in my trunk. But formerly I had the direction of the Philharmonic Society, of which I have again been appointed director this year. A meeting was held, and I offered all your music, if they would pay the price which I thought it deserved. They replied that one after the other should be rehearsed, for unfortunately the overtures had not pleased—and that then a sum would be offered. I opposed the idea of holding a kind of auction on your works, and left the meeting. My decision was to give a concert for your benefit, and myself to take all risk. You know the cause why this fell through. But as director I will make my influence felt this year. Since then I have offered your sonatas to a publisher; he said they were too difficult, and that he could not offer anything likely to be accepted. I will now play them, and when they are better known among artists, a better offer will be forthcoming. Money is very tight here, and the times are unusually wretched. The symphony you read about in the *Morning Chronicle was*, I believe, the one in C minor—the one in A has not as yet been produced. I shall insist on its being given this season—perhaps at the very first concert. I am glad that you are on terms of intimacy with Sir George Smart: he is a man of his word, also, my friend and your friend. Had it been otherwise, it might have affected, and to my injury, my whole career. Meanwhile, I am quite ready, if you insist on it, to deliver up every sheet of music. Sir George Smart will write by next post and confirm this. You say I have not even recognised your friendship, yet, when in Vienna I never ceased speaking of your friendship, and how proud I was of it. Also you may remember that I offered you the little I possess, which, however, you magnanimously declined. I have taken great trouble about the dedication of your Trio, and only found one lady who offered ten guineas in return. If you are satisfied with this, please let me know. Sir G. S. will give you his opinion with regard to a concert for your benefit. He understands such matters better than I do. I hope, however, the Philharmonic will organise a concert for you—free of expense. I again assure you that you have no two better friends than Sir G. S. and myself. Whatever is done in London to your advantage and honour will take place through us. I now hope you will think better of me. I am once again, as formerly, a free man.

"Write to me in French or German with Latin letters. I will write by next post to Häring.

"My address: CHARLES NEATE, Esq.,

"No. 10, High Row,

"Knightsbridge, London."

It was necessary to give the whole of this letter, so as clearly to establish the relationship between Neate and Beethoven, also Beethoven's business relations with English publishers. There was a third friend, Stumpff, who, together with the noble Englishmen Smart and Neate, remained faithful friends of Beethoven until his premature death.]

221. To CHARLES NEATE

[At Beethoven's dictation.]

VIENNA, 18th December, 1816.

MY DEAR SIR,

Both letters to Mr. Beethoven and to me arrived. I shall first answer his, as he has made out some memorandums, and would have written himself, if he was not prevented by a rheumatic feverish cold. He says: "What can I answer to your warmfelt excuses? Past ills must be forgotten, and I wish you heartily joy that you have safely reached the long-wished-for port of love. Not having heard of you I could not delay any longer the publication of the Symphony in A which appeared here some few weeks ago. It certainly may last some weeks longer before a copy of this publication appears in London, but unless it is soon performed at the Philharmonic, and something is done for me afterwards by way of benefit, I don't see in what manner I am to reap any good. The loss of your interest last season with the Philharmonic, when all my works in your hands were unpublished, has done me great harm; but it could not be helped, and at this moment I know not what to say. Your intentions are good and it is to be hoped that my little fame may yet help. With respect to the two Sonatas, Op. 102, for pianoforte and violoncello, I wish to see them sold very soon, as J have several offers for them in Germany, which depend entirely upon me to accept; but I should not wish, by publishing them here, to lose all and every advantage with them in England, I am satisfied with the 10 guineas offered for the dedication of the Trio, and I beg you to hand the title immediately to Mr. Birchall, who is anxiously waiting for it; you'll please to use my name with him.

I should be flattered to write some new works for the Philharmonic —I mean Symphonies, an Oratorio or Cantatas, &c. Mr. Birchall wrote as if he wished to purchase my *Fidelio*. Please to treat with him, unless you have some plan with it for my benefit concert, which in general I leave to you and Sir George Smart, who will have the goodness to deliver this to you. The score of the Opera *Fidelio* is not published in Germany or anywhere else. Try what can be done with Mr. Birchall or as you think best. I was very sorry to hear that the three Overtures were not liked in London. I by no means reckon them amongst my best works (which I can boldly say of the Symphony in A) but still they were not disliked here and in Pesth, where people are not easily satisfied. Was there no fault in the execution? Was there no party-spirit?

"And now I shall close, with the best wishes for your welfare, and that you enjoy all possible felicity in your new situation of life.

"Your true friend,

"LOUIS VAN BEETHOVEN."

[According to I. Moscheles (*Life of Beethoven*), who, in reference to the sentence, "I mean Symphonies, an Oratorio, or Cantatas," states that, "In consequence of this offer, the Philharmonic Society ordered a Symphony for one hundred guineas, and he accordingly sent them his Ninth Symphony."—TR.]

222. To FRAU NANETTE STREICHER, NÉE STEIN

December 28, 1816.

Already yesterday N. ought to have given you the New Year's note; she, however, did not do so. The day before, I had business with Maelzel, who is very pressed for time, as he is soon going away from here; hence you will quite understand that otherwise I should, without fail, have hurried up. Yesterday your dear good daughter came to see me, but I was very ill, worse than I can ever remember. It took my nice *servants* from seven to ten o'clock in the evening before they could get the oven alight. The excessive cold, especially in my state of health, brought on a chill, and all day yesterday I could scarcely move a limb. A cough, worse pains in my head than I have ever had, lasted the whole day. Already in the evening, about six o'clock, I had to go to bed, and I am still there, although I feel somewhat better. Your brother dined with me, and showed me great kindness. On the same day, as you know, namely December 27, I gave B. notice. The low behaviour of these persons is unbearable, and I wonder whether N. will behave better when the other has gone; but I doubt it, and in that case she will have to *clear out* at a moment's notice. For a housekeeper she has not sufficient training, is too *beastly*; you can tell by the face of the other that she is *lower than a beast*. As New Year's Day is approaching, I think six florins will be enough for Nannie; I have not given her the four florins for *getting her spencer made* on account of her *bad behaviour to you*. The other does not *really deserve a New Year's present*; besides, she had nine florins in advance, and when she goes away I shall only be able at most to deduct 4 or 5 fl. I hope you will *approve* of all this, and now my best thoroughly sincere wishes for your prosperity. I am in so many ways indebted to you that I often feel ashamed. Farewell; continue to be my friend.

As always,
Your,

To Countess Streicher,   L. v. Beethoven.
née v. Stein.

[with Beethoven's visiting card.]

[This is the first letter of the master to his noble-hearted friend, Nanette Streicher, wife of Joh. Andreas Streicher, the youthful friend of Fr. v. Schiller. As daughter of the well-known Augsburg pianoforte manufacturer Stein, she received a careful musical education. The married couple settled in Vienna in 1793, where they founded the Streicher pianoforte manufactory which afterwards became so celebrated. As both were excellent musicians, they naturally made friends with Beethoven, and they had already made the acquaintance of the youthful Beethoven in 1787. Nanette may be called Beethoven's good Samaritan. In the year 1813, when, like Beethoven, she was spending the summer away from the hot city, she took care of the neglected musician. Schindler was informed by Nanette Streicher that at that time Beethoven, "as regards bodily wants of all kinds, was in a pitiable condition. He had no good clothing, and was very short of linen." As with v. Zmeskall there were now endless complaints concerning the male servants, so with Frau Streicher, and in more forcible manner, concerning housemaids and cooks, as in the present letter concerning N. and B.=Nany and Baberl. The letters of Beethoven to Nanette Streicher in Otto Jahn's manuscript are sixty-two in number.]

223. To TOBIAS HASLINGER

[1816.]

Herr Adjutant, *guilty* or *innocent*, is requested to send the corrections of the Symphony in F and of the Sonata in A major, for just now I am staying in, and can get on sooner with the matter. Some people are especially worrying me about the *Sonata* so difficult

to play; who can help writing such difficulties ○ ▬ 𝄆♪♪♪♪ ! It is hoped that the health of the Adjutant, who is as uncouth as he is polite, will improve, so that at last he will be able to get on.

L. v. BETH.

[The Sonata (Op. 101) dedicated to Baroness Ertmann, appeared in 1817. Like all the last five Sonatas, it is difficult to perform, but there are no quarter-demisemiquavers in it.]

224. To STEINER & CO.

[December 1, 1816.]

It was arranged that in all the complete *copies* of the quartet, etc., the faults were to be *corrected*; notwithstanding this, the Adjutant is shameless enough to sell the same uncorrected. Even to-day I shall know how to resent and to punish this. I see that the lists are treated with simple derision; but here again I shall know what my *honour* demands, and certainly not give way. For the moment send me the song " A Schüsserl und a Reindl"; I want it. Take note that unless between to-day and to-morrow I am convinced of the warmer zeal of the Adjutant, he is threatened with a second disgraceful dismissal, although we should have liked, in accordance with our magnanimity, rather to have promoted him.

The song "an Schüsserl und a Riendl" will be found in the catalogue separately, or with variations.

G—s.

[The Quartet was the one in F minor (Op. 95). With regard to the song, we can only say that it was not by Beethoven.]

225. TO THE SAME

[1816.]

The whole business with this Symphony is very annoying to me, for now, neither the *score* nor the printed parts are free from faults; in these already printed *copies* the faults must be corrected with Indian ink, for which purpose Schlemmer must be employed. Then a list of all faults without exception must be printed and sent off; the roughest copyist might have written out the score just as it is now printed; such faulty, incomplete work, I have never yet seen the like of in anything of mine which has appeared in print. This is the result of *not* being willing to correct, of not having sent it to me sooner to look over, or even given me notice of it. The same copies which I am now sending have to be returned to me as soon as possible, together with the one already corrected, so that I may see what you have done correctly or incorrectly. Obstinacy punishes itself and innocent people have to suffer from it. I do not wish to know anything more about this mangled, wheel-broken *Symphony*. Faugh!

So *you* have really made it a matter of principle to treat the public without esteem, also, without any conscience, to detract from the *author's* reputation!

That I was ill, and am still so, and the longing of the public to have this work, etc., these are excuses which you might allege when you announce the list of the faults.

Heaven watch over you—the devil take you.

226. To TOBIAS HASLINGER

[1816.]

DEAR ADJUTANT,

I have seen nothing of the ruddy non-commissioned officer, probably he did not wait any longer at cashier Dam's, although he had to bring me back a note from him. I beg you therefore to send him once again to the cashier, for I have to receive money from there. The ruddy one has also to come straight to me from Herr Dam's. I am very sorry to have to be so troublesome to the G—l l—tnant, but I cannot employ my people for a thing of that kind. I therefore beg you to send the ruddy one to Cashier Dam and from there to me. I also beg you not to show the letter to Hebenstreit concerning the germanising of *Pianoforte*, but to send it back to me; as I am neither a learned nor an unlearned man, I am already in the habit of consulting him.

Farewell.

H—r H—

2ten " — "—Klchen

To Herr Adjutant.   mpr. 𝅝 𝅝 ♪ ♪ ♪ ♪ !

[The "ruddy one" must have been a messenger or an employé of the Steiner firm. Beethoven wished the term "Pianoforte" in the Sonata (Op. 101) to be replaced by "Hammerklavier." The abbreviations "H—r H." etc., stand for "Herr Haslinger, second little ragamuffin." . . . Who Hebenstreit was cannot be determined, although the name is known in musical history; he may have been related to the inventor of the Pantaleon.]

227. To STEINER & CO

[1816.]

By chance I have hit upon the following dedication for the new Sonata:

Sonata for the Pianoforte
or . . . Hammerclavier
composed and
dedicated to
Baroness Dorothea Ertmann, *née* Graumann
by
Ludwig van Beethoven.

If the title is already made, I have the two following proposals: either I pay for *the one title, that is at my cost,* or it is to be kept *for another new Sonata of mine,* for which the mines of the G—l l—t, especially *pleno titulo* G—l l—t and first State Councillor, have only to be opened so as to bring it to the light of day.

The title must first be shown to an expert linguist. Hammerclavier is certainly German, moreover the invention also is German; honour to whom honour is due. How comes it that I have had no news of the punishments which no doubt were carried out? As always your best

Amicus
ad amicum
de amico

I beg you to observe the strictest silence with regard to the dedication, as I wish it to come as a great surprise.

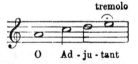

O   Ad - ju - tant

[Beethoven kept the German title "Hammerklavier" only for Op. 101 and Op. 106; after that he went back to the term in general use, Pianoforte or Klavier.]

228. To the Same

[1816 *end?*]

The painful matter is thus ended, and indeed to our mutual satisfaction, and this can only serve as pleasant knowledge to our dear faithful G—l l—t. Concerning the title of the new sonata, all that requires to be done is to transfer the title given to the Symphony in A in the *Wiener Mus. Zeitung*. The Sonata in A, my good G—l l—t, which is difficult to perform, will startle folk and make them reflect that the term "difficult" is a relative one; what is difficult for one person is easy for another. Consequently nothing should be said, although the G—l l—t must know that with this *everything is said ; for what is difficult, is also beautiful, good, great,* etc.; besides, every one perceives that this is the *strongest* praise which can be given; for *what is difficult makes one sweat.* As in talk the Adjutant has again shown himself treacherous and rebellious, his *right ear* ought to be roughly taken hold of and well pulled; further execution we reserve to ourselves, so that it may be fully carried out in our presence, and in that of our worthy G—l l—t. We hope our dear G—l l—t will have everything that is of use to him, especially a better Adjutant.

229. To GIANNATASIO DEL RIO

[1816, *February*?]

I tell you with great pleasure that at last I shall bring to you the dear pledge entrusted to me. For the rest, I once again beg you not to allow the mother in any way to influence him. How or when she may see him, all this I will arrange with you in detail in the morning. You ought even to have to some extent your eyes on your servants, for, in another matter, *mine* was bribed *by her*! All details by word of mouth, although silence on this subject would be most to my liking—for the sake, however, of your future citizen of the world these communications, to me so sad, are necessary.

With high esteem,
Your most humble servant and
friend, BEETHOVEN.

[The letter probably belongs to February 1816, in which year nephew Carl was sent to Giannatasio's Institution.]

230. TO THE SAME

[1816.]

I send you, dear Sir, my Carl's cloak, also a school-book, and I beg you to send me the list of the clothes and effects he brought with him, so that I may make a copy for myself; for as his guardian, I have to in every way look after his interests. To-morrow about half-past twelve I shall fetch Carl to go to a little concert, and after he has had something to eat with me, I will bring him back to you. With regard to the mother, I entreat you, *under the pretext that he is busy,* not to let her see him. No man knows and can judge better than I; all the plans that I have thought out for the child's welfare would in a measure be disturbed thereby. I will myself arrange with you how the mother in future can see Carl; I hope that in no case what happened yesterday will occur again. All responsibility in the matter I take on myself, and so far as I myself am concerned, the law court has given me full power to set aside, regardless of consequences, everything which is hurtful to the welfare of the child.

Had it been possible to look upon the mother as legally entitled, she certainly would not have been excluded from the guardianship. Whatever she may say, nothing has been made use of in an under-hand way against her; in full council, all were unanimous. I only wish I had no further doubts; the load, as it is, is heavy to bear. From my interview yesterday with Adlersburg, it may last ever so long before it is decided what belongs to the child. Am I again to be oppressed by the cares and by the doubts, which *through your Institute, I thought, had been finally dispersed*? Farewell.

> With esteem,
> Yours very truly,
> L. v. BEETHOVEN.

231. To the Same

[1816, *September?*]

If you have nothing to say against it, I beg you at once to send Carl to me. Being in a hurry, I forgot to say that all love and kindnesses shown by Frau A. G. to my Carl during his illness, has been entered in my great book of debts, and further, I will soon show that I shall ever have them in mind. Perhaps I may see you to-day with Carl. In haste,

> Yours truly,
> L. v. BEETHOVEN.

[In an unknown hand:]

Which is the more useful, painting or music?

[BEETHOVEN.] Both in painting and music a pair of snuffers is needed. Both exert a good influence; the latter, however, can also be of great use to ladies. Yes, of great use to them, in that with the receipts from concerts one can buy one's self a pair of snuffers.

232. To Frau NANETTE STREICHER

[1816?]

I thank you for your interest in me. Matters are already better —meanwhile I have endured much to-day from N., but have thrown half a dozen books at her head as a New Year's gift. We are trimming off the leaves (by sending B. away), or the branches, but we must get right down to the *roots*, so that nothing is left but the soil. I think I saw Frl. Sophie, and when I came home in the evening, the pain was so bad that I could do nothing but lie down on the sofa. I hope to see you soon either here or at your house.

In haste,

Your friend,

BEETHOVEN.

[The N. and B. are Nany and the housemaid Baberl. Frl. Sophie was probably one of Streicher's two daughters.]

233. TO THE SAME

[1816?]

So far as B. is concerned, she goes off early on Monday, so *the other can also come in either in the afternoon about 2 o'clock or 3 o'clock*, whichever you think best. N. asked me to-day, whether B. *was going to stop*. I said *no*, she could at latest remain till the first thing on Monday. For the rest I have good ground for thinking that N. and the other one continue their spying in your house. The evening before last, N. began to jeer at me for ringing the bell, after the manner *of all low people*, so she already knew that I had written *to you* about it. Yesterday the infernal tricks recommenced. I made short work of it, and threw at her my heavy chair which stands by the bed; for that I was at peace the whole day. So often however as they have to take a letter, or otherwise notice anything between us, they at once take vengeance on me. As for N.'s *honesty*, I can't say much for it; she likes to pick at dainties, and this may be the cause of it. As soon as the other maid arrives, I will, the first time you pay me a visit, call her in, and *in your presence* express my doubts about the kitchen-book. Monthly accounts will not begin at my house until every day a certain number of persons take their meals here; also the getting in of provisions made this impossible; but that I alone should want almost as much as if 2 persons were taking their meals, that was all very well, but———. At the midday meal we shall probably always be three in number, and also the 2 servants, as my nephew's tutor will always take his midday meal with us. I must thank Heaven in that I always find people who, especially now, take interest in me. For instance, I have found *one of the most distinguished* professors at the University here who attends most carefully to everything *connected with Carl's education*, and helps me with advice. If you should happen, when at Czerny's house, to meet those Giannatasios, *don't know anything that's being done about my Carl. Tell people it's not my habit to chatter about my plans; for every plan that is the matter of common talk, is no longer one's own. They might want to have a say in the matter, and I want these every-day sort of people as little for myself as for Carl.* I believe that you willingly forgive N., I certainly think so, but I can't but look on her as an *immoral* person. We shall see how matters go on, but usually when anything has happened between masters and servants, it is no longer any good. I beg you so to instruct the kitchen-maid about to enter my service, that she *must take sides* with you and me against N.; for that purpose I will often write something which the other need not know about. Besides, she may not be so greedy as N. and B.; in short, the kitchen-maid must always be in *opposition* to N., and so the extraordinary cheek, wickedness, and low-mindedness of N., who indeed is now somewhat subdued, will decrease. I assure you that what I have experienced with N. exceeds the behaviour of many servants I have had. I have strictly forbidden N. to have strange visitors, and especially from the first floor. And now farewell. As to servants, there is but one opinion everywhere, about their immorality, which must partly be ascribed to the general bad state of affairs here, and so you need never suffer or expect injury on my part about this. I shall always thankfully acknowledge what your friendship has brought me. I am only sorry that I should have been the innocent cause of unpleasantness in your house. I bless you in place of the Klosterneuburg clergy.

In haste,
Your friend,
BEETHOVEN.

N. just now asked me if I was going to have some one in place of B.; I answered yes.

[The Klosterneuburg clergy are named, because Frau Streicher lived in Klosterneuburg near Vienna, on the right bank of the Danube.]

234. TO FRAU ANTONIE VON BRENTANO

VIENNA, *the 6th February*, 1816.

HONOURED FRIEND!

I seize the opportunity through Mr. Neate, as distinguished an English artist as he is an amiable man, to recall myself to your remembrance, also to your good husband Franz. At the same time

I send an engraving on which is imprinted my countenance, many also see in it clearly my soul, let that be as it may. Meanwhile I have fought in order to snatch a poor unhappy child from an unworthy mother—and I have succeeded—*te deum laudamus*—but it causes me many sweet anxieties. I wish to you and Franz all earthly happiness with your souls united, in thought I kiss and embrace all your dear children, and wish that you may know this; but I commend myself to you, and only add, that I shall never forget and always willingly recall, the hours which I have spent in company with you both.

(I know that you will   With sincere respect,
receive Mr. Neate kindly   Your admirer and friend,
as one of my friends.)   LUDWIG VAN BEETHOVEN.

[Address in Beethoven's handwriting:]

For Frau von Brentano and Herr Franz v. Brentano, Frankfort.

[On the side of the address is written:]

"Demandès à la poste la maison de
Mr. François Brentano."

[The engraved portrait was most probably the Letronne-Höfel of 1814–15. The victory of Beethoven over his sister-in-law, Johanna, was no lasting one, for the lawsuit concerning the guardianship recommenced, and only came to an end, to Beethoven's satisfaction, in 1818.]

235. To Frau NANETTE STREICHER

[1816?]

The conscious criminal has got her sentence to-day—she behaved almost like Cæsar under Brutus's dagger, only with the difference, that in the first case there was truth at bottom, but with her, hopeless perfidy. The kitchen-maid appears more capable than the former *bad beauty-faced one*, she keeps quite out of sight, a sign that she does not expect a good character, which, however, I had thought of giving her. Now I want a new housekeeper. I beg you, however, to think over what is best, good cooking so that one can have good digestion, she must likewise be able to patch (not in State matters) shirts, etc. She must be useful, and have as much brains as are *necessary* for the wants of our persons, and at the same time be *sufficiently* careful of our purse. The new kitchen-maid made an ugly face when asked to carry up wood, but I hope that she will remember that our Saviour dragged His cross to Golgotha. I shall probably see you to-morrow.

In haste,
Your friend,
BEETHOVEN.

To Frau von Streicher, *née* Stein.

236. To GIANNATASIO DEL RIO

[1816?]

. . . As regards the mother, she has expressly wished to seek Carl at my house. You have seen me several times hesitate whether I should place confidence in her. You must attribute this to my feeling against inhumanity, all the more as it is not possible for her to do any harm to C. For the rest, you can easily imagine how to a man like myself, accustomed to live in freedom, all these anxious circumstances in which through Carl I am placed, often appear to me unbearable, and among them those concerning his mother; I am glad when I am not compelled to hear about them, and this is the cause why I generally avoid speaking about her to you. As regards C. I beg you to enjoin strictest obedience on him, and when he does not obey you or those whom he has to obey, to *punish* him. Treat him rather as you would your own child, and not as a pupil; for I have already remarked to you that during his father's lifetime he was forced to obedience by blows; that was very bad, but it cannot be changed all at once, and one must not forget this. For the rest, if you do not see me often, ascribe this to nothing else than my small inclination to go into society. That inclination is often stronger, also now and then less strong; this could be ascribed to a change in my feelings, but it is not so. Only the good apart from unpleasant circumstances is always present to me, and you must accuse this iron time if I do not show my thankfulness with regard to Carl in a more active manner; but God can change everything, and so also my circumstances may improve, in which case I certainly shall hasten to show you how much I am, as always, with high esteem your thankful friend,

L. v. BEETHOVEN.

I beg you to read this letter over to Carl.

237. To the Same

[1816?]

Carl must go to-day at 4 o'clock to H. B., I beg you therefore to ask his professor to let him leave about 3.30; if this cannot be done, he will have to remain away from the class; in the latter case I would come and fetch him, but in the former, meet him at the upper passage at the University. So that there may be no confusion, I beg you for a clear answer which of the two it shall be. As you have the reputation of being partial, I go out [illegible]—with Carl. If you do not see me, ascribe it to my grief, for I am now feeling very strongly this terrible occurrence. In haste your,

BEETHOVEN.

[The occurrence referred to concerns the change in the lawsuit with regard to the guardianship. The suit was transferred from the lower Austrian Court to the magistrate. Then, on remonstrance from the sister-in-law, Beethoven's "van" was not recognised as a sign of nobility, and the suit had to be sent back to the Lower Court.]

238. To the Same

[1816?]

The gossip of this bad woman has so worried me that I cannot answer everything to-day. To-morrow you will receive information on all matters, but do not let her in any case get at Carl, and insist on her only seeing him once a month; as it has been, so shall it go on for the future, and in no other way. In haste, your

L. VAN BEETHOVEN.

[According to the *Grenzboten* of 1857. The bad woman is naturally the "Queen of Night," Johanna van Beethoven.]

239. To the Chamberlain Baron Von SCHWEIGER

[1816 *or the end of* 1815?]

BEST, DEAREST, FIRST GYMNAST IN EUROPE!

The bearer of this is a poor devil (and there are many such! ! !)

You can help him by speaking to the gracious master, and asking whether he would perhaps buy one of his very small, but neat, well-made pianos? Then I beg you to recommend him to one or other of the chamberlains or *adjutants* of the Archduke Carl, to see whether it were not possible to get H.I.H. to buy one of these in-

struments for his wife? I also beg from the first gymnast an introduction to those chamberlains or *adjutants* for this poor devil.

Likewise your poor devil,

L. v. BEETHOVEN.

[The Archduke Charles married the Princess Henrietta of Nassau on
17 September, 1815, so this letter must anyhow be of later date. Who was
the poor pianoforte maker who is recommended? Von Koechel was surely right
when he remarked that it would be difficult to find out. Beethoven at times
praises Baron G. von Schweiger in extravagant manner; he once positively
declares him to be his "best friend."]

240. To GIANNATASIO DEL RIO

[1816?]

This, my dear friend, is the substance of *yesterday's conversation*
with H. v. Schmerling: Under no pretext whatever may Carl be
fetched from the institution without permission. *The mother can
never visit him here*—if she wishes to see him, she must apply to the
guardian who will make arrangements for that purpose.

In this way will the document from the court be drawn up—
for the present you may take this as a safe rule as to how the
woman should be treated. To-day about 12 o'clock I, together
with my friend Bernard, must trouble you by calling, for the
document must at once be drawn up, and also what you wish must
be inserted. S. likewise wants your letter enclosed. Last night this
Queen of Night was at the artists' ball till 3 o'clock, not only wanting
in sense, but even decency. . . . Oh, terrible, and into these hands
ought we, even for a moment, to entrust our precious treasure? No,
certainly not. I cordially embrace you as my friend, and likewise
as Carl's father.

Your

LUDWIG VAN BEETHOVEN.

241. To STEINER & CO.

[23rd January, 1817.]

To the worshipful G—l l—t von Steiner, to be delivered into
his own hands.

Publicandum.

We have, after due examination and after hearing our council,
resolved that henceforth all our works which have German titles
are to have *Hammerclavier* instead of Pianoforte, and of this our

excellent G—l l—t, together with his Adjutant and all others whom it concerns, are to take notice and act upon it.

Instead of Pianoforte *Hammerclavier*.

And so shall it be henceforth. Given, etc., etc., the 23rd, January, 1817.

From the
G—s.
m.p.

[The German *Hammerclavier*, instead of Pianoforte, was used in the titles of the Sonatas in A (Op. 101) and B flat (Op. 106).]

242. To Frau NANETTE STREICHER

[*27th January*, 1817.]

You surprise me, and with my quick power of imagination transport me at once to Bremen. Meanwhile it is somewhat too far to betake myself there at this moment. I have not Oberon's horn, and, besides, I am to-day at the Landstrasse and can pay you my long-intended visit, as I have to speak to you about something. About 3 o'clock this afternoon I shall tell you how much I am,

Your friend and servant,
L. v. Beethoven.

(In haste.)
27th Jan., 1817
for Frau von Streicher.

243. To Baron ZMESKALL

[*30th January*, 1817.]

Dear Z. You have wished to associate me with a Schuppanzigh, etc., and have disfigured my pure honest work. You are not my debtor, but I am yours, and now you have made me all the more so. I cannot write how much this gift pains me, and honest as I am, I must add that I cannot grant you a friendly look *on that account*. Although you are only an executive artist, yet you sometimes use your power of imagination, and it seems to me that at times it puts unnecessary whims into your head; so at least I judge from your letter following my *dedication*. However good I am, and prize all that is good in you, still I am angry, angry, very angry.

Your new debtor who however knows how to avenge himself,
L. van Beethoven.

[In December 1816 the Quartet in F minor, dedicated to his friend, had been published. Zmeskall thought that he must acknowledge the dedication by a present, which the sensitive Beethoven took amiss.]

244. To the Same

[31st January, 1817?]

Dear Z. of D—Z, etc., etc., etc., together with Burgundian grapes. I send here the Trio with the 'cello clef to it, and I beg you to keep it. In addition, I should be very glad if you would send your servant early the day after to-morrow, and indeed, if it was possible, between 11 and 11.30, up to 12 I am sure to be at home. Kindly at the same time ask him, if he finds any one for my service, to tell me of it. I have already made inquiries elsewhere, for it is too annoying with such people; I could really at any time get into great perplexity through them, both are of the same kidney, and only compassion, which they in no wise deserve and really do not need, has caused me to be patient so long. Farewell master and lord of all Buda and Burgundian mountains.

Yours,
L. Beet[hoven].

[The trio was probably the one (Op. 97) published by Steiner during the summer of 1816. The worries about the maid-servant are so aggravating to Beethoven that he is intending to have a man-servant.]

245. To Frau NANETTE STREICHER

13th February, 1817.

My dear worthy Streicher,

I dare not go out to-day, but to-morrow about 10 o'clock I will come to you, only arrange that the landlord on the first floor gives us some idea of the upper rooms; if I then find them suitable I will at once take them—yesterday several things made it impossible for me to see you. Arrange also that we get one day's grace

In haste,
Your friend,
Beethoven.

246. To Baron ZMESKALL

Dear Z.,   [21s *February*, 1817.]

It is only a single question about the servant, then I will go at once myself to the police station, and Master Strauss instead of a nosegay [*Sträusschen*] will be locked up for 24 hours. I beg you therefore to let me know when I can see you for a moment to-day, the afternoon I should like best; however if you are not able, fix another hour. It would be well for you *to ask the former servant about where he lives*; do not say anything about the police until we have spoken on the matter together.

In haste,
Yours,
BEETH(OVEN).

[The name is half torn off.]

Herr von Zmeskall.

[According to the original manuscript in the Vienna Court Library; first printed by Nohl.]

247. TO THE SAME

[22nd February, 1817.]

Only let me know whether it was the same person, *in case it was not*, I would perhaps only go to-morrow to the police, for I have got pressing work for the moment; only a few words about it.

Yours, in haste,
BEETHOVEN.

To Herr von Zmeskall.

248. To GIANNATASIO DEL RIO

[February 1817.]

HONOURED FRIEND!

The Queen of Night took me by surprise yesterday, uttering a real anathema against you. Her usual boldness and insolence towards me showed itself again this time, and for a moment made me hesitate, and almost believe what she said might perhaps be correct. But later on when I came home, there was the following result from the decision of the Law Court which has turned out as desired, and of which I now give you what is most important, although perhaps by this evening you will have a *copy* of it.

"A decree of the Law Court handed to me, orders that with regard to visits of my nephew to his mother, or fetching him away out of the house, positively nothing ought to take place but what has been arranged, approved of, and allowed by myself; also, that every time the arranging and ordering of such things are absolutely left to my judgment. The mother of the boy has therefore only to address herself to me if she wishes to see him, when, according as I find good, I will fix when and how, and whether it is to be done."

Carl received the enclosed little book from his mother secretly yesterday, ordering him *not to say anything about it*. You therefore see that we must give it back to her, also how careful we must be. If you think right, I will fetch *my little Carl to-day about one o'clock to dinner*, so that he may see something of the *carnival* which will also be celebrated at your house, and (as he says) by his *school-fellows*. I heartily embrace you to whom I readily ascribe all that my Carl may bring forth of good and great.

In haste and esteem,
Your friend,
BEETHOVEN.

(*Kindly tell me whether I may venture to fetch Carl to dinner.*)

[Nephew Carl remained in the Institution of Herr Giannatasio del Rio until 1818.]

249. To CHARLES NEATE

VIENNA, *19th April*, 1817.

MY DEAR NEATE,

Since the 15th October I have had a severe illness, I am still feeling the effects of it, and am not quite myself. You know that I can only earn my living by my compositions; since my illness I have been able to do very little in the way of composition, and so have been able to earn very little indeed; all the more welcome would it have been to me if you could have done something for me. Meanwhile I presume that the result of everything is *nothing*.

You have indeed written *complaints about me to Hering*, which, considering my fair dealing with you, are by no means deserved. Meanwhile I must justify myself in the matter: namely, the opera *Fidelio* had already been written several years ago, but the book and the text were very faulty; the book had to be thoroughly recast, and owing to that, several of the numbers had to be lengthened, others shortened, while again others needed entirely fresh music. So, for instance, the Overture is quite new, and so are several of the other numbers; but it is possible that the opera may be in London, in its *original* shape, in which case it must have been stolen, for such a thing in theatres is scarcely possible to avoid. So far as the Symphony in A is concerned, as you have not written any satisfactory answer, I shall probably have to publish it. I would willingly have waited three years, if you had written to me that the Philharmonic Society had taken it—but everywhere nothing—nothing. Now as regards the *pianoforte Sonata with 'cello*, I gave you *a month*, if I then receive no answer from you, I should publish it in *Germany*; as likewise I have heard as little from you about the other works, so I have given them to a German publisher, who begged me for them, yet I *have agreed for myself by writing* (*Hering has read this document*), *that he shall not publish the Sonatas until you have sold them in London.* You ought to be able to get at least 70 or 80 ducats in gold for these two Sonatas; the English publisher can fix the day when they are to *appear in London, on the same day then* they will also appear in Germany. In this way Birchall bought and received from me the Grand Trio and the pianoforte Sonata with violin. I also beg you as a last kindness to *send me an answer* as *quickly as possible about the Sonatas*. Frau v. Jenny swears about all that you have done for me, I also, that is, I swear *that you have done nothing for me*, that you are doing *nothing* for me, and again will not do *anything* for me, *summa summarum Nothing! Nothing!! Nothing!!!*

I assure you of my perfect respect, and I hope at least as a *last kindness, a speedy answer.*

Your most devoted servant and friend,

L. V. BEETHOVEN.

[This important letter gives further explanation of the connection between Beethoven and Charles Neate. The master feels compelled to read a lesson to his otherwise "dear English countryman" and friend. On the other hand, there are many exaggerations, and inaccuracies too, on the side of Beethoven. First of all the remark that Beethoven could only live by his compositions. That leads to misunderstanding. In this we trace something of a mental reservation. Beethoven personally means his own personal wants, whereas his real annuity—the one he receives from his three known patrons—was to be devoted to the education and keep of his nephew. In comparison with other periods, the winter quarter 1816-7 was, however, very poor as regards compositions.

Frau von Jenny was really a Countess von Genney, of whom indeed, in all the biographies of Beethoven—at any rate up to 1902—there has been no mention, yet her name often occurs in the Conversation Books of 1822-3. Her name is mostly connected with that of Baron von Pronay, especially at a time when Beethoven wished, in the spring of 1823, to rent the villa at Hetzendorf from this baron. In a Conversation Book of April to May 1823, we find the following: "To Schindler the baroness said that 'her daughter was a very great admirer of you (Beethoven), for she plays all your compositions on the violin, and extremely well.'" There were many intrigues about the house in Hetzendorf in the year in which the Ninth Symphony was written. Finally, thanks to this lady admirer, everything was settled as desired. We read: "Genney thinks that there has been a misunderstanding; she at once took steps, ordered Pronay to write to him, that he would bring him next morning the key." So finally Beethoven got the Hetzendorf villa at a reasonable price.]

250. To Countess M. Von ERDÖDY

HEILIGENSTADT, *19th June*, 1817.

My honoured, suffering friend! most worthy Countess. I have been worried all along, am too much loaded with cares, and since the 6th October, 1816, I have been constantly ill; moreover, on the 15th October I caught a very severe cold which forced me to keep my bed for a long time, and many months passed before I could venture to go out, even a little. I *still feel the effects* from it. I changed doctors, as mine, a crafty Italian, had such strong underhand designs on me, and lacked both honesty and intelligence. This was in April 1817. I had now from the 15th April to the 4th May, to take every day six powders, six cups of tea; this lasted up to the 4th May; after that, I received again some kind of powder which I had to take again six a day, and I had to rub myself three times with a volatile ointment. Then I journeyed here, where I am taking the baths. Since yesterday I have received a new medicine, namely, a tincture, of which I have to take twelve spoonfuls a day. Every day I hope that the end of this wretched state has come; although I feel somewhat better, it seems that it will be a long time before I am quite restored to health.

You can imagine how all this affects my life! My hearing has become worse; already, formerly, I was not able to look after myself and my wants, and it is now as then . . . and my cares have been increased through my brother's child. Here I have not even found proper rooms. As it is difficult for me to look after myself, I have to turn now to this person now to that, but I am none the better, and a *prey* to wretched men. A thousand times have I thought of you, dear honoured friend, as I do now, but my own grief has cast me down. C. gave me Linke's letter, he lives with Schwab, I lately wrote to him to inquire how much the journey would cost to come to you, but I have received no answer. As my nephew has *holidays* from the end of August up to the end of October, I could then, health permitting, come to you; we should probably get rooms for study and comfortable living, and if really I were for some long time among old friends who, notwithstanding rascally people, have remained so, I might get well again and happy. Linke must write and tell me the cheapest way I could make the journey, for, unfortunately, my expenses are so great, and owing to my illness, as I can only do a little writing, my income is small, and this small capital, through the fault of my dead brother, I must not touch; as my annuity grows less, is, in fact, almost nothing, I must keep this. I write frankly to you, dearest

Countess, but on that account you will not misunderstand me. In spite of all, I want nothing, and would certainly not accept anything from you; it is only a question as to how I can come to you in the most economical manner; everything in my present position has to be thus considered, hence, my friend, be not concerned about it. I hope your health is better than I formerly heard. May Heaven preserve the excellent mother for her children's sake; yes, on that account alone you deserve the best of health. Farewell! best, most honoured Countess, let me soon have news of you.

Your true friend,

BEETHOVEN.

[This remarkable letter is really the last one which we possess from the composer to his musical countess. We do not learn from it where the Countess Erdödy was at that time. In 1819 a musical greeting to this friend is mentioned, and then, from what we read in the Conversation Books, came the tragic fate which overtook the Erdödy house. The doctor, the "crafty Italian," was probably Dr. Malfatti, uncle of Therese Malfatti. It came to a complete break with this doctor, who, however, gradually became one of the most noted doctors in Vienna. Only when the composer was on his death-bed did Anton Schindler, by his earnest efforts, bring Dr. Malfatti to the composer, and effect a complete reconciliation. The wish to spend the late summer and autumn in the unnamed residence of the countess does not appear to have been fulfilled. The small capital which, owing to the prosperous year 1814 to 1815, Beethoven had been able to put aside, was not to be touched; it remained the inviolable property of his nephew Carl.]

251. To Frau NANETTE STREICHER

NUSSDORF, 7th July [1817].

MY WORTHY FRIEND!

I received your letter here with mention of your bad fall. I hope that you will soon be better; tepid baths heal all wounds. The bad weather the day before yesterday, when I was in town, prevented me coming to you. I hastened back here yesterday morning, but found that my servant was not at home, and that he had even taken with him the key of the rooms. The weather was very cool; coming from town, I had nothing but a thin pair of trousers on, and so I was obliged to wander about, three long hours; this did me harm, and I felt ill for the whole day. You see how servants attend to the house!—so long as I am ill, a different connection with different people would be necessary. However much I like solitude, it especially pains me now, as it is scarcely possible, with all the medicines and baths, to work as formerly; and then there is the anxious fear that perhaps I shall never be better again, so that I even lose faith in my present doctor, who now at last declares my complaint to be disease of the lungs. I will consider about a house-keeper; if with this total moral corruption of the Austrian Government one could be assured of getting an honest person, it would be easily settled, but—but—! ! ! Now a great *request* to Streicher; ask him in my name to be kind enough to prepare a pianoforte especially adapted to my weak hearing; I want the tone to be as strong as possible. I have long had the intention to buy one, but at the moment it is very difficult for me; perhaps later on it will be easier for me. Until then. I should like you to *lend me one*, but certainly not gratis; I am ready to pay you ordinary charge for six months in convention coin, and in advance. Perhaps you do not know that although I have not always had a *piano* of yours, I have always preferred your instruments ever since 1809. Streicher is the only person who could give me such a *piano* as I really want. I am extremely sorry to be troublesome to any one, as I am accustomed rather to do things for other people than to get other people to do anything for me—whatever proposition you make to me with regard to this matter, I will accept, and willingly fulfil your conditions. Many thanks for the 20 fl. you lent me, also for the spoon, which I here send back. I shall see you soon for a moment —kind remembrances to you all.

Your friend and servant,
L. v. BEETHOVEN.

To Frau v. Streicher.

[This letter also shows that in addition to the female servant, there was a man-servant. His present physician was Dr. Staudenheim or Staudenheimer. Towards the improvement of the pianofortes in the Streicher manufactory, Beethoven himself contributed much.]

252. TO FERDINAND RIES

VIENNA, 9th July, 1817.

DEAR FRIEND!

The offers made to me in your honoured letter of the 9th June are very flattering. From the present letter you will see how highly I think of them. Were it not for my unfortunate illness, whereby I need more nursing and money, especially in journeying to a foreign country, I should have accepted the offer of the Philharmonic Society *without conditions*. Place yourself, however, in my position, think how many hindrances I have to fight against more than any other artist, and then judge whether my demands are unfair. Here they are, and I beg you to communicate them to the directors of the named Society:

(1) I will be in London at latest in the first half of the month of January.

(2) The two great Symphonies which I have just composed will be ready by then, and will be and remain the sole property of the Society.

(3) The Society is to give me for them 300 *guineas*, and 100 *guineas* travelling expenses, which, however, will amount to much more, as I must really have some one to accompany me.

(4) As I shall at once begin to work at the composition of these great Symphonies, the Society after accepting my proposal, is to send me here the sum of 150 guineas, so that, without delay, I can provide myself with a carriage and see to other necessary preparations for the journey.

(5) The conditions about not appearing at the head of another orchestra and publicly, about not conducting, and about showing preference to the Society under equal conditions, have been accepted by me, and with my love of honour are all self-understood.

(6) That I may venture to hope for the assistance of the Society in arranging and carrying out one or, according to circumstances, several *benefit concerts*. The special friendship of some of the directors of your esteemed Society, also the kind sympathy shown by all artists for my works, are guarantees that I shall all the more zealously endeavour not to fall short of what the Society expects.

(7) I still ask for the consent or agreement to the above in English, signed by three Directors in the name of the Society.

That I look forward to making the acquaintance of the worthy Sir George Smart, and to seeing you and Mr. Neate again, you can well understand. If only instead of this letter I could myself fly over!

Your sincere admirer and friend,

[Postscript on a separate sheet:]

L. v. BEETHOVEN.

DEAR RIES!

I heartily embrace you! I have intentionally had the answer to the Society written out by some one else, so that you might read it the easier, and put it before the Society. I am convinced of your good intentions as regards myself. I hope that the *Philharmonic* Society will accept my proposal, and I can assure them that I will use all my powers to show myself worthy of such an honourable offer from such a distinguished society of artists. What is the strength of your orchestra? How many violins, etc., etc., with single or double wind? Is the hall big, good for sound?

[This joyful letter of the master is the answer to the very enthusiastic letter of his pupil Ferdinand Ries of 9 June, 1817. I here give a fairly long quotation from it:

"DEAREST BEETHOVEN!

"For a long time I have again been quite forgotten by you, although I cannot think there is any other reason than your being very busy. . . .

"Indeed, dear Beethoven, the thanks that I owe you *must ever remain a debt*, which, I think I may say with open heart, I have never forgotten; although many a time I have been represented to you by my enemies as thankless and envious, and so I have always had the strongest wish to give you a proof of it by something more than words. This ardent wish is now at last, so I hope, about to be fulfilled, and I trust again to find in my old teacher my old loving friend. The Philharmonic Society, of which our friend Neate is now a director, and where your compositions are preferred to all others, wishes to give you a proof of the high respect and recognition for the many beautiful moments which we have so often enjoyed through your extraordinarily gifted works—and I feel it as a most flattering compliment to myself to be commissioned, together with Neate, to write first to you about the matter. In short, dear Beethoven, we should much like to have you next winter amongst us here in London." . . .

(Next follow the conditions made by the Philharmonic Society, which were nearly all repeated in Beethoven's answer to Ries.) Then follows:

"Now you are free to deal as you like with publishers, also with Sir George Smart who has offered you 100 *guineas* for an oratorio in one act, and especially commissions me to remind you to send an answer. . . . The Intendant of the Grand Italian Opera, G. Ayrton, is an especial friend of ours." A. promises to give a commission for an opera. Then follow these very important words:

"We still want some one here who will set things going once again, and who will keep the gentlemen of the orchestra in order.

"Yesterday evening was our last concert, and your beautiful Symphony in A was given with extraordinary success. It makes one afraid even to think of writing a Symphony when one reads and hears such a work! Only write to me very soon a detailed answer, and give me the hope of soon seeing you here. I remain ever

"Your sincere and grateful friend,

"FERD. RIES.

"My hearty greeting to Zmeskall, Zizius, Krumpholz and others."

Nothing came of the planned journey towards London either in this or in any later year. A diary—probably belonging to this year—contains the following: "Something must happen—either a journey and for that purpose the necessary works must be written, or an opera—if you still remain here next winter it would be better to decide what opera, in the case only of fair conditions—the summer residence here, everything must be decided, how, where?" And a little lower down, the following touching words of despair: "Oh God, help, Thou seest that I am abandoned by all men because I will do nothing unjust, hear my prayer, yet only for the future, to be together with my Carl, as nothing for the present seems to show it possible. O hard fate, O cruel lot, no, no, my wretched condition never comes to an end." . . .

253. To WILHELM GERHARD, Leipzig

NUSSDORF, *July* 15, 1817.

DEAR SIR,

You once honoured me with a request that I should set to music some of your anacreontic songs. Being very busy, my not answering it was impossibility rather than lack of courtesy. To gratify your wishes was still more difficult, as those poems which you sent me do not in the least lend themselves to vocal music. Pictorial descriptions belong to painting; even the poet in this respect may, in comparison with my art, esteem himself lucky, for his domain in this respect is not so limited as mine, yet the latter extends further into other regions and to attain to our kingdom is not easy. My illness, for nearly 4 years, is partly the cause of my answering many applications by silence. Since last October, 1816, my illness has increased. I had a severe cold which led to inflammation of the lungs; I say all this in order that you may not think me discourteous, or else, like many others, misjudge me.

With respect,

Yours truly,

LUDWIG VAN BEETHOVEN.

To Herr Wilhelm Gerhard in Leipzig (Saxony).

[The merchant Gerhard often came to Vienna on business. On one of his visits Beethoven made him a present of the autograph of *Gretels Warnung*. The above letter is of special interest, as Beethoven seldom broached æsthetic questions.]

254. To FRAU NANETTE STREICHER

VIENNA, *July* 30, 1817.

WORTHY FRIEND!

On account of bad weather I could not get here sooner than Thursday, and you had already left. What a *trick* [*Streich*] on the part of Frau v. Streicher!!!! to Baden???!!! so in Baden. I have spoken to your husband; the interest he takes in me has brought about both weal and woe, for he almost shook my resolve to be *resigned*. God knows what will happen, but as I have always helped others, whenever I was able, so I also trust that he will deal mercifully with me. As regards the housekeeper, whom you know and at any rate have found honest, it might be seen what she can do in the way of *cooking* before she came to me. This, however, cannot be managed, until you return to town, when? For the rest do not be *led away by your husband to play certain tricks.* There's time, too, about the house. In the Gärtner street there are houses on the opposite side where one could really enjoy an extraordinary fine view; everything depends on your return. *How ever did you send your letters to me at Nussdorf?* Insist on your daughter being diligent, so that she may become a good wife. To-day happens to be Sunday. Shall I read you something out of the Gospels: "Love one another," etc., etc. I stop, and with kind regards to you and your excellent daughter, I wish that all your wounds may be healed. If you go to the old ruins, think that Beethoven lingered there; if you wander through the mysterious fir-forests, think it was there Beethoven often poetised, or, as it is called, composed.

In haste,
Your friend and servant,
BEETHOVEN.

[Enclosure.]

BEST FRAU V. STREICHER!

The enclosed letter, as you will see by the date, ought to have been sent to you last Sunday. As regards Frau v. Stein, I beg her not to let Herr v. Steiner be petrified, so that he may still be able to serve me; or, Frau von Stein might not be too much of a stone as regards Herr v. Steiner, &c.

As for my health, it is certain that there are signs of improvement, but the chief complaint is still there, and I fear that I shall never be rid of it. My Good Frau Streicher, play no tricks on your dear husband, but rather be Frau v. Stein towards everybody!!! Next Wednesday and Thursday I shall spend in town, where I shall again have a chat with Streicher. About the housekeeper, I wish you were here, i.e. as if by chance, however much I rejoice at your enjoying the Baden air; meanwhile when will you again rejoice me here with your presence?

All kind wishes to your dear
daughter and Fr. v. Streicher,
Your friend and servant,
BEETHOVEN.

Where are my blankets?

Where? Where?

[Frau v. Streicher's maiden name was Stein (Stone).—Tr.]

255. To the Same

[*Summer* 1817.]

I beg you, worthy Fr. v. Streicher, to accept from me these 6 bottles of genuine *Eau-de-Cologne*, which you cannot easily get here, even by paying. I hope to see you soon, if only a second deluge is not approaching; anyhow we are *bound* to get dripping wet, after rain continually pouring down from the sky.

In haste,

Your friend and servant,

BEETHOVEN.

To Frau v. Streicher.

256. To XAVER SCHNYDER Von WARTENSEE

August 9, 1817

You remember once having been to my house in Vienna, and having given me written proof of it; such things from a noble nature like yours does me good—continue to climb up into your heaven of art, for there is no calmer, purer joy than that which it offers. You once wished to see me gazing in astonishment at the grandeur of nature in Switzerland. I myself also, if God restore me to health, which for several years has been getting worse, really hope to go there. Herr v. Bihler, the bearer of this, who is on his travels with his pupil, v. Puthon, ought, even without me, really to expect a friendly reception by you. Meanwhile I fancy you lay great stress on my introduction to him, and strongly enjoin upon you to show him as much kindness as possible.

Your friend and servant,

L. v. BEETHOVEN.

To Herr Xaver Schnyder von Wartenstein (?) in Lucerne (Switzerland).

[Wartensee, poet and musician, was born at Lucerne in 1786. He came to Vienna in 1810 or 1811 to study music seriously, but did not succeed in becoming Beethoven's pupil. In 1817 he settled in Frankfort, where he died in 1868. Among Schindler's papers in the Berlin Library there is a most respectful letter from W. to Beethoven with important comments on certain passages in the Arietta of the Sonata in C minor (Op. 111).]

257. To Frau NANETTE STREICHER

26th August [1817.]

WORTHY FRAU VON STREICHER!

With pleasure I received your invitation which I accept, to-day and to-morrow I cannot trouble you, as in spite of the bad weather I have to go to Vienna. Your *patent piano* is not in any need of recommendation from me, but for my sake I have long had the wish to see it; in a few days I will inquire when you are at home, and when I may have the pleasure of visiting you.

(J. 1817)
On the 26th August
I have received the
letter to Elise Müll.
For Frau von Streicher,
née Stein
at merchant Perger's
the [three?] stairs
in the court.

As always,
Your friend,
BEETHOVEN.

[Fräulein Elise Müller, the famous pianist, was a daughter of the great Beethoven enthusiast, Dr. C. W. Müller, of Bremen. Thanks to the Müller family and to Dr. Iken, there was at a very early period a flourishing Beethoven cult in Bremen.]

258. To the Archduke RUDOLPH

NUSSDORF, *1st September*, 1817.

YOUR IMPERIAL HIGHNESS!

I always hoped that I should be able to betake myself to Baden, but my indisposition continues, and though there is improvement, I am not quite well again. What I used and still use as a remedy are means of all kinds, of all shapes; now I shall probably have entirely to give up the hope which I have nourished, of being perfectly restored. I hear that Y.I.H. looks wonderfully well, and from such false premises one might conclude excellent health, yet I hear that you *are* in the very best, and that creates in me most lively sympathy. I hope likewise that when Y.I.H. comes back to town, I shall be again able to help in your offerings to the Muses. God will probably hear my prayer, and once again free me from so much adversity, for I have trusted Him from childhood onwards and I have done good whenever I could; I therefore trust in Him alone, and I hope that the Almighty will not let me, amidst all my misfortunes, go utterly to ruin. I wish Y.I.H. all that is beautiful and good, and

as soon as you are back again in town will betake myself at once
to Y.I.H.

Your Imperial Highness's faithful
and most obedient servant,

L. v. BEETHOVEN.

[Beethoven's religious feelings, his true resignation to the will of God,
could scarcely be more clearly expressed than in this letter to his revered
archduke.]

259. TO BARON ZMESKALL

11th September, 1817.

Dear Z. The answer came already yesterday from London, but
in English. Don't you really know some one who could read it off
for us?

In haste,
Yours,

BEETHOVEN.

[This was a new answer to Beethoven's letter to Ferdinand Ries with
regard to the projected journey to London. The Fischhoff manuscript states
that the whole scheme failed on account of the condition made by Beethoven
that he must have some one to travel with him. We read further: "There
were many important obstacles [to the journey to England], of which one,
the most important, the most impossible, was to find a travelling companion
agreeable to him, Even his deafness was less a hindrance than this. Three
persons at least were necessary, namely, his physician, a friend and a servant.
But propositions were made by his sympathetic friends; even his brother
[Johann] offered to accompany him. Friend Zmeskall had recommended
to him a highly trustworthy man, but he would accept nothing, and said
he would rather travel all alone, which was equally impossible; and so the
journey was given up. Yet he always retained the wish to go to England."]

260. TO FRAU NANETTE STREICHER

NUSSDORF, *25th September*, 1817.

In spite of wind and rain, I arrived here early about 7 o'clock
to-day. Although I tried to start out yesterday evening in the rain,
but—fire cannot resist water. I found the *servant* with the *medicine*,
but *not* your letter—yet I very much wished to read your explanations about game in housekeeping. I could still give notice for the
rooms in the Gärtnergasse if it could be mathematically calculated
how long both routes were from the town—what do you think?
&c., &c. Your shoemaker might send me some good *boot-polish*
which does not smudge like the stuff that my *fidelis* cheated me
with—his account of 27 fl. I will pay in a day or two in town. If

you would kindly lend me 25 fl. for a few days, that would be very nice, for I yesterday forgot the key of my cash-box, when I again wanted money. I should like to *read* something explicit about game and about the housekeeper. Greetings from us to your well-behaved daughter.

Tantus quantus lumpus L. v. BEETHOVEN.

N.B.—We want a few dusters as preliminary to our future housekeeping.

261. TO THE SAME

NUSSDORF, *2nd October*, 1817.

To-morrow I will come to you in the afternoon; if you would kindly tell the housekeeper to come, you would greatly oblige me. Yesterday I reckoned up future expenses with some one, and *he* painted everything to me in terrible colours; he counted for servants 2 fl., and for the housekeeper 2 fl. for food alone; in this way the servant would have 20 fl. a month, and the housekeeper 120 fl. yearly, the total per year for both would alone cost 1704 fl.! —ought it really to be so? Heaven have mercy upon us. Farewell, I hope to see you to-morrow, for I come *especially for that purpose* from the *country* to the Landstrasse.

In haste,
Yours,
L. v. BEETHOVEN.

262. TO THE AULIC COUNCILLOR VON MOSEL

[1817?]

I heartily rejoice in the same opinion, which you share with me in regard to the terms indicating time-measure which have been handed down to us from the barbarous period of music. For, only to name one thing, what can be more senseless than *Allegro* which, once for all, means *merry*, and how far off are we frequently from such conception of this time-measure, in that the music itself expresses something quite contrary to the term. So far as the four principal movements are concerned, but which are far from having the truth or importance of the four principal winds, we consider them last. It is another matter with words indicating the character of a piece; these we cannot give up, as time refers rather to the body, whereas *these are already themselves related to the soul of the piece*. As for me, I have often thought of giving up these senseless terms,

Allegro, Andante, Adagio, Presto, and for this Maelzel's Metronome offers the best opportunity. I herewith give you *my word*, that I will *no more* use them in my new compositions. It is another question whether by this means we shall bring the M[etronome] into the so necessary *general* use. I scarcely think so. I have no doubt they will call out that I am a *despot*; anyhow, that would be better than to accuse us of *feudalism*. Hence I am of opinion that the best thing for our country, when once *music* has become a National Want, and every village schoolmaster would have to promote the use of the Metr., would be for Maelzel to seek to bring out by subscription a certain number of metronomes at the higher price; and when the number covers his expenses, he will be able to supply the other necessary Metron. for the Musical National Want, and at so cheap a rate, that we may expect them to become in general and widespread use. It is, of course, understood that some persons must place themselves at the head of such a movement to give a stimulus to it; so far as I am of any influence you may certainly count on me, and with pleasure I await the post which you will herein assign to me.

Sir,

With high esteem,

Yours most devotedly,

Ludwig van Beethoven.

[After the numerous letters of lamentation about domestic matters, the "Queen of Night," and matters concerning mere earthly wants, the present letter dealing with æsthetics, addressed to the author of the *Salieri Biography*, is quite refreshing. Here an energetic word is spoken in favour of German terms in place of the Italian words expressing *tempo*. Maelzel had become reconciled with Beethoven, as we learn from a letter of his of the year 1818. Other composers were in sympathy with these efforts; they could not, however, succeed in suppressing the Italian expressions. In regard to the Maelzel Metronome, Schindler informs us that there were two kinds, radically different from each other in construction. This accounts for the different metronome figures given by Beethoven himself, e.g. for the A major Symphony.]

263. To TOBIAS HASLINGER

[1817?]

See about the little house once again, and let me know; also I should very much like you to get me the *article on education*. It is a matter of moment to me to be able to compare my ideas on the subject with other people's, and still more, to improve on them.

Beethoven at the age of forty-seven (1817)

From a portrait by A. von Kloeber

As regards the little Adjutant, I think I have now adopted the right way with regard to his education.

Your
Contra Fa,
m.p.

[This letter appears to belong to the year 1817, in which, on his nephew's account, the subject of education deeply engaged Beethoven's attention.]

264. To STEINER & CO.

[1817.]

The G—l l—t firm must do what they can for this young artist, Bocklet from Prague, the bearer of this. He is a performer on the violin, and we hope that our writing will be taken notice of, all the more as we with the wildest devotion call ourselves

Your
G—s.

265. To GIANNATASIO DEL RIO

[1817?]

You here receive, my worthy friend, the coming quarter's money through Carl. I beg you to take into greater consideration his feelings and temperament, as the latter is especially the lever to all that is good, and however derisively and meanly temperament has often been looked upon, yet it is considered by our great writers, as, for instance, Goethe, etc., as a special quality; yes, without temperament, many assert that there cannot be a really distinguished man, and that no depth can be in him. The time is too short to say more on the subject; more by word of mouth as to how I mean to deal with Carl.

Your friend and servant,

L. v. BEETHOVEN.

Alser suburb near the Apple 2 stairs, door No. 12, Leibertz, dressmaker.

266. To the Same

[*Probably* 1817.]

It is, at any rate, the first time that I have had to be reminded of a duty, to me a pleasing one; being busy both with my art and with other matters, made me entirely forget the account; it will, however, not happen again. With regard to my servant bringing Carl home of an evening, the arrangement is made; I thank you, meanwhile, for your kindness yesterday in letting him be fetched by your servant; as I knew nothing about it, it might easily have happened that Carl would have had to stop at Czerny's. His boots are too narrow, and he has complained about it several times; indeed, it has been so bad that he could hardly walk, and it would take time to set the boots right. A thing of that sort spoils the feet, so I beg you not to let him put on these boots any more until they have been stretched. As regards *pianoforte practice*, I beg you to keep him to his work, otherwise there is no use in his having a teacher. Yesterday Carl was not able to play the whole day, I myself have found that out already several times when I intended to go through music with him, so that I, without having attained my object, was obliged to leave off.

La musica merita d'esser studiato.

The few hours which are allowed him for his music are not sufficient, and I must therefore all the more impress upon you that they are kept. It is by no means an unusual thing for attention to be paid to this matter in an institute; a friend of mine had likewise a boy at a school who intends to devote himself to music, and he is given every facility: I was, indeed, not a little surprised when I found the boy in a distant room practising all alone, and being neither disturbed nor disturbing others. I beg permission to send for Carl about half-past ten o'clock, as I have to go through his music, also to take him to see some musicians.

With all conceivable respect,
Your friend,
L. v. BEETHOVEN.

267. To CARL CZERNY

[1817?]

MY DEAR CZERNY!

I beg you to exercise as much patience as possible with Carl; even if he does not get on as both you and I wish, he will otherwise accomplish still less, for (this one cannot venture to tell him) through the bad distribution of hours he is too much on the stretch. This cannot be at once changed; hence be as kind as possible to him, yet serious. In these truly unfortunate circumstances such treatment will succeed better with C. With regard to his playing, I beg you, if once he has got the right fingering, plays in good time, with the notes fairly correct, then only pull him up about the rendering; and when he is arrived at that stage, don't let him stop for the sake of *small faults*, but point them out to him when he has played the piece through. Although I have done little in the way of teaching, I have always adopted this plan; it soon forms *musicians*, which, after all, is one of the first aims of art, and it gives less trouble both to master and pupil. With passages such as:

etc., I like at times all fingers to be used, also in the following:

so that they may be played in gliding style! Certainly they sound, as it is said, "played in a pearly" (with few fingers), or "like a pearl," but at times one wants a jewel of a different kind. On another occasion I will say more on the subject. I hope that you will receive all this with the kindly feeling with which I say it to you; for the rest, I am and ever remain your debtor. May my sincerity, for the rest, serve as a true pledge of future payment, so far as lies in my power,

Your true friend,

BEETHOVEN.

[According to the original manuscript in the archives of the *Gesellschaft der Musikfreunde*, Vienna. This letter concerning the art of teaching the pianoforte is of high importance. It was probably first published by August Schmidt in the *Allgemeine Wiener Musikzeitung* in 1845. Czerny also wrote in that paper during the same year: "In the year 1815 at his (Beethoven's) request I began to teach his adopted nephew Carl, and from that time onward I saw him almost every day, for as a rule he came to my house with the young fellow. I still possess many letters of that period, of which I here communicate one, remarkable from a musical point of view, and a faithful copy of the original."]

268. To FRAU NANETTE STREICHER

[1817?]

I am at work sorting my papers, now and then reflecting on what change is necessary for the future, so if your accounts have not been settled, and if I have not been to see you, this is the cause. It needs a *fearful lot of patience* to put things like my papers in order, but if it comes to a fellow like myself, he has to stick to it, otherwise it *never* gets done; this also is connected with what we want in the way of tools. Many *thanks* for your recommendation of the new parlourmaid, and for your continued kindness to us, without which I shall always be in suspicion, although with three it is easier to discover everything. I hope to see you to-morrow or the next day.

> In haste,
> Your friend,
> BEETHOVEN.

269. TO THE SAME

[1817?]

I only say to you that I am better; last night I often thought about my death, also such thoughts are not unusual to me even in the daytime.

Concerning the future housekeeper, I wish to know whether she has a *bed* and bedroom furniture? By *bed* I mean partly the bedstead, partly the bed, the mattresses, etc., etc. And do speak to her yourself about the washing, so that we may be certain about everything; she must also have earnest-money, which I will give to her. About all other matters we must talk to-morrow and the day after. My musical and unmusical papers are now almost in order; it was one of the seven labours of Hercules!

> In haste,
> Your friend,
> BEETHOVEN.

270. TO THE SAME

[1817?]

You cannot judge how things are at home, and will be later on, etc. We have the parlour-maid, and indeed not such an elephantine creature as the Peppi, but much cleverer, and I hope she will be all right. With the housekeeper it is not so, and we wish for a better one, but it will be as well to wait until we find a better one— and for that there is time. The enclosed letter is to be delivered at the Institute of Herr Giannatasio, Zimmerplatz, 379, that, at least, I think is the number. There is written over the porch in golden letters "Educational Institute," but it should be called *Non-Educational*. I earnestly beg you to send your pianoforte there about 11 o'clock in the morning, and to tell her to ask for this Herr Langer, *and deliver the letter to him, herself*. *He* is not to know that either you or I send it. You will wonder when I tell you what I have experienced this time, my poor Carl was only persuaded just for the moment, but there are men more like cattle—among them is the *priest* who deserves cudgelling.

> In haste,
> Your friend,
> BEETHOVEN.

You can only send Friday morning, about 11 to Langer, for Thursdays he is not there. Your number I do not know, hence I must send this letter through a former commissioned officer; I hope soon to hear that it has been received without having received anything.

To Fr. v. Streicher together
with a parcel.

[The priest mentioned was probably the one at Mödling, where Beethoven was staying.]

271. TO THE SAME

[NUSSDORF, 1817?]

How indebted I am to you, worthy friend, for I have become such a poor man that I cannot in any way make up for it to you. Monday or Tuesday I shall come to town, when we can talk together about the house; the one on the other side of the Gärtnergasse would probably be better, and as regards rent the same as the one opposite. I thank Streicher very much for the trouble he has taken, and only beg him to continue; God will no doubt let me once again be in a position to repay good with good, for the contrary is most distressful to me. I send you the washing, also 11 fl. which I still owe your washerwoman; but don't let the servant go to her. As regards a new servant, I think for the moment, as I have given notice to him, to stick to it. To whomsoever we may ascribe the loss of all the things, his bad nature, how he slandered the *master* to the people of the house, and took upon himself many other things; all this has made me lose all confidence in him, and I hold him rather the thief than any other. I beg you only to say to him that you thought that *a pair of socks has been lost, this is clear from the letter which you wrote to me about it*; he is always telling me that you had found the socks again. The washerwoman received two pairs of stockings, as the *two washing-bills, yours and mine, showed; and this would not be so had she not received them.* So I am convinced that she gave him the two pairs of stockings, as she certainly received them, so that they must have got lost only through him. He talks everywhere about my distrust, and invents things which have never happened, so as to clear himself and again to get a character there, so as to remain in my service. Only on one occasion I wished to speak to him about the stockings, but I had forgotten all about it, and only through his chatter have you had to hear something about the trashy story; for the rest, of what he offers most excuses, he is guilty. So I thoroughly know him, and do not speak without being firmly convinced. Away with him. You told me of a man whom you know, he could enter my service the first day of next month; as it is inconvenient for him to have to wait a *whole month* at your expense, *I will pay him per day 2 fl. 20 kr.*, so long as I remain here in Nussdorf. If he wants to cook, i.e. for himself, he can use my wood; and as he will have to go into town two or three times a week, I will give him for that a fitting remuneration, for instance I will give him *what it costs to vamp a pair of boots.* Perhaps the people in the house will see to his meals, for with these persons I want to have *as little to do* as probably you; about the housekeeper nothing will probably be arranged until I come to town. Now, God be thanked, I have fortunately got over these periods with *great trouble*; God grant that I may not have to speak, write, or think about anything about it, for *swamp and mire* in the region of art are more profitable for a man than all such devilry.

Farewell.

BEETHOVEN.

Kind regards to Streicher and his wife.

[The servant may have been the "Wenzel Braun" mentioned in the diary, of whom it is said: "Left on May 17, 1817."]

272. TO THE SAME

[1817.]

First of all it is clear, that if you do not kindly see to things, I with my infirmities shall meet with the *same fate* with all people. *Ingratitude* towards you is what has most lowered these two servants in my estimation. What otherwise you say about chattering, I do not understand; just once I remember, with regard to a third matter, to have forgotten myself for a moment, but this was with *people of quite a different stamp*—that is all which I have to say on the matter. I on my side neither take notice nor ever listen to the chattering of *common people*; I have often given you a hint on the subject, *without saying a word* of what I have heard—away, away, away, with such people.

Several times I have sent Nanni to you that you might forgive her, and since your last visit I have certainly not scolded her, but I have not spoken a single word or syllable to her, and thus gave her clearly enough to understand my will; for I must say that of *persons* who behave so *against* you I cannot think well, and I care for neither. I shall give notice to B. to-day, perhaps she will ask

Nanni's forgiveness, as she has already taken a step towards it. For the rest, if some one does not take this matter under his care, *we shall not fare better with other servants.* For the rest, I trust to the human kindness which prompts you to be good, I cannot agree with you in this case; unfortunately I have already felt this, and I hope that none the less you will continue to act for me, for your friend and servant.

Nanni wants a person over her, a more *reasonable* one; a person who would not require this would suit us probably better, *yet not altogether without supervision,* but we will not push excuses too far, for "every man *errs, only in a different way.*" Only engage the other one at once, and forgive all the trouble that I am causing you. As soon as you come from Klosterneuburg, I beg you to be very kind. I have told Nanni that I have *engaged a servant,* leave her under this delusion.

[The N. and B. are the housemaids Nany and Baberl, who have often been mentioned. The sentence of the poet: "Every man, etc.," was evidently one of Beethoven's favourite sayings. Not only does it occur almost word for word in another letter, but he even set it to music, almost at the close of his life, in a letter to Carl Holz of December 1826, in which the thought is thus expressed: "We all err, only each in a different way."]

273. To Baron ZMESKALL

[1817?]

Again unfortunate with a servant and *probably also robbed.* Already on the 4th I gave him 14 days' notice, but he gets drunk, stays whole nights out of the house, and is so bold and coarse that I would like to send him away still sooner; I should like to pay him the fortnight and let him go his way. Now the question is, if I dismiss him in this way whether I must pay him for the previous days from the 1st of this month, or from the 4th up to the day (which might be to-morrow) when I pay him 14 days? His month begins with each month and ends with the same. Forgive me dear Zmeskall, kindly send the answer early in the morning through your servant. I hope to see you soon.

[On the side of the address:]

I beg you not to say anything about the note to your servant, I shall know what measures to take.

[The year 1817 was a terrible year with his servants *masculini et feminini generis.*]

274. To Frau NANETTE STREICHER

[1817]

I have not forgotten—I am more inclined to *forget what is owing to me than what I owe others*. I did not like to overload the servant as the last time he had so many commissions—here is the florin which you were kind enough to give to the washerwoman; the spoon which the servant returns with thanks was likewise since I went away to the Landstrasse lying ready, but it was too much for him the last time, hence he will probably bring it to-day; with kind remembrances at home and especially to Streicher.

[At the top of the letter:]

I beg you to send to the washerwoman so that the washing may come home on Sunday.

275. To the Same

[1817?]

WORTHY FRAU V. STREICHER,

Forgive me, if I perhaps offended you to-day by my mission. My illness and my truly sad situation in this respect do not let me ponder over things as formerly. I will explain further when we meet. I hope soon to see you.

Please let me have
the bed-clothes.
Excuse me, I am worn
out.

Your friend,
BEETHOVEN.

[According to Jahn; first printed by Nohl.]

276. To the Same

[1817]

WORTHY FR. V. STREICHER!

Please give the bed-covers to the bearer of this, and pay no attention to his gossip—this man is not pure-minded. I also ask you kindly to see that the washerwoman delivers the washing at latest Sunday. My waistcoats, two of which have gone to the devil, and other not numerous articles cause me to express this wish. For the rest I do not wish you to imagine that I think that in any way through carelessness on your part anything has been lost. This would pain me, do not judge of my usual way of thinking from what bad *servants* say. Concerning another servant, or how, otherwise I shall arrange, I will tell you when we next meet. I must have cooking for myself, for in these bad times there are so few people in the country, that it is difficult to get a meal in the inns, still more so to find what is beneficial and good for me.

In haste,
Your friend and servant,

To Fr. v. Streicher   L. v. BEETHOVEN.
Ungergasse.

277. TO THE SAME

[1817.]

I beg you, worthy Fr. v. Streicher, not to say a word to any one about my decision to engage a *tutor* for Carl, so that it may do no harm either to him or to Carl, until the matter is quite settled. For my existence, indeed, I require better nursing and waiting on, and that means a *housekeeper*. As we have found a good tutor, we shall now probably not want the Frenchwoman, because Carl must have a scientific training in French, and for that our Frenchwoman would be of no use. On the other hand the *tutor* and his *wife* would cost too much. I hear, however, that for 100 florins per year, together with keep and room, one could probably get a housekeeper. Think over this and help

Your
To Streicher the   poor suffering
most affectionate   friend,
To Fr. v. Streicher.   BEETHOVEN.

[Beethoven's decision respecting a tutor for Carl renders it probable that the letter was written at the end of 1817, or even the beginning of 1818. Carl left the Giannatasio Institute, January 1818.]

278. TO FRAU MARIE PACHLER-KOSCHAK

[1817.]

I am very happy at your granting an extra day; we shall still have a lot of music. You will play me the Sonatas in F major and C minor? will you not?

I have never met with any one who interprets my compositions so well as you. The great pianists not excepted: they are either mechanical or affected. You are the true foster-mother of the children of my intellect.

[The autograph is written in pencil on a long strip of paper, and is very difficult to decipher. Schindler quotes from a diary of 1817 or 1818, and also gives a facsimile: "Only love—yes, that alone can procure for you a happier life. O God! let me at last find her who shall make me happy in virtue—her who will be lawfully mine—Baden, July 27, as I saw M. (?!) drive past, and it seemed as if she looked at me." Schindler adds: "The object of this autumnal love was well known to the writer, and among Beethoven's papers I have still two letters to Beethoven of the years 1825 and 1826 from Marie L. P—r, who was afterwards married at Graz." Marie Leopoldine Pachler-Koschak was born at Graz, 2 February, 1794, the daughter of the lawyer Dr. Aldebrand Koschak. Her pianoforte teacher appears to have been Herr Heimrich. Through unfortunate circumstances she had to renounce her wish to devote herself entirely to music. In 1816 she married the lawyer Dr. Carl Pachler. His brother Anton Pachler had already made the acquaintance of the composer. In 1816 he placed before the master a composition (Fantasia for pianoforte) of his sister-in-law Marie, and on 17 October, 1816, he wrote to her: "Beethoven had returned from Baden a few days before, so I flew post-haste to him and luckily found him at home. I kept my promise to you and named no composer. He looked through the piece very carefully, and at the end said it was really very good for some one who had not studied composition; but that it would be too long to explain by writing, also that after careful study of composition the composer himself would become alive to the fact." During the summer of 1817, Marie made the personal acquaintance of the master. After his death she wrote about it to a friend: "I do not know whether you are aware how much I admired him also as a man. I made his acquaintance during my first stay in Vienna; we spent much time together."]

279. To Dr. PACHLER

[1817.]

MY DEAR P!

According to my doctor's opinion the very best thing for me would be a journey to turn my thoughts in another direction. It is not improbable that I may make use of your offer, but, it is understood, I will willingly pay my share of the expenses, so that I need not be a burden to any one in Graz. I am still here to-morrow or perhaps the next day; I live at the Landstrasse, No. 268, second floor—you will always find me at home early in the morning, especially about 8 o'clock.

Your friend,

BEETHOVEN.

To Herr v. Pachler
at the Golden Ox
    No. 14

[The journey to Graz did not take place, either now or later on. Frau Pachler-Koschak died 10 April, 1855.]

280. To Frau NANETTE STREICHER

[1817.]

Best Frau von Streicher!

This servant is *scarcely* honest, though I will not *condemn him straight off*. I think, meanwhile, of keeping him still here, with the *housekeeper*. *What do you think?* It will probably not be easy to find another one at once, and yet I fear the *fellow* might have a *bad influence over an honest person*.

I send you here the two keys, so that you can inspect everything. Tell me whether it would be possible for the housekeeper to come here at latest Tuesday? or even Monday afternoon? Dusters are wanted—even here, for the devil has already always carried off 2 or 3 times my household things. Farewell, my worthy friend.

In haste,

Your friend,

L. V. BEETHOVEN.

N.B.— Do not curse me for troubling you so often.

281. To the Same

[1817.]

Kindly send to your haughty tailor. He has had two pairs of trousers of mine for a fortnight, and they would be of service just for the cold weather, but he does not condescend to let me have them.

282. To the Same

[1817.]

I am still unwell, and there is little comfort in the house; the food yesterday and to-day was really *bad*. This person lacks reflection—more about her when we meet. I know she is willing, and indeed both are probably not the worst; but N., especially, does not attend to me properly; no good is done by violence and over-haste. But I fear that you would have far too much to do to bring about order or method here, and how would it be when you are ill or away. We must have *some one* on whom we could rely without other aid. Besides it is hard lines to be in a condition to have to make use of so many persons. Hearty thanks for your purchase. I shall certainly see you the day after to-morrow, for if I only feel better, I shall be very busy to-morrow.

In haste,

Your friend,

BEETHOVEN.

[Some calendars which have been preserved give a dismal picture of these household miseries.]

283. TO THE SAME

[1817.]

I had to pay dearly for the last conversation with you, for after it N. behaved to me in such a way that on Saturday evening I became wild with rage, and then she certainly was good again—but *your* help is of no avail, the bad side of this person, her *stubbornness* cannot be cured, and she has already lost my confidence. Then seeing that the time is gradually approaching when Carl will certainly live with me, I think you will agree with me to exchange both persons for other and better ones. Perhaps I may see you to-morrow, *certainly the next day*.

In haste,
Your friend,
BEETHOVEN.

To Frau von Streicher,
née Stein.

284. TO THE SAME

[1817.]

I thank you. It seems already to be much better. I also send the *speaking-tube*; please send it back to-morrow, as my observations have now gained thereby.

Your grateful
BEETHOVEN.

[In addition to Maelzel, now again reconciled with Beethoven, Andreas Streicher also made ear-trumpets for the composer.]

285. TO THE SAME

[1817.]

Pardon. Scissors, knives, etc., are wanting. I think the rags are too bad, and that it would be better to buy a *linen cloth*. The neckties also want *patching up*—more by word of mouth, and indeed by word of mouth, again to ask for indulgence.

In haste,
Your friend,
BEETHOVEN.

286. To the Same

[1817?]

Many thanks for the kindness shown to me. I will betake myself one of these days to S., and hear how it stands with the whole *matter*. I am frightfully busy, and it has been practically impossible to see you. Carl desires to be remembered to you; we shall very soon pay you a visit.

In haste,
Your friend,
BEETHOVEN.

Do not quite
desert your post of
mistress of the household.
It will always have a
rare good effect.
For Fr. v. Streicher.

287. To the Same

[1817?]

I have only *one* emetic powder, must I after this take tea *oftener*? Please let me have a tin spoon.

In haste,
Your friend,
BEETHOVEN.

[The autograph belongs to Miss E. A. Willmot.—Tr.]

288. To the Same

[1817?]

Dear lady, I am ready to go with you to-morrow, to see this instrument, what time I will arrange when I call on you this afternoon. For the rest, have patience with me; in my present state I can no longer *drive a bargain, as I could formerly*, although my name is still <u>Beethoven.</u>

To Fr. v. Streicher.

[Written with pencil.]

289. To the Same

[1817?]

Yes, indeed, all this housekeeping is still *without keeping*, and much resembles an *allegro di confusione*. If I read rightly, you will give me the pleasure of a *visit* this afternoon at 4.30, or is it to be 2.30? This needs an answer, so you must once again send out your little *letter-carrying pigeon*, for the women are washing for themselves to-day, by turns, in the washing trough.

In haste,

Your friend,

BEETHOVEN.

To Frau von Streicher *née* Stein.

[The "letter-carrying pigeon" was probably Frau Streicher's daughter Sophie.]

290. To J. N. BIHLER

DEAR BIHLER!　　　　　　　　　　　　　　　　　　　[1817?]

I only announce to you that I am now in Baden and feel extremely well, not owing to the company there, but to the truly beautiful Nature.

[According to the reprint in Th. Frimmel's *Beethoveniana*, from the Vienna *Presse* of 21 December, 1889. The philologist and musical enthusiast, J. N. Bihler, travelled in 1817 as tutor to the son of the Baroness von Puthon. This Bihler, according to Dr. Pachler, was tutor to the children of H.I.H. the Archduke Carl.]

291. TO THE SAME

DEAR BIHLER!　　　　　　　　　　　　　　　　　　　[1817?]

Dr. Sassafrass, concerning whom I spoke to you, is coming to-day about 12 o'clock. I beg you therefore, to come to me also, and in order that you may not go wrong, I give you the number of the house and the floor, so that you can see everything before you, before you get there. On the 3rd floor of 1241 lives this poor, persecuted, despised Austrian musician.

BEETHOVEN.

[Sassafras is the name of a tree in North America, the bark of the root of which is used for medicinal purposes. Beethoven may have used the term to indicate a quack doctor; anyhow, in 1861, there was a drama by Count Franz Pocci entitled *Doctor Sassafras; or Doctor, Death and Devil.*]

292. LETTER OF RECOMMENDATION FOR HERR VON KANDELER

[1817?]

It is certainly the duty of every composer to be generally acquainted with all ancient and modern poets, and, with regard to vocal music, to be able himself to choose the best and most suitable for his purpose. As this, however, is not usually done, this praiseworthy Collection of Herr von Kandeler will always be useful for many who wish to compose songs, and it will also stimulate good poets to do something towards this.

LUDWIG VAN BEETHOVEN.

M.p.

I entirely agree with Herr van Beethoven.

JOS. WEIGL.

293. To THOMAS BROADWOOD

VIENNE, le 3me du mois Février, 1818.

MON TRÈS CHER AMI BROADWOOD!

j'amais je n'eprouvais pas un plus grand Plaisir de ce que me causa votre Annonce de l'arrivée de cette Piano, avec qui vous m'honorès de m'en faire présent, je regarderai cõme un Autel, ou je deposerai les plus belles offrandes de mon Esprit au divine Apollon. Aussitôt cõme je recevrai votre Excellent jnstrument, je vous enverrai d'en abord les Fruits de l'inspiration des premiers moments, que j'y passerai, pour vous servir d'un Souvenir de moi à vous mon très cher B., et je ne souhaits ce que, qu'ils soient dignes de votre jnstrument

Mon cher Monsieur et ami
recevés ma plus grande
Consideration
de votre ami
et très humble serviteur

LOUIS VAN BEETHOVEN.

[The contents concern a grand piano from Broadwood. The instrument, after it had been tried by Clementi, Cramer and Ferdinand Ries, was sent to Vienna to Beethoven on 27 December, 1817. The artists named and other distinguished men had written their names inside the instrument. Thayer also adds that the Court of Exchequer most generously made no charge for import duty. Schindler wrote a short account of the pianoforte manufacturer to Beethoven on 17 July, 1818.]

[Among the Schindler papers is the following letter:]

LONDRES, au 17th Juillet, 1818.

MON CHER MONS. BEETHOVEN,

Mon ami Mon^r. Stumpff porteur de cette Lettre a intention d'aller à Vienne, je n'ai pas besoign de vous dire, qu'il l'envie generalle de tout ceux qui ont jamais entendue la Musique de faire votre connaissance, ou même de vous voir seulement de vous parler, et si vous voulez lui permettre d'accorder et de regler le piano que j'ai eu le plaisir de vous envoyer et que j'espère a merité votre approbation,—je suis extremement fache d'entendre dire la semaine passe que vous avez été encore malade mais j'espère que le nouvelles prochaine que je recevrez de vous, ou de mon respectable ami Mon. Bridi [i.e. the merchant Joseph Anton Bridi] me dira que vous vous portez bien encore.

> Toujours à vous,
> Mon cher Mons. Beethoven,
> Votre ami sincère,
> THOMAS BROADWOOD.

Je vous prie de faire bien mes
Compliment respectueux à mon Bridi.

[It was Stumpff who sent Handel's works (40 vols.) to Beethoven shortly before the composer's death.]

294. TO FERDINAND RIES, LONDON

VIENNA, 5th March, 1818.

MY DEAR RIES!

In spite of my wishes, it was not possible for me to come to London this year; I beg you to tell the Philharmonic Society that my weak health prevents me from doing so. I hope, however, this spring to be quite restored, and then, in the latter part of the year, to make use of the Society's proposal to me and to fulfil all the conditions therein named.

Ask Neate not to make use of the many works he has of mine —at least in public—until I come myself; however matters may turn out with him, I have reason to complain of him.

Botter visited me several times; he appears to be a good man and has talent for composition. I hope and trust that your good fortune may daily increase; unhappily I cannot say that of myself. . . . I cannot see any one in want, I must give; so you can also imagine how greatly I suffer about this matter. I beg you to write to me soon. If it is in any way possible, I shall get away from here still sooner, in order to escape complete ruin, and then I shall arrive in London during the winter at latest. I know that you will help an unfortunate friend; had it only been in my power, and had I not, as always here, been tied by circumstances, I certainly should have done much more for you. Farewell, greetings to Neate, Smart, also to Cramer—although I hear that he is a counter-subject of yours and mine; meanwhile I understand already something of the art of dealing with such matters, and in spite of him we shall bring about a pleasant harmony in London.

I greet and embrace you from my heart.

> Your friend,
> LUDWIG VAN BEETHOVEN.

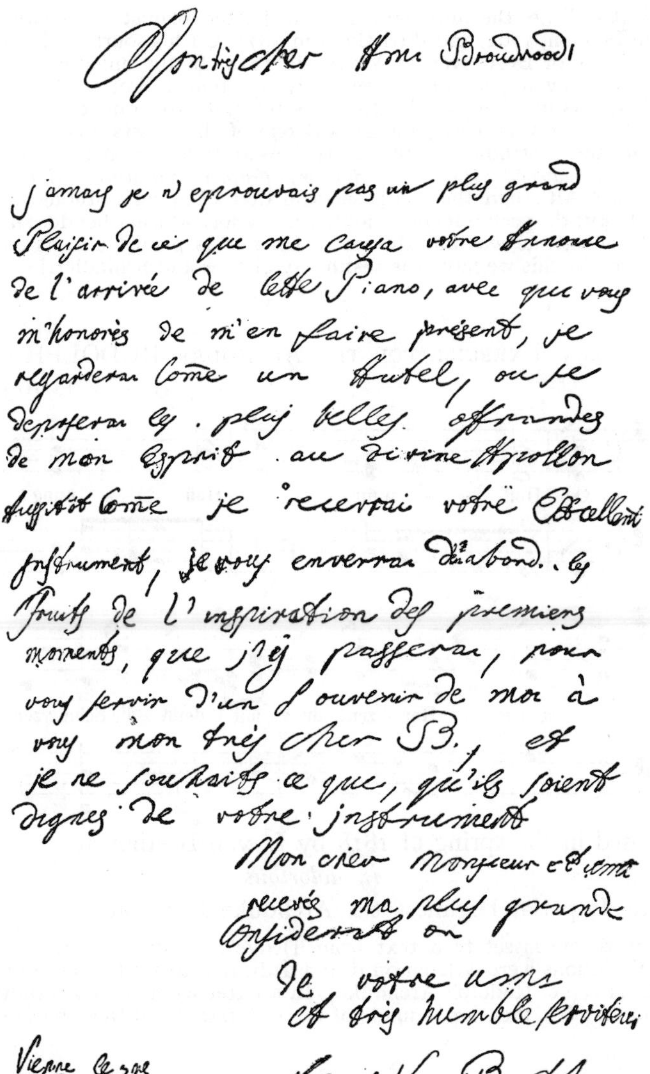

LETTER TO THOMAS BROADWOOD, 1818

All that is pleasant to your dear and (as I hear) beautiful wife.

["Botter," i.e. the musician, Cipriani Potter, pianist and composer, was born in London, 1792, and died there in 1871. On his journeys he made the acquaintance of Beethoven at Vienna in 1818. In the unlading and testing of the Beethoven pianoforte previously mentioned, Potter, together with Streicher, was most active. Beethoven's reference to Cramer as a "counter-subject" is not very clear, for he was one of the artists who inscribed his name in the instrument. Here is the inscription: "*Hoc instrumentum est Thomæ Broadwood (Londini) donum, propter ingenium illustrissimum Beethoven.*" Although the composer said that "Cramer's Studies render the touch sticky; the performer does not learn any staccato, neither does he acquire a light touch," he was an admirer of Cramer as pianist and as an Étude-composer; for this we have the testimony of Ries and Schindler.]

295. EXERCISE FOR THE ARCHDUKE RUDOLPH

[*Spring* 1818.]

composed in the spring of 1818 by L. van Beethoven
in doloribus
for His Imperial Highness the Archduke Rudolph.

[The theme is set to a text from Tiedge's *Urania*. According to Nohl, forty Variations were written on it and dedicated to Beethoven by his pupil, "R. E. H." (i.e. Rudolph Archduke). In a letter written by Beethoven from Mödling in 1819, mention is made of these Variations of the Archduke's.]

296. To CARL CZERNY

MY DEAR WORTHY CZERNY!   [1818?]

I learn this very moment that you are in a position which I have never suspected; you really might place confidence in me and just show me in what way perhaps your affairs can be bettered (without any vulgar patronage on my part); as soon as I have time to take breath, I must have a talk with you; be assured that I esteem you, and of this I am ready at any moment to give you practical proof.

With true respect,
Your friend,
BEETHOVEN.

For Herr Carl von Czerny.

[Zellner's explanation of the letter is given by Nohl as follows: "In 1818 Beethoven wrote to Czerny, asking him to play his last concerto in E flat (Op. 73) at one of his concerts in the Redoutesaal. Czerny, however, answered frankly that he depended on teaching the pianoforte for his living, and that for many years he had given more than twelve hours' lessons per day. Hence he had been compelled to neglect his own playing, so that he could not venture within a few days (as Beethoven requested) to give a worthy performance of the work in public. In return he received the above letter, a touching proof of Beethoven's sympathy."]

297. TO THE FISCAL COUNCILLOR, VINCENZ HAUSCHKA

[1818?]

BEST AND CHIEF MEMBER OF THE SOCIETY OF MUSICAL FIENDS OF THE AUSTRIAN IMPERIAL STATE!

I have only a *sacred* subject, but you want a heroic one, and that also suits me, only I think I shall mix a little sacred with it, which for such a mass would be in the right place.

Herr von Bernard would suit me very well, but mind and pay him; for myself I say nothing, as you already call yourself music-friends, so it is natural that on this score you will act liberally!!!

Now farewell my good fellow (I wish you open bowels and

convenience), so far as I am concerned, I wander here among the mountains, clefts and valleys with a sheet of music paper, and I scribble a lot for the sake of bread and money, for to this pitch have I arrived in this all-powerful Phæacian Land, that in order to win time for a great work, I am always compelled beforehand to do so much daub-work for the sake of money, so that I may stand the strain of a great work. For the rest my health has greatly improved, and if haste is required, I can already serve you.

Ex. 3.

ich bin be - rei - - - - - - t   ich bin be -
rei - - - - - - - - - - t

If you want to speak to me, write, and then I will arrange all about it. My best respects to the Society of Musical Fiends.

In haste, your friend,

BEETHOVEN.

[The address on the wrapper reads:]

To Herr von Hauschka
Chief Member of the
Society of Musical Fiends of the
Austrian State, and also Grand Cross
of the Order of the Violoncello, &c. &c.

[This letter appears to be an answer to Hauschka's proposal "to write an *heroic* oratorio for the Musical Society." Schindler goes on to speak of the great success which Stadler's heroic oratorio, *Die Befreiung von Jerusalem*, had met with when performed by the Society a short time previously, and he was of opinion that this created the desire among the members to have a similar work from Beethoven's pen. The "Phæacian Land" stands for Austria; Beethoven commonly spoke of the Viennese as his Phæacians. To his very intimate friend Hauschka he could venture to repeat his joke about the "Musical Fiends' Society." The Grand Cross of the "Order of the Violoncello" refers to Hauschka's great skill as a performer on that instrument.]

298. To Frau NANETTE STREICHER

[1818?]

I am glad that you yourself feel that I cannot possibly enter your house any more—the enclosed note was written this morning, I wished to send it to you when yours reached me through your

Viennese servant. I await you with pleasure Tuesday morning—you will certainly find me at home. From Carl's physician I learn that it goes well with his body; as regards his soul, that must be left to Heaven.

In haste,
Your friend,
BEETHOVEN.

299. TO THE SAME

[1818?]

It will be well that you and also myself do not *let the two servants notice that I unfortunately can no longer have the pleasure of coming to your house,* this if it were not carried out would have *very bad consequences* for me, likewise if you should entirely keep away from here. I beg you kindly to let me know what you spent for me, and I will at once send it to you with many thanks. Likewise will you kindly let me know where your goldsmith's shop is? I have given a scolding to Nany and to the other one on account of their behaviour to you; nevertheless the younger one yesterday was so insolent and bold, that I threatened her, in case she should again say nasty things about other people and also about me, I would drive her out of the house *on the spot.* You see that from both we *experience like treatment,* this lies probably in the nature, and in the thoroughly bad nature of the *younger one*—for this *you* are as little to blame as I am. As soon as you are able, do me the pleasure to come here, or even to come and dine here. Every little kindness on your part I shall keep in remembrance, and always call myself

Your grateful,

For Frau von Streicher,   L. v. BEETHOVEN.
née Stein.

300. TO THE SAME

[1818?]

I beg you, my worthy friend, to settle about buying the silver. It would be too long before I could manage it. First of all, we must know whether we have to spend any money besides? how much? The *sugar-basin we will in any case return,* and in addition I will give *three tea-spoons* of mine; if only for these we could get a pair of table-spoons and a light ladle, without paying much besides; and then our wants will be seen to, for a poor Austrian, very poor, very poor musician cannot think of anything further. In haste—

compliments on account of the exemplary conduct of yourself and your daughter.

Your friend,
BEETHOVEN.

For Frau von Streicher,
with the bill for the
silver sugar-basin, and three
tea-spoons.

[Beethoven's frequent sigh about being a "poor Austrian musician" has now risen to the superlative.]

301. TO THE SAME

[1818?]

I was just on the point of writing to you when I received your letter together with the silver, we will talk over all other matters. Carl is not allowed to go out as yet, and not for some days, and with the arranging there will be work for several days; on account of all this I could not see you, I hope however to be able to manage it to-morrow or the day after. P— cooks well, and for that I must be eternally thankful to you; if you only continue to care a little about us, the whole thing will be tolerable, and perhaps something still better. It will be still some days before I am quite in order. It was for me a Herculean piece of work, God only grant that I may once again be able to devote myself entirely to my art. Formerly I was able to keep all other matters entirely subordinate to this, now truly I have become somewhat disturbed in this; more by word of mouth. Carl sends kind regards.

In haste,
Your friend and servant,
L. V. BEETHOVEN.

For Frau von Streicher,
  née Stein.

[P. is the elephantine Peppi. The oft-mentioned diary of these years of tribulation contains Pliny's remark: "Tametsi quid homini potest dari maius (in Fischhoff 'magis') quam gloria et laus et æternitas?"]

302. TO THE SAME

MÖDLING, 18th June, 1818.

BEST FRAU VON STREICHER!

It was not possible to answer your last letter sooner. I had already some days ago written to you before the servants were sent away, but I always hesitated about my decision until I perceived that especially Frau D— kept Carl back from confessing everything. She said to him that "*he ought to spare his mother*," and Peppi joined in in the same strain; naturally they did not wish to be found out. *Both disgracefully played into each other's hands, and allowed themselves to be used by Frau van Beethoven; both received coffee and sugar from her, Peppi money, the old woman probably also; but there is not the slightest doubt that she went herself to the house of Carl's mother.* She also told Carl that if I sent her away, she would at once go to his mother. This occurred on an occasion when I was reproaching her with her behaviour, for I had often cause to be dissatisfied. Peppi, who often listened when I was talking to Carl, seemed disposed to confess the truth, but *the old woman told her she was a fool, and gave her a good blowing up*—and so she again was stubbornly silent and sought to lead me on a wrong track. The story of this horrible deception may have lasted for about six weeks, both of them would have had a worse time of it with a less magnanimous man. Peppi borrowed from me 9 or 10 fl. for stuff for shirts, and I afterwards made her a present of the money, and instead of 60 fl. she received 70 fl.; she might at least have denied herself those wretched bribes. As for the old woman who behaved worse, hate may have had something to do with it, as she always thought herself thrust into the background (although she received more than she deserves), for through her *scornful face* one day when Carl embraced me, I suspected *treachery*, and how disgraceful in such an old woman, and how backbiting she could be. Imagine, two days before, when I betook myself here, Carl went without my knowledge one afternoon to his mother, and both the old woman and Peppi were aware of it. But now hear the triumph of a hoary-headed traitress; when I drove hither with Carl and her, I spoke to Carl in the carriage about the matter, although I did not know everything, and indeed I expressed fear lest we might not be quite safe in Mödling, she called out I need only rely on her. Oh, how disgraceful! Only twice has anything of the sort happened to me with people of an otherwise venerable age. Several days before, when I sent them both about their business, I arranged with them by writing that neither should dare to accept anything from Carl's mother for him. Peppi, instead of repenting, sought secretly to take vengeance on Carl, because he had already confessed everything, and this they clearly discovered, for I had written on the above sheet, *everything has been discovered*. I expected that after this they would both ask me to forgive them; instead of that they both played bad tricks with me, now one now the other. As there was no hope of improvement from such obstinate sinners, and as I every moment had to expect new treachery, I resolved to sacrifice my bodily sense of comfort for the good of my poor deluded Carl, and out they went as a terrible warning to all future servants. I could have made the characters less good, but I didn't; I stated that they had been full six months with me, although it was not so. I never indulge in vengeance; in cases in which I have to act against other people, I never do so more than necessity demands to preserve myself from them, or to prevent them from future evil. On account of Peppi's general honesty, I am sorry to have lost her, hence I made her character more favourable than the one for the old one, and she also appears to me to have been practically led astray by the old woman. But that it was not as it ought to be with Peppi's coniscience, s clear, because she said to Carl, *that she was afraid to return any more to her parents, and as a matter of fact I understand that she is still here.* I long had suspicion of treachery, when the evening before my departure, I received an anonymous letter, which owing to its contents filled me with terror; however they were only suppositions. Carl, whom I once tackled in the evening, confessed at once, but not everything. As I often treated him roughly, not without cause, he was too frightened to confess everything. During this struggle we arrived here. As I often questioned him, the servants noticed this, and especially the old traitress sought to prevail on him not to confess the truth. But when I solemnly assured Carl that all would be forgiven if he would only tell the truth, since lies would only plunge him into a deeper abyss, everything came out into the light of day. Now connect the dates previously given you about the servants with this, and you have the whole shameful history of both traitresses clear. Carl has been at fault, but—mother—mother—even a bad one still remains a mother. In so far he is to be excused, especially by me, as I know too well his resentful passionate mother. The priest here knows already that I know about him, for Carl has already told me. Probably the latter was not aware of everything, so that he would be on his guard, but in order that he may not be ill-treated by the priest who appears to have been somewhat rough, I let the matter rest for the present. But as Carl's virtue was being tested, for without temptation there is no virtue, so I pass it over purposely, until once again (which I certainly do not expect) it happens, and then I will so mercilessly treat the reverend priest with such spiritual cudgelling, amulets, and with my exclusive guardianship and the privileges connected with it, so that the whole parish shall tremble. My heart has become terribly touched by this affair, and I find difficulty in recovering from it. Now the housekeeping matters; they need your help. How we want it you well know. Do not be alarmed; such a thing can happen anywhere; but if it has for once happened, and one can put *this* as a warning before the next servants, it is scarcely likely to happen again. What we want you know, perhaps the French girl, and one who will suit as parlour-maid. Good cooking is an essential—even as regards economy. For the moment we have some one here who cooks for us, but badly. I cannot write any more to-day. You will at least see that I could not have acted otherwise; things had gone too far. I do not yet invite you here, for everything is in confusion; *yet there will be no necessity to have me put into the lunatics' tower.* I can say that I have already terribly suffered in Vienna on account of this affair, and therefore kept silent. Farewell, do not talk about anything, as it might be prejudicial to Carl, as I who understand all the ins and outs of things can bear witness for him, that he was most terribly led away. I beg you soon to write something consoling about the cooking, washing, sewing art. I am not at all well and I soon require something to restore digestion.

In haste, your friend,
BEETHOVEN.

[The Fischhoff manuscript has the following characteristic words: " June 8, 1818, at Mödling the new housekeeper arrived"—"troglodyte, inhabitant of hell."]

303. TO THE SAME

[1818.]

From enclosed you see the state of things. As your cousin from Cracow will be so kind, he ought to inquire of Hofrath Anders at the chief custom-house, who will give him information, and to whom I desire to be kindly remembered, as his pretty daughter likewise is musical. The principal thing is for *an order to be sent to the custom-house at Trieste from the one here, for the instrument to be sent on. As soon as I have the order from the office here, I will give it to Henikstein and Co., asking them to look after the instrument.*

In haste,
Your friend,

To Frau v. Streicher. BEETHOVEN.

[This note to Frau Streicher, with whom a lively correspondence was carried on during the spring of 1818, refers to the looking after an instrument from the custom-house at Trieste." Nothing is known of Nanette's cousin beyond the name. The banker Henikstein (Joseph) was very musical, and frequently gave musical evenings.]

304. To the Same

[1818?]

In haste, with haste, and through haste, I beg you to ask Streicher for us to be alone to-day about 12 o'clock.

In most hasty haste,

Your friend,

To Fr. v. Streicher.　　　　　　　　　　　BEETHOVEN.

305. To Frau JOHANNA Van BEETHOVEN

VIENNA, 1818.

So far as I am concerned, you have my full consent, in selling your house, to leave the 7000 fl. belonging to your son as a mortgage on it. But we must obtain the consent of the worshipful Law Court so that we may be able to give assurance to any purchaser that the capital of 7000 fl. cannot be called in for three or four years. In my opinion there is nothing in this either harmful or unjust to your son Carl, and I do not in the least doubt that the upper guardianship will grant your request.

As stated, I know nothing against it, and hope and wish that the upper guardianship will fully endorse my view of the matter.

306. To the Fiscal Councillor, VINCENZ HAUSCHKA

[1818?]

My dear H., I send you 8 basses, 4 violins, 6 second and 6 first, together with 2 *Harmoniums*. I cannot send a score, as I have only mine, the writing in which, for any one except myself, is too fine. It is, however, well to have a score, and you could get one at Steiner's, Vaterunsergässl.

I am again unwell, but will certainly come and have a talk with you very shortly.

Your friend,

BEETHOVEN, M.P.

N.B.—You can have still more copied parts from me.

[Pohl states that Beethoven's *Mount of Olives* was performed at the Society's concert of 23 February, 1823, for the first time there; so in spite, therefore, of the date "1818" on the copy, the letter may really refer to this performance.]

307. To the Archduke RUDOLPH

January 1, 1819.

Your Imperial Highness!

All that can be encompassed in one wish, and whatever can be termed beneficial—prosperity, happiness and blessing, all this is offered to Y.I.H. to-day, I hope my wish for myself will be accepted most graciously by Y.I.H., viz., that I may still enjoy the favour of Y.I.H. A terrible event has recently taken place in my family affairs, so that for a time I lost all power of thinking, and this alone accounts for my not having come to Y.I.H., also for not having mentioned the masterly variations of my highly honoured, exalted pupil, and favourite of the Muses. For the surprise and favour with which I have been honoured, I cannot venture to express my thanks either in writing or by word of mouth, as I occupy too *humble* a position; neither, even if I wanted, or desired ever so ardently, could I repay *like with like.* May Heaven hear and truly grant my wish for Y.I.H.'s health. In a few days I hope to hear Y.I.H. play the masterpiece sent to me, and nothing could rejoice me more than to assist in obtaining for Y.I.H., as speedily as possible, the place already prepared for you on the summit of Parnassus.

To your Imperial Highness,
With love and deep respect,
From your most obedient servant,

Ludwig van Beethoven.

[The Variations of the Archduke were published by Steiner and Co. in 1819. The "terrible event" was the moment in the lawsuit when it was sent down to the Lower Court, the sister-in-law having declared that Beethoven was not a *nobleman.* On the appointed day the composer appeared in court and declared, pointing to his head and heart, "that his *nobility was here and there.*" But, as Schindler remarks: "For such nobility, neither in Austria, nor in other countries, is there even to the present day any tribunal." When, however, Beethoven, who was deeply pained, put his case into the hands of the trusty advocate, Dr. Joh. Bach, matters improved. In the above letter, the composer, referring to the dedication to himself of the Variations, spoke of himself as being in too humble a position to repay *like with like,* he had only for the moment lost his proud, though justifiable self-respect.]

308. To the Same

[*January* 1819?]

. . . . and though appearances may be against me, everything one day will be cleared up for me. The day on which a High Mass of mine will be performed at the ceremony for Y.I.H., will be for me one of the grandest days of my life, and God will enlighten me, so that my weak powers may contribute to the glorification of this festive day. With deepest thanks I send the *Sonatas*, only the 'cello part is wanting. I have, therefore, taken the liberty of adding a printed copy, together with a Violin Quintet. In addition to the two movements in my own handwriting composed for Y.I.H.'s name-day, there are two more, the latter of which is a great *Fugato*, so that they all form one grand Sonata which will soon be published, and which, in my heart, has long been intended for Y.I.H.; *with this, the most recent appointment of Y.I.H. is not in any way concerned.* In asking for forgiveness for my letter, I pray that the Lord may send down His richest blessings on the head of Y.I.H. The new calling of Y.I.H., which fully encompasses the *love of mankind*, is probably one of the most noble, and through it Y.I.H., both in a *secular* and in a *sacred* capacity, will always offer one of the finest examples.

[The festive day referred to by Beethoven was the installation of the Archduke as Archbishop of Olmütz. The sonatas with 'cello are Op. 102 in C and D. The Sonata is Op. 106, published by Artaria in 1819, and dedicated to the Archduke.]

309. To the Vienna Magistrate

VIENNA, *Feb.* 1, 1818 [? 1819].

WORSHIPFUL MAGISTRATE!

As I have to speak of future education, it appears to me most fitting to commence with the actual state of things, whence it is evident that any change whatever can only be *prejudicial* to my nephew. It has already been mentioned that he has a private tutor who is still with him, but in order to stimulate still further his zeal, I let him, accompanied by his tutor, continue his studies at Herr v. Kudlich's, the principal of an Institute in the Landstrasse in my neighbourhood. He has as companion only one boy, the son of Baron Lang, and, whilst there, he is under constant supervision. Then, a specially good thing for him, Herr v. Kudlich teaches according to the thorough method used at the University, or carries it out practically; and all who know about such matters, and also myself, consider it the best. Every tutor does not follow it, hence a candidate at examination is sometimes puzzled. Then, in addition, he receives special instruction in French, in drawing, and in music, so that he is usefully and pleasantly employed the whole day; *but he is also under constant supervision which is so necessary.*

In addition, I have found a reverend father who instructs him in his duties as a Christian, and especially as a man, for on this basis only can *genuine men* be reared. Later on, towards summer he will also do a little Greek. It will be seen that I have spared no cost, having in view the excellent aim, viz., to give to the State a useful and well-mannered citizen; the *present arrangement* leaves nothing to be desired. *No change, therefore, is needed,* but if I were to perceive the necessity for such, I would improve on it, and *propose and carry it out most conscientiously.* Every man who does not become trades- man, let him be what he will, must have passed through at least 5 to 6 standards; during that time it will be seen what his inclina- tion and capability are. Whether he become a state official or a learned man, the foundation *can only be laid in this way.* The exceptional capability of my nephew, and to a certain extent, his peculiarities, call for exceptional means, and I never acted in a more beneficial and more magnanimous way, than when I took my nephew to live with me, and myself looked after his education. A Philip did not esteem it below his dignity to direct the education of his son Alexander, and to give him as teacher the great Aristotle, because he did not consider the ordinary teachers sufficiently qualified for that purpose. Did not even Laudon himself direct the education of his son; and why should not such excellent, noble examples be followed by others. My nephew, even during his father's lifetime, was entrusted to me by him, and I confess, that I feel more than any one else called, by my own example, *to incite him to virtue and activity.* At *Convict-schools and Institutes* there would not be the necessary supervision, and all learned men, among whom I include Professor Stein and Simerdinger, Professor of pedagogy, agree with me that it would *not be at all suitable for him* there; they even assert, that most youths are ruined when they leave; yes, even many who go in *morally good,* come out *the reverse*; and *unfortunately* I agree with the *experiences and opinions* of these men, *also of many parents.* If the mother had been able to suppress her evil disposition, and permitted the quiet development of my plans, there would have been really a favourable result from my direction hitherto. But when a *mother of this kind* seeks to involve him in the secrecy of her vulgar and even bad surroundings, and leads him in his tender years (a pestilence for children ! ! !) to deceive, to bribe my servants, *to tell falsehoods, and laughs at him* when he speaks the truth, even gives him *money* to awaken carnal desires, which are harmful to him, and such things would be *accounted in me and others grave faults,* then this already difficult matter becomes more difficult and more dangerous. But let it not be thought, that when my nephew was in the Institute, she behaved differently, but *against that*, a new *barrier* has been raised. In addition to the tutor, a lady of position will be at my house and look after the housekeeping, and will never allow herself to be bribed by her. Secret meetings of son and mother always have bad consequences, but that is *just what she wants*, because she appears to *find herself by no means at ease* among *well-mannered and well-meaning* persons. So many dishonourable accusations have been raised against me, and *by such persons* that I ought not to have *even* to mention; for not only is my moral character generally and publicly recognised, but even special writers such as Weissenbach, etc., thought it worth while to write about it, and only partiality can ascribe to me *anything low-minded*. Nevertheless, I hold it necessary to explain many things connected with this. As regards my nephew's fortune, he has 7000 fl., Vienna value, on his mother's house which has been sold, of which the mother has the usufruct; in addition he has 2200 fl., Vienna value, in mint bonds, and the half of the mother's pension. As regards the 2200 fl., they were only worth 2000, Vienna value, which, however, I (as shown to the Law Court) changed into money, 2200 fl., including costs. Both the half of the pension and the 2000 fl. are only as compensation for the 4th part of the sold house, and for the 4th part of the house rent of which he never received anything. So long as the mother had the house, which she alone occupied from Nov. 15 until Jan. 1818, and probably 7 to 8 months longer, she *kept all for herself*, notwithstanding that the 4th part of the house rent was due to the son. From this it may be seen that the arrangement was by no means the most advantageous for him, for if the mother were to die or get married, he would lose his whole share of the pension. There was, however, nothing to be done with men whose dishonesty was perceived by the Law Court in the matter of the inventory, and one had still to rejoice that *this* was saved for the child. Besides, I have always kept in mind the *salvation of his soul*, i.e. to withdraw him from the influence of the mother. Gifts of fortune may be acquired: *morality*, however (especially when a child already has the misfortune to suck *in such mother's milk*, yes, and has under her very guidance for several years become *entirely corrupted*, *even* had to help *deceive* the father), must be *implanted* at an early age. Further, he will inherit; already now I should leave him sufficient, so that *without being in want* he could continue his studies until he obtained a post. All we need is *rest, and no further interference* from the mother, and certainly *the fine aim which I set before me* would soon be attained. As one has spoken about what I received, it is easy to calculate. In May 1817 the arrangement was made; in the month of October 1817 the arrears of the pension were paid out to the mother, but she would not pay up, and I was forced to go to law to compel her. The accounts are likewise amongst the papers from the Law Court, and only an inconsiderable portion remained over. On the 19th of May, 1818, I drew the first instalment of the pension, and likewise in February 1818 the first of the interest of the mint bonds, and now for six whole months I have not received a farthing from the pension; for she herself did not apply for it as formerly, and I myself can only apply after her; one sees from this that my nephew, in my arrangements for his education, does not *in the least* suffer. It may also be seen that many a count or baron need not be ashamed of these institutes with regard to education, and there are noblemen who neither *spend* nor are able to *spend* as much. I did not count at all on this paltry contribution. My former proposition was to pay the whole amount of the pension money out of my own pocket, but her immorality, her bad behaviour towards *her own child* and myself, has taught me that this would only be the means of still further *deteriorating* her character. From the will of my poor brother who became so unhappy (through her), it can be seen how fully therein are recognised the benevolent actions which I showed to him, and how thankful he was. Now I have transferred these to his son; for immediately after his father's death, which took place in 1815, on the 15th of November, I even looked after him, even when he was staying with his mother, and at considerable expense, when he left her and went into the Institute, and I *incurred the whole expense* of his education almost until 1818. What good would it be to me to have this miserable contribution which is here deposited. Of what selfishness can I be accused; certainly of no other than that which I showed to my brother, *to do good*, and the double consciousness of having *acted* well, and of having brought up for the state a worthy citizen! Even after the opposition to my *guardianship* it may be seen from the will that my brother therein appointed me *sole* guardian. A codicil was extorted from him when in the death throes, and my *oath* and the *oath* of a lady will confirm that he sent me *several times* to town to Dr. Schönauer to withdraw *it*, Dr. Adlersberg, whom the Law Court proposed as *co-curator*, because they had *no trust in the former*, did not hesitate to regard these circumstances, although there was not the requisite number of witnesses, as entirely *legal and valid*, and to quote them as *points* in his request *against the codicil*; although apart from that, the law excludes the mother from the guardianship, and in consequence, was excluded by the Law Court from exercising *any influence on the education and from all intercourse.* If any change were made, great danger would ensue for the boy, and—there is no hope of *any improvement in the mother, she is* too corrupt; but my nephew, that tender plant in its blossoming might be destroyed by a *poisonous breath*, and it would be a heavy responsibility to *place him in such a position.* I might become easy-going and finally weary of so many intrigues and slanders; but no, I will show *that he who acts well and nobly, can also endure maltreatment on that account, and must never lose sight of the noble aim he has in view.* I have sworn to do *my best for him to the end of my life*, and, anyhow, only that can be expected from my *character and feelings* which in every respect *is most advantageous for my nephew.* And now need I still refer to the intrigues of the court draughtsman Huschowa, or of the *Mödling priest* who, despised by his community, is in disrepute owing to *illicit intercourse*, who orders his pupils to be placed, in military fashion, on the form to be thrashed, and could not forgive me for having found him out, and refused to let my nephew be caned in a *brutal manner.* Must I tell of such things? No, already the connexion of these two men with Frau von Beethoven is *sufficient evidence* against them *both*, and *only such* men would *unite with her against me.* I here repeat that, *undaunted*, I will pursue the noble aim I have in view, viz., the *intellectual, moral, and physical welfare of my nephew.* Education, however, needs to go on *quietly*, and so Fr. v. Beethoven must, *once for all*, be sent about her business. This was the aim of the *last commission* of the Law Court, for which I made request, and which *I* helped to form, so as to do on my part what might ensure the desired quiet. And so *I* will propose a *co-guardian*, and would by this time have already named him, had I not been *uncertain concerning as to whom I should select.* As regards *an appeal*, that naturally stands open to *all.* I certainly do not fear *it*, yet as soon as the welfare of *my nephew* which is connected *with me* in the close manner, is in danger, I shall likewise at once appeal. *Between a law and its consequences nowhere would a difference be established.* A *total setting aside* of Frau v. Beethoven would certainly bring about a *different and favourable result*; for if she could be made to see that her intrigues were *powerless to suppress the good*, she would no longer despise the magnanimity and mercy *so often tried on her by me*, and this unpleasant *gloom*, so far as circumstances permit, *could be turned into the brightness of day.* May the outcome of everything be that as I was formerly the benefactor to the father of my nephew, so may I deserve to be called a still *greater benefactor to his son*, yes, I might say *his father.* No private, no public interest can be ascribed to me in this but *only the good*; the Law Court saw this, and thanked me for my fatherly care.

Ludwig van Beethoven,
Guardian
of my nephew,
Carl v. Beethoven.

To the Worshipful Magistrate of the Imperial Royal City
of Vienna.
Ludwig van Beethoven
In the matter of the guardianship
(with enclosure).

[The letter is one of the few in which the composer expounds his theories on education. The date (1818) is an evident error; it should be 1819. With regard to Carl's training, we here read something which causes astonishment. Beethoven states that he let Carl continue his studies at the institute of which Herr von Kudlich was principal, and in company with the son of Baron Lang. The only biographer who has mentioned this Kudlich Institute is Nohl; the Conversation Books of 1820, however, contain much about Carl's training there.

Gideon Ernst Freiherr von Loudon was in every respect a great hero and personality; Haydn, by the way, dedicated to him one of his symphonies. Beethoven, however, appears to have confused the baron with his father, Gerhard Otto von Loudon, who according to Janko was a "pious, honourable, Christian man, who in conformity with his principles, made it his chief duty to instil into his son Gideon the observance of religious duties."]

310. To FERDINAND RIES, London

Vienna, *April* 16, 1819.

Here, dear Ries, the *tempi* of the Sonata.
1st Allegro, Allegro only, the *assai* must be taken away.
Maelzel's Metronome, minim = 138
2nd movement, Scherzoso. M. Metronome, minim = 80
3rd movement, M. Metronome, quaver = 92
Notice here that a bar is to be added at the beginning thus:

4th movement, Introduzione largo, Maelzel's Metronome,
  semiquaver = 76
5th movement, ¾ time,

and the last, Maelzel's Metronome, minim = 144.

Excuse the muddles; if you knew what a state I am in, you
would not be surprised at them; rather at what I am able to do
in spite of them. I cannot keep back the Quintet any longer, and
it will shortly appear; but not the Sonata, until I receive a final
answer from you, and the honorarium for which I am longing. De
Smit is the name of the courier from whom you have received the
Quintet and Sonata—please send a speedy answer. More shortly.
In haste.

Your BEETHOVEN.

[The Sonata in B flat (Op. 106) referred to in this and the following
letter, was published in 1819.]

311. TO THE SAME

April 19, 1819.

DEAR FRIEND!

Forgive all the trouble I am causing you. I cannot conceive
how so many faults got into the copy of the Sonata; they are
probably owing to my no longer being able to keep a copyist of my
own. Circumstances have brought all this about, and may the Lord
send improvement until the —— is in a better state! But for that
a full twelvemonth is needed. It is really terrible, how this affair
has been going on, and what has become of my annuity, and no
one can say what will be, until the said year is over. If the Sonata
(Op. 106) should not be the right thing for London, I could send
another, or you could also leave out the Largo, and begin at once
with the Fugue in the last movement, or the first movement, Adagio,
and for the third, the Scherzo and the Largo and All°. risoluto.
I leave this to you to do as you think best. The Sonata was written
under painful circumstances. For it is hard to write almost for the
sake of bread; and to that I have now come.

As to London, we will correspond further on the subject. It
would certainly be the only salvation for me, so as to extricate
myself from this wretched, oppressive plight. I am never well,
and never able to accomplish what, under better conditions, would
be possible.

312. To the Same

Dear Ries,

I have only just recovered from a severe attack, and am going into the country—I wish you could see your way to induce a publisher in London to take the 2 following works, a grand solo pianoforte sonata, *and a pianoforte sonata transcribed by me as a Quintet for 2 violins, 2 violas, 1 'cello*. It will probably be easy for you to get 50 ducats in gold for them.

N.B. (if you can get more, all the better. Surely you can manage that ! ! ! !)

In order to receive both works, the publisher need only say when he wishes to publish both works, then I could also publish them here at the same time, and I should at least get more than if I only published them here. I could also publish a new Trio for pianoforte, violin and 'cello, if you found a publisher for it—of course you know very well that I have never acted illegally, and therefore you can negotiate the matter without your or my honour suffering. The publisher will inform me as soon as he has received the works when he wants to publish them, and then they will also come out here.

Pardon my troubling you; my request is a special one, for I have to try in every direction to provide for my sad existence. Potter says that Chappell in Bond Street is one of the best publishers. I leave everything to you, only I beg you to give me an answer as quickly as possible, so that the works may not lie idle here.

Please ask Neate not in any way to make known the many small works which I gave him, until I myself come to London. I certainly hope to do so next winter, and this I *have to do* if I don't want to become a beggar here. Best regards to the Philharmonic Society.

Will shortly send more news,
and beg you once again to send
a speedy reply.
As ever your true
friend,

Kind regards to your
handsome wife.　　　　　　　　　　　　　BEETHOVEN.

[Was the Quintet arranged from a *Sonata* a slip of Beethoven's pen? In the above letter the firm of Chappell and Co. is mentioned for the first and only time in Beethoven's letters.—Tr.]

313. To the Same

— — — Meanwhile I have been worried with cares such as I never had before in my life; and all through excessive kindness to other men.

Continue to compose diligently! My dear little Archduke Rudolf and I also play your music, and he says that the former pupil does honour to the master. Now farewell. Your wife, as I hear she is handsome, I will kiss, only mentally; I hope, however, next winter to have the pleasure of doing so personally. Do not forget the Quintet and the Sonata and the money, I wanted to say: the honorarium, *avec ou sans honneur.* I hope to hear good news from you very soon, not *allegro* time, but *Veloce Prestissimo.* The bearer of this letter is a most intelligent Englishman, who for the most part are all smart fellows, with whom I should like to spend some time in their country.

Prestissimo—Responsio, il suo amico e Maestro.

BEETHOVEN.

314. To the Archduke RUDOLPH

YOUR IMPERIAL HIGHNESS!

I receive with regret the news that Y.I.H. is again unwell, but not having received any further and more definite news, I am very anxious. I was in Vienna to look in the library of Y.I.H. for something, and *quick finding* is an essential (and with *better art-union* in which, however, *practical intentions* may form exceptions), for which the ancients are of double service to us, since for the most part in them alone is real, valuable art (among them only the *German* Handel and Seb. Bach possessed genius). The aim in the world of art, as indeed in the whole creation, is freedom, *progress*; if we moderns have not the same *firmness* as our ancestors, yet the refinement of our manners has in many ways enlarged our sphere of action. My worthy pupil himself, now striving for the laurels of fame, cannot be accused of one-sidedness, *et iterum venturus judicare vivos—et mortuos.* Here are three poems, from which, perhaps, Y.I.H. might select one to set to music. The Austrians now know that the *spirit of Apollo* has revived in the Imperial family. From all quarters I receive requests to obtain something. The *proprietor of the Modezeitung* will *apply* to Y.I.H. *by writing.* I hope that I shall not in any way be accused of *bribery*—I am at the court, yet no courtier; *what is the good of all that ??!!!* In looking for the music in Vienna, I met with some opposition from *his excellency the chief steward.* It is not worth while to trouble Y.I.H. by writing details, but I only want to say this much, that through things of this kind, many a good and noble man, not being fortunate enough to have full knowledge of your excellent qualities of head and heart, might be frightened away. I hope Y.I.H. that you will very soon be restored to health, also that I shall receive news to *ease my mind.*

[The passages concerning the æsthetics of the art are, unfortunately, not clear. The sentence within brackets beginning "and with better" was declared by Koechel to be "incomprehensible." In translation, therefore, it is equally so.]

315. TO THE SAME

MÖDLING,
Aug. 31, 1819.

YOUR IMPERIAL HIGHNESS!

Only yesterday did I receive fresh news which increases the *value and splendour of your excellent qualities of head and heart.* Graciously receive my congratulations, and accept them; they come from my heart—and are thoroughly genuine. I hope that things will soon go better with me, so much misfortune has acted unfavourably on my health, and I find myself far from well. Since some time I have had to take medicine, so that for only a few hours in the day can I give myself up to Heaven's noblest gift, my art, and to the muses. I hope, however, to complete the Mass, so that it can be performed on the 19th if that date still stands. I should at least fall into despair, if through circumstances connected with my bad health, it should fail to be ready by that time. I hope, however, that my inmost wish to accomplish this will be fulfilled. Concerning the masterly Variations of Y.I.H., I think they could be published under the following title, viz.:

> Thema oder Aufgabe
> gesetzt von L. v. Beeth.
> viertzigmal verändert
> u. seinem Lehrer gewidmet
> *von den durchlauchtigsten Verfasser*

There are so many inquiries for them, that incorrect copies of this honourable work might be sent out into the world. Y.I.H. will be compelled to give copies away here and there, and thus, if God will, together with the numerous consecrations which your Y.I.H.

is now receiving and becoming acquainted with, will also be counted the consecration of Apollo (or the Christian Cecilia). Y.I.H. might, perhaps, accuse me of *vanity*, but although this dedication is dear to my heart, and I am really proud of it, this alone was certainly not my object.

Three publishers have announced themselves: Artaria, Steiner, and a third whose name I cannot for the moment recall. So to which of the first two shall the Variations be given? I await the orders of Y.I.H. Both of them have undertaken to *engrave at their own cost*. It is now a question whether Y.I.H. is *satisfied with the title*. As to whether they should be published, I think Y.I.H. should not trouble. If they appear in print Y.I.H. may consider it a misfortune; *but the world will think the reverse*. God preserve Y.I.H. and scatter His horn of plenteous mercy on your sacred head, and may He ever preserve to me your gracious favour.

Your Imperial Highness's
most obedient,
most faithful,

[Outside: L. v. BEETHOVEN.

Y.I.H. will, I hope, owing to my illness, excuse this untidy letter.

[The fresh news here referred to was the Grand Cross of the Order of St. Stephen bestowed by Kaiser Franz. In spite of holy vows and protestations, the Mass was far from ready for the enthronisation of the new Archbishop (1820); it was only completed in 1823. But the delay did not cause Beethoven to despair ; also the Archduke and Archbishop graciously accepted the dedication of the *Missa solemnis*.]

316. To CARL ZELTER, BERLIN

VIENNA, *September* 18, 1819.

HONOURED SIR!

It is not my fault that you, as we say here, were made a fool of; unforeseen circumstances prevented me having the pleasure of spending some highly enjoyable, and for art, profitable hours with you. I hear, unfortunately, that you are leaving Vienna the day after to-morrow. My country life on account of my weak health is not this year so beneficial as usual; hence I may return to town the day after to-morrow, and then in the afternoon, if you have not gone, I shall hope to tell you by word of mouth, and most cordially, in what high esteem I hold you, and how I wish to be near you.

In haste,
Your most devoted friend,
BEETHOVEN.

[Carl Zelter, the intimate friend of Goethe, changed from a captious fault-finder to an enthusiastic admirer and worshipper of the master's. A few days before this letter, Zelter wrote to Goethe (14 September): "The day before yesterday I wished to pay a visit to Beethoven in Mödling. He was going to Vienna and so we met in the Landstrasse; stepped out of our carriages and cordially embraced each other. He is unfortunately almost stone-deaf, and I could scarcely refrain from tears. I drove on to Mödling and he to Vienna." To the left of the signature at the end of Beethoven's letter, Zelter wrote: "To see the countenance of this man once again, who provides joy and edification for so many good persons, among whom I most willingly class myself, that was the reason, my worthy friend, why I wished to pay you a visit in Mödling. You met me, and my intention was at any rate not quite frustrated, for I gazed on your countenance. Of the infirmity which oppresses you I have been informed, I sympathise with you, for I suffer in a similar way. The day after to-morrow I return to my calling, but I will never cease to hold you in high esteem and love you. Vienna, October 7, 1819. Your Zelter."]

317. To Countess Von ERDÖDY

19th December, 1819.

All that is good and beautiful to my dear honoured friend,
from your true friend who esteems you,

L. v. BEETHOVEN.

In haste the 19th December, 1819.
I shall soon come myself.   Vi=

[The Countess, after this year, quite vanishes from Beethoven's circle and, indeed, from Vienna. Mystery surrounds her fate and that of her household. There are enigmatical statements on the matter in a Conversation Book of 1820. So much is certain, viz., that the Countess was banished from Austria; that she lived first at Padua, then in Munich, where she died, aged fifty-seven, in 1837.]

318. To the Archduke RUDOLPH

[1819?]

Your Imperial Highness!

I have the honour to send you through the copyist Schlemmer, Y.I.H.'s masterly Variations. I myself will wait upon Y.I.H. to-morrow, and heartily rejoice that I can guide my distinguished pupil along the path leading to high fame.

Your Imperial Highness's most
devoted and faithful

L. v. BEETHOVEN.

[The Variations of the Archduke appeared this year at Steiner's.]

319. To the Same

[1819?]

Your Imperial Highness!

I unfortunately must accuse myself, I went out yesterday for the first time and felt pretty well—but as a convalescent patient I forgot about, or paid no attention to returning home early—and through that I have again suffered an attack. However, by staying at home to-day, it seems as if I shall be in the best order to-morrow, and I certainly hope to be able to wait on my most revered and distinguished pupil. I beg Y.I.H. not to forget Handel's works, as they always offer the best nourishment for your ripe musical mind, and will at the same time lead to admiration for this great man.

> Your Imperial Highness's faithful and most
> obedient servant,
> Ludwig van Beethoven.

[Beethoven was never tired of praising Handel.]

320. To the Painter STIELER

[1819?]

Most worthy Friend!

To-day it is impossible for me to come to you, but to-morrow I will be with you punctually at 11. Please forgive.

> In haste,
> With deepest respect,
> Yours very truly,
> Beethoven.

[This note to the portrait-painter, Carl Josef Stieler, may belong to the years 1820–21.]

321. To the Lower Austrian Law Court

When the summons of the L.A.L.C. was sent to me on the 22nd of this month to my present residence at Mödling, I was just at that moment in Vienna on business, and so could not appear at the appointed time to answer the summons. I therefore send a written explanation which I herewith place before the L.A.L.C.

The mother of my ward, who on account of her moral incapacity was properly and strictly excluded by the L.A.L.C. from taking any part in his education, has made several unsuccessful attempts to prevent me from carrying out the education plan which I had sketched out, but by interference she has again ventured on a step to which I, as exclusively appointed guardian of my nephew Carl van Beethoven, can in no wise agree.

In order to attain her aim, she has recourse to means which in themselves show her low-mindedness, for, as regards the education of my nephew, she casts a disadvantageous light on my deafness, as she calls it, and my alleged illness.

As to the first point, it is well known by all who are acquainted with me, that all communication by word of mouth between me and my nephew, likewise other people, is carried on with no difficulty, so that cannot be brought forward as an obstacle. Then again, my health was never better than it is at the present moment, so from that side there is no thought or fear of my nephew's education suffering.

After I had placed him in the Institute of Herr Giannatasio, where he remained for two years at my expense, he came home to me in order that I myself might perceive whether he showed more inclination to music or to science.

Here under my eyes he had every opportunity to display his talent for music, in which I myself instructed him daily for $2\frac{1}{2}$ hours, also at the same time to continue his school studies.

I found that he showed inclination rather to scientific subjects. The certificates enclosed under Letter A offer abundant proof that during this summer when he was with me in the country, he devoted himself to his studies with the same zeal as in Vienna itself; I beg that those certificates be returned to me. As to the intention of the mother of my ward to get him into the Convict School, I must most clearly state my reasons for objecting to this proposal.

I. Those relationships settled by the Court, namely, that the mother was not only excluded from the guardianship, but also from *all* influence in the matter of education, and from all intercourse with the ward, are still in force.

II. Therefore, if the ward went to the Convict School, the object of the Court would be frustrated, in that the special restrictions with regard to *this* mother would not be known there, so that she might easily manage to ask for the boy and to take him away to her home.

Attempts of this kind she had already made at my house, by bribing the servants, and by leading the boy to tell untruths, also to carry on deception, although she has been allowed to see and to speak with her son in my presence, whenever she expressed a wish to do so, and whenever circumstances allowed of it.

III. The enclosures under B and C sufficiently show that the mother of my ward, already during his residence in the Institute, made secret attempts, and that her intercourse with the ward was recognised by the Principal of the Institute himself as highly injurious to the same.

IV. Since the time when the exclusive guardianship of my nephew was entrusted to me by the Law Court, I have not only paid all costs for education (for the small contribution from the mother which I have lately received as compensation, is too small to be taken into consideration), but I have also continually taken all care and trouble to do everything to turn him into a good and useful citizen of the state, and to have him educated as well as possible, so much so indeed, that the tenderest father could not do more for his own child. I do not for all this expect the thanks of the mother, but I hope that it will be recognised by the legal guardianship.

V. The scheme for the future, higher education of my nephew has long been planned and followed. A harmful disturbance in the course of education would therefore arise, if suddenly a totally new plan were followed.

For the rest, I intend to give the proper notice to the Law Court at every proposed change with regard to my nephew, in order to do what is most fitting in unison with the same. For this it would be more and more necessary, so as to avoid all disturbance and hindrance on the part of the mother of the boy, and to remove her from all influences, as it has been decreed in the case in point by § 191 of the Civil Law Code—certainly a very wise determination. Also because she, through her intellectual and moral character, appears to me least fit, owing to the advancing age of the boy, to have any influence on his education, and therefore on his future career as a man. But in such a manner, Frau Johanna van Beethoven, after the decision of the Court by which she was excluded from taking part in the education of her child and of intercourse with him, likewise after the decision of the Law Court of the 19th January, 1816, whereby the sole and exclusive guardianship of my nephew was entrusted to me, how, I say, she can venture to come forward as the guardian of her son, who is a minor, is sufficiently understandable by me from her bold behaviour in all matters.

VIENNA, 25th September, 1818.

LUDWIG VAN BEETHOVEN,
as guardian of my nephew, Carl van Beethoven.

I. DAS LIEBE KÄZCHEN

Munter

Un - sa Käz had Ka - z'ln g'habt drai und sex si nai - ni

van's häd a Aeu-gerl af däs is schön das mai - ni.

II. DER KNABE AUF DEM BERGE

'Sist just so a

Bia - berl wiä du! Komm ä - ba main Bia - berl zu miar i

zähl drae 'n Biar i zähl dr' a Nüss mid an'm kna'n, könnst

D. C.

glai wölst main Bia - berl no wea'n.

322. To Herr SIMROCK, Music Publisher, Bonn

VIENNA, 18th March, 1820.

DEAR HERR SIMROCK!

I do not know whether I clearly explained myself about everything in my former letter—I therefore write to you briefly that I will also, if you think it necessary, prolong the term for the publication of the Variations. As to the Mass, I have carefully thought over the matter, and could give it to you probably for the honorarium of 100 louis d'or, offered to me by you, if, perchance, you agree to some conditions which I will propose to you, and which, so it seems to me, you will not find troublesome? We have already, when you were here, gone through the plan for the publication, and thought that the matter, with certain *modifications*, could soon be set going, which is very necessary; so will I hasten and propose as soon as possible the necessary changes—As I know that merchants like to save post money. I add here two Austrian folk-songs in exchange; you can do whatever you like with them, the accompaniment is my own. I think a hunt after folk-songs is better than a hunt after men of the so praised heroes.

My copyist does not happen to be here, but I hope you will be able to read it. You could have many things of the kind from me, in return for which you could show me kindness in a different way.

In haste,
Yours,
BEETHOVEN.

[On the reverse side of the cover is written: "Ouvrés la lettre avec bien de ménagement." In spite of this warning, a piece was torn off a sheet of music paper with the superscription: "Der Knabe auf dem Berge," so that the first four bars can no longer be clearly made out.]

323. To MORITZ SCHLESINGER, Music Publisher, Berlin

VIENNA, 5th March, 1820.

DEAR SIR,

· I remember that you came to see me in Mödling, and wished to have some of my works, and if I remember rightly, you wanted small rather than big ones. I am now on the point of publishing several works, among which I offer you the two following, which I think most suitable to you—25 Scotch Songs with pianoforte accompaniment (violin or flute and 'cello) (violin or flute and 'cello are *ad libitum*). Each song is provided with *ritornelli*, several of them are for two, three voices, and with chorus. The text is by the best English poets, and they could with advantage be translated into German, and published with the English as well as the German text. Eight themes, among which Scotch and Russian songs, with variations for pianoforte, each of which forms a small work with flute *ad libitum*. I ask you as honorarium for the 25 Scotch Songs, 60 ducats in gold, for the 8 themes with easy variations for pianoforte, and flute *ad libitum*, an honorarium of 70 ducats in gold. I cannot agree to any lowering of the terms. You will have these works as your property for the whole Continent, Scotland and England being excluded; yet on the understanding, that I refrain from publishing these works in both countries until I know when you will publish them on the Continent. For this time I want the publishing of the said work to be hurried on, and I therefore beg you to let me know as quickly as possible your intentions in the matter, otherwise I should lose time! In expectation of an answer very soon.

Yours very truly,
BEETHOVEN.

N.B.—You need only put this address, "To Ludwig van Beethoven, Vienna."

[The twenty-five Scotch Songs were accepted and published as Op. 108 towards the end of 1821. The work was dedicated by the publisher to Beethoven's friend, Prince Anton Heinrich Radziwill.]

324. TO SENATOR FRANZ BRENTANO, FRANKFORT-ON-MAIN

VIENNA, November 28, 1820.

DEAR SIR,

Your kind nature lets me hope that you will not refuse to see that this enclosure is sent to Simrock, as in it my views concerning the whole matter are given. There is now nothing to do but to take what he offers, namely the 100 pistoles and what extra, as an expert, you can gain for me through the state of the money market, so I am in anticipation convinced of your honest opinion. I am in such a hard and harassed position just now, but that one can *least of all write to a publisher*. It is not my fault, thank God, it is my great devotion to others, especially to the weak Cardinal who has brought me into this slough, and knows not how to help himself. As soon as the transcription is ready, I will trouble you again about the sending of the Mass, and I then beg you, if possible, to devote a little attention to my advantage against this Jewish publisher. I hope that I may in some way be of service to you or to yours.

With high esteem, your grateful friend and servant,

BEETHOVEN.

Please excuse my apparently careless scrawl, it is owing to hurry—best regards to all of you.

[The contents of this letter concern the great Mass in D which many publishers wanted, and among them Schlesinger of Berlin. The "weak" Cardinal, who brought Beethoven into this "slough," was the formerly high-esteemed, highly-honoured Cardinal Archduke Rudolph, for whom the Mass was intended; the Jewish publisher was Schlesinger of Berlin.]

325. To SCHLESINGER, DEALER IN WORKS OF ART, BERLIN

VIENNA, *March* (?) 7, 1821.

DEAR SIR,

You will probably think badly of me, but you ought soon to change your opinion, when I say to you that I have been laid low for the past six weeks with a severe attack of rheumatism, but I am now better. You can imagine that a stop was put to many things, but I shall soon make up for lost time. Now let me briefly tell you what is most important. On the songs is marked Op. 107, and, if I mistake not, the names of the English authors, amongst whom are Moore, Byron, Scott, &c., are not added; they shall be sent to you very shortly. It is open to you to dedicate to the Crown Prince of Prussia, although I had intended it for some one else. So I give way—but as regards the Sonata which you must now have had for some time, I beg you to add the following title together with the dedication, namely,

Sonate für das Hammerklavier

Verfasst u. dem Fräulein Maximiliana Brentano

gewidmet von Ludwig van Beethoven

109tes Werk.

Will you also add the year, as I have so often desired, but which no publisher has ever been willing to do?

The other two Sonatas will soon follow—and I will let you know in good time about the honorarium. I have not your letters to hand; if I am right, you wanted some other works. If you will soon let me know about this, I can arrange, and so as to produce, and at leisure, works worthy of myself, the public, and my art. I wish you all that is profitable. Probably my manuscript will be legible. If you find corrections necessary, I beg you to send both the songs and the Sonatas, only you must send with them the manuscript of the songs, which indeed is only a hurriedly made copy of my manuscript, the latter however I do not possess.

Farewell, my honoured friend,

Yours very truly,

BEETHOVEN.

[Beethoven here speaks expressly of the Opus No. 107, which was to be put on a vocal work given to the firm. As contents of the work Beethoven mentions songs, from which it appears doubtful whether the Scotch Songs published by Steiner as Op. 108 are meant. The present Op. 107 consists of ten themes with variations for piano alone or with flute or violin. In a former letter to Schlesinger there was a question of such a work. According to Thayer and Nohl, these themes with variations were composed between 1818 and 1820 for G. Thomson of Edinburgh.]

326. To TOBIAS HASLINGER

BADEN, 10th September, 1821.

VERY BEST ONE!

Yesterday as I was on the way to Vienna in my carriage, I fell asleep, all the more so, seeing that scarcely ever (on account of the early rising here) have I had a proper sleep. Now while slumbering I dreamed that I was taking a far journey, as far as Syria, as far as India, back again as far as Arabia; finally I came, indeed, to Jerusalem. The Holy City prompted thoughts about Holy Writ, when, and no wonder, I thought of the man Tobias, and naturally that led to my thinking of our little Tobias and our *pertobias*; now in my dream journey the following Canon occurred to me:

O To - bi - as

But I had scarcely woke up, when the Canon was gone, and I could not recall any of it. However, as I (a poor Austrian musician) was returning next day in the same carriage, while awake, the dream journey went on, only think, according to the law of association of ideas, the same Canon came back to me. Now being awake, I held it fast as once Menelaus Proteus, only allowing it just to change itself into a three-part one:

O To - bi - as

Farewell! Soon I will send something on Steiner in order to show that he has not a stony heart. Farewell, my best one, we always hope that you will never answer to the name of publisher, and that you will never be in perplexity, but as publishers, who are never embarrassed either in taking in or giving out. Sing every day the Epistles of St. Paul, go every Sunday to Pater Werner, who will point you to the little book by which you may at once get to heaven. You see my anxiety for the salvation of your soul, and with greatest pleasure I remain for ever and ever

Your most faithful debtor,

BEETHOVEN.

[The year must be 1826, instead of 1821, as written by Nottebohm and Nohl. The musical jokes against Tobias Haslinger continued in the following years, and led finally to controversy with the publishers of *Cäcilia*, of which we shall hear more in the years 1825 and 1826. The command in the letter to go every day to Peter Werner refers to the preaching of the dramatic poet, F. L. Zacharias Werner. From the time of the Congress of Vienna, Werner had lived in that city, where—having gone over to Roman Catholicism in 1811—he preached to great crowds. In the summer of 1814 he was ordained priest, hence the expression "Pater Werner." He died at Vienna in 1823.]

327. TO STEINER & CO.

[1821.]

To the most famous music firm in Europe, Steiner & Co. (*Paternoster* (*miserere*)-Gässel).

I am asking Gebauer for a few tickets, as some of my friends wish to go to this little *musical corner*—you *yourselves* perhaps have entrance cards, so send me one or two.

Your f. amicus,

BEETHOVEN.

The State belongs to
the chorus, for which Bauer
has the parts.

["Geh Bauer." ("Away, peasant," a joke of Beethoven's on the name "Gebauer."—TR.) Which particular Gebauer is referred to—for there were several of that name in Vienna—is not certain. It was probably Franz Xaver Gebauer, who conducted the first performance in Vienna of Beethoven's Mass in C. He founded the famous *Concerts spirituels,* and it seems as if it were to one of these that Beethoven is referring.]

328. For Herr Von PETERS

[1821?]

What are you doing? Are you well or unwell? What is your wife doing? Will you allow me to sing to you:

[On the second page.]

What are your young princes doing?

Shall you be at home this afternoon about 5 o'clock, perhaps I will come to see you with my *state*-brother.

> In haste,
> Yours,
> Beethoven.

329. To the Music Seller M. SCHLESINGER

Vienna, 1st *March,* 1822.

Dear Sir!

You will by now surely have received the Scottish songs which were here delivered at Diabelli's. Concerning the last movement of the 3rd Sonata, here is the receipt, I hope that you will now have the music, I beg you once again to sign it and to destroy the first copy received. Concerning the 2nd Sonata in A flat, I have decided to *dedicate it to some one* whose name I will send you by the next post—the 3rd can be dedicated to any one you please. Thank God I am better in health; as for the Mass, I beg you now to bring everything into order, as other publishers have asked for it, especially from here many offers have been made to me, yet I have for a long time determined that it shall not be published *here*; for this time it is a matter of great importance to me. For the moment I beg you to let me know whether you accept my last offer with respect to the Mass and the two added songs. So far as concerns the draft for the honorarium it must not be for longer than four weeks. I must insist upon a definite answer as especially two other publishers wish the Mass to be in their catalogue, and already, for a long time, they have been begging me for a definite answer. Farewell, and write at once to me, I should be very sorry *if I had not to hand over to you just this work.*

With esteem, yours very truly,

To Herr Ad. M.
BEETHOVEN.

Schlesinger *celebrated*
Art and Music Publisher,
in Berlin.

[In the history of the Mass, this letter is of importance. The Scotch Songs mentioned were published by Schlesinger (Op. 108) at the end of 1821. The Sonatas were Op. 109–11, in the last of which the dedication to the Archduke Rudolph was added by the publisher. A note in the composer's handwriting shows that it was "for Frau Antonie Brentano." Why, therefore, the Sonata bore no dedication has yet to be explained. The Mass, after all, was not published by Schlesinger. Peace, however, was restored, for Schlesinger published the Quartets (Opp. 132 and 135).]

330. To FERDINAND RIES, LONDON

VIENNA, 6th April, 1822.

DEAR, BEST RIES!

Already for the last six months being again poorly, I could never answer your letter. I received the £26 all right, and thank you heartily for it; of your Symphony which you have dedicated to me I have received nothing. My greatest work is a grand Mass which I have recently written, etc., etc.; time is too short to-day, so only what is most necessary. . . . What do you suppose the Philharmonic Society would offer me for a Symphony?

I still entertain the thought of coming to London, if only my health permits, perhaps next spring? You would find in me the true appreciation of my dear pupil, now a great master, and who knows what further good would arise for art in union with you. I am, as always, entirely devoted to my Muse, and only in it find the happiness of my life, also work and act also for others when I can. You have two children, I one (my brother's son), but you are married; and what I have to pay is more than enough for both of you.

[Beethoven never came to England, neither did he dedicate any work to Ries.]

331. To his Brother, JOHANN Van BEETHOVEN

3rd July, 1822.

BEST LITTLE BROTHER! A POWERFUL LAND PROPRIETOR!

Yesterday I wrote to you, being tired, however, owing to much exertion and many occupations, and having moreover a bad pen, you may have found my letter difficult to read. Write to me first of all how quickly the post goes from you to me and from here to you. I wrote to you that the Leipzig publisher takes the Mass for 1000 fl., I only wish that I could send you all the letters, there is too much detail to write. It would be better if you were present at everything, for I think that I have given him many of the other small pieces too cheaply; he still receives 4 Marches for 20 ducats, 3 songs 8 ducats each, 4 Bagatelles, one at 8 ducats. In order to avoid all formalities, I wrote to him that he might pay the money in silver coin. As however he did not yet know how many Bagatelles he receives, he has, as you will see from the enclosed note, assigned to me at once 3000 fl. I cannot, however, send the Bagatelles off at once, as the copyist is busy with the Mass, which is the most important thing, and for which, as soon as I write some days before that the Mass will go off, I shall receive at once the 1000 fl., which, had I wished it, I might have already received. Everything shows the strong desire of the man for my works. I would not however willingly compromise myself, and I should be very glad if you would write to me whether you can spare me something, so that I may not be prevented going in good time to Baden, where I must remain at least a month. You see there can be no uncertainty in the matter, for you will receive back the 200 fl. in September and with thanks. I beg you will at once send me back the enclosed note. For the rest, as a merchant, you are always a good adviser. The Steiners are driving me into a corner. They really want to have in writing that I will give them all my works. They will pay per sheet, but now I have declared that I will not enter into any such undertaking until they cancel the debt. I have proposed two works to them which I wrote in Hungary, and which may be regarded as a pair of small operas, from which they have already taken four numbers. The debt amounts to about 3000 fl. but, horrible to say, they have added interest to which I do not consent. I have undertaken herewith to pay some of Carl's mother's debts, as I willingly show to her all kindness so that no harm may come to Carl. If you were here, these things would soon be arranged; only necessity forces me to sell my soul in this way. If you come, and could only go with me for a week to Baden it would be delightful, only you must write at once what you think of doing. Meanwhile see that the kitchen and cellar are in the best order, for probably I and my little son will take up our quarters at your place, and we have the noble intention to eat you out of house and home. You understand that this is only from September.

Now farewell best brother! read the Gospel every day; take to heart the Epistles of Peter and Paul, travel to Rome and kiss the Pope's slipper. Hearty greetings to the family. Write soon. I heartily embrace you.

Your faithful brother,
LUDWIG.

I the secretary likewise heartily embrace you and hope to see you again soon.

CARL.

[In Beethoven's hand:]

I do not enclose the draft for 300 fl. convention coin, as I am afraid lest something might happen to it.

[It was only signed by the composer, the rest is in the nephew's hand.]

332. To C. F. PETERS, LEIPZIG

July 6, 1822.

DEAR SIR,

I have only just read your letter thoroughly, and I see that you wish for some of the *Bagatelles* for pianoforte alone, also a *Quartet* for 2 violins, etc. So far as the *Bagatelles* are concerned, I ask 8 ducats in gold for one; many of them are of *fair length*. You could also publish them separately, and under a German and more suitable title, viz.—*Kleinigkeiten* [Trifles, or Small Pieces].

No. 1, No. 2, etc.

e.g. *Kleinigkeiten*, No. 1 separately

—*Kleinigkeiten*

No. 2, &c., as you think best.

As to the *Viol. quart.*, which is not quite finished, as something else came in between, I could scarcely accept a smaller honorarium for it, as things of that kind are paid best for, I am almost inclined to say to the injury of the general public taste, which in the world of art often stands below individual taste. Later on, perhaps, another *quartet*, if possible. Concerning the ducats, you can reckon the same at 4 fl. 20 kr. at the 20-kreutzer rate, I do not mind. As you can have at once the songs as well as the Marches and also the *Bagatelles*, I beg you to write *soon* concerning them, so that I may not run short in the distribution of them, as I have been approached from several quarters for such trifles. Steiner's conduct *requiescat in pace*. He seems to be very anxious about it. I cannot *excuse* means of this kind, but—one has, willy-nilly, to take people as they are; if not, one finds oneself continuously in hot water. I have already written to you everything concerning the Mass, and we will leave it at that. Do not forget about the edition of the complete works, etc., etc. And now please answer soon all that still concerns me.

I wish you every good possible.

Respectfully,
Your
devoted,
BEETHOVEN.

[It is interesting to learn that already in the year 1822 Beethoven was working at the first of the last five quartets, which was only completed after the Ninth Symphony, and which was published by Schott in 1826 as Op. 127.]

333. TO HIS BROTHER JOHANN

DEAR BROTHER,   VIENNA, *July 22, 1822.*

Extremely busy, and most comfortable as regards home and my servants, who are both as awkward as they can be, I could not manage to write to you. I am better in health. I have had to drink for the last few days Johannes-Brunnen-Wasser, take powders four times a day, and now I must go to Baden and take thirty baths; if it is possible to arrange, I shall betake myself there and remain up to the sixth or seventh of August. If you could only come and help me for a few days, but you would find the dust and the heat too strong; if it were not for that, you could come and spend a week with me in Baden *ad tuum libitum*. Here I have still to look after the corrections of the Mass; I receive for it 1000 florins, C. C. from Peters, and he has already ordered 300 fl. C. C. to be sent for some other small works. If you could only read the letter, but I have not yet received the money. Also Breitkopf and Härtel have sent their Saxon *Chargé-d'affaire* to me about works, also from Diabelli in Vienna; in short, they are scrambling for my works. What an *unfortunate fortunate* man I am! ! ! Even this Berliner has appeared. If only my health keeps good, I am on the road to good fortune.

The Archduke Cardinal is here; I go to him twice a week. There is nothing to expect from him in the way of magnanimity or money, but I am on such good familiar footing with him, so that it would pain me not to be nice to him; besides, I don't think his apparent parsimony is his own fault. Before I go to Baden I want clothes, because I am very short of them, even of shirts, as you have already seen. Ask your wife what she thinks of this linen; it costs per ell 48 kreutzer. If you can come without harm to yourself, do so. In September I will come to you with Carl, if I do not go to Ollmütz to the Cardinal, which he much desires. Concerning the rooms which you have already taken, so let it be, but whether it will be equally good for me is a question. The rooms lead into the garden, but garden air is the worst possible for me, and then the entry is through the kitchen, which is very unpleasant and unhealthy. And now I have to pay a quarter for nothing; therefore Carl and I, if possible, will come to you at Krems, and have a jolly time of it till the money is made up, i.e. if I do not go to Moravia. Do write as soon as you receive this. Greetings to your household. If I had not to go to Baden I should certainly have come to you next month. But now things can't be changed, so if you can come, do so; it would be a great relief to me. Write at once. Fare right well. I embrace you from my heart, and am, as always,

Your faithful brother,

LUDWIG.

334. FOR HR. ARTARIA

August 22, 1822.

As I am just very busy, I can only say briefly that all the kindnesses shown to me by you, I will repay so far as I possibly can. As regards the *Mass*, 1000 fl., convention coin, has been offered me. My circumstances do not admit of my taking a smaller sum from you; all I can do is to *give you the preference*. Rest assured that I will not take a *farthing more* from you *than is offered to me by others*; I could show you this in writing. You can think over the matter, yet I must beg you to let me have an answer by *midday to-morrow*, as to-morrow is post-day and my decision is being waited for elsewhere. As regards the 150 fl. convention coin, which I owe you, I will likewise make you a proposal, as I am very much in want of the 1000 fl. I beg you, for the rest, to keep secret about the Mass.

As always your grateful friend,

BEETHOVEN.

[Simrock, Schlesinger, Probst, Peters, Artaria and Schott were all wanting the Mass; the last-named acquired it.]

335. To FERDINAND RIES

VIENNA, *December* 20, 1822.

MY DEAR RIES!

Overloaded with work I have only just found time to answer your letter of November 15. I accept with pleasure the proposal to write a symphony for the Philharmonic Society, although the honorarium from the Englishmen cannot be compared with that of other nations. If I were not always the poor Beethoven, I myself would willingly write free of charge for the first artists in Europe. If only I were in London, what would I not write for the Philharmonic Society! For Beethoven, thank God, can write; of all else, indeed, he is incapable. If only God will restore to me my health, which to say the least, has improved, I could do myself justice, in accepting offers from all cities in Europe, yes, even North America, and I might still prosper.

[According to the Biographical Notices of Wegeler and Ries. There was a request from Boston that Beethoven should write an oratorio for the Musical Society of that city. Letters passed, and the matter is mentioned in the Conversation Books, but nothing came of it.]

336. To ANTON DIABELLI

[1822?]

DEAR D——!

Patience! I am not *human yet*, still less accustomed to doing what is necessary and fitting for me—the *honorarium* for the Variations would be at most 40 ducats, if they are carried out on the same large scale as at present is planned; but should this not be so, then they would be less. Now about the Overture, in addition to this, I would have given 7 Nos. from the *Weihe des Hauses* for which I have been offered here an honorarium of 80 ducats. I would add a *Gratulations Menuet* for full orchestra, in short, the Overture and 7 Nos. from the *Weihe des Hauses* and the *Gratulations Menuet*, and all for 90 ducats. My housekeeper is going to-day into town before 12 o'clock. Please give me an answer concerning my offer. I hope by the end of next week to set to work on your Variations. Farewell, my good friend,

Yours always,

B——N.

As soon as the Sonata has been corrected, send me the same with the French copy. With regard to the metronome, next time

—kindly look over it yourself, for my eyes can scarcely bear such work without doing them harm.

Your friend,

Please send the Variations   BEETHOVEN.
to be corrected.

[The principal point in this letter is the set of Variations on a Diabelli waltz. This delightful episode in Beethoven's life deserves to be given here in fuller detail. The publishing firm, Diabelli and Co., in the winter of 1822, proposed to get various composers to write Variations for the pianoforte. The theme was by Diabelli. Each composer was to contribute one Variation. Beethoven himself was invited to take part. This suddenly awoke in him a remembrance of the collective vocal settings of the text, *In questa tomba oscura*, of the year 1808. At the same time the master recalled all the bitterness which was caused thereby. He now declared that he had resolved never again to take part in a collective work, in the present case the triviality of the theme invited ridicule; he did not care for it nor for its rosalias. Hence he seemed to have declined the invitation. But not long after this decided declaration, Beethoven sent his amanuensis Schindler to ask Diabelli whether it would be agreeable to him if he worked out the theme by himself, and what fee D. would be willing to offer. The publisher, delighted, at once offered eighty ducats, and notified the master at once of this resolve in a few lines of writing, only asking for six or seven Variations. Beethoven, on his side, was not less agreeably surprised at the unusually high fee for a few Variations on a theme which was new to him, and he wrote back at once agreeing, remarking to Schindler: "Well, he shall have some Variations on his cobbler's patch!"—In May of the year 1823 Beethoven rented, as is well known, the magnificently situated villa at Hetzendorf, belonging to Baron von Pronay. The next thing was setting to work at the Diabelli waltz, which amused him very much. Soon ten, then twenty, then twenty-five Variations were completed, and still the end was not in sight. Diabelli began to get very anxious about the inordinate length of the work, and wanted it to be cut short, but the composer, who had on him a fit of composition, wanted to show all that he could make out of a fairly commonplace theme, especially one with rosalias, and he told Diabelli that he must still be patient for a while. And thus arose the *Thirty-three Variations on a Waltz* (Op. 120), in which, as Schindler remarks: "One can easily see in what a *couleur de rose* mood they were written."]

337. To the Grand Duke, LUDWIG I. Von HESSE

VIENNA, *February* 5, 1823.

YOUR ROYAL HIGHNESS,

The undersigned has just finished his latest work, which he considers the best of his musical products.

It is a grand solemn Mass for 4 solo voices, with choruses and full orchestra. It can also be performed as a great oratorio.

He therefore desires most submissively to send a copy of this Mass in score to Your Royal Highness, and therefore dutifully begs Your Royal Highness to give your most gracious consent.

As, however, the copy of the score entails considerable expense, the undersigned ventures to inform Your Royal Highness, that he has fixed the moderate honorarium of 50 ducats for this great work, and flatters himself that he will have the distinguished honour of counting Your Highness among the number of his most noble subscribers.

[On the 26th of the same month, Schleiermacher, cabinet secretary, wrote at the head of the above letter: "Answered, with request to send the score."]

338. To FERDINAND RIES, London

February 5, 1823.

My dear good Ries!

Up to now I have not received further news about the *Sinfonie*, meanwhile you can safely count on it, for I have made the acquaintance here of a very amiable educated man who holds an appointment at our Imperial Embassy in London, so he will undertake later on to help to forward the *Sinfonie* from here to you in London; so it will soon be there. If I were not so poor as to be compelled to live by my pen, I would really accept nothing from the Phil. Society; as matters stand I must actually wait here till the honorarium is sent; in order, however, to show my love for and trust in this society, I have already given the new *Overture* mentioned in my last letter to the above-mentioned gentleman of the Imperial Society. As the latter starts from here in a few days, he will himself hand it over to you in London. They will know your address at Goldschmidt's, if not, give it to them so that this kind-hearted man may lose no time in looking for you. I leave it to the Society what they will arrange concerning the *Overture*; they may keep it, likewise the *Sinfonie*, for 18 months—only after that period shall I publish it. Now another request. My brother here, who keeps his *carriage*, also wished to borrow from me, and so without asking me, he has offered this same Overture to a publisher named Boosey in London; keep him waiting, and tell him that, for the present, one cannot definitely say whether he can have the *Overture*; that I would write about it myself—everything depends on the Philharmonic Society; only please say that as regards the *Overture* my brother has made a mistake. Other works for which he had written to him, he may possibly have. He bought them of me in order to make a profit by them, as I have found out, *o frater*. I ask you especially to write at once about the *Overture* as soon as you receive it, whether the Philharmonic Society will take it; as otherwise I should soon publish it.

Of your *Symphony* dedicated to me I have received *nothing*. If I did not look upon the *dedication* as a kind of *challenge* which I am bound to accept, I should already have dedicated to you some work; but up to now I have always thought I ought to see your *work* first, and would willingly show my gratitude in some way or other. I am greatly indebted to you for the great affection and kindness shown to me. If my health improves through a course of baths during next summer, then I shall embrace your wife in London in 1824.

Ever yours,
BEETHOVEN.

339. To Director ZELTER, Berlin

VIENNA, *February* 8, 1823.

MY GALLANT BROTHER ARTIST!

A request which I wish to make to you induces me to write, as being so far apart, we cannot speak to each other; but, unfortunately, writing can also not be frequent. I have written a grand Mass, which could also be given as an oratorio (for the benefit of the poor, according to the good custom now in vogue). I do not wish to publish it in the ordinary way, but to get it accepted by the principal courts. The honorarium is 50 ducats, and with exception of those copies which have been subscribed for, no others will be given away, so that the Mass is practically manuscript. There must, however, be a fair number, if the author is to derive any benefit from it. I have addressed a petition to the Royal Prussian Embassy here, that his Majesty the King of Prussia may condescend to take a copy; I have also written to Prince Radziwill asking for his interest. I beg you yourself to bring your influence to bear in the matter. A work of that kind would also be of service for the Singakademie, for with very little change the vocal parts could be performed alone; with those parts doubled and multiplied, in combination with the instruments, the effect would, however, be more imposing. Also as an oratorio, as benevolent societies require such things, it might be useful. Already for several years I have been always ailing, and therefore not in the most brilliant position, and so I had recourse to this means. I have indeed written much—but *gained*—almost 0. My thoughts are rather directed heavenwards, but, for his own sake and that

Beethoven

*From a portrait by Robert Krauss after the original of Waldmüller
and the cast of his face*

of others, a man must look earthwards, yet even this pertains to
the destiny of mankind.

With high and genuine esteem,

I embrace you,

my dear brother in art,

Your friend,

BEETHOVEN.

340. TO J. W. VON GOETHE, WEIMAR

YOUR EXCELLENCY,   VIENNA, *February* 8, 1823.

From the days even of my youth I was familiar with your
immortal, ever new works, also I have never forgotten the happy
hours spent in your company. And now an opportunity occurs
in which I have to call myself to your remembrance. I hope you
will have received the dedication to my setting of Y.E.'s *Meeres-*
stille und glückliche Fahrt. Both, on account of the contrast
which they offer, seem to me most fitting to be expressed musically.
And how thankful I should be to know whether my harmonies
are in unison with yours. Advice, which I should value as truth
itself, would also be most welcome; for the latter I prize above
all things. Never shall it be said of me: *Veritas odium parit.* Soon
may appear some of my settings of your poems which will always
remain unique, and among them *Rastlose Liebe*, and you cannot think how much I should value some general comment on
composing, or setting your songs to music. Now for a request to
Y.E. I have written a grand Mass, which as yet I do not intend
to publish, but have merely decided to send it to the principal
courts. The honorarium is only fifty ducats. And with this intention
I have applied to the Grand Ducal Embassy at Weimar, where
the petition to his Serene Highness, the Grand Duke, has been
accepted, and a promise given that it shall be put into his hands.
The Mass can also be performed as an oratorio, and, as everybody
knows, societies for the benefit of the poor are in need of such
works got up by subscription! My request consists in this, that
Y.E. would call the attention of his Serene Highness to this
matter, so that the Grand Duke might become a subscriber. The
Grand-ducal Embassy gave me to understand that it would be
very advantageous if the Grand Duke could be induced to show
favour to the undertaking already beforehand.—I have written
much, but have scarcely gained anything by it. Now, however,
I am no longer alone; already for over six years I have been
a father to a boy of my late brother's, a promising young fellow

in his sixteenth year, and entirely devoted to art and science. With the rich literature of Greece he is already quite familiar.

But in this country such matters are expensive, and with young students thought must be given not only to the present but to the future; and however much formerly I only thought of my art, I must now direct my looks earthwards,—my income is from no settled appointment. My illnesses for several years have prevented me from making concert tours, and generally from seizing hold of everything which tends to earn money. Could I fully recover my health, I might venture to expect a more prosperous state of things. Y.E. must not, however, think that just on account of the above request for myself, I had dedicated to you the *Meeresstille u. glückliche Fahrt.* That was already done in May 1822, and at that time there was no thought of making known the Mass in this manner; it is the outcome of only the last few weeks. The respect, love, and high esteem which I have entertained from my young days for the unique, immortal Goethe have not diminished. That, however, cannot be expressed in words, especially by a bungler like myself. My sole thought has been to devote myself to music, but a peculiar inward feeling strongly prompts me to say so much to you, seeing that in your writings the Good is at all times clear to us, so that I feel assured Y.E. will not refuse my request. I believe that you will not fail, for once, to use your influence for an artist who has only felt too much how *mere gain* has nothing to do with *art.* Necessity compels him *owing to others* to think and to work *for others.*

A few words from you would spread happiness around me.

To your Excellence, who inspirest
With the utmost esteem,
Your worshipper,
BEETHOVEN.

[The letter bears no address. It is well known that no answer was vouch-safed to this very humble letter full of ardent hopes. Goethe and Beethoven remained great, but separate. Many passages in this letter remind one of the epistle of the master to Zelter written on the same day.

Concerning *Meeresstille* (Op. 112), the work was produced on 25 December, 1815, and was published in 1822, under the title, "Meeres Stille und glück-liche Fahrt. Poem by J. W. von Goethe. Set to music and most respectfully dedicated to the immortal Goethe, author of the poem." On the reverse side of the title-page is printed:

Alle sterblichen Menschen der Erde nehmen die Sänger
Billig mit Achtung auf und Ehrfurcht, selber die Muse
Lehrt sie den hohen Gesang, und waltet über die Sänger.
From Voss's version of HOMER's *Odyssey.*

In Goethe's diary, under 21 May, 1822, we find, "Score received from Beethoven."]

341. To FERDINAND RIES, London

VIENNA, *February* 25, 1823.

MY DEAR WORTHY RIES,

I seize this opportunity through Herr v. Bauer, secretary of the Imperial Royal Embassy, to write to you. I do not know how to act with regard to the Symphony. As soon as I hear further from you, it would be at the same time necessary to receive notification about the money. This very same Herr v. Bauer, who is as intelligent as he is kind, has promised that it will be sent from here to London as quickly as possible, as I have only to leave it at Prince Esterhazy's house. You receive also with this the promised Overture. If the Philharmonic Society wish also to keep it for 18 months, it is at their service. Nobody as yet has it, nor will they get it until I receive an answer *from you* about it. If the Philharmonic Society is as poor as I am, it need not give me anything; but if it is richer, as I am inclined to believe, and heartily wish, I should gladly leave to it to settle with me the Overture. At the same time you will receive 6 *Bagatelles* or *kleinigkeiten*, and *again* 5 in 2 parts connected together. Drive as good a bargain as you can with them; I hope you have *received* the 2 *Sonatas*, and beg you to drive as good a *bargain* with them; for I am in need of it. The winter and several circumstances have pulled me back, and to have to live almost always by one's *pen*, is no small matter. Next spring, 1824, I shall be in London to embrace your wife. About that we have still time to write to each other. Had I only received your Dedication, I should at once dedicate to you this Overture, if it turns out a success in London. Now farewell, my dear friend. Hurry up with the Symphony, and whatever money you receive for the *Sonatas* and *Bagatelles*, send it soon; it will be very welcome. Heaven bless you, and grant me an early opportunity to show you a kindness.

With kindest remembrances,
Your
BEETHOVEN.

342. To CHARLES NEATE, London

VIENNA, *February* 25, 1823.

MY DEAR FRIEND,

Ries tells me you wish to have three Quartets of me, and I now write to beg you will let me know about what time they are to be ready, as I am fully satisfied with your offer of a hundred guineas for them; only let me beg of you to send me a cheque for that sum upon one of our banking-houses, so soon as I shall let you know that the Quartets are finished, and I will, in my turn, deliver them to the same banker upon the receipt of the hundred guineas. I trust you are enjoying to the full the blessings of a family life; would I could have the pleasure of becoming an eyewitness to your happiness! I have sent Ries a new Overture for the Phil-harmonic Society, and am only waiting the arrival of a cheque for the new Symphony, to forward him that too, through our Austrian Embassy. You will find in the bearer, Mr. A. Bauer, a man equally intelligent and amiable, who can give you a full account of my doings. Should my health improve, I mean to visit England in 1824; let me know what you think about it. I should be delighted to write for the Philharmonic Society, to see the country and all its distinguished artists, and as to my pecuniary circumstances, they too might be materially benefited by this visit, as I feel that I shall never make anything in Germany. My name on the address of letters is sufficient security for their reaching me. With every kind wish for your welfare, believe me

Your sincere friend,
BEETHOVEN.

[According to Moscheles' *Life of Beethoven*, vol. ii. p. 161.]

343. To LUIGI CHERUBINI

VIENNA, March 15, 1823.

HIGHLY HONOURED SIR!

With great pleasure I seize the opportunity of approaching you by writing. In spirit I am often with you, in that I value, more than any other, your stage works. But artists regret that it is so long, at any rate here in Germany, since a new opera from your pen has appeared. However highly your other works may be prized by genuine connoisseurs, it is still a real loss for art, to possess no new product of your great mind for the stage. True art is im-perishable, and the true artist feels inward pleasure in the pro-duction of great works. I, likewise, am also filled with delight whenever I hear that you have composed a new work, and take as great an interest in it as in one of my own; in short, I honour and love you. Were it not for my continued illness which prevents me from seeing you in Paris, it would afford me the utmost pleasure to talk over matters of art with you. I am about to ask a favour of you, but do not think that I say all this merely by way of prologue. I hope, nay, I feel convinced, that you would not expect me to be so low-minded.

I have just completed a great solemn Mass, and I desire to send the same to the European Courts, because for the present I do not wish to publish it. Through the French Embassy here I have also sent an invitation to His Majesty, the King of France, to subscribe to this work, and I am convinced that the King, on your recommendation, will take a copy. *Ma situation critique demande, qui je ne fixe pas seulement comme ordinaire mes vœux au ciel, au contraire, il faut les fixer en bas pour les necéssités de la vie.* Whatever may be the outcome of my request to you, I shall still always love and honour you, *et vous resterez tourjours celui de mes contemporains, que je l'estime le plus. Si vous mes voulez faire un estréme plaisir, c'était, si vous m'ecrivez quelques lignes, ce que me soulagera bien. L'art unit tout le monde,* how much more true artists, *et peut-être Vous me dignez aussi, de me mettre* also among such.

Avec le plus haut estime,

Votre ami et serviteur,

BEETHOVEN.

[Luigi Cherubini (1760–1842) was in Vienna in 1805, writing a new opera (*Faniska*) for the Theater an der Wien. He then made the acquaintance of Beethoven. Schindler, who was in Paris in 1841, relates much of interest about his conversations with Cherubini and his wife about old times in Vienna. The following letter from Cherubini to Schindler contains a reference to Beethoven:

PARIS, *le juin* 11, 1841.

MONSIEUR,

Je vous remercie infiniment de la complaisance que vous avez eue de m'envoyer le Programme du grand festival célebré à Cologne le jour de la Pentecôte dernière, dans lequel on a exécuté ma 4ème Messe solennelle, avec des paroles latines. Je ne crois pas mériter, Monsieur, tous les compliments que vous voulez bien m'adresser au sujet de cet ouvrage et je vous réitère mes remerciments pour les choses bonnes et aimables que vous avez la bonté de me dire.

Mme Cherubini a été fort sensible, Monsieur, à votre souvenir et à la promesse que vous voulez bien lui faire de disposer en sa faveur d'un autographe de Beethoven. Nous serons charmés, elle et moi, de vous revoir à Paris l'hiver prochain, ainsi que vous nous en donnez l'espoir.

Agréez, Monsieur, l'assurance de mes sentiments les plus distingués,
j'ai l'honneur d'être,
votre devoué serviteur,

L. CHERUBINI.]

344. To CARL ZELTER, BERLIN

VIENNA, 25th March, 1823.

SIR!

I seize this opportunity to send you all good messages from myself. The bearer has asked me to recommend her to you, her name is Cornega, she has a fine mezzo-soprano voice, and is also an able singer; she has already acted, and with success in several operas.

I have carefully thought over your proposition for your "Singakademie." If the Mass should be printed, I will send you a copy without asking anything for it. It is certain that it can be almost entirely performed *a cappella*, the whole would have, however, to be somewhat modified, and perhaps you would be patient enough to do it. For the rest, there is one number in this work quite *a cappella*, and really this style might be especially designated, the one true Church style. Thanks for your readiness. From such an honoured artist as yourself I would never accept anything. I honour you, and only wait for the occasion to give you practical proof of this.

With the highest respect,
Your friend and servant,
BEETHOVEN.

[The lady through whom Beethoven sent this letter to Zelter was Nina Cornega, an Italian singer; she was a pupil of Salieri, and had appeared with great success on Italian stages. She is often referred to in the Conversation Books, which record many interesting talks between Schindler and Beethoven about her.]

345. To ANTON SCHINDLER

[1st Quarter] 1823.

Very best one! In pursuance of the following Hati-Sherif you have to present yourself at 3.30 this afternoon in the Mariahilf coffee-house, in order to be cross-examined about your various punishable acts. Should this H.S. not find you to-day, you are commanded to appear before me to-morrow at 1.30, where, having partaken of water and bread, you will have to undergo confinement for 24 hours.

L. V.!! BTHVN.

[Address:]

a Monsieur de Schindler, premier membre engagé et attaché aux Faubourg de J——stadt.

[Beethoven always addressed Schindler in a tone of sovereign authority, which, however, the receiver of the letters did not take in bad part. He was frequently addressed as "Samothracian L—k" (scamp). The expression "Samothracian" had reference to the Samothracian mysteries in Greece, which in part were based on music. As silence was imposed upon the youths in the Greek mysteries, so Schindler had always to be silent. He was also called, after the musical hero in Mozart's *Zauberflöte*, Papageno. Many ways in which the addresses on Schindler's letters were written show Beethoven's humour at its merriest. For instance: "Herr A. von Schindler, Moravian cranium," another is "Pour Monsieur Papageno de Schindler." L.V. stands for *Lumpenkerl vale*, that is, "Farewell, scamp."]

346. To the Same

[*1st Quarter*, 1823.]

I am just off to the coffee-house, where you could come—there are only two ways with the Mass, namely, that the publisher does not publish the same for a year and a day, or if not, then we cannot get any *subscriptions*.

I beg you to taste this beautiful soup, which the housekeeper has prepared.

[In Beethoven's housekeeping, soups play a very important rôle; one can go so far as to say that he was a kind of oracle on the subject. If a soup had once been condemned by him, no appeal was possible, the soup simply remained bad. If Schindler had declared a bad soup good, after some time he would get a note to this effect: "I do not value your judgment about the soup in the least, *it is bad.*" But Beethoven even judged the character of his cook or housekeeper according to the way it was prepared. One who could not make pure soup could not have a pure heart; that was a fixed dogma in the life-catechism of the unique Beethoven.]

347. To FERDINAND RIES

VIENNA, *April 25*, 1823.

DEAR RIES,

The four weeks' stay here of the Cardinal (Archduke Rudolph) to whom I had to give lessons every day for 2½, even 3 hours, robbed me of much time—for after such lessons one is scarcely able the next day to think, much less to write. My constant sad position, however, forces me to write down immediately what brings me in so much money, that I may have it at once. What a sad revelation I am making to you! ! Now, owing to all the worries I have undergone, I am not well, even my eyes are bad! Meanwhile do not trouble, you will get the Symphony shortly; this wretched situation is really the only cause. You will also receive in a few weeks 33 new Variations on a theme (*Walzer*, Opus 120) dedicated to your wife. Bauer (Chief Secretary of the Imperial Royal Embassy) has the score of the

Battle of Vittoria—dedicated to the former Prince Regent, for which I have still to receive the copying costs. Only I beg to say, my dear friend, I shall be satisfied with what you can get for it. Only take care that the [Sonata] in C minor is printed at once. I will be answerable to the publisher for its not appearing anywhere before; if necessary, I will let him have the copyright for England, but then it must be printed at once. As to the other in A flat, even if it should already be in London, it has been printed incorrectly; he may therefore, if he prints this one, announce it as a correct edition. I should really think that a thing of this kind deserves the recognition of an English publisher (of course in ready cash)—however, we two know what publishers are, they are most deserving scamps. Now farewell, my dear R., Heaven bless you, and I embrace you heartily. Greet all who care about it from me— as to your tender-hearted helpmate, *you yourself* will always find me a kind of *opposition*, that is an opposition to *you* and a *proposition to your wife*.

As ever,
Your friend,
BEETHOVEN.

348. To LOUIS SCHLOESSER

VIENNA, *May 6th,* 1823.

You receive here, my dear Schlösser, a letter to Cherubini and one to Schlesinger. The house of the latter you must find out by inquiring here at Steiner's in *Paternostergässerl.* Say only that I send you there together with a recommendation to Herr Haslinger. Say to Cherubini all the good things you can think of; tell him that I most ardently wish to receive soon a new *opera* from him; that, altogether, I have the greatest respect for him above all our contemporaries; and that I hope he has received my letter and ardently desire to receive a few lines from him. Inquire also of Schlesinger whether he has delivered the letter to Cherubini, and why I have not received for myself any copies of the Sonata in C minor. I beg you very much indeed to write to me at once from Paris about both items, regarding Cherubini and Schlesinger. At the *Paris* post office, where letters are simply put into a letter-box, one must above all not forget to add the *porto*, else the letters are kept there, and cannot be got except by writing to Paris for them, Heaven bestow upon you all that is good, I shall always with pleasure take interest in you.

Your devoted,
BEETHOVEN.

[Louis Schlösser, Court Capellmeister at Darmstadt, was at Vienna in the spring of 1823, when he held frequent and pleasant intercourse with the composer.

(Towards the end of May he paid a farewell visit to Beethoven, but on the day before his departure for Paris he was surprised by a visit from the composer. Beethoven then gave him the letter to Cherubini and one to the Paris publisher, Schlesinger, also a special letter, i.e. the above one, to Schlösser himself, which, uncertain as to whether he should find him at home, he had written for S.'s special instruction.)

On the same day Beethoven wrote in his album the six-part Canon in E flat, *Edel sei der Mensch*, and on the reverse side, "Pleasant journey, Herr Schlösser, may all your wishes be gratified."]

349. To ANTON SCHINDLER

HETZENDORF, *May or June*, 1823.

From my note-book I see that you have your doubts about Diab[elli] in the matter concerning the Mass. I ask you, therefore, to come soon; the Variations will not be given to him even then, as my brother knows somebody who will take both, one can therefore speak with him about it.

Amicus

BEETHOVEN.

[The Diabelli Variations were finished here at Hetzendorf, and much of the "Ninth" sketched. Beethoven at this time was staying at the villa of Baron Pronay, and could walk about the splendid park to his heart's content. Diabelli did not acquire the Mass, but Schott and Sons at Mayence.]

350. To THE SAME

[HETZENDORF, *probably June* 1823.]

There are very many mistakes in the Variations at Diabelli's. Please fetch them back again from Diabelli's, but the corrected *copy* must also be sent with them. The faults in the *Sonata*—after it has been printed, you must find out the places where it will be sold here. I think it will not cost much, if they are printed or engraved, but everything must be done at once, and then inform the publishers how many copies they have, but all must be done quickly, very quickly. The matter in hand concerns the said mistakes which Schlemmer copied.

If Schlemmer is satisfied with 5 fl. he might as well earn it; however, as many leaves as copies; but here you have to be careful—everything quick, as quickly as possible.

[The Sonata mentioned was most probably the one in C minor (Op. 111) published by Schlesinger in 1823. According to Schindler, it was reprinted, after being corrected by Beethoven, by Cappi and Diabelli.]

351. To the Same

18th June, [1823?].

Be so kind as to send the *invitation* for subscriptions to the Mass in German and in French. There seems to have been some mistake either in the copies, or in the way in which it has been drawn up.

In great haste, your *Ami*,

LUDWIG VAN BEETHOVEN.

P.S. The Tokay is not for summer but for autumn, and indeed for a fiddler who is able to *return* its noble fire, and can walk straight.

[In the month of June a musical friend sent Beethoven six bottles of the best Tokay wine, so that it might serve him for the strengthening of his weak stomach. Schindler, who was just at that time in Beethoven's house, informed him of this costly present sent to Hetzendorf. Some days after, Schindler received from Beethoven the above letter with its postscript referring to the matter. The "fiddler" is Schindler, who was acting as an orchestral player in Vienna. The housekeeper had orders that Schindler was to deal with the wine according to his pleasure. Our amanuensis ordered a bottle to be sent to Hetzendorf; the other five bottles he disposed of otherwise, but whether in favour of himself he does not say.]

352. To the Same

SAMOTHRACIAN L—l!   *From* HETZENDORF, 1823 [*June*].

How is it with the trombone part, it is quite certain that the fellow still has *it*—for he did not give it up, when handing over the Gloria; on looking hurriedly at the bad scribbling, one forgot all about taking back from him the trombone part. If it must be so, I will go to the Vienna police station to-morrow morning. Here follows for Rampel first, the *theme* of the Variations which is to be written for me on a separate sheet—then he has to write the others up to Variation 13, or to the end of Variation 12, and that is all. You must get from Schlemmer what is missing from the *Kyrie*; show him the postscript, and herewith *satis*—with such rascals there is nothing else to be done. Farewell, attend to everything—I must bandage my eyes of a night, I must use them sparingly, otherwise Smettana writes to me that I shall not be able to write much more music. Best remembrances to Wocher whom I shall visit as soon as I come to town, and are the *Variations* now ready?

BT.

farewell.

POSTSCRIPT.

Diabelli receives here the old and a portion of the new. My

eyes, which are rather worse than better, compel me to do every-thing very slowly; as soon as Diabelli has done this, send it out, and he will at once receive all the rest. That one [i.e. a publisher] must have the manuscript in order to show that it belongs to him, is to me something quite new; I never heard of such a thing. The manuscripts which I have are proof to the contrary, and which have been returned to us after the same have been printed. A document concerning the copyright of a work has been sometimes asked from me, and that D. can also have. D. might have claimed a copy, but you know the state of things, all the more as one wanted to hand over the D. Variations as quickly as possible.

[The police affair had to do with the sordid family concerns of Brother Johann. The Variations which were given to the copyist Rampel were the already-mentioned Variations on a waltz by Diabelli (Op. 120), who is here indicated by the initial D. With regard to proprietary rights, Diabelli was mistaken, whereas Beethoven was thoroughly clear about the matter. We also perceive very clearly that Beethoven understood the value attaching to his manuscripts. This letter further offers testimony concerning Beethoven's malady of the eyes.]

353. To the Same

HETZENDORF, *Summer* 1823 [*June*].

I answer quickly what is of chief importance—Schlemmer was there, but in order that the matter may go on in proper order, *as is now required*, he will always have to *come here to me*. You will therefore not need any more to gallop up the four flights of stairs—nor make any further visits about the subscriptions at the Embassies. I will write the thing out as best I can to all four, and shall know how to explain the cause of the delay. I beg you to put the Varia-tions by themselves in the room, so that the landlord can take them. Perhaps I shall have another opportunity of sending to London. As soon as the rain really comes in, you can have the windows closed, otherwise not—kick the impudent landlord at once out of the door.

I cannot now accept the attractive invitations. I am busy so far as my bad eyesight permits, and if it is fine weather I am out of doors. I will myself render thanks for the amiability of the two fair ladies. Nothing from Dresden—I still wait up to the end of this month, and then a lawyer in Dresden; about Schober-lechner to-morrow.

VALE.

[Some of the Embassies which had subscribed for a copy of the Solemn Mass complained that they had not yet received the manuscript. The invitations mentioned in the concluding portion of the letter were from the eminent vocalists, Fräulein Caroline Unger and Fräulein Henrietta Sontag, who took part in the production of the Ninth Symphony and sang the solo parts in the Solemn Mass. Beethoven was angry and sarcastic at the long delay over the answer from the King of Saxony with regard to the Mass manuscript; this letter shows that he seriously intended to get a lawyer in Dresden to look after his rights.]

354. INVITATION LETTER TO THE EUROPEAN COURTS

[VIENNA, 23rd January, 1823 (Delayed).]

The undersigned entertains the wish to send his latest work, which he regards as the most successful of his productions, to the Court of . . .

It is a Grand Solemn Mass for four solo voices, with *choruses* and full *orchestra*, in *score*, it can also be used as a Grand *Oratorio*.

He therefore begs the High Embassy . . . to graciously work so as to procure him the necessary permission of *Your* most noble Court.

As the copying of the score is very expensive, the author does not think that a fee of 50 ducats in gold for it will be too high.

The work mentioned, however, will not for the present be published.

LUDWIG VAN BEETHOVEN.

[The above is addressed to the Courts. Similar letters of invitation only signed by Beethoven were also sent this year to other cities, Petersburg, etc.]

355. TO THE ARCHDUKE RUDOLPH

VIENNA, 1st July [?], 1823.

YOUR IMPERIAL HIGHNESS!

Since the departure of Y.I.H. I have been for the most part unwell; yes, now I have been suffering from severe pain in the eyes, which has only so far improved, that for the last eight days I have been again able to make use of my eyes, though sparingly. Y.I.H. will see from the enclosed *receipt* of the 27th June that some music was sent. As Y.I.H. seemed to take pleasure in the *Sonata* in C minor, I did not think that I was taking too much upon myself, if I surprised you with the dedication of it. The Variations have been copied for at least five or even six weeks, nevertheless my eyes would not allow of my looking through the whole of it; in vain did I hope to get all right again, so, finally, I had to get Schlemmer to look over it, and it ought, though not very neatly written, to be correct. The *Sonata* in C minor was printed in Paris in very faulty fashion, and as it was here reprinted therefrom, I took as much care as I possibly could in correcting it.

Of the Variations I will shortly send a beautifully printed *copy*. With regard to the Mass, which Y.I.H. wished to become more generally known, my bad state of health which has now continued for several years, and through which I incurred heavy debts, compelled me to refuse invitations to go to England, and rendered it imperative to think of a way in which I could somewhat better my position; so the Mass appeared to me suitable for this. I was advised to offer it to several Courts, and however unpleasant, I thought that if I did not do so, I should draw down reproaches on myself. I therefore sent an invitation to several Courts to subscribe to this Mass, fixed the fee at 50 ducats, as it was thought that this would not be too much; also, that if several more subscribed, it would not be altogether unprofitable. Up to now the subscription has brought honour, for their Royal Majesties of France and Prussia have accepted, and I have also recently received a letter from my friend Prince Nicolas Galitzin at St. Petersburg, in which this truly amiable Prince announces that His Imperial Russian Majesty had also accepted the subscription, and that I soon should have news from the Imperial Russian Embassy here. Notwithstanding all this, I do not receive, although others too have *subscribed*, by any means as much as a publisher would have given. I have, however, the advantage that the work remains *mine*. The costs of copying are already great, and will become still greater as three new movements will be added to it, and these, as soon as I have finished them, shall be sent to Y.I.H. Perhaps Y.I.H. will not mind graciously speaking about the Mass to His Imperial Highness the Grand Duke of Tuscany, so that the same may also take a *copy* of the Mass. The invitation was sent some time ago now to the Grand Duke of Tuscany through von Odelgha, the agent here, and he sincerely assures me that the invitation will certainly be accepted; however, I do not place much faith in this, as several months have passed without any result. As the matter is now in progress, it is natural that one should do everything that is possible to accomplish the aim in view. This undertaking was unpleasant for me, and still more so to inform Y.I.H. about it, or to notify you of anything, but *necessity knows no law*. I, however, thank Him Who dwells above the stars, that I can again begin to use my eyes. I am now writing a new Symphony for England for the Philharmonic Society, and I hope to complete it within a fortnight. I cannot strain my eyes for long at a time, hence I beg Y.I.H. graciously to be patient about the Variations which seem to me to be very charming, but which still demand further looking through. Let Y.I.H. continue specially to accustom yourself to note down at once, when at the pianoforte, any ideas that may come to you; for that purpose you ought to have a small table near the pianoforte. By such means not only will imagination be strengthened, but one learns also how to fix at the moment the most out-of-the-way ideas. To write without pianoforte is likewise necessary, and often to develop a choral melody with simple, and again with various contrapuntal figures, and even beyond that. This will certainly not give Y.I.H. a headache, but rather, when one finds oneself absorbed in art, a great pleasure. Gradually grows the power of representing just what we wish to feel, an essential matter to noble-minded men. My eyes order me to stop. All kind and good wishes to Y.I.H., to whom I commend myself,

with deepest respect,
most faithful servant,

L. v. BEETHOVEN.

[Mention is made of Prince Galitzin, through whom an invitation was sent to the Czar of Russia. Nohl adds the following interesting information: "There lies before me a fragment of a letter from Prince Galitzin, now in the possession of the widow of Johann Beethoven; on the post-stamp can clearly be read 1822, and the month appears to be October. In it is: '. . . *grand admirateur de votre talent je prens la liberté de vous ecrire pour vous demander de vous ne* [?] *pas à composer un, deux ou trois nouveaux Quatuors, dont je me ferais un plaisir de vous payer la peine,*" etc. And a detailed list of the letters of the Prince, notes four others, in which the commission for the quartets is particularly mentioned, and in which news is given with regard to the subscription for the Mass. One may perhaps wonder at the whole affair of the subscription and the correspondence with so many potentates, considering Beethoven's former political opinions; but this letter gives the sad explanation: "necessity knows no law."]

356. To THE SAME
Postscript (to the foregoing letter)

HETZENDORF [*Beginning of July*], 1823.

If Y.I.H. would gladden me with a letter, I would ask you graciously to address it to "L. v. Beethoven, Vienna," when I shall certainly receive all letters even here through the post. Would Y.I.H.—provided it is in keeping with your connections—kindly recommend the Mass to Prince Anton at Dresden, so that His Royal Majesty of Saxony may subscribe to the Mass, which he certainly would do if Y.I.H. only showed interest in the matter. As soon as I get the news that you have been kind enough to show this favour to me, I would at once address myself to the *General Director* of the Royal Theatre and of the music, who looks after such matters, and send him the *subscription* invitation for the King of Saxony, which, without a recommendation from Y.I.H., I should not like to do. My opera *Fidelio* was performed with great success during the festivities when the King of Bavaria was at Dresden, when these Majesties were all present. This news I received from the above-mentioned *General* Director, who through Weber asked me for the score, and who afterwards actually made me a very nice present for it. I hope that Y.I.H. will excuse me troubling you with such requests, for Y.I.H. knows how little importunate I am as a rule. But if there is the slightest objection, so that it would be unpleasant for you, you will, of course, understand that I shall not be on that account less convinced of your magnanimity and grace. It is not for greed, not as *speculation*, which I have always avoided—but necessity forces me to do everything in my power to extricate myself from this position. Publicly, so as not to be unfavourably judged, is probably the best thing. Owing to my constant illness, which prevents me from writing as I could formerly, I have incurred a debt of 2300 fl., which can only be met by exceptional effort. If things only go somewhat better with this subscription, and there is every hope of it, I shall be able, through my compositions, once again to place myself on a firm footing. Meanwhile I hope Y.I.H. will condescend not ungraciously to receive my frankness. If I should be accused some day of not being so active as formerly, I should, as I always have done, keep silence. As regards the recommendations, I am anyhow convinced that Y.I.H. will everywhere do what is possible to work in my favour, and that in this matter he will not make an exception.

With the deepest respect,
Your Imperial Highness's most faithful servant,
L. v. BEETHOVEN.

357. To FERDINAND RIES

MY DEAR RIES!   HETZENDORF, 16th *July*, 1823.

With much pleasure I received your letter the day before yesterday. By this time you will probably have received the Variations. I could not write out the dedication to your wife myself, as I do not know her name. So please do that in the name of your wife and your wife's friend; surprise her with it; the fair sex likes this. Between ourselves, to surprise the fair sex is the best thing in the world! As regards *allegri di bravura*, I must look through yours. To be frank, I do not care about such things, as they only serve to improve technique, at any rate those with which I am acquainted. Yours I do not know, but of ——, with whom I beg you to deal cautiously, I will also inquire about it. Could I not be of some use to you here? These publishers, whom one should always perplex, so that they may deserve their name, reprint your works, and you get nothing from it; perhaps some other arrangement could be made. I will surely send you some choruses, even though I have to write new ones; such things are my pet fancy.

Thanks for the fee for the *Bagatelles*. I am quite satisfied. Do not give anything to the King of England. Take whatever you can get for the Variations; I am satisfied anyhow, only I must make a condition, that for the dedication to your wife the only thing I will accept is a kiss, which I have to receive when I come to London. You often write about guineas and I only receive sterling; I hear, however, that there is a difference between the two. Do not be angry with a *pauvre musicien autrichien* for this; truly my lot is still a heavy one. I am likewise writing a new Violin Quartet. Could one perhaps offer this to the musical or unmusical Jews in London?—*en vrai juif?*

Heartily embracing you,

Your old friend,

BEETHOVEN.

[Beethoven assures us in this letter that he is no friend of the *allegri di bravura* of those days. What would he have said had he known the *allegri di bravura* of a Rosenthal, a Godowsky, etc.? Concerning the dedication of the Variations to Frau Ries and what came of it, I promised to say more. Anton Schindler referred to it in detail in the 'forties, in an article from which I extract the following: "In 1821 and 1822 Beethoven was repeatedly requested by Ferdinand Ries from London to dedicate to him one of his new works. This wish, innocent enough in itself, gave rise to many conversations with Beethoven in the Conversation Books, which give us manifold and living testimony with regard to many circumstances otherwise unknown to us, and prove that Beethoven's brother and nephew likewise took part in them. With regard to the many services which Ries rendered to his former teacher in the sale of his manuscripts in London, his wish was supported by us all. It was proposed to dedicate to Ries one of the last Sonatas (Op. 109, 110, 111). Beethoven agreed to it. However, the day after this decision, I received the following cabinet order: 'The two Sonatas in A flat and C minor are to be dedicated to Frau Brentano, *née* von Birkenstock —Ries—nothing'—but the master changed his mind. The Sonata in C minor he dedicated to the Archduke Rudolph, and the one in A flat, after further consideration, remained without dedication, probably a mere whim. Later on Ries changed his request into: 'that Beethoven would dedicate a work to his wife,' to which the composer showed himself inclined. He settled upon the thirty-three Variations, which he at that moment was writing. Meanwhile Beethoven had become acquainted with Ries's *Farewell Concerto to London,* and there followed an explosion. Beethoven would have nothing to do with a dedication either to Ries or his wife and declared that any mention of the subject was a case for punishment." Schindler, in his *Biography,* says: "The dissatisfaction of Beethoven with that work was so extraordinary, that it induced him to write a hot letter about it to the editor of the Leipzig *Musikalische Zeitung,* in which he ordered Herr Ries no longer to call himself his pupil. Kanne and Schuppanzigh, to whom I related this circumstance, together with myself, managed to prevent the angry master from carrying out his intention." I will only recall one saying of Schuppanzigh: "Ries steals too much from Beethoven. All steal, but Ries by handfuls."]

358. To the Archduke RUDOLPH

VIENNA, *July* 30*th* [?], 1823.

YOUR IMPERIAL HIGHNESS!

I have just heard that Y.R. Highness will arrive here to-morrow. If I cannot comply with the desires of my heart, I beg you to ascribe it to my eyesight. I am much better, but for several days I must not breathe the town air, which would still have a bad effect on my eyes. I desire only that Y.I. Highness will graciously inform me when you next return from Baden, and also at what hour I shall put in my appearance, when I shall again have the pleasure and happiness to see my most gracious Lord. But as naturally Y.I. Highness will not stay here much longer, it will be necessary to make use of the short time to commence again our musical discussions and performances. My great thanks I shall render myself, or they shall come to Baden. Herr Drechsler thanked me to-day for having taken the liberty of recommending him to Y.I.H. Your I.R. Highness has received him very graciously, for which I also render my ardent thanks. May it also please your Royal Highness not to hesitate, for Abbé Stadler is trying, as is said, to procure this post for somebody else. It would also be very advantageous for Drechsler if Y.I. Highness would condescend to speak about it with Count Dietrichstein. I again beg most submissively for the favour of letting me know of your return from Baden, when I shall hasten to town to wait upon the only master I have in this world. The health of Y.I. Highness seems to be good. I thank Heaven in the name of so many who desire this, among whom I also am to be numbered.

Your Imperial Highness's
most faithful,
most obedient,
servant,
BEETHOVEN.

[Schindler, in the first edition of his Beethoven biography, gives the Archduke's reply:

DEAR BEETHOVEN,

I shall be again in Vienna, Tuesday, August 5, and stay there several days. My only wish is that your health will also allow you to come to town. I am generally at home from four to seven in the afternoon. My brother-in-law, Prince Anton [afterwards King of Saxony], has already written to me that the King of Saxony is expecting your fine Mass. Concerning D . . . . r I have spoken to our most gracious monarch, and also to Count Dietrichstein. Whether this recommendation will be of any use I do not know, as there will be a competition for the post, when every one who wishes to obtain it must show his capabilities. I should be very glad if I could be of service to this able man whom I, with great pleasure, heard play the organ at Baden, and all the more as I am convinced that you would only recommend one who is worthy.

I do hope you have written out your canon, and beg you, if it should do you harm to come to town, not to exert yourself too soon out of attachment to me.

Your well-disposed pupil,
RUDOLPH.

Beethoven in his letter speaks about the pleasure of serving "his only master." His occasional utterances about the burden of his service are not, therefore, to be taken too seriously. In this letter mention is made of the Canon *Grossen Dank*. Nottebohm, in his *Zweite Beethoveniana*, gives a sketch:

Gros-sen Dank, gros-sen Dank ___:___ für sol - che Gna - de.

but no trace of the Canon has been found. Drechsler, born in 1782, studied thoroughbass and counterpoint under Grotius. In 1807 he came to Vienna, where he taught music. He became conductor at the Baden and Pressburg theatres. After Gänsbacher's death in 1844 he became Capellmeister at St. Stephen's.]

359. To ANTON SCHINDLER

HETZENDORF, *July 1st*, 1823.

Please see about Rampel, or, if you have already got it, send it off to me; If Diabelli has his ready also, you can send it too at the same time. Kindly give Schlemmer some fine paper for the *trombone* parts, as it will be easier to write them on it. To Wocher I wrote myself, and as Carl just then drove up, in order to be quicker, I sent through him the invitation to Prince E[sterhazy]. Very little has been changed in the letter—instead of *Euere : Eure*, etc., instead of *Nicola, Nicolas*, as you are not a very good speller.

You can now make inquiries about the result, I have my doubt about it being a good one, as I do not think him well disposed towards me, at least judging from former times. I think one is only successful with him through the influence of women.

Thanks for your kind exertions; at any rate one now knows how to correspond safely with this worthy Scholz. The bad weather and the worse air in town prevent me from visiting him. In the meantime, farewell till I see you.

Your amicus,
BEETHOVEN.

Postscript.—It will all go right by post, as I have given orders in town to push it forward in order not to overlook *anything*.

From Dresden—Nothing.

Just now Schlemmer came to ask again for money. Now he has received 70 fl. in advance. Merchants, of course, *speculate*, not such a poor devil as myself. Up to now the result of this wretched speculation has only been more debts. Have you seen that the *Gloria* is done?

If only my eyes were good enough to enable me to write things would go better.

Have the Variations been already sent off to London?

[On the outside:]

N.B.—As far as I can remember, nothing is mentioned in the invitation to Prince Esterhazy about the Mass only being delivered in manuscript; what mischief may not arise through that; I suspect that Herr Artaria aimed at offering the Mass to the Prince gratis, etc., and so thus for the 3rd time steal a work of mine; Wocher's attention has to be drawn to this.

[At the side in pencil:]

Of course Papageno in such a matter is not *obbligato*.

[Nicolas was probably Prince Nikolas Esterhazy. With regard to Prince Paul von E., Beethoven refers to his meeting with him at Eisenstadt in 1807, when his Mass in C was performed. Scholz was a musical director at Warmbrunn in Silesia. He wrote German words for the first Mass. In 1824 Schindler was commissioned to write to Scholz about words for the second Mass, but learnt that he was dead.]

360. To the Same

From HETZENDORF, *Summer* 1823 [*July*].

SCAMP OF A SAMOTHRACIAN!

You were told yesterday that you must go to the South Pole whilst we were betaking ourselves to the North Pole, for the small difference has been settled already by Captain Parry. But there were no potato-cakes there—Bach, to whom give my kind regards, with many thanks for his care for me, is begged to say how high the charge for rooms might be in Baden. At the same time one must see how every fortnight (cheap) (Good Heavens—poverty and cheapness) Carl could come here. That is your business, as you have admirers and friends among the patrons and the country coachmen. If this letter still reaches you, it would be well if you went even to-day to Bach, so that I might have the answer to-morrow morning before 12 o clock. Else it will be almost too late. You might also surprise the rascal of a copyist to-morrow, I do not expect anything good from him; he has had the Variations for a week.

Your friend,

BEETHOVEN.

[Sir W. E. Parry appears to have been in Vienna in 1823, and to have made the personal acquaintance of Beethoven. Possibly he gave a lecture in Vienna on the music of the polar regions. Anyhow, the *Leipziger Allgemeine Musikalische Zeitung* of May 1824 has an article: "Captain Parry on the Music of the Esquimaux," from the polar traveller's great work, *Journal of a Second Voyage in Search of a North-West Passage.* So it can be understood how Beethoven went to the North Pole while Schindler carried out certain commissions at the South Pole. The "patrons" were Beethoven's own patrons, those who had granted him the annuity. The copyist mentioned was Rampel.]

361. To CARL BERNARD

[1823, *July*.]

DEAR BERNARD!

S. will show you the present from the King of France. You no doubt will see that it is worth while, both for my honour and for that of the King, to make it known. It can be seen that H.M. did not wish *merely* to decline, for H.M. has paid for his *copy*. I find herein a magnanimous and refined king. I leave entirely to you how you will make known this event in your valuable paper.

Concerning your *oratorio* we will soon have a chat; you formerly quite misunderstood me, but I was so overwhelmed with many things, that it is difficult for me always to enter into the details of life; I hope however——

[Where the letter breaks off, the sheet was torn. S. at the beginning of the letter stands for Schindler. Schindler writes: "The chief Chamberlain of the King, the Duc d'Achâts, announced in the most flattering way that H.M. had granted a gold medal with his effigy as subscription price for the Mass." This honourable gift weighed twenty-one louis d'or and bore on the reverse side: "Donné par le roi à Monsieur Beethoven."]

362. To his Brother JOHANN

BADEN, *August* 19 [1823.]

I am glad about the improvement in your health. As for myself, my eyes are not yet quite right, moreover I came here with an impaired digestion, and a terrible cold—the former through that arch-pig the housekeeper, the other from a beast of a kitchen-maid, who though formerly dismissed, I have taken back again—you ought not to have applied to Steiner. I will see what is to be done; with the songs *in puris* it might prove difficult, as the text is German, but the Overture might have a better chance.

I received your letter of August 10 through the wretched scoundrel Schindler. You need only post your letters, and I shall receive them quite safely, for I avoid this despicable fellow as much as possible. Carl can only come to me on the 29th, when he will write to you. It will not remain unobserved what the two scoundrels, Glutton and Bastard, are doing to you, also you have received letters about this matter from me and Carl. For however little you deserve it of me, I shall never forget that you are my brother, and a good spirit will, I hope, come over you, to free you from these two scoundrels, and from this former and present whore whose lover was with her three times during your illness, and who, besides, has entirely in her hands the spending of your money. O! infamous disgrace—is there not a spark of manhood in you! Now of something else. You have some numbers of the *Ruins of Athens* in my own handwriting, and these I particularly want, because the copies were made from the Josefstadt score in which several things were left out which are in these manuscript scores. I am just writing something of the same kind, so it is most important for me to have them. Please write and say when I can have these manuscripts. Do please see to this. About coming to you; I'll write another time. Ought I to so lower myself, so as to be in such bad company? but perhaps this can be avoided, and we shall be able to spend a few days with you. About the affairs mentioned, I will write another time. Invisibly I hover around you; I work through others so that these blackguards may not strangle you.

As ever,
Your true brother.

[In all these unfortunate affairs poor faithful Schindler was always the scapegoat.]

363. To his Nephew, CARL Van BEETHOVEN

BADEN, *August* 23, 1823.

Little rascal! . . .
Best little rascal!

Dear child, I receive to-day your yesterday's letter. You are speaking about 31 fl. As I have also sent the 6 fl. you wanted, the lot of tittle-tattle among the leaves must have prevented you from seeing them. S.'s receipt ought to have been drawn up thus—

      10 fl. the household expenses of B.
       9 ,,   my   ,,   ,,
      31 ,,   enclosed
      ——
Total 50 ,, which I, the undersigned, have received.

S—dler [Schindler.]

He was only here one day with me, to take rooms, as you know, slept in Hetzendorf and went in the morning, so he says, again to the Josephstadt; but do not get gossiping against him, it might do him harm, and is he not already sufficiently punished? As he is such a fellow, the straight truth must be told to him, he has a bad crafty character, and must be dealt with seriously. If your clean linen is not very urgent, leave it until I come on the 29th, for if you send it here first, it will be scarcely possible for you to have it back on the 28th, the day of the examination. In case of need give the servant a pair of trousers, which can easily be washed in the neighbourhood. I remember the advertisement of the *Petiscus*. If it is worth the money it must be bought, the expense for anything useful ought not to be considered. The Lord will not forsake us, the expenses are really heavy, and there is still Blöchlinger's bill. If there is anything else to be remembered, do not forget it, so as not to be detained on the 29th. As to the servant, he is to remain for a time until we are together again, for the whole housekeeping with the old woman can no longer go on, she can no longer see, smell or taste—my poor stomach is always in danger. The former house-keeper of the Josephstadt has already offered her services again; she would be more suitable together with a man-servant, but this *old* one needs waiting upon and helping, and the kitchenmaid whom I have sent away is a big swine. At present the man-servant has a proper room, in many other situations he would not have that, but whether he leaves or remains he ought to let us know where he will be, and we can talk about it when we are together again. Consider that a kitchenmaid costs only 10 fl. 44 kr. and her bread-money per month, 128 fl. 48 kr. per year, the man-servant 20 fl. per month, boot-money and livery—with the old one we should want another woman to help. My health is better, but yet not so good as formerly. Now farewell.

The every day's work exhausts me. I wish you every good, my dear son. Czerny, your former master, dines with me to-morrow. You will find many people here who will be interesting to you— your affectionate Father.

[Address:]
        To Carl van Beethoven
            in Vienna.
To be delivered in the Josephstadt
Kaiserstrasse in Count Kotheck's house
at the Training Institute
        of Herr Blöchlinger.

[Considering Schindler's activity and zeal as amanuensis, the remarks about him in this and the previous letter are one of the mysteries in Beethoven's life. *Petiscus*, i.e. the popular Petiscus Mythology.]

364. To ANTON SCHINDLER

[BADEN, *Summer* 1823.]

N.B.—Schlemmer is to receive the little sheet of paper; stop a little longer at home to-morrow. With this you get the parts of the *Gloria*: "Ternione" is quite a new instrument to me. Do not forget the answer about the Diploma, as I am going to look after it myself, to-morrow I come myself to hand over the *Credo*. Trusty one, I kiss the hem of your coat.

[The term "Ternione," from the Latin *ternio*, was possibly put by Schlemmer to indicate the trombone group, instead of writing the word trombone three times.]

365. To FERDINAND RIES, LONDON

BADEN, *September* 5 [1823].

MY DEAR FRIEND!

You say I ought to look about for some one to see to my affairs; well, this was just what happened with the Variations, viz., my brother and Schindler looked after them, and how? The Variations were only to appear here after they had been published in London; but everything went wrong. The dedication to Brentano [Antonie von Brentano, *née* Baroness v. Birkenstock] was only to be for Germany, as I was under deep obligation to her, and for the moment had nothing else to publish; for the rest only Diabelli, the publisher here, received them from me. But everything was done through Schindler, a greater wretch on God's earth I have never known, an arch-scoundrel, whom I have sent about his business. In its place I can dedicate another work to your wife. You must by now have received my last letter. As regards the *Allegri di Bravura*, perhaps they would give me 30 ducats for one; I should, however, like to be also able to publish them here at once, which could easily be managed. Why should the rascals here have the profit? It will not be given here until the news arrives that it has reached London; for the rest I leave you to arrange about the fee, as you best know London conditions.—The score of the Symphony has just been copied, and Kirchhoffer and I are only waiting for a good opportunity to send it off. I am here, where I arrived very ill, for my state of health is still most uncertain. Good heavens, while others are enjoying themselves at this watering-place, my poverty compels me to write every day, and in addition to baths I have to take mineral waters. The copy will soon go off. I am waiting to hear from Kirchhoffer about an opportunity; it is too large to send by courier. From my last letter you will have understood about everything — —. I will send you the choruses. Let me know soon about any orders for oratorio, so that the time can be at once fixed. I am sorry for ourselves . . . about the Variations, as I wrote them rather for London than for here. It is not my fault. Answer soon, very soon, about details and also time. Kind regards to your family.

[Kirchhoffer must be the merchant of that name, the well-known friend of Schubert.]

366. To ANTON SCHINDLER

BADEN, *September* 1823.

Signore Papageno! I beg you, together with my housekeeper, to deliver the two indicated parcels, and see that they do not cost too much. So that your bad scandal may do no more harm to the poor Dresdener, I tell you that to-day the money has been sent to me with all marks of honour. However willingly I would have shown to you my *active* gratitude for your [? scratched through, and quite illegible] I cannot as yet put an end to this matter which I have so much at heart, but I hope in a few weeks to be more fortunate.

Is not the Russian Ambassador Count Golovkin? Would you kindly inquire there, whether or not there is a courier who could take with him a parcel for Prince Galizin? If not, it must go on Tuesday by the mail coach.

Your entirely devoted,
(BEETHOVEN).

[At the side:]

N.B.—As regards the Russian Ambassador, I want to be set right about his position, name, on account of the sending off of the said parcel.

[Address:]

Per il Signore nobile Papageno Schindler—C sharp—

[The "poor Dresdener" is the King of Saxony, who now, through Prince Anton of Saxony, sent a highly satisfactory answer with regard to the Mass. The short, interesting letter of the Prince is herewith published:

DRESDEN, 12*th September*, 1823.

HERR KAPELLMEISTER!
    I have received your letter, together with the enclosure to the King my brother, and I do not doubt that he will grant your wish, especially as I have already spoken with him in the name of my brother-in-law, the Cardinal [Rudolph]. The new work, of which you speak, and which certainly will be a masterpiece, will, like your others, be admired by me when I hear it. I beg you to remember me kindly to my dear brother-in-law, and on your side to be assured of the good feeling with which I for life remain

Your affectionate
ANTON.

Prince Boris von Galitzin received likewise a copy of the Solemn Mass in manuscript.]

367. To FRANZ GRILLPARZER

[1823.]

HONOURED SIR,
    The management wishes to know your conditions *re* your *Melusine*; so far it has declared itself, and this is probably better than to be importunate in such matters. My household affairs have been for some time in great disorder, otherwise I should already have looked you up, and asked you to return my visit. For the present write yourself to me or to the management your conditions, I will then hand them over myself. Overloaded with work, I could neither become acquainted with you earlier nor can I come now; I hope, however, that I shall manage it one of these days—my No. is 323. This afternoon you will find me at the coffee-house opposite the Golden Pear; if you will come, come *alone*; this

importunate appendix of a Schindler has long been, as you must already have noticed at Hetzendorf, altogether offensive to me—*otium est vitium*—I heartily embrace and honour you.

Yours truly,
BEETHOVEN.

[In 1823, Beethoven, owing to the successful revival of *Fidelio* with the youthful Wilhelmine Schröder, was to compose a new opera, and thus arose the intercourse with Grillparzer; the Conversation Books are full of it. The poet visited the composer again in the autumn of this year.]

368. To KING GEORGE IV. OF ENGLAND

[Rough Draft]

While presuming to present herewith to your Majesty my most humble request, and with all due respect, I venture at the same time to add a second one.

As early as the year 1813 the undersigned, at the desire of several Englishmen residing here, took the liberty of sending to Y.M. [Your Majesty] his work entitled *Wellington's Battle and Victory at Vittoria*, at which time no one possessed it. Prince von Razumowsky who was then Russian ambassador here, undertook to forward this work to Y.M. through a courier.

For many years the undersigned entertained the dear wish that Y.M. would most graciously let him know that it had been duly received; but up to now, he has not been able to boast of this good fortune, and had merely to content himself with the short account of his worthy pupil, Herr Ries, who informed him that Your Majesty had most graciously condescended to hand over this said work to the then music directors Mr. Salomon and Mr. Smart in order to have it publicly performed in Drury Lane Theatre. The English newspapers announced this, and, further, added, as did Herr Ries, that this work was accepted with extraordinary success in London and everywhere.

The undersigned has felt offended at being obliged to hear about this from an indirect source. Your Majesty, therefore, will certainly forgive his sensitiveness in this matter, and most graciously allow him to state that he spared neither time nor money to present this work to Your Majesty in the most becoming manner, and by its means to afford you pleasure.

From all this, the undersigned has come to the conclusion that everything has been placed before Your Majesty in a wrong light, and as this most submissive request again offers him opportunity to approach Your Majesty, he takes the liberty to forward to Your Majesty the here enclosed printed *copy* of the score of the *Battle of Vittoria*, which in 1815 was already written for this special purpose, and was only kept back so long, on account of the uncertainty the undersigned always felt about this matter.

Convinced of the high wisdom and grace with which Your Majesty has known how to esteem art and artists, and to gladden them, the undersigned flatters himself that Your Majesty will take this into consideration, and will most graciously grant to him his most humble request.

[In another handwriting:]

Convaincu de la haute Sagesse dont Votre Majesté a toujours su apprécier l'art, ainsi que de la haute faveur qu'elle accorde à l'artiste le soussigné se flatte que Votre Majesté prendra l'un et l'autre en considération et voudra en grace condescendre sa très-humble demande.

[The letter itself was sent to the King, but no invitation to subscribe to the Mass. Nothing is known of a reply from the English Court.]

369. For Frau JOHANNA Van BEETHOVEN

8th January, 1824.

Many business matters have prevented Carl and myself from sending you our good wishes for the new year. I however know that without this you are well aware that we have only the purest good wishes for your prosperity.

As regards your difficulty, I should like to help you with money, but unfortunately I have too many expenses, debts, and only the expectation of various sums, so that I cannot at once show my willingness to assist you. Meanwhile I assure you by writing that you may continue to draw Carl's half of your pension; we will hand you the receipt every month, and then you can yourself draw it out, as it is no disgrace (and I know several of my acquaintances who draw their pension every month) to draw the pension yourself every month. If later on I should be able to improve your circumstances by sending you a sum out of my pocket, it shall certainly be done—the 280 fl. 20 kr. which you owe to Steiner, I have long undertaken to pay, which probably has been told you. So you will not be compelled to pay any interest for some time.

You have received from me through Schindler two months' pension money. This month on the 26th, or somewhat later, you will receive the pension amount for this month—with regard to the law-suit I will personally speak with Dr. Bach.

We wish you all possible prosperity, Carl also myself.

Your most ready to oblige,

L. v. BEETHOVEN.

[The self-restraint and humanity displayed by Beethoven towards his brother's widow is astonishing. But his nephew Carl's widow (Caroline van Beethoven) relates how "by her letters she moved heaven and earth, and understood how to present her poverty and despair in burning colours and with dramatic effect."]

370. TO THE DIRECTORS OF THE "GESELLSCHAFT DER MUSIKFREUNDE"

VIENNA, 23rd January, 1824.

DEAR SIRS!

I am exceedingly busy and still troubled with my eyes, so kindly excuse my late answer—as regards the oratorio, I hope that *veritas odium non parit*. I did not select Herr von B[ernard] to write it. I was assured, that he had been commissioned to do so by the Society, for as Herr von B. has to edit the newspaper, it is exceedingly difficult to get much conversation with him. It must therefore become a long story, indeed very vexatious for me, as Herr von B. has only written the *Libussa* for music, which then was not even performed; but I know it since 1809, since which time very much was altered in it, so I could scarcely place full confidence in any undertaking with him. I was obliged all the more to insist on having the whole. At length I certainly received the first part, but according to B.'s statement the same had to be altered again, and I had to give it back to him, so far as I can remember. Finally, again about the same time, I got the whole from the Society, but other engagements which I had undertaken and which, owing to my former illness, I could not carry out, compelled me to hasten to keep my word, all the more as it is known to you that I *unfortunately can only live by my writing*. But now there are *several* and *many things* in B——'s [Bernard's] *oratorio* which have to be changed; I have pointed out some of them, and shall soon finish with it, and then make it known to B.; for *as it now stands*, although the stuff is of good invention, and the poem has a certain value, it cannot remain as it is. The *Mount of Olives* was written by me, together with the poet, within a fortnight, but the poet was musical and had already written several things for music, and I could at any moment consult him. Quite apart from any value of such poems, we all know how we have to take them; the good lies here in the middle, but as far as I am concerned, I would rather set to music Homer, Klopstock, Schiller, although even these would cause difficulties, but *these immortal poets* are worth it—as soon as I have done with the changes of B[ernard]'s oratorio I shall have the honour to point this out to you, and at the same time let the Society know exactly when they may count upon it; for the moment that is all that I can say in the matter. As concerns these 400 fl., Vienna value, which were sent to me *unasked for*, I should long ago have sent them back if I really had seen that this affair of the oratorio would have lasted so much longer than I could have imagined. It was very painful for me not to be able to express any opinion about it. As regards this, I had the idea of procuring for the Society at least the interest of this sum; as to a combination with the Society for a concert, neither Herr Schindler nor my brother had any commission to communicate with you about it; and it was very far from my thoughts that it should be done in such a way. I also beg you to tell Herr L. von Sonnleitner that I thank him most heartily for the offer of the platform, and generally of the help which the Society has given me; and at the proper time shall make use of it. With pleasure I shall hear whether, after my concert, the Society will make use of the works, among which a new Symphony, for the Grand Mass is more in oratorio style, and was really thought of specially for the Society. I shall feel special pleasure if my unselfishness in this matter is recognised, and at the same time my zeal to serve the Society, in whose benevolent deeds for art I have always taken the greatest interest. I specially acknowledge my high esteem for you in all respects.

LUDWIG VAN BEETHOVEN.

[The composer had been invited by Hauschka, the artistic director of the concerts of the *Gesellschaft der Musikfreunde*, to compose an oratorio for the Society, which was to belong to them exclusively for one year, and for which Beethoven was to receive an honorarium of 300 ducats. From the foregoing letter we perceive that Beethoven had received an advance of 400 fl. from the Society without having asked for it. Negotiations dragged on from year to year. At last, in 1823, the poet C. Bernard could write to the Society that Beethoven had received the complete poem *Der Sieg des Kreuzes*. The Society then wrote a respectful letter to the *tone-master* at the beginning of January 1824. In it Beethoven is requested "to tell the Society definitely whether he will set to music the poem of Bernard which has been delivered, and at what time they may venture to hope to receive this work, for which all friends of music and admirers of your great talent have been waiting." Beethoven's answer is, in many respects, highly interesting and instructive, though in many points not exactly a happy one. First, the fact that the Bernard poem needed much alteration is of weight, and yet it was not sufficient to inspire the composer. Then the statement of Beethoven that unfortunately he could only live by his writing, was exaggerated owing to his intense love for his nephew Carl.

With regard to the advancing of 400 fl., we learn that Schindler and his brother had mixed themselves up in the matter without authority, also that the Music Society had many a time helped him. Beethoven was, indeed, reminded several times of his promise, and finally, at the session of the Society on 31 January, 1826, it at last resolved: "to remind him to hand over at least one other composition for the sum already advanced." Beethoven, however, composed neither this nor any other oratorio, nor any new Mass, but only his last five great quartets; yet he always had the intention to compose a great work for the Society. The sketches for the Tenth Symphony, likewise those for a great Mass in C sharp minor, finally the idea, zealously entertained, of collaborating with the poet C. Kuffner in an oratorio, *Saul and David*, give proof of this. Beethoven, however, in the year 1826, was named honorary member of the Society. In the diploma awarded on 26 October, 1826, the Society says, among other things: "It feels itself honoured to count among its members a composer of such high reputation." Complaints about his eyes do not occur in the letters beyond the summer of 1823. If, then, the excuse in this letter is to be taken seriously, and not simply to be regarded as retrospective, one must suppose that at the beginning of the year 1824 Beethoven was still troubled.]

371. To B. SCHOTT & SONS, MAYENCE

SIRS!   VIENNA, *the* . . . *May*, 1824.

In answer to your honoured letter of the 27th of this month, I have the honour to tell you that I am not unwilling to let you have my Grand Mass and the new Symphony. The price of the former is 1000 fl., convention coin, and of the latter 600 fl., convention coin, according to the 20 fl. scale. The payment can be arranged in this way, you can send three bills to a safe house here, and they would be accepted. I would send the works at your expense, or hand them over to any one here whom you might appoint. The bills can be drawn as follows, one for 600 fl. at one month, 500 fl. at two months, and 500 fl. at four months from the present date. If this suits you I should be very glad if you would bring out a fine edition. Meanwhile I have the honour to remain with highest esteem, and readiness to oblige,

Your

LUDWIG VAN BEETHOVEN.

[This was the commencement of the important correspondence between Beethoven and the famous publishing-house of Schott and Sons in Mayence. The relationship was of a noble character from this moment up to the end of the master's life. Never before had there been such harmonious relationship between author and publisher as that between Beethoven and the Schott house, nor one that was more honourable to both parties. Beethoven could not and need not change his personality. The Schotts knew and acknowledged his noble nature.

The person "recommended" was Capellmeister Rummel, who was travelling with the Duke of Nassau. Schott and Sons wrote in one of their highly creditable letters to Beethoven—who was usually addressed by them: "An Seine Hochwohlgeboren Herrn Hofkapellmeister," etc.—on 19 April, 1824: "At the same time we take the liberty to recommend to you Capellmeister Rummel, who is travelling with His Highness the Duke of Nassau to Vienna, and who will hand you the present letter; he is a great admirer of your works. The chief object of his journey is to perfect himself in composition, and, seeing that he has already distinguished himself by his early works, his deep and great industry can only be profitable to the world of art: wherefore we take the liberty to recommend this young man to your friendship and good-will, since you alone know how to show him the right way which he has to pursue as an art disciple, and how worthily to imitate so great a master as yourself." This Christian Rummel, who became a friend of Beethoven, was born in 1787 and died at Wiesbaden in 1849. From 1815-41 he was conductor at Wiesbaden; he became distinguished as a pianist, violinist and performer on the clarinet, and composed various works for wind-instruments. His son Joseph was a famous pianist, and Court pianist to the Duke of Nassau. Franz Rummel, who died in Berlin in 1901, was a nephew of Christian Rummel.]

372. To ANTON SCHINDLER

[*May* 1824.]

Beginning. *Papageno*, don't talk of what I said about Prussia. It is of no importance, only something like Martin Luther's Table-talk. I likewise request my brother to keep silent and not to say anything about it at the upper or lower end of Selchwurstgasse.

The Variations were left behind, send them by the housekeeper. Also send those ordered to London—do not act according to your self-conceit, otherwise everything will go wrong.

[Continuation:]

I beg you kindly to write down where the diploma was last, before it goes to the government office, and how long it will be before it gets there. What is that wretched story again about Prince Esterhazy?

End. Inquire of that arch-rascal Diabelli when the French copy of the Sonata in C minor will be printed, so that I may have the proof to correct. At the same time I have stipulated for four *copies* for myself, of which one is to be on fine paper for the *Cardinal*. If he should act as usual in his churlish way, I will sing to him personally the bass aria in his vaulted hall, so that the vault and the Graben shall resound with it.

Your most obedient servant,
BEETHOVEN.

[The reference to Prussia at the beginning probably relates to the answer which Beethoven had received from the Chancellery of the Prussian Embassy with regard to the subscription for the Mass. The Director Wernhard had given the master the option of fifty ducats or a decoration. When the Prussian official had gone away, Beethoven, according to Schindler, gave vent to a thundering philippic against the bad system of fishing for decorations and such things. He certainly had good reason for not letting this outbreak be known, and hence reminds Schindler-Papageno to keep his mouth shut. When, in 1824, negotiations about the concert in Vienna were not progressing favourably, Beethoven turned to the General Intendant, Count von Brühl, at Berlin, to arrange a performance of the new works there. The result was that remarkable address to Beethoven from the highest circles in Vienna, and all that resulted from it. Already, in 1823, Beethoven had taken the necessary steps with the Austrian Government for permission to accept the membership of the Royal Swedish Academy. The answer, which finally was a favourable one, had long to be waited for. Hence this question to his factotum Schindler. The reference to the "arch-rascal" Diabelli is explained by Schindler as follows: Diabelli is named an "arch-rascal" because he had refused to take away from the printers the manuscript of the Sonata in C minor (Op. 111) and thus to hinder them in their work. Beethoven had already had it back several times so as to look through it and make corrections, but he kept on wanting to see it once more. Diabelli put up quietly with all his hard words, and wrote to the angry composer that he would note down the bass aria which had been sung to him, and then publish it, but also pay for it. After that, Beethoven was more patient. This affair shows the painful conscientiousness and care taken by the composer in the publication of his works. The Sonata itself was dedicated to the Cardinal and Archduke Rudolph.]

373. To TOBIAS HASLINGER

BADEN, 12th June [1824.]

DEAREST FRIEND!

Something has been sent to you, take good care of it; a proper tip, together with payment for your *expenses* will not fail. With regard to the March with Chorus, the last proof must be sent to me —likewise the one of the Overture in *E flat*—The *terzet*, the *Elegy*, the cantata, the *opera*, get them out, otherwise I shall use no ceremony, as your rights have already expired; only my magnanimity gives you a greater *honorarium* for them than you give to me. I want the score of the *Cantata* for a few days, as I should like to write a kind of *overture to it*; mine is all in pieces, so that I cannot find it. I must have it copied from the parts. Has the Leipzig musical Mass paper [*Messzeitung*] not yet contradicted the lies about my medal from the late French King? for it will be *mean* enough not to send me the newspaper any more; if it is not withdrawn, I shall have the editor, together with his consumptive principal, harpooned in the Northern Waters among the whales.

Even barbarous Baden is brightening up. *Guten* Brun is now written instead of, as formerly, Guttenbrunn—but what about the *p. n. gässler* folk who still write *Grossen* instead of *Grosse*. And now I am, with highest esteem, *i.e.*, I have no esteem whatever for the *p. n.* gässler folk.

Yours truly (*in Comparativo*),

B——N.

P. n. gässl Primus will again, like Mephistopheles, let fiery flames issue from his jaws. To be delivered in *pater noster Gässel*, Graben, to the Steiner Art and Music firm.

374. TO THE SAME

[*May–June* 1824?]

DEAR FRIEND!

You would do me a real injustice, if you thought that through carelessness I did not send you any tickets. I have thought over the matter, but like so many other things it was forgotten; I hope that a fresh opportunity will occur to let me show what I think of you. Of all that Duport has indeed done I am quite innocent, for instance, he gave out the Terzet, as new, *not I*. You know too well my love of truth, but now it is better to be silent about it, for every one does not know the actual state of the case, and I, though innocent, shall be misunderstood. I don't care at all about the other offers of Duport, as I have only lost time and money in connection with this concert.

In great haste, your friend,

BEETHOVEN.

"Pour Mr. de Haslinger géneral musicien et géneral lieutenant."

[Beethoven here gives the true honest explanation about the date of the Terzet, which was announced as "new."]

375. TO THE COURT BARRISTER, DR. JOHANN BAPTIST BACH

BADEN, GUTENBRUNN, 1st *August*, 1824.

MOST HONOURED FRIEND!

My hearty thanks for your recommendation, I am truly in good hands. Regarding my will concerning Carl, I must remind you that I sometimes think I shall have a stroke of apoplexy, like my worthy grandfather whom I somewhat resemble. Carl is to remain sole heir of everything which is mine and what is found after my death; but as relations, even though they are not really related to one, also have to receive some legacy, let my *Bruderé* receive my French piano which came from Paris. On Saturday Carl might bring the will with him, if it does not in any way give you trouble. With regard to Steiner, he will be satisfied to see his debt fully cleared off at the end of this and the month of September—for if anything comes off with Mayence, it will take all that time; and the first 600 fl. are to be given to two of the noblest of men who, when I was well-nigh helpless, generously came to my assistance with this sum, and without interest. Farewell, I embrace you.

With kind regards,

Your friend,

BEETHOVEN.

[Address:]

To Herr Dr. B. Bach

[The letter is a document showing the master's love for his nephew Carl. Already, on 6 March, 1823, Beethoven had sent his wishes with regard to the will in favour of his nephew. The French piano from Paris, which brother Johann was to inherit, was Beethoven's so-called "Paris Klavier." It was exhibited at the Vienna Exhibition of 1873 with the inscription: "Fortepiano, with which the city of Paris honoured the composer L. van Beethoven, the laurel-crowned hero of instrumental music. Donor: Johann van Beethoven, private gentleman at Linz, his brother. The Museum Francisco-Carolinum at Linz." The piano is possibly still in that museum. With regard to the "Bach" music, we may recall the fact that the composer thought of writing an Overture on the name; there are many sketches, the following is among some for the Tenth Symphony:

Is the final é in "Bruderé" perhaps intended for donkey (*Esel*), a term often applied to his brother by Beethoven?—TR.]

376. To ANTON DIABELLI

BADEN, 24th August, 1824.

DEAR DIABELLI!

It was not possible to write to you sooner, you want a Grand Sonata for pianoforte duet. It is not in my line to write a thing of the kind, but I willingly show my readiness in this matter, and will write it. Perhaps if my time permits I shall be able to let you have it sooner than you expect. As regards the honorarium, I fear it will surprise you, but considering that I shall have to put off other works which bring me in more, and are more to my liking, you will perhaps not find it too much if I fix it at 80 ducats in gold. You know that, like a brave knight by his sword, I must live by my pen; my concerts, too, have involved me in a great loss. You can write to me on this matter, but if you agree I must soon know it; so far as the key is concerned, I have already settled.

Farewell,
As always your friend and servant,
BEETHOVEN.

To Herr von Diabelli and Co.
Art and Music Publishers, Vienna
To be delivered at No. 1133 Graben.

[The foregoing letter appears to be Beethoven's answer to the following letter of Diabelli:

"VIENNA, 7th August, 1824.

"As I have neither received a letter from you nor seen anything of you personally, I am bold enough herewith to inquire whether I can definitely count on receiving a *grand four-hand Sonata* in F of your own composition. As I settle my business matters according to the works which are to come in, and as I am very anxious to have a grand four-hand Sonata, I beg you to let me know as soon as possible whether *still in this year* I may count on receiving it. At the same time I wish to know the price. In expectation of a speedy answer, I remain with the highest respect.

"Your most willing servant,
"ANT. DIABELLI,
"m.p."

(In Schindler's Beethoven Papers.)

Later on, in August, Diabelli writes again to the composer:

"With pleasure I see from your honoured letter that you think of fulfilling my wish. I therefore most politely beg of you to write for me a four-hand Sonata, the sooner the better. As regards the honorarium, I agree with your request to pay you for it eighty ducats in gold, for I am convinced that your works are not created for the moment, but for eternity. At the same time, it is doubly valuable to me as you have not yet written any grand pianoforte Sonata for four hands, and you will be able to work here in a much freer and less constrained manner, seeing that the whole key-board stands at your command and, so to say, a whole army of tones is subordinate to you. In full confidence of the promise you have given, I remain, with the highest respect,

"Your most willing servant,
"A. DIABELLI,
"m.p."

(Also in Schindler's Beethoven Papers.)

In the passage about the "key-board," Diabelli, no doubt, had something good in his mind, but it is not very clear. In spite of the brilliant honorarium, nothing came of this planned four-hand Sonata.]

377. To the Archduke RUDOLPH

BADEN, 23*rd August*, 1824.

Your Imperial Highness!

I live—how?! the life of a snail; the very unfavourable weather always throws me back, and it is impossible at these baths to be master in one's own house, as formerly. A few days ago the musical author and writer Nägeli of Zürich, and a man of some note, writes to me that he is publishing 200 poems, among which some musical poems, and he has strongly requested me to beg Y.I.H. graciously to *subscribe* to this collection. The price is very small, namely, 20 groschen or 1 fl. 30 kr. If Y.I.H. would subscribe for *six copies*, that would cause the work to be talked about, although I know that my gracious master does not care for such a thing. For the present it is sufficient if Y.I.H. will graciously inform me that the money will be paid as soon as the *copies* arrive, which will be at latest in a few months. Herr Nägeli has begged this of me, and now I myself must beg for him. Everything cannot be measured according to rule, but Wieland says: how easily can a small book be got for a few groschens; put the crowning stone on these poems, by adding your worthy name as subscriber, and so help this man. They will certainly not be entirely without merit—Whilst I am convinced of the sympathy of Y.I.H. for all that is noble and beautiful, I hope not to have made a useless request for Nägeli, and I only beg that Y.I.H. will give me written permission to announce to him that Y.I.H. consents to subscribe.

Ever your Imperial Highness's
With love and obedience,
Your faithful,
BEETHOVEN.

378. To C. F. PETERS, Leipzig

[*August–September* 1824.]

I have written to you, that a quartet [scratched through "and a really grand one"] is lying ready for you; so as soon as you write that you accept it for 360 Fl. convention coin, or 80 ducats, I will send it at once to you. I now get higher terms than ever for my works; for the rest the fault of the whole affair is yours. *Your letters* show what you formerly asked, and what I sent was *the real thing* (the frequent reprints show that this is true). The quartet too will teach you that I am not taking my revenge *on you*, but that I am giving you something better than I could give to my best friend.

I beg you to make haste, otherwise there will be nothing to do but to send you back the 360 Fl. convention coin. Besides, I am in perplexity, since some one wants to have this one as well as another new one which I have completed, but he does not care for a single one.

This is really done out of consideration for your long waiting, for which you alone are in fault. That I at this moment should separate this quartet from the next following one also completed (do you think that I could offer the latter work here? Sharp, very sharp, yes, like Löffel *comme Marchand coquin*). For the rest don't be apprehensive of my sending you something in order to get into closer business connection with you. No, I assure you on my art-honour that you will have a right to consider me the most disgraceful of men if you do not find that it is an art-work worthy of me.

[We notice that the differences are becoming acute and that nothing definite can be arranged with Peters. The quartet in question was the E flat (Op. 127).]

379. To HANS GEORG NAEGELI, Zurich

Under the signature address me "in Vienna" as usual.

BADEN, *9th September,* 1824.

MY VERY WORTHY FRIEND!

The Cardinal Archduke is in Vienna and I am here for my health; only yesterday did I receive a letter from him promising that he would with pleasure subscribe to your poems, owing to the merit you have won through your furthering of the art, and he will take six copies. I will send on the title. There is likewise an anonymous subscriber, and that is myself; as you honour me by being my panegyrist, I really cannot venture to give my name. Willingly would I have subscribed for more copies, but my circumstances are too limited. Father of an adopted son, the child of my late brother, I have to think and act for the *present* as well as for the *future.* I remember that you wrote to me formerly about subscription, but then I was not well, and my illness lasted over three years, now I am much better. Just send me your collected lectures, also to the Archduke Rudolph, and, if possible, dedicate them to him; in any case you will receive a present, though it certainly will not be a large one, but that's better than nothing. Put a few flattering words about him in the preface, for he understands music and is heart and soul in earnest about it. I am really sorry, for he is

talented, that I have not so much time as formerly to take interest
in him.

I have here and there made inquiries about subscriptions to
your poems; if I receive them, I will at once let you know. I wish
that you would also send me your lectures, likewise the five-part
Mass of Sebastian Bach; what both cost I will at once forward to
you. Do not think that I am saying anything from interested motives;
I am free from all small-minded vanity; only the divine art, in it
alone is the main-spring which gives me strength to devote the best
part of my life to the heavenly Muses. From childhood onwards,
it has been my greatest happiness and pleasure to be able to work
for others; you can therefore imagine how pleased I am to be in
some way useful to yourself, and to show you how I value your
merit. As a votary of Apollo, I embrace you, yours most cordially,

BEETHOVEN.

Concerning the Archduke write to me soon, because then I will
set the matter going; you need not trouble about permission for
the dedication; it will, and ought to be, a surprise.

[It was a favourite plan of Nägeli's to publish every year the score of an
important Church work by subscription.]

380. TO HIS NEPHEW, CARL VAN BEETHOVEN

BADEN, *Evening of the 14th September* [1824 ?]

DEAR SON!

It may rain to-morrow and perhaps heavily, or it may not,
either is disadvantageous to me. The terrible dust also the rain
—it really pains me to know that you have to be with that old
devil so long, keep at a distance from her—you must write a
letter for her in my name to the Superintendent of the hospital,
and say that she did not come at once, partly because she was
not very well, and partly because several people came to see me
here—*Bastà*

cosi—here are the 40 fl. for the *tutor*, get it confirmed by a
written receipt. How many errors does one thus avoid, and it is
done by every one who has to pay for another person; did not
Holz, unasked, bring the receipt from Rampel, do not others act
likewise!—take the white waistcoat, and have the other one made
for me—you could bring the metronome with you, it can't be got
here—you might bring with you the bed sheets and two coverlets

—pencil, pens, but the former not from the Brandstatt, and now farewell dear son

[Pages 3 and 4 of this letter are almost wholly torn away. Only a few words, the signature and postscript remain.]

this
best
whom will
the finest fruits

as always
Your true,
FATHER.

There was nothing else to do than to send you with the old woman in the *Zeiselwagen*,[1] and that even costs 8 fl. 36 kr.,—do not forget anything, certainly not your health.

381. To ANDREAS STREICHER

VIENNA, 16th September, 1824.

I willingly comply with your wish, my worthy friend, to send to several choral societies the vocal parts of my last great Mass, together with a score for organ or piano, because these societies at public, and especially at sacred festivals, can produce a powerful impression on audiences; and in writing this great Mass, it was my chief aim to awaken, and to render lasting, religious feeling as well in the singers as in the hearers.

But as the copies, also the frequent revision, cost a lot of money, I cannot ask less than 50 ducats, and I leave it to you to make inquiry, so that I may devote my whole time to the music.

Yours very truly,
LUDWIG VAN BEETHOVEN.

[Andreas Streicher, husband of Nanette Streicher, sent, together with this Beethoven letter, a note to the "Honourable Committee of the Choral Union at Zurich." In it he says: "The great Mass of Herr Ludwig van Beethoven, which was performed here for the first time on the 7th of May, is unanimously regarded as the most extraordinary sacred work which has appeared since Handel's *Messiah*, both on account of its novelty—and this is of special importance—and also on account of the pious resigned feeling which is expressed in every note. And in conformity with the spirit which should pervade Church music, Arias and duets, which only attract attention to the solo singers, are entirely avoided, and in their place a quartet of voices is used, and this either alternates with the chorus of voices or joins in with it." It is not known whether the offer of the Solemn Mass was accepted by the great Choral Society; probably not.]

[1] This was a long carriage in which people sat back to back.—TR.

382. To B. SCHOTT & SONS, Mayence

17th September, 1824.

I only announce to you that I have not received your letter of the 19th August, how it happened is not for the present clear to me. As regards your last letter containing the notice to the Fries and Co. firm, you may rest assured that as soon as I go from here to Vienna, which at latest will be the end of the month, the work in question shall be at once seen to.

Also you will for certain receive the quartet by the middle of October. I am very busy, and my health is poor, so you must be patient with me. I am here for my health, or rather for my indisposition, yet I am better. Apollo and the Muses will not yet hand me over to the Scythe Man, for I still owe them much; and before my departure to the Elysian Fields I must finish what the spirit suggests to me and commands me to finish. It is to me as if I had only written a few notes. I wish you all good success in your efforts for art, which, together with science, gives intimation and hope of a higher life—more news soon.

In great haste,
Yours very truly,
BEETHOVEN.

383. To ANTON SCHINDLER

[Autumn 1824?]

I ask you with all courtesy for the testimonial, the original and the copy—as we have much to talk about, we should lose least time if you would come to dinner one day, but this must be certain, for to invite oneself and not to come belongs, etc., as indeed you are, and as you ought not to be!

dixi

[Schindler, in the margin of this letter, seeks to justify himself. He was violinist in the Josephstadt Theatre orchestra, and the rehearsals often lasted until past two o'clock. To get from there to Hetzendorf would take a good hour, and then he had to be back by seven o'clock in the theatre, so "there was no question of keeping a promise." He adds: "but Beethoven did not willingly take into consideration these hindrances, or engagements with other people. Hence there were numerous disputes and, indeed, even disturbances." Schindler, however, knew exactly how things were with the orchestra and the theatre, and must therefore have known what he could venture to promise and what not.]

384. To B. SCHOTT & SONS, MAYENCE

[*November* 1824.]

DEAR SIR!

I am *sorry* to announce to you that the sending off of the work will be somewhat delayed. It was not so much the looking over the copy, but as I did not *spend the summer here*, I have now every day to give a two-hours' lesson to H.I.H. the Archduke Rudolph. This so fatigues me that I am unfit for anything else, and besides, I cannot live on what I receive, so that my pen has to help me; in spite of that, no thought is given either to my health or to my valuable time, I hope that this state of things will not last long, and then I will look over what remains, and will at once forward to you both works.

Some days ago I received a commission which concerns you, in which it was said "that a foreign music-publishing house thought of having 50 copies of both works from you, and further, to join with you, so as to prevent re-printing." I place no belief in the whole thing, for I have often had bitter experience of such matters (perhaps only spying). If you care for anything of the sort, I will with pleasure make further inquiry. And now another commission. To my brother, to whom I am indebted for kindnesses, I have, in place of paying a sum I owe him, handed over the Grand Overture which was performed here, 6 Bagatelles or *Kleinigkeiten* for pianoforte, many of them being considerably developed, and probably the best of their kind which I have written. Three songs, of which two with choruses, and one with accompaniment of pianoforte alone, or with wind instruments alone; the other two have accompaniments for full orchestra or for pianoforte only. Of the Overture there are already two pianoforte transcriptions, one for two and the other for four hands, both of which you will receive. My brother wants for the lot 130 ducats as honorarium; as he is a landowner and well-to-do, it is quite indifferent to him how you arrange with him about the payment; he will leave all this to your convenience. Only I very much beg you to send me an answer at once about this, for some one else would like to have these works (I do not boast, for that is not my habit). There is, therefore, no time to be lost, I thought that you might perhaps like to possess a larger series of my works, and for that purpose would ask my brother for delay in this matter. Do not trouble either about the quartet or about the two other works; by the beginning of next month everything will be sent off. My open character is a guarantee to you; do not think there is any trick, afterthought, etc. Who knows what a great connection may take place between us!

Yours as always,

BEETHOVEN.

[The small works here offered are: (1) Matthisson's *Opferlied* for voice and chorus, also a setting with pf. different from that of 1802; (2) The *Bundeslied* of Goethe. These appeared as Op. 122 at Schott's in 1825, at the same time as the Bagatelles (Op. 126).]

385. TO THE SAME

DEAR SIRS,   VIENNA, *December* 5, 1824.

The works will be delivered without fail this week to Friess and Co. For the rest, be quite at your ease; you may, perhaps, have heard about a pianoforte score for which I have been asked; *there is no truth in it and nothing of the kind will be done.* It was only talked about so long as I was not certain about *you,* for some one here tried to dissuade me from having dealings with you; this *somebody,* whom *you would have difficulty in guessing, is also a publisher.* But as soon as one of my friends inquired at Friess and Co., and found that everything was all straight, there was an end of this whole matter, and I give you my word of honour, *that nothing has taken and nothing will take place.* I was also asked from Leipzig to send this work for performance for a fee, but I roundly refused it. I wished to tell you this, as I notice that there are men here who are bent on disturbing the understanding with you, perhaps on both sides. I will contribute to your journal. Pray do not say anything in it about the lessons with the Archduke Rudolph, Cardinal; I have, meanwhile, again sought to free myself from this yoke. One might, indeed, exercise *authority, but this up to now has not been thought of,* which, however, these new times seem to be bringing it about. We thank God for the expected steam-cannon, and for the already existing steamships. What swimmers to far-off regions will there not be to procure for us air and freedom?! The letters, unless they have been swallowed up by the floods, you will probably have received by now. You may count safely on the correct sending off of both works still during this week.

Heaven bless you.

Yours very truly,

BEETHOVEN.

[In all creations of an intellectual kind the composer retains his interest, as now for steam-cannon. James Watt's attempts to fire cannon or guns by the expansion of steam were unsuccessful.]

386. To TOBIAS HASLINGER

[1824?]

To - bi - as   pa - ter nos - ter gäss - ler

To - bi - as   pa - ter nos - ter gäss-le - ri - scher bier-häuss-le - ri-scher

Mu - si - ka - li - scher Phi - li - ster ;

Notice what Carl says
Consider yourself as a fire-station,
only instead of water think of money—
the receipt to Prague *prestissimo*—
If it does not come soon I must act as advanced post
farewell. The office [or decree?] as great seal-bearer shall soon
be given to you—

B——N.

387. To the Same.

Best One !   [1824?]

To - bi ° - - - as   To - bi - - - - as

Fill up the space between, but if you praise me shamefully,
I shall come out with the truth. The proofs are enclosed. Kindly
return them to me to-morrow after the faults are corrected. Please
never forget this kind of little stroke = = = after *cresc.*
Take care of yourself.

Your etc., etc., etc.,
Beethoven.

[Address:]
To Herr *Tobias Hass*
and Messrs. *lin*
and also *ger*
of good or low birth
In this place.

388. To ANTON SCHINDLER

[1824?]

I do not accuse you of anything wrong as regards the concert, but many things have been spoilt through your imprudence and arbitrary conduct. But anyhow, I have a certain fear that some great misfortune will befall me through you. Stopped drains often open suddenly, and to-day when in the Prater I thought that I had been in many respects insulted by you. In fact I would often rather seek to return your services by a little present rather than by dinners, for I must confess that it worries me too much; if you see a glum countenance, you think at once, "it's going to be ugly weather again to-day." With your commonplace understanding you are bound to mistake anything out of the common run?!!! In short I love my liberty too much. I shall often invite you to dinner, but constantly is impossible for me, as that disturbs my whole peace of mind.—Duport has promised next Tuesday for the concert, for he will not let me have the singers for the Constitutional Hall which I could have had to-morrow evening. He has again applied to the Police, so please go there with the note and hear if they have anything to say against the second time. I would never have accepted gratis these kindnesses shown to me and never will. So far as friendship is concerned it is a difficult matter with you. I should not like in any case to trust my welfare to you, as you lack judgment, and act in an arbitrary way, and already before I learnt to know you in a manner by no means to *your* credit, and in like manner *others*. I confess the purity of my character does not suffer me to be your friend in return for your kindnesses, although I am ready and willing to serve you in what concerns your welfare.

B.

[Concerning the differences between the master and his faithful amanuensis, Schindler, we leave the latter to give his own explanation: "After more than eight years of unbroken intercourse with the master, this incident brought about the first sensible rupture; it also produced a harsh dissonance in the small circle of faithful friends and adherents. Beethoven thought that he ought in some way to thank Umlauf, Schuppanzigh and me for the trouble we had taken, and so a few days after the concert he ordered a banquet at the 'Wild Man,' in the Prater. Accompanied by his nephew, he appeared amongst us with gloomy brow, and he was cold, snappy and fault-finding in everything he said. There was every reason to expect an explosion. We had scarcely taken our places at table when he turned the conversation on to the pecuniary result of the first concert, and bluntly blurted out that the administrator Duport and I had swindled him. In spite of the endeavours of Umlauf and Schuppanzigh, Beethoven stuck to his insulting assertion.

"It was now high time to assert my dignity. I quickly went off with Umlauf, but Schuppanzigh, after enduring some sarcasms at the expense of his bulky body, soon followed us. At the Inn of the Golden Lamb, in the

Leopoldstadt, we continued in peace the interrupted banquet. The furious master could vent his anger on the waiters and the trees, and as a punishment had to consume the banquet with only his nephew.''

Friendly feeling was soon restored with Schindler, for about this time, when Charles Neate was pressing the master to come to London, the journey was to be undertaken in the autumn, and Anton Schindler was to be his companion.]

389. To CHARLES NEATE
VIENNA, *Jan.* 15, 1825.

Ce fut avec le plus grand plaisir que je reçus votre lettre du [20 Dec.] par laquelle vous avez eu la bonté de m'avertir que la Société Philharmonique distinguée d'artistes m'invite à venir a Londres. Je suis bien content des conditions que me fait la Société, seulement je désire de lui proposer de m'envoyer, outre les 300 guinées qu'elle me promet, encore 100 guinées pour faire les dépense du voyage; car il faudra acheter une voiture; aussi dois-je être accompagné de quelqu'un. Vous voyez bien que cela est necessaire; d'ailleurs je vous prie de m'indiquer l'auberge ou je pourrai descendre a Londres.

Je prendrai un nouveau Quatuor avec moi. Quant au bruit dont vous m'écrivez, qu'il existe un exemplaire de la 9ième Symphonie a Paris, il n'est point fondé. Il est vrai que cette Symphonie sera publicé en Allemagne, mais point avant que l'an soit écoule, pendant lequel la Société en jouira.

Sur ce point il faut encore vous avertir de ne faire que de petites preuves de cette composition, en Quatuor par example, car c'est la seule manière d'etudier bien une belle œuvre; les chœurs avant tout doivent être exercés. Il y a encore quelque erreurs, dont je vous enverrai le catalogue par la poste prochaine.

Il me semble avoir été oublié dans la 2de partie de la Symphonie, qu'à la repétition du minor aprés le Presto il faut commencer de nouveau du signe ❆ et continuer sans répitition jusqu'à la Ferma, alors on prend aussiôt la Coda. Je vous prie de me répondre au plus vite possible, car on demande de moi une grande composition nouvelle, que je ne commencerai cependant pas, sans votre réponse. Il faut que j'écrire toujours pas pour me faire des richesses— seulement pour pourvoir à mes besoins.

Or je dois avoir de la certitude sur ce point. Je serai bien charmé de vous voir, et de connaitre la noble nation Anglaise. Je suis ayec la plus haute consideration,

Monsieur,
Votre sincere ami,
LOUIS VAN BEETHOVEN.

[Neate, in his invitation letter of 20 December, 1824, expresses the pleasure it will be to see Beethoven in England, and tells him that the Society, the Philharmonic, is ready to give him 300 guineas for his visit, etc. Further on Neate says: "If you bring the quartet about which I wrote to you, it is as good as a hundred pounds more; and you can be quite sure, I see no obstacle to it, that you could earn a sufficient sum of money to take back with you, enabling you to pass your whole life pleasantly and free from care," and also: "Your new symphony has arrived and will be rehearsed for the first time on January 17. I hope, however, that you will be here so as to conduct it yourself at our first concert."]

390. To B. SCHOTT & SONS, MAYENCE

VIENNA, *January 22*, 1825.

DEAR SIR,

On the 16th of January both works were delivered to Friess; what I have still to notice I reserve for my next letter. Both are bound, and by Friess, where warm interest is taken in them, they will certainly be properly forwarded. That the Mass is already printed does not appear to me to be possible. A certain Brockhausen, who is forming a choral society, may, as I hope, have spread this report. He wrote many kind things about the Mass, and said the court placed *faith* in him, and had ordered him to get a copy for his society, where they are sure to make proper use of it. This was probably through the influence of the Duke of Blacas who attended these fine performances *parceque les grands sont le plus faibles—*

I did not feel quite at ease, but I hope there is no reason for it. Neither is Schlesinger to be trusted, as he takes money as he can. Both *Père et fils* have bombarded me about the Mass. I did not condescend to answer either, as on closer acquaintance with their ways, I have done with them. I should be very glad if you yourselves would send me something to sign in which I should declare that you alone are owners of these correct editions, but it must be without delay.

I, the undersigned, bear witness by my signature that B. Schott and Sons at Mayence are the sole lawful publishers of my great Solemn Mass as well as of my great Symphony in D minor.

[Here follow some lines, afterwards scratched through, concerning the *Overture* and Bagatelles.]

I also recognise only these editions as *legal* and *correct*.

VIENNA, *January* . . . 1825.

LUDWIG.

Schlesinger wished also to publish a complete edition of my quartets, and to have from me for that purpose each time, *periodically*, a new one. He was willing to pay what I asked, but as this might have done harm to my idea of an edition of my complete works, I also left this unanswered. This matter you might think over, for it would be better to be done *by me* now, than after my death. I have already had offers about it, I even receive plans; these transactions, however, do not appear to me suitable for so great an undertaking. I would rather trust you, and what I should like best would be a lump sum. I would indicate the usual small unimportant changes, and to each species of works such as *Sonatas*, *Variations*, etc., I would add a new work of the same kind. Here follow a few *Canons* for your paper. Three more will follow, and as supplement, a romantic description of the life of Tobias Hasslinger in 3 parts. First part: Tobias is an assistant of the celebrated authority, Capellmeister Fux—and holds the ladder to his *Gradus ad Parnassum*. As he is now inclined to practical joking, through shaking and pushing the ladder he causes many of those who had got fairly high up to fall headlong and break their necks, etc. He now bids farewell to our clod of earth and reappears in the days of Albrechtsberger.

2nd part. The already existing Fuxian *nota cambiata* is now treated in conjunction with A. and the changing notes thoroughly expounded; the art of creating a musical skeleton is carried on to the highest degree, etc.

Tobias, now a caterpillar, is turned into a chrysalis, is developed, and appears for the third time on this earth.

3rd part. The scarcely formed wings now hasten to the Paternostergässl; he becomes Paternostergassler *Capellmeister*, and having gone through the school of the changing notes [*Wechselnoten*] he retains nothing of them but the change [*Wechsel*], and so gains the friend of his youth, and finally becomes a member of several inland *empty-headed* societies, etc. If you ask him, he will certainly allow this account of his life to be published.

In greatest haste and as speedily as possible,

Yours,

BEETHOVEN.

391. TO THE SAME

DEAR SIR,   [VIENNA, *Jan.* 26, 1825.]

Just a few hasty reminders. The best and clearest way of printing the Mass would be if, between the wood and brass instruments, also the drums, a space were left; then follow the two violins, violas, the four solo voices, the four chorus parts, 'cello part, double-bass part, and finally the organ part. That is how the score was grouped by my late copyist.

The organ part might be placed somewhat differently from what it is in your copy. The old score was too bescribbled to send to you. The new one has been looked through most carefully, truly no small trouble with a copyist who scarcely understands what he writes. It would have taken too long for you to have waited for the Symphony to be all copied again, and, as a matter of fact, I could not find any copyist able even to a moderate degree to understand what he is writing; hence for some of the worst pages I have had new leaves inserted. Frequently the dots are wrongly placed,

instead of after a note , somewhere else, perhaps

Please tell the printer to take care and put all such dots near the note, and in a line with it.

Where in the first allegro, first part, this passage occurs in the two violins, viz.,

non ligato must be indicated above them, likewise in the second part.

Then there is to see whether in the *dona nobis* in the *allegro assai*, the flat before the D has been forgotten in this passage, viz.,

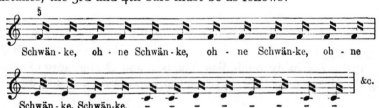

The Tempo of the *Benedictus, Andante molto cantabile e non troppo mosso* has, perhaps, also not been indicated. In the Canons which I sent to you and copied out myself, when I always make mistakes, the 3rd and 4th bars must be as follows:

Do write about Paris, I could also send you at once from here a French explanation, but I will fully agree with what you decide in this matter. My brother has not yet received the draft. Send it quickly, for he is somewhat greedy after money, all the more as the money for it was assigned here, and I was in a difficult position with the other publisher; also a firm a long way off wanted these works; I say this without boasting. The quartet will go off in at latest eight days as I am very much pressed with another work.

With cordiality and esteem,
Your friend,
BEETHOVEN.

In the *Dona Nobis* instead of quaver appoggiaturas there must always be semiquaver appogiaturas in the following passages

Vno. 1mo. *Allegretto vivace.*

Dona Nobis —2do. Viola. Bars 5, 6, 7, 8, 9, 10, 11.

Where in these bars there are quaver appogiaturas they must all be changed into semiquaver appoggiaturas. n.b. In the violin 2do quaver appoggiaturas only begin at the 6th bar. After the Allo assai Tempo primo $\frac{6}{8}$ Vno 2do bars 7, 8, 9, 10, 11, 12, 13, 14, 15, 16, 17, 18, 19, 20, 21, 22, and in the Viola from the 10th to the 22nd bar likewise quaver instead of semiquaver appoggiaturas, likewise after the Presto Tempo primo $\frac{6}{8}$ measure Oboe 1mo bars 9, 10, 11, and Flauto 1mo bars 10, 11, instead of quaver, semiquaver, appoggiaturas —likewise Vno. 1mo and Viola in bars 14, 15, 16, 17, 18, 19, 20, there must be quaver instead of semiquaver appoggiaturas. From this you can see what sort of a copyist I have now, the fellow is a downright Bohemian, a pandoor; he does not understand me; at first he wrote crotchets! for the appoggiaturas, and then finally quavers; as I did not look through it any more, I only noticed it when hastily packing it up.

392. To the Copyist WOLANCK

[January 1825?]

HERRN. HERRN. LUDWIG V. BEETHOVEN!

I can only finish inserting the *Finale* into the *score* by Easter, and as by that time you will not want it any more, I send you all the parts together with the already commenced Finale.

I am grateful to you for the honour shown to me by giving me work. So far as the otherwise disagreeable behaviour towards me is concerned, I can regard it smilingly as merely an assumed outburst of temper. There are many *dissonances* in the ideal world of tones. Why, then, should it not be so in the real world?

The firm conviction that to me, in my capacity as copyist, the same fate has been dealt by you as to those celebrated artists, Haydn and Mozart, is a consolation to me.

I therefore request you not to rank me among those common copying fellows who, even when treated like slaves, think themselves lucky to be able to earn a living.

For the rest, be assured that I have not the slightest cause to blush on account of my behaviour to you.

With high esteem,

Yours truly,

FERD. WOLANCK.

[Below this Beethoven wrote:]

To such a rascal, who really robs one of one's money, am I to pay compliments instead of pulling his ass's ears?

[On the other side:]

Scribbler!

Stupid fool!

Correct your own faults caused through ignorance, arrogance, self-conceit and stupidity. This is far better than to try to instruct me; for this would be just like the sow trying to teach *Minerva*.

It was resolved yesterday, and even earlier, not to engage you any more to copy for me.

Honour Mozart and Haidn by not mentioning their names.

[The whole of Wolanck's letter is scratched through, and in big letters over it is written: " Stupid fool, conceited ass of a fellow."]

393. To B. SCHOTT & SONS, MAYENCE

VIENNA, February 5, 1825.

DEAR SIRS,

You will soon have all the works—and I will sign a document stating that you are sole owners of the Josephstadt *overture* and pianoforte score of the same, as also of my 6 *bagatelles*, or *Kleinigkeiten* [trifles], and 3 songs of which two are with wind instruments or pianoforte alone, and an arietta with pianoforte; also that your editions of these works are the only correct and legal ones, and revised by the *author*.

LUDWIG VAN BEETHOVEN.

You will do well to publish at once the pianoforte score of the *overture*. You are, as I see, already informed about the mischief caused by Herr Henning, for I was just going to tell you about it. The Königstadt theatre had the overture *only for performance, not for printing or publishing*: this was settled by writing with Beht-mann. But you probably know that they have *quarrelled* with him, and now perhaps think themselves right *in not adhering to what had been settled with him*. I had news at once about it from an acquaint-ance in Berlin, and wrote off to Henning, and he wrote back at once that the *pianoforte duet edition* had been issued, and that it was impossible to withdraw it, but that I could reckon on nothing further being done. I will send you the letter, but after all, it is not necessary. Only publish the pianoforte edition at once, under my name or that of Carl Czerny, *who really arranged it*. I should also like to know that the overture was in the hands of the public, the Josephstadt title holds good. The dedication is to His Highness Prince Nicolaus Galitzin, *i.e.*, only on the *score*—you will do well to announce this everywhere, also in Paris, etc. With regard to it you have full authority from me to further your interests in the best and most likely way; I shall approve of any step you may take. I have sent you some *Canons* for your *Caecilia*. But if you would prefer some-thing else, write to me. You have no need to be anxious about Brockhausen in Paris, I will be sure to write to him. Do play the joke on Tobias to get him to ask from me the romantic account of his life. That is the way to manage with men of this sort, *Viennese without any heart*—it was really he who tried to *dissuade me from doing business with you*. *Silentium*. There is no other way. The real Paternoster Steiner here is a skinflint, a rascal of a fellow. Tobias is somewhat weak-minded, and rather *obliging*, and for many things he is *useful* to me. They make talk as they like, you need not trouble about my intercourse with them. As soon as you feel inclined to undertake a complete edition of my works, hurry up, for here and there in this matter much is to be expected; a new though not *exactly great* work of each kind would be of great advantage—and in the announcement you could say that the future edition (I mean of the new works which you have undertaken; nb., the Mass which has been reprinted in Paris is an early Mass of mine) will all be revised by me personally.

I have not received either the 4th or 5th number of *Caecilia*.

Fare right well, and let me soon have a friendly line from you.

With true esteem,

Your

BEETHOVEN.

[Behtmann was theatre director at Berlin. With this letter another one was sent to Schott's from Johann van Beethoven. It was as follows:]

With enclosed you receive clearly written copies of my brother's seven works which have just been looked through and corrected by him, so that they could be at once printed. With regard to them I give you notice not to send all the works you have in hand to my brother, but to the well-known, able Herr Gottfried Weber, so as not to seriously delay the edition. I fully believe that out of love to the author and to the works, he will willingly undertake the correcting.

I further point out to you in my name and in that of my brother that you can regard the above seven works as your legal property, and this my brother will confirm in his next letter.

I sign myself,
With high esteem,
Yours very truly,
JOHANN VAN BEETHOVEN.

VIENNA, *February* 5, 1825.   Landowner.

[Below this letter was written, probably by the firm, to Gottfried Weber: "They are making a heavy claim on you." And Weber writes: "I cannot possibly undertake the proof-reading, and have no desire to be Herr Beethoven's proof-reader. Cursed cheek of the Tom-fool."]

394. TO THE SCHUPPANZIGH QUARTET

MY DEAR FELLOWS!   [*March* 1825.]

With this each one receives his due, and is bound to undertake on his word of honour, to behave in the best possible manner, to distinguish himself, and to vie each with the other.

Every one who takes part in this said matter, must sign this sheet.

BEETHOVEN,
SCHINDLER,
Secretarius.

Schuppanzigh
Weiss
Lincke cursed
'cello of the great Master
Holz
the last, yet only
in this signing.

[For the rehearsal of the E flat quartet (Op. 127) this document was placed before the performers for signature. The original is among Schindler's

Beethoven papers; only the signature is Beethoven's, and on the left the signatures of the four players are likewise autograph.]

395. To FERDINAND RIES

Vienna, 9th April, 1825.

WORTHY, DEAR RIES!

Only what is most necessary in haste! In the score of the Symphony sent to you (it was the 9th with Choruses), there is, so far as I remember, in the first Oboe, and at the 242nd bar:

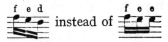 instead of

I have looked over all the instruments (except the brass, these only in part), and therefore think that it is tolerably correct. I would gladly have sent you my score, but I have a concert in prospect, and the manuscript is the only score which I possess. If, however, my health allows of it, I must now soon go into the country, where alone I am well at this time of the year. You will now soon have received the *Opferlied* copied for the second time, and mark it at once as corrected by me, so that it may not be used with the one which you already have. Here is an example of the miserable copyists I have had since Schlemmer's death. One can hardly trust them for a single note. As you have already received the written-out parts of the Finale of the Symphony, I have also sent you the chorus-score-parts. You can easily have these put in from the parts into the score, before the Chorus begins; and where the singing commences it is quite easy with a little care to have the instrumental parts placed over the vocal parts. It was impossible to write all this at once, and in the hurry you would have received nothing but faults with this copyist. I have sent you an Overture in C, ⁶⁄₈ time, which has not yet been performed in public; you will also receive the printed parts next post day. The *Kyrie* and *Gloria,* two of the best numbers (from the Solemn Mass in D) are likewise already on the way to you, together with an Italian vocal duet. You now receive, in addition, a Grand March with Chorus, very suitable for large bands. A Grand Overture, never performed in public, might have been added, but I think you will have enough with these. . . . Farewell, to you who live in the Rhine district ever dear to me. I wish you and your wife an entirely happy lot in life. All good and kind greetings to your father from your friend

BEETHOVEN.

[In this year Ries returned to Germany and settled on his estate at

Godesburg, near Bonn, where, as he himself tells us, "I invited Beethoven, pressing him to come to me, and so spend some time in his native city." The *Opferlied* mentioned is Op. 121*b*. The Overture in C is Op. 115, and the unperformed Overture was the one in C, Op. 124.)

396. To his Brother, JOHANN Van BEETHOVEN

BADEN, *May* 6, 1825.

The bell, together with the bell-pulls, etc., etc., is certainly not to be left in the rooms. No offer has been made to these people to take anything over from me. My illness prevented me from sending at once from here to town, as the locksmith did not come to take down the bell when I was there. It could have been taken down, as the people had no right to keep it. However it may be, I shall certainly not leave the bell there, as I want one here, and will use it, for the same bell would cost me here twice as much as in Vienna, since locksmiths charge the highest price for bell-pulls. In case of need go at once to the police. The window in my room was in the same state as when I went in, however, that will be paid for, also the one in the kitchen—for the two, 2 fl. 12 kr. I shall not pay for the key, as we did not find one, but the door was nailed up or bolted when we moved in, and so it remained till I moved out. No one had a key—indeed, neither my predecessor nor myself ever used one. If a collection should be arranged I will put my hand in my pocket.

LUDWIG VAN BEETHOVEN.

397. To Prof. Dr. BRAUNHOFER

May 13, 1825.

Dr. : How are you, my patient?—*Patient :* We are still in the same bad state—still very weak, vomiting, etc. I think a strengthening medicine will be required, one, however, which will not bring on constipation—white wine mixed with water I have been allowed to take, as the mephitic beer is repugnant to me—my cathartic state shows itself in the following way, namely, I spit a good deal of blood, very likely only from the windpipe, but oftener from the nose; and this was also often the case last winter. But that my stomach has become very weak, and also my whole constitution, there is no doubt whatever; and so far as I know my own constitution, my strength will scarcely be restored to me by nature alone.—*Dr. :* I will quickly help you (and be now a Brownianer and now a Stollianer, etc.)—*Patient :* Please consider that I should be glad to be able to sit again at my writing-desk, feeling somewhat stronger.—*Finis*. As soon as I come to town I shall call on you; only tell Carl when I can find you at home, but if you could inform Carl what is to be done, it would be very beneficial; the last medicine I only took once and then lost it.

With high respect
and gratitude,
ever
your friend,
BEETHOVEN.

Dok - tor sperrt das Thor dem Todt No - te hilft auch aus der Noth Dok - tor sperrt das Thor dem Todt No - te hilft auch aus der Noth

Written on May 11, 1825, at Baden, Helenthal, on the second Anthony bridge towards Siechenfeld.

[Dr. Braunhofer was Beethoven's physician during his long and severe illness of the winter 1824–5; the great quartet in A minor is connected with the composer's recovery. Nottebohm tells us that the Brownianers and the Stollianers represent the adherents of two methods of healing opposed to each other. John Brown, a Scotchman by birth, a pupil of the distinguished Professor William Cullen, was a physician of great note, and adopted the irritation theory. Max Stoll was the representative of humoral pathology.]

398. To his Nephew CARL

BADEN, May 22.

Although I have been informed by somebody that again there have been secret meetings between you and your mother, up till now I have only suspected it—have I once more to suffer the most abominable ingratitude?! No, if the tie between us is to be broken, let it be so, but you will be hated by all impartial people who hear about it. The statements of my *Herr Bruder* and those of Dr. Reissig, as he says, and yours yesterday concerning Dr. Sonleitner who necessarily must feel offended with me, as the law court decided exactly the opposite of what he demanded, do you think that I would risk once more to be mixed up in those vulgarities?—no, never more—if the *Pactum* is irksome to you, then, let it be so, I leave you to Divine Providence; I have done my part, and can appear fearless before the highest of all judges. Do not be afraid to come to me to-morrow, I still only suspect. God grant that *nothing* of it is true, for in truth there would be no limit to your unhappiness, lightly as this scamp of a brother of mine and perhaps your mother, may think of your gossiping with the old woman. I shall expect you with certainty.

399. To the Same

BADEN, *May* 31, 1825.

I intend coming to town on Saturday, and returning here again on Sunday evening or Monday morning. I ask you, therefore, to inquire of Dr. Bach at what hour he generally can be seen, also to get the key from my *Herr Brother, the baker* to see whether in the room which my unbrotherly brother occupies, there is sufficient furniture so that I can stay there overnight, whether the bed-linen is clean, etc. As Thursday is a fête-day, you will scarcely come here; indeed I do not demand it. You might undertake these few errands, and could report to me Saturday on my arrival. I do not send any money, for in case of need you can borrow 1 fl. in the house. Moderation is necessary for the young, and you do not seem to have paid enough attention to this, since you had money *without my knowing it*, and *without my knowing from whom*. Nice goings-on. To go to the theatre is not advisable just yet, on account of its great distraction, so I think. The 5 fl. laid out by Dr. Reissig, I shall pay off punctually every month—and that is done with. Spoiled as you have been, it would do you no harm at last to study *simplicity* and *truth*, for my heart has suffered too much through your crafty behaviour towards me, and it is difficult to forget and even if, like a yoke-ox drag along without murmuring, yet if you behave towards others in the same manner, it will never win for you people who love you. God is my witness that I dream only of you, of my wretched brother, and of the joy of having nothing more to do with this deceiving, abominable family foisted on me. May God hear my prayer, for I can never trust *you* any more.

Sorry,

YOUR FATHER,

or better still, not your father.

400. TO THE SAME

[*June* (?) 1825.]
Tuesday morning.

MY DEAR SON!

The upper or lower sample for 21 fl. seems to me the best, the landlord perhaps can advise you—trousers 88—

$$4\tfrac{1}{2}—$$

You receive herewith 62 fl. Vienna value, 30 kreutzers, give a correct account about it. It is earned with great trouble—however for the sake of *one* fl. (per ell) it is wiser to have the best. Choose yourself, or let anybody else choose between the two at 21 fl., but it must be the best.

For the trousers also the best! However, do not put on your best clothes when at home. One need not be fully dressed when anybody calls; so as soon as you come home, take off your coat and make yourself comfortable in the clothes meant for that purpose.

Meanwhile farewell,

Your true FATHER.

POSTCRIPT

The wench left yesterday, and has not come back, but you will see how this turns out; the old woman is troubled that she has to go, because like a wild beast without aim and sense, she cannot rest. God have pity on me, it has already commenced with the *cooking* yesterday.

401. TO THE SAME

[*June* 1825.]

The old goose follows this with—she has given you the pens, and you have told a lie—alas!—farewell, I only expect your report about the book. She goes to-day to Tatel, she has little time to commit any stupidity—God will set me free from them, *libera me domine de illis, etc.*

402. TO THE SAME

[*June* 1825.]

DEAR SON—DEAR LAD,

The point of *Bonheur* is to be touched upon, which I already found out with Lichnowsky, that these so-called grand gentlemen do not like to see an artist, who otherwise is their equal, also well-

to-do. *Voilà le même cas—votre altesse!* in the context sometimes
V. A. On the letter *à son Altesse Monseigneur le Prince, etc.*—one
cannot know whether this is a weakness—here follows a sheet,
already signed by me—you could add this, so that he may not be
disturbed by newspaper gossip, which, if I wished, would give me
no little praise. The Quartet was a failure the first time that Schuppanzigh played it, for he, being so very stout, wants more time
than formerly before he can grasp anything, and many other circumstances were the cause of its not succeeding. This was also pre-
dicted by me, for although Schuppanzigh and two others draw their
pension from Princes, this *Quartet* is no longer what it was when all
were constantly playing together; on the other hand, it has been
performed six times by other artists in the best possible manner,
and received with the greatest applause. On one evening it was
played twice consecutively, and yet once more after *supper.* It
will also be given for the benefit of a violin player named Böhm.
And now I have still to give it to others—in *Peters's* letter to Leipzig
Grand Quartet—hurry up with it, so that he may soon send an
answer—these fatalities are not to be avoided, as we must defend
ourselves—close this letter to my brother and post it. Tell the tailor
in the Kärntnerstrasse to fetch the cloth for a pair of trousers, and
to make them long in the legs, yet without straps, a kerseymere
cloth pair of trousers; he can also get the? [*Untzer*] at Wolf's. The
cobbler has his shop in the town, in the Spiegelgasse, straight before
you as you are going from the Graben. His name is: *Magnus Senn*
near the Town Hall, No. 1090—*go* to Hönigstein and *be frank,* so
that one may *know how this wretch has acted*; it would be well before
sending the letter to Galitzin to be informed. I really think that
something else is being planned for you in the winter, we will speak
about it. Before you come here on Saturday, inquire in the Nagler-
gasse about knives, these you could hand over first. The old woman
has been playing the fool—yesterday when I drove here I found
Clement, Holz, Linke, Retschaschek [Rzehaczek] at Neudorf, they
had all come to my house while I was away in the town, they wished
to have the Quartet again. Holz drove back here from Neudorf, and
had supper with me when I then gave him back the *quartet*—with
the *overture* remember that there is a letter to Galitzin announcing
to him that when it is printed it will be dedicated to him.

The attachment of able artists is not to be despised, moreover
it affords one pleasure—as soon as you have spoken to Hönigstein,
write at once to me—on the Overture in C write the *dedication* to
Galitzin, let the H. servant undertake the delivery, and give it
them, but folded up. God be with you. I expect safely to have a

letter from you, my dear son, God be with you and with me. There will soon be an end of

Your faithful FATHER.

Farewell ragamuffin!

[Very interesting are the communications here concerning the performances of probably the first of the last quartets, and the reminiscences about Prince Lichnowsky, of whom Beethoven very naturally thought himself the equal. These reminiscences occur to him just at the moment when he is preparing to write to Prince Galitzin.]

403. TO THE SAME

DEAR SON!   *[Summer, 1825.]*

You see everything from the enclosed—write this letter to Schlesinger

to Schlesinger in Berlin,

to be delivered at the Schlesinger Art and Music warehouse, but first of all improve many things in it. I think that one might well reckon on 80 ducats. If *necessary*, keep back the letter to Galitzin, but see that Schlesinger's goes off on Saturday—you will have received the *parcel*. I beg you to bring me some shaving soap, and at least a couple of razors, and here are 2 fl. for the knife-grinder if there is something to pay, if not, for housekeeping; for you always have too much money—but a Viennese remains a Viennese. I was glad when I could help my poor parents; what a difference in my behaviour to you, and yours to me—thoughtless fellow, farewell.

Your faithful FATHER.

Bring anything in the shape of a newspaper with you.

This time you have too much to do, you will probably write before Sunday. The *wretches*, do not flatter them.

He is a weak patron, etc. I

embrace, etc.

not better.

[According to the original manuscript in the Royal Library, Berlin; first printed by Nohl.]

404. TO PRINCE N. BORIS VON GALITZIN

VOTRE ALTESSE!   *[Summer 1825.]* BADEN.

With regard to the *contestation* Jenner a parfaitement raison—

la Viola a un ré ♭ dans cet passage c'est a dire  les

mot ff se trouvent deja dans le thême d écrire ainsi, and, besides, on account of the melody, which is always of prime consideration.

For the rest, this passage is based on [music notation] in spite of the G flat. [music notation] in the first *Violin*, which is only a Nachschlag or *Antici-pation*, which every good singer would make, for just as in art there is nature, so again there is nature in art. If, however, I had written

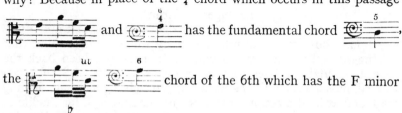

[music notation] the whole melody would have become disjointed, and

why? Because in place of the [music notation] chord which occurs in this passage

[music notation] and [music notation] has the fundamental chord [music notation],

the [music notation] [music notation] chord of the 6th which has the F minor

chord [music notation] as fundamental chord, would have arisen, and this

would have been foreign and contrary to the whole course of the melody and harmony. In short, Jenner *a parfaitement raison,* and I am pleased at finding myself at once understood by this able artist. The new quartet in A minor is already finished, and I shall try to send it as quickly as possible to Your Serene Highness. In my next letter I will write to you more fully, and hope in this way to scatter the clouds which seem to come between me and Your Serene Highness. Believe me, that it is my most ardent wish that my art may find favour with the noblest and most highly educated men; unfortunately, and in a manner none too gentle, one is dragged down from the heaven of art to what is of the earth earthy. As to those who belong to us and who neither wish nor are able to heap up riches, we must see to it that they bless our memory, since we are not all of us grand princes who, as is well known, leave the welfare of their families to the future and to God. In conclusion I have only to mention one thing more. I hear of considerable difficulty in having to deal with rubles and ducats, etc. I ask Your Highness, therefore, not in the least to trouble about this; I am quite satisfied to leave it the same as it has been up to now, and all the more since you permit me to publish these quartets at once.

So I have already made use of this permission with the first quartet, and have given it to a publisher. I beg you also not to take amiss the mistake of 4 ducats, as I am very conscientious, yes, I must even confess that there is another mistake of 2 ducats, but, as I said before, I am quite content with the honorarium for the quartet. A person of so high a position has to give on all sides, so graciously grant me the pleasure of leaving everything else to your magnanimity. I now hand to Hönigstein 2 *Overtures*, one of which I have taken the liberty to dedicate to Your Highness, and it will give me great pleasure if you think the dedication worthy of you. Heaven bless you and your family; myself I beg you to count among the most grateful of your acquaintances, and so I am Your Highness, etc. The 3rd Quartet is also nearly finished.

[In the Fischhoff manuscript copies of the letters of the Russian prince to Beethoven occurs the following passage: "As yet I have heard this piece played on the pianoforte only, for M. Jenner, who has the good fortune to be recommended to you, and who is one of your greatest admirers, pays me a visit every day, and I never let him go away until he has played me something of yours." With regard to the musical examples, it is difficult to say to which of the late quartets it refers, possibly to the *Allegretto* section before the last movement of the C sharp minor quartet. [Or why not to the *Allegro con moto* at the close of the E flat quartet, Op. 127?—Tr.] The name of the Russian prince will for ever be associated with the history of the late quartets. In one of his letters to the master (8 April, 1824) he says: "Truly your genius is centuries in advance, and at the present time, there is scarcely one hearer who would be sufficiently enlightened to enjoy the full beauty of this music, but posterity will pay homage to you, and bless your memory more than your contemporaries are able to do." The Prince was a performer on the 'cello, and his wife (*née* Princess Soltykoff) an excellent pianist. The former arranged pianoforte compositions of Beethoven which he could not play, for strings. When he entered into correspondence with Beethoven, he was twenty-eight years of age.]

[The following is from the same volume:]

A Monsieur
Monsieur LOUIS Van BEETHOVEN
à Vienne

Monsieur!   St. Petersburg, 9 *Novembre*, 1822.

Aussi passionné amateur de musique, que grand admirateur de votre talent, je prends la liberté de vous écrire, pour vous demander, si vous ne consentirez pas à composer un, deux ou trois nouveaux Quatuors, dont je me ferais un plaisir de vous payer la peine ce que vous jugerez à propos de marquer. J'en accepterai la dédicace avec reconnaissance. Veuillez me faire savoir à quel banquier je dois addresser la somme, que vous voulez avoir. L'instrument que je cultive, c'est le Violoncello. J'attends votre réponse avec la plus vive impatience. Veuillez m'adresser votre lettre à l'adresse suivante: Au Prince de Galitzin à St. Petersburg aux soins de Messrs. Stieglitz et Co. Banquiers. Je vous prie d'agréer l'assurance de ma grand admiration et de ma considération distinguée.   Prince Nicolas Galitzin.

405. To his Brother, JOHANN Van BEETHOVEN

BADEN, 13*th July*, 1825.

WORTHY BROTHER!

As you have taken such care of the *book*, I beg you to send it back *here* to the *owner*—again a pretty story. I have long ago explained myself clearly about your wish to see me at your house. I beg you to let me hear nothing more about it, for you will find me firm as a rock in this matter, as always; spare me from going into particulars, as I dislike repeating anything unpleasant. You are happy, and indeed this is my desire; let it remain so, for each is best *in his own sphere*. I only once used your rooms; but the oven almost made me ill, therefore it was only for once—as I now have lodgings, I shall probably hardly ever make use of the other room which you offer me. If you write, at least *seal* the letters and *address* them to Carl at Vienna, as such a letter costs too much here. I once again beg you earnestly for the return of the book belonging to mechanician Kunst in the Graben, for such a thing is really quite unheard of, and I find myself in no little perplexity—therefore the *book*, the *book*!—send it swiftly and speedily to Carl at Vienna.

Farewell, my worthy brother.

God bless you,
Yours,
LUDWIG.

To Herr Johann v. Beethoven,
Landowner at Gneixendorf Post Krems.

[Beethoven's resolve not to go to his brother's house was, alas! not adhered to. He went in the following year to Gneixendorf, where he caught the illness which soon put an end to his life.]

406. To his Nephew CARL

BADEN, *Aug.* 11, 1825.

DEAR SON

I am in deadly fear about the quartet. The 3rd, 4th, 5th and 6th movements Holz took with him, but the opening bars of the 3rd movement were left here; the number of sheets is 13.

I get no news from Holz, I wrote him yesterday. As a rule he writes. What a terrible misfortune if he should have lost it; he is a *heavy drinker, this between ourselves*. Do set my mind at ease as quickly as possible. You can find out about Linke's rooms at Hasslinger's. Hasslinger was here to-day and very friendly; he brought the parts and other things and was very anxious to have the new quartets; don't enter into any details about the matter; it leads to vulgarities. For God's sake put me at ease about the *quartet*, it would be terrible loss—the rough copy was all written on odd bits of paper, and I should never be able to write out the whole again.

Thy true FATHER.

[At the top stands the following:]

I also remind you that *next* Sunday and Monday are 2 holidays, so you can arrange accordingly. You could, perhaps, come here on Saturday evening with me, if I come to town, so that you would have the whole of Sunday morning to the good.

[The quartet may have been the one in C sharp minor or the last one in F, as each has six movements.]

407. To CARL HOLZ

BADEN, *August 24, 1825.*

Yes Yes! *Paternoster*gässel and our directors are nicely in for it. It is a pretty story to know about, even if one does not gain anything by it.

Best mahogany wood! we know nothing about pens, be satisfied with that. Your letter made me laugh, but Tobias remains a T——, but we will certainly *out-tobias* him. Yes yes! Castelli must have his share in it. The thing will be printed and engraved for the benefit of all poor Tobiases.

I am just writing to Carl to keep back the letters to P and S., i.e., I also expect the answer of Herr A. in Manheim.

BADEN, *August* 24.

It is indifferent to me what hell-hound licks or gnaws my brain, because it must be so. Only don't let the answer be waited for too long. The hell-hound in L. can wait, and meanwhile amuse himself with Mephistopheles, the editor of the *Leipziger Mus. Zeit.*, in Auerbach's cellar, the latter of whom will soon have his ears pulled by Beelzebub, chief of all devils.

My good friend, the last quartet also contains six movements, and I think I shall finish it this month, if only some one would give me something for my poor stomach. . . . My brother has been again to P. n. G. But, my good friend, we must see that all these new-coined words and expressions are preserved down to the third and fourth generation of our posterity.

Come on Fridays or Sundays, come Fridays, when Satanas in

the kitchen is at her best. Yes, fare right well, a thousand thanks
for your devotion to and love for me; I hope that you will not be
punished through it. With love and friendship.

Your,
BEETHOVEN.

n'oubliez pas de rendre
Visite à mon cher
    benjamin
Do write again,

Better still, come.

[Address:]
An Seine Wohlgebohren Hr. v. Holz in Vienna Molker-Bastay,
No. 96.
Four steps up in the Bergerstamm House.

[This humorous, sarcastic letter is the precursor of a joke at the expense
of the music publishers, and Castelli was to help. This poet and writer on
music relates how Beethoven wanted him to help in the matter. He also
refers to his 1000 *Sprichwörter*, which he showed to the composer, who thought
some might be set to music as canons; and so he gave him a copy of the
book interleaved with music paper. After a time, Beethoven told the poet
he had already written down some, but after the composer's death there
was no trace of the volume. Mention is made of "new-coined words and
expressions." Schindler says that Beethoven and Holz used to amuse themselves by finding German equivalents for certain technical terms. It is evident,
however, from the above letter, that Beethoven did not exactly consider
them as nonsense words. Here are a few specimens: Composer: *Tonsatzwerker*
(Composition - worker); Instrument: *Klangmachwerkzeug* (Clangmaking-
machine). There seems, however, no doubt whatever that Toneflightwork
for *Fugue*, and Art-lover-to-pass-away-the-time for *Dilettante*, were mere
jokes.—TR.)]

408. TO HIS NEPHEW CARL

BADEN, *5th October* (?) [1825].

[At the top stands:]

For God's sake do come home again to-day, who knows what
danger might be threatening you, hasten, hasten.

MY DEAR SON!

Only nothing further—only come to my arms, you shall hear
no harsh word. For heaven's sake do not rush to destruction—you will
be received as ever with affection—as to considering what is to be
done in future, we will talk this over in a friendly way, no reproaches
on my word of honour, for it would be of no use. You need only
expect from me the most loving help and care.

Only come—come to the faithful heart of your father,

BEETHOVEN.

Come home at once on receipt of this

Volti sub.

[Address:]

For Carl van Beethoven.

[Underneath:]

*Si vous ne viendrez pas
vous me tuéres surement*

[On the side of the address:]

*Lisés la lettre et restés a la maison chez vous, venez de m'embrasser
votre pere vous vraiment adonné soyez assurés que tout cela restera
entre nous.*

409. TO C. F. PETERS, LEIPZIG

VIENNA, *25th November*, 1825.

DEAR SIR!

When I offered you the *Quartet,* the answer of your *partner* was
not quite clear and decided. It is the same with your last two letters;
as soon as you plainly state the sum, namely 360 *fl.* convention
coin, which I have received from you, and assure me that you will
take the *Quartet* for this amount, you can have one shortly. If you
had done that at once, you could have had two new *quartets,* for
you cannot desire that I should suffer loss. If I chose to take a still
higher tone, I might demand an even larger sum for a *quartet.*

Therefore, as soon as you write to me, I will as speedily as
possible put you in possession of a new *quartet;* but if you prefer
your money, you can have it back without delay, for it has long
been lying ready; moreover I send nothing more on approval.

I await a prompt reply as to this.

Yours truly,

L. V. BEETHOVEN.

[The letter was written by his nephew, and only signed by Beethoven,
and with it all intercourse between Beethoven and Peters came to an end.
In his reply Peters said that he gave up the idea of the quartet, and requested
Beethoven to return the money with interest due. This Beethoven did, and
received in due course the receipt.]

410. To B. SCHOTT & SONS, Mayence

DEAR SIRS!   VIENNA, 25th November, 1825.

The *tempo* indication, according to Mälzel's metronome, will follow next time; I send you here the title of the Mass:

Missa
composita et
Serenissimo ac Eminentissimo Domino Domino Rudolpho Joanni
Cæsareo Principi et Archduci Aistriæ, S. R. E. Tit. s. Petri in monte
aureo Cardinali et Archiepiscopo Olomuensi profundissima cum
veneratione dicata
a
Ludovico van Beethoven.

The subscription lists must be put before the dedication.

1. The Czar of Russia.
2. The King of Prussia.
3. The King of France.
4. The King of Denmark.
5. The Crown Prince of Saxony.
6. Grand Duke of Darmstadt.
7. Grand Duke of Tuscany.
8. Prince Galitzin.
9. Prince Radziwill.
10. The Caecilia Society of Frankfort.

The dedication of the Symphony I beg you to postpone for a time, as I am still undecided about it; but I really beg you to delay the publication of these works for another three months; you will greatly oblige me by doing this. What is wanting shall be seen to as quickly as possible.

I again entreat you to be good enough to send me a copy of the improved bassoons.

You may not yet have received any assurance of your right to the possession of the Quartet in E flat; I enclose it herewith.

Yours truly,
LUDWIG VAN BEETHOVEN.

I hereby certify that Herren B. Schott and Sons have received from me a Quartet in E flat for 2 violins, viola and violoncello, and that the same is their sole property.

As witness my hand.

LUDWIG VAN BEETHOVEN.

[The word *dicata* instead of the usual *dedicata* deserves note. Dr. Hans Volkmann gives a very interesting account of August Mittag (1789–1867), performer on the bassoon in the Hofkapelle at Vienna, who, through Holz, became acquainted with Beethoven. There is much about this intercourse in the Conversation Books. In one occurs (September 1825) the following: "Have had a talk with Mittag about the improved bassoon," and again: "Mittag begged me to tell you that the hour he spent with you was the happiest of his life."]

411. To?

DEAR SIR!   1825 (?).

Your mother not long ago was sent away through the stupidity of my housekeeper, without any one having told me a word of her coming here. I have rebuked this unbecoming behaviour, for she was not even shown into my room; the *incivility and rudeness* of these people whom I am so unfortunate as to have about me, is known to every one. I therefore beg to apologise.

Your obedient servant,

L. V. BEETHOVEN.

[In 1825 a musical amateur published a volume of Waltzes. It was so successful that he ventured to ask Beethoven, with whom, through his father and grandfather, he had made acquaintance, to write something as a supplement. The composer promised to do so, and told the gentleman to call again in about four weeks. But as the latter fell ill, he asked his mother to call for the music, and to express his thanks. The housekeeper, however, to whom the lady gave her name and address, would not let her in, saying that the master was again off his head. At that moment Beethoven's head appeared at the door. "Hide yourself," said the housekeeper to the lady, pushing her into a dark room, "you cannot speak with him to-day." So she had to go away without the music. A few days after Beethoven sent the music, with this letter.]

412. To the Bankers HENIKSTEIN & CO., VIENNA

[1825.]

I beg you earnestly to tell my Carl what happened then about Prince Galitzin's bill, and whether you really could only give 215 fl. instead of 225 for it, for I am not always satisfied with my brother's transactions, and I should be sorry if on that account you felt somewhat hurt. I should also like to know whether you received a letter of the 29th April from Prince Galitzin to yourselves or no letter at all from him, as he wrote to me that he had *also written to you*. Lastly, I beg you kindly to arrange for a parcel to Petersburg, as it is too large to be sent by letter post. I am also having my quartet for the Prince written, the sooner H.H. receives it the better. I find it too troublesome by letter post. I await your kind information about this, and am with entire esteem.

Yours very truly,

BEETHOVEN.

[Baron Henikstein attended to the business correspondence between Beethoven and Prince Galitzin.]

413. To CARL HOLZ

BEST ONE!   [1825?]

I told you already yesterday that I have already found out that she [i.e. the cook] cannot cook daintily, nor in a way beneficial to health. She behaved at once very pertly when told about it, but in my sweetest manner I told her that she should pay more attention to it. I did not trouble any more about her, went for a walk in the evening, and on my return found she had gone, leaving this letter behind. As this is leaving without giving notice, the police perhaps will know how to make her return. I ask your help, and it would be nice if you could come just for a moment.

Yours,

BEETHOVEN.

For Herr von Holz.

414. To CARL HOLZ

BEST *violino secundo*   [1825.]

Read *Violino 2do*! The passage in the first *Allegro* in the 1st violin, so

play it thus; also in the first *Allegro* just follow these marks of *expression* in the four parts:

The notes are all right—only understand me rightly.

Now about your copy, my good friend. *Obligatissimo—ma,* the signs p < > etc., are terribly neglected, and often, very often, in the wrong place—no doubt owing to hurry. For heaven's sake please impress on Rampel to write everything as it stands; now only look carefully at what I have corrected, and you will find all that you have to say to him; where · is over the note, there must be no ! also vice versa!

 are not the same thing. The < are often

intentionally placed after the notes, for instance,

The slurs just as they now stand! It is not a matter of indifference

whether you play   or

Mind, this comes from a high quarter. I have spent no less than the whole morning and the whole of yesterday afternoon over the correction of the two pieces, and am quite hoarse with swearing and stamping.

In great haste, yours,
BEETHOVEN.

Excuse more for to-day, it is just four o'clock.

[The owner of the letter could not decipher the last sentence, but he traced the letters with pencil. It is something like this: "To go to Carl about four o'clock, we were very pleased."]

415. TO B. SCHOTT & SONS, MAYENCE

28th January, 1826.

DEAR SIRS!

In reply to your last letter I inform you that you will soon receive everything with metronome marks; I beg you not to forget that the first Quartet is dedicated to Prince Galitzin. So far as I know, Math. Artaria has already received from you two copies of the Overture. Should it have happened that I have not yet thanked you for the former copies, this only occurred from forgetfulness; moreover, you ought to be convinced that I neither sell nor deal in copies; only some artists esteemed by me have received a few of them, and this can do you no harm, as they could not procure these works for themselves.

I must also know whether Prince Galitzin, when he made known to you the title for the dedication, at the same time asked you for the necessary copies of the Quartet and the Overture, otherwise I shall have to send them to him from here.

I also beg you to send to me in future through Math. Artaria and no longer through Steiner, as I think I shall receive everything sooner through the first-named firm.

On the title-page of the Mass the subscription lists should be printed first, and then the dedication to the Archduke which I have already sent you, should follow.

With regard to the dedication of the Symphony, I will let you know my decision before long; it was settled to dedicate it to the Czar Alexander; but circumstances have occurred which cause this delay.

Do you want any more works of mine?

BEST ONE!

You have *grossly offended me! You have committed several falsa!* You have, therefore, first to exculpate yourselves before my judgment-seat; as soon as the ice has thawed, Mayence has to betake itself here; also the critical councillor of the High Court of Appeal will have to appear, and render an account; and now farewell!

You are by no means specially in our good books. Given without giving anything on the heights of the Black Spaniards, the 28th January, 1826.

BEETHOVEN.

[According to the original manuscript in the nephew's hand-writing, in the Town Library, Mayence; first printed by Nohl. On the letter is written, probably in the publisher's hand: "The explanation *re* Schwarzspanier we found by chance in some blotting-paper. It is a piece of luck, otherwise no one would have understood what the joke about the Black Spaniards meant." Later on he writes: "Our reply to his last letter appears to have been forgotten, in which we showed him how unpleasantly he had compromised himself, as if we wanted to prove through the printing of his original letters that no syllable is (false?). You may write that to him." It is evident that Beethoven would have become compromised, had not the publishers been very indulgent. The music notes at the end of the letter are in Beethoven's handwriting.]

416. To the Same

[*Delayed*]

VIENNA, *March*, 1825.

GENTLEMEN!

Here follow the numbers of the 3 great songs, No. 121 *Mass* No. 123.

Overture — 124
Symphony — 125
Bagatelles — 126
Quartet — 127

The metronome *tempos* will soon follow; my own is ill and has to recover its *even* steady pulse at the watchmaker's. The Symphony, as you know, must not be published before the end of July. I should also be glad if the quartet, which is ready, did not appear for some time yet. People speak in extremely favourable terms of the quartet and *ut dicunt* it is the best and finest I have ever written, the best virtuosi vie with one another in their desire to play it. Enough for nothing to-day can be invented to multiply one's words by stereo-typography without having need of *sticks* of copyists.

More next time.

Your, with love and esteem,

devoted BEETHOVEN.

[The quartet in question was the Quartet in E flat (Op. 127).]

417. To ABBÉ MAXIMILIAN STADLER, VIENNA

February 6, 1826.

HONOURED REVEREND SIR!

You have really acted well in rendering justice to the *manes* of Mozart by your truly admirable and profound essay, and learned as well as unlearned, in fact all who are musical, or are only counted as such, owe you thanks for it.

Either no knowledge or a great deal is required to talk on the subject as Herr W. has done. If one further considers that, so far as I know, a man of that sort has actually written a treatise on composition, and yet writes such passages as

and wants to ascribe them to Mozart, and if to that one adds W.'s patchwork, such as

W.'s astounding knowledge of harmony and melody reminds one of the late old imperial composers, Sterkel, Naumann, Kalkbrenner (père), André (not the other one), etc.—*requiescant in pace*. Let me thank you specially, my worthy friend, for the joy you give me by sending your article. I have always counted myself among the greatest admirers of Mozart, and shall remain so until my last breath.

Reverend Sir, *your blessing next time.*

With great respect,
Yours truly,
BEETHOVEN.

[From 1825 to 1829 there was great discussion about the genuineness of Mozart's *Requiem*, in which Abbé Stadler and Gottfried Weber played the principal parts. Weber inserted in *Caecilia* a slanderous attack on Beethoven and Stadler, but he was effectively answered by A. B. Marx.]

418. To?

3rd April, 1826.

Holz assures me that you want to have the engraving representing Handel's monument in St. Peter's Church in London, printed in larger size, and published. This gives me great joy, to say nothing of my having been the cause of it. Accept my thanks for it in anticipation.

Your obedient servant,
BEETHOVEN.

[The monument referred to is the one by Roubiliac in Westminster Abbey, also called the "Collegiate Church of St. Peter."—TR.]

419. To CARL HOLZ

WORTHY FRIEND!
26th April, 1826.

You may rest assured that I think no more of what occurred recently, and that my gratitude to you will never alter; I therefore beg you not to show anything with regard to it in your behaviour. You will always be welcome to me.

Next Sunday I hope that you will not despise my table. I have too much to do this week, and have no rest until everything is completed; but in such cases *meal*-times are very uncertain with me, and as a rule ever since my thirteenth year I have been accustomed to take my midday meal very late. I became still further confirmed in this habit by respectable men of business here, and it is now difficult entirely to relinquish the habit. Do not take this ironically, remember that I am dependent on the Muses, and then you will certainly not blame me; I have long ago thought of a means of proving my gratitude to you, which I shall put into practice as soon as possible.

If you can find time to call on me this week, it will give me pleasure if you will do so. You will find me unchanged, as usual. I expect you Sunday for certain.

As always, your friend,
BEETHOVEN.

[Beethoven's "rule" from his "thirteenth" year, must be taken *cum grano salis.*]

420. To BARON CARL AUGUST VON KLEIN, COMPOSER

VIENNA, *May* 10, 1826.

Through Court Councillor von Mosel, I received your letter which, on account of much work, I could not answer at once. You desire to dedicate a work to me; little as I lay claim to such distinction, I will accept with much pleasure the dedication of your fine work. You also wish me to be a critic, but you do not consider that I myself must submit to criticism. But I think, with Voltaire, "that a few gnat-stings cannot arrest a spirited horse in his course." I beg you to imitate me in this. However, to meet your wishes, not indirectly, but frankly, as is my wont, I only tell you that you might pay a little more attention to the separate conduct of the parts in future works of this kind. I shall always consider it an honour if I can be of service to you in any way, and commending myself to your kind thoughts, I am, with the greatest respect,

Your most devoted,
BEETHOVEN.

[Von Klein was born at Mannheim. Dr. Prieger also sent me the following letter from von Klein to the Peters publishing house:

Honoured Sir,

Herr Heinrich Gugel, of Petersburg, who stayed here not long ago, recommends you to me as a very active business man, and advised me to offer you a violin quartet which I wrote and *dedicate* to our worthy Beethoven. How this great composer received this little work, you will see from the enclosed copy of his own letter. If you feel inclined to publish this quartet I will send you the manuscript through the bookseller Kupferberg, when an opportunity offers itself. As regards the honorarium, I should only ask for some copies and some other music.

Awaiting a kind and speedy reply,

I remain,

Your obedient servant,

Frhr. v. Klein.

Beethoven and von Mosul had many artistic interests in common, especially as regards the employment of German instead of Italian music terms.]

421. To B. SCHOTT & SONS, Mayence

Vienna, 20*th May*, 1826.

Messrs. B. Schott and Sons in Mayence.

Overwhelmed with business, and constantly suffering in my health, I could not answer your favour of the 6th April sooner. Moreover, the quartet was not finished at that time; it is now completed. You can well imagine that I do not willingly take less than 80 ducats, which were offered and paid to me for the two earlier quartets which immediately followed yours (in E flat). But as you have already agreed to this fee, I accept with pleasure your proposal that it shall be paid in two instalments. Kindly, therefore, send me two bills, one for forty ducats at sight, the other for the same amount payable in two months. As you, no doubt, know of the misfortune which has overtaken the Fries firm, I should prefer you to draw the bills on Arnstein and Eskeles.

The metronome marks you will receive in a week by post. Things go slowly, as my health requires care. Of the quartet in E flat I have not yet received anything from you; the same remark applies to the Minerva. I must again beg you never to think that I would sell a work twice over. How it was with the Overture, you know yourselves. I could not possibly answer you about the accusation of having sold your quartet again to Schlesinger. Such a thing would be too bad for me to care to defend myself. Such a reproach could not be washed out, even with the best Rhine wine. For that purpose *Liguori penances*, such as we have here, would be necessary.

Yours very truly,

L. v. Beethoven.

N.B.—Please answer this at once.

[Alfonso Maria de Liguori (1696–1787) was the founder of the Liguorians, or Redemptionists. His *Moral Theology* in eight volumes created a sensation.]

422. To STEPHAN Von BREUNING

Summer 1826?

You are, as I myself, overwhelmed with work. At the same time, I am not yet quite well. I should have already invited you to dinner, but up till now I need several people, to whom a cook is the ablest of authors, and whose most pungent works are not in their own cellars, but in other people's kitchens and cellars; with their society you would not be pleased. However, there will soon be a change. Do not get Czerny's Pianoforte School at present; in a few days I shall receive more precise information about another one.

Enclosed you will find the journal of fashions promised to your wife, and something for your children. The journal can be sent back to you at any time, *and you need only ask for anything else you want from me.*

With love and esteem,

Your friend,

BEETHOVEN.

[The passage in this letter about dinner, and the pregnant form of expression, show that Beethoven was acquainted with Kant's works; it appears to me to be a reminiscence of that author's *Anthropology*.]

423. To HIS NEPHEW CARL

[*Summer* 1826.]

Since you at least have followed my advice, all is forgiven and forgotten, more about it with you by word of mouth. To-day quite calm. Do not think that any other thought weighs with me than that of your welfare, and judge my actions from this—do not take a step which may bring you into trouble and may shorten *my* life. I only got to sleep about 3 o'clock, for I was coughing the whole night. I embrace you heartily, and am sure that you will soon *misunderstand* me no longer, thus do I also judge your behaviour of yesterday. I expect you without fail to-day at one o'clock, give me no more trouble and anxiety, meanwhile farewell.

Your true and faithful father.

We are alone, I would not let H. come on that account, all the more as I wish that nothing may be said about yesterday, come then —let *my poor heart bleed no longer.*

["H." is Carl Holz. In this letter an unknown name occurs: Frl. Salomon. As Beethoven wrote a letter to his nephew in her house, she must be regarded as one of his friends.]

424. To CARL HOLZ

[*Summer* 1826.]

MOST ASTONISHING ONE! ASTONISHING ONE

You have dared to let me know that you do not consider me good enough to cut my own hair, and have actually sent me a real haircutter.

Ha! it is really too bad! you will have to pay, therefore, a fine of 2 ducats and a 3rd one besides, and again ½ a ducat, thus the one ducat will become two ducats, and altogether it will be a *brilliant* salad. It would be very good of you to come to an early breakfast to-morrow, but not to a late breakfast—think of the *miserabilia* of life. And that is by no means all—therefore, as early as possible. I shall wait till you come, but do not forget to pay the ½ ducat fine.

Your amicus fidelis,

BEETHOVEN.

425. To THE SAME [?]

[*Summer* 1826.]

Have you returned home to-day from the kingdom of love, as I have written to you and Breuning? If not, could you go, after your chancery, with the letter to Breuning—but if you—— *quel. Resultat?* I cannot say more, the copyist has come. I hope, therefore, to see you this afternoon about 5. Mind you always take a *droschke*, whenever you can. How sorry I am to have to trouble you, but Heaven will help. Carl has only 5 or 4 days to stay here.

In haste,

Your friend,

BEETHOVEN.

[The sentence about Carl having to stay five or four days refers to the hospital to which the young man was taken after his attempted suicide.]

426. To THE SAME

[*Summer* 1826.]

You had scarcely gone, when I found the spoons still on the box. As *she* [the servant?] was busy, I placed them on the table.

Lyser's sketch of Beethoven

But it occurred to me to look once more through them after the used ones had been cleared away, and again one was missing. I therefore said at once that I would take and keep your spoons until you returned my spoon. Now, God forbid that at our venerable age we should make away with spoons. The best of them, is in fact, gone; if not too troublesome to you let it be made the day after to-morrow. *To-day is Sunday*, so we can look forward to a right good *Sunday* meal. You see, so far as the spoon is concerned, it is as far off as the day before yesterday. If you could come to me to-morrow morning for a moment, that would be the best. You could have breakfast—the best is to end the matter as quickly as possible, otherwise something worse might happen.

Friday

Your

primus and

ultimus

[This unprinted letter to Holz was copied by me from the autograph in the Royal College of Music, London. The writing was difficult to decipher; some words are therefore doubtful.—TR.]

427. To B SCHOTT & SONS, MAYENCE

VIENNA, 26th July, 1826.

From the postscript of your honoured letter of the 8th, I perceive that you want to send two copies of the Symphony to the King of Prussia. I beg you to put this off for a time, as I am thinking of sending a manuscript copy to the King from here by courier, which could be done in this way without any danger. Now I beg you to keep back the edition until I give you notice that the King has received the copy; you understand that with the publication of a work, the value of the copy ceases. Please see that the two copies for the King are printed on fine paper.

In my last of the 12th, which, no doubt, you have received, I wrote to you that on account of my uncertain state of health I intended to take a little journey; I am still expecting your bill on Herr Frank, so that on receipt of it I may carry out my plan without delay.

I beg also for a speedy answer.

With esteem, yours very truly,

BEETHOVEN.

Postscript. Tobias now *primus*, lately *secundus*, is troubled at many inquiries after the quartet in E flat, and he has therefore written *two months ago* about a supplement, nevertheless he has not received it—this belongs to the books of the Black Spaniards, which will now soon appear.

[Both letter and signature are in the nephew's handwriting, but the postscript was written by Beethoven. The Symphony to which reference is made is the Ninth, which was dedicated to William III. of Prussia. The autograph is one of the treasures of the Berlin Library. "Tobias *primus*" means that Tobias was now head of the firm of Steiner and Co.]

428. To Dr. A. SMETTANA

[*August* 1826.]

MOST HONOURED HERR A. SMETTANA.

A great misfortune has happened, which Carl by chance has inflicted on himself. I hope that it will be possible to save him, you can do so if you appear soon. Carl has a bullet in his head, how, you will soon learn—only quickly for God's sake, quickly.

Yours respectfully,
BEETHOVEN.

To hurry on matters he had to go to his mother, where he is now. The address follows herewith.

[The letter belongs to the period of the catastrophe; in August 1826 Carl attempted suicide. The physician, Dr. Smettana, soon appeared on the scene to help, and Carl's life was saved, but he remained for a long time in the city hospital, to which Beethoven now addressed a number of letters.]

429. To CARL HOLZ

[*Summer* 1826.]

Holz!—Bring wood! to-morrow very early the least dangerous of all persons will bring money for that purpose. Must it be Herr C——l and agent? It must be!

Do your part, as we ours.

Amicus BEETHOVEN.

[Written with pencil.]

[The "least dangerous person" was the old housekeeper. Here we have the "Muss es sein, es muss sein," which we find in the Finale of the F major quartet (Op. 135). A great deal has been written about the real meaning of this phrase; Schindler attributed it to the housekeeper, "Frau Schnaps," or to an episode with the court agent, von Dembscher.]

430. To the Same

Do not forget the money, I shall soon have nothing left. Carl is steadily getting better. This afternoon Frau Table-Queen will sing at my house.

[The "Table-Queen" who sang to the master can only have been the famous Nanette Schechner, who made her *début* at Vienna in 1825, and was still there in 1826. The Conversation Books make this perfectly clear. In one Schindler writes: "I come to ask permission to introduce to you *Delle* Schechner, who longs to make your personal acquaintance.

"A true *portentum naturæ*.

"Milder is very inferior to her.

"To-day is *Don Juan*, and then will come *Fidelio*.

"You will not find her a beauty, but she is a very *honnette* and staid maiden, who, in addition to art, gives herself up entirely to looking after the house, for she keeps and instructs ten children, whom she supports with her income."

The result was, as the letter informs us, that Schechner could venture to pay her visit, and she was very soon invited to dinner.]

431. To the Same

August 1826.

Please be kind enough to leave the name of the police reporter where we were. A pretty story. Yesterday Carl was fetched away by the police, and why—they are not satisfied; I am running about to see if I can find some one.

[This note also concerns the suicide catastrophe. The zealots (*Zionswächter*) wished to reproach Beethoven for not having sufficiently cared for the salvation of his nephew's soul.]

432. To STEPHAN Von BREUNING?

Midsummer 1826.

With regard to Carl there are, I think, 3 points to be observed: (1) he must not be treated as a criminal, for that certainly would not be what is most desirable, but the very reverse; (2) in order to be advanced to a higher grade, one certainly cannot afford to live in a poor insignificant style; (3) too much restriction as regards food and drink would be hard lines for him; but I will not dictate to you.

[Nohl showed that it was not written to Holz, but to St. v. Breuning, who now, in the Schwarzspanierhaus, took the deepest interest in all the composer's troubles and joys.]

433. To CARL HOLZ

[*Midsummer* 1826.]

AMOROUS SIR,

I send you the Symphony, tell the bearer where Haslinger's warehouse is, so that she may give it to him to bind, without giving up herself.

Could I send *to you* this afternoon for the copies of the Clementi Pianoforte School? If I receive one gratis, I will take one, and it shall be duly paid for; if not gratis, I take *only one*, and *duly pay for it*.

Carl begs you for *Cigarro*, if you could manage all this and that, it would be of consequence this afternoon. If you thought how necessary it is to go with me once more to the hospital, let it be at least the day after to-morrow, for we could still learn something. I believe that Herr Brother will not come, so at least you would bring *one-fourth* of your *ego* to Döbling the day after to-morrow, and be with me about 7 o'clock—the afternoon would not be convenient.

Infatuated Lover,
I bend my knees before the
power of love
Your devoted
B——N.
†
memento mori

P.S.

It would be nice if you told the book-binder to see that it is properly bound and cleaned.

Inf. L——r.

[The housemaid was to take the Ninth Symphony to be bound to Haslinger in the Paternostergässel; this was probably the copy with the dedication to the King of Prussia, which is now in the Royal Library, Berlin. The Clementi Pianoforte School, which Beethoven prized so highly, was intended for Gerhard von Breuning.]

434. To THE MAGISTRATE'S COUNCILLOR, VON CZAPKA

[*August* 1826.]

I entreat you, as my nephew in a few days will be well, to give orders that he is only to leave the hospital in the company of myself and Herr v. Holz. It is impossible to allow him to be with his mother, that most depraved person. Her bad and wickedly crafty character, yes, indeed, the inducing Carl to get money from me, the probability that she may have shared moneys with him, likewise her intimacy with Carl's dissolute companion, the sensation which she caused with her daughter for whom the father is being sought, yes indeed, the presumption that at his mother's house he made the acquaintance of ladies none too virtuous—all these things justify my anxiety and my request; the very fact of being with such a person cannot possibly incline a young man to become virtuous. I entreat you to take the matter to heart, and with my kindest remembrances to you, I only add, that although the matter is a painful one, it affords me the highest pleasure to have made the acquaintance of a man of such distinguished intellect and such noble qualities.

I remain, dear sir, with high esteem,

Yours,

BEETHOVEN, m.p.

[Von Czapka, to whom Beethoven offers such striking testimony, displayed both love and zeal on the composer's behalf. "Carl's dissolute companion" was a young man named Niemetz, who also, in the Conversation Books of this sad period, is severely condemned.]

435. TO THE SAME

[August 1826.]

DEAR SIR!

Herr Court Councillor von Breuning and I have carefully considered what is to be done, and have come to the conclusion that, for the present, the only thing is for Carl (on account of his leaving here for the army) to spend a few days with me. He still talks in an excited way of the impression which my rebukes have made on him, when he was already in the act of putting an end to his life; but after this period he also showed himself full of affection for me. Rest assured that even fallen humanity remains sacred to me. A warning from you would have a good effect, and it would also do no harm to let him notice that he is secretly watched whilst he is with me.

Accept the expression of my high esteem for you, and regard me as a loving friend to humanity, who, where it is possible, has its welfare at heart.

Yours very truly,

BEETHOVEN, m.p.

436. To B. SCHOTT & SONS, Mayence

VIENNA, 29*th September*, 1826.

On the point of starting off to the country, I announce to you hastily that you will shortly receive the metronome marks for the Symphony.

You will probably already have the Quartet in C sharp minor; do not be alarmed at the four sharps. The work will shortly be given here for the benefit of an artist.

Finally, I beg you to hasten on what is necessary concerning the publication of my complete works. I cannot hide from you that, did I not firmly adhere to my promise, you might easily suffer some loss through proposals made to me by other publishers.

In the hope of hearing very soon from you.

Yours truly,
BEETHOVEN.

P.S.—I must still point out that in the second movement of the Symphony, after the last bar of the *Maggiore*   Viol. 1mo.

the D.S. is forgotten.

Yours truly,
BEETHOVEN.

[The letter was written by the nephew; the only words by Beethoven are: "Ihr ergebener Beethoven." Beethoven was now on the point of going to his brother's estate at Gneixendorf, near Krems—unfortunately, for it was there that he contracted his mortal sickness.]

437. To KING FREDERICK WILLIAM III. of Prussia

[*Beginning of October*, 1826.]

YOUR MAJESTY!

The gracious permission of Your Majesty to dedicate to you, in all humility, the present work, affords me great happiness.

Your Majesty is not only the father of your subjects, but also the patron of arts and sciences; so much the more, therefore, must your gracious permission rejoice me, as I am myself fortunate enough to count myself, as a citizen of Bonn, amongst your subjects.

I beg your Majesty to accept this work as a trifling token of the high esteem which I entertain for your virtues.

Your Majesty's most humble and obedient,

LUDWIG VAN BEETHOVEN.

[Schindler preserved the reply from the King, which is as follows:

To the Composer Ludwig van Beethoven

Recognising the value of your compositions, I was much pleased at receiving the new work which you have sent me. I thank you for this gift, and send you the enclosed *diamond ring* as a token of my sincere esteem.

BERLIN, 25 *November*, 1826.

FRIEDRICH WILHELM.

Much has been written about the story of the diamond ring, in which Prince Hatzfeld was concerned. We will only give an unprinted letter of Beethoven's taken from a Conversation Book:]

438. Uncertain

DEAR SIR,

While offering you my best thanks for the letter sent to me, I must beg you kindly to forward me the ring intended for me by H.M. the King of Prussia. I much regret that indisposition prevents me from receiving in person this token of the love of H.M. for art. I should, however, be sorry to entrust it to strange hands. At the same time, I beg you to let me have a few lines to say whether the worshipful Embassy would have the goodness to receive and forward a letter of thanks for H.M. the King.

B.

[This letter, however, must have been sent to Prince Hatzfeld. At length the supposed diamond ring came into Beethoven's possession. It is said that the composer was not a little astonished to find, on opening the case, not a diamond, but some reddish stone, valued by the court jeweller at 300 fl. in paper money.]

[Sir George Grove, in his *Beethoven and His Nine Symphonies*, wrote: "How it came to pass that, after the engagement and payment of the money by the Philharmonic Society, Beethoven should have allowed the Symphony to be first performed in Vienna, and have dedicated it to the King of Prussia, is a mystery which must be left to Mr. Thayer to unravel." There is another mystery connected with the Symphony. The Philharmonic Society offered fifty pounds, and the money was at once advanced (i.e. end of 1822 or beginning of 1823). But there is a receipt (British Museum), signed by Beethoven, dated 27 April, 1824, acknowledging receipt of £50 for Symphony composed for the Philharmonic Society. Nohl states that Beethoven received 100 guineas for the work.—TR.]

439. To Dr. FRANZ WEGELER

VIENNA, *7th October*, 1826.

MY DEAR OLD FRIEND!

I cannot tell you how much pleasure your letter and that of your Lorchen gave me. Certainly a reply ought to have been sent with lightning speed, but I am generally somewhat careless about writing, because I think that the better sort of men know me

FACSIMILE OF BEGINNING OF VARIATION V., SONATA IN A FLAT (OP. 26)

without this. I often compose the answer in my mind, but when I wish to write it down, I usually throw the pen away, because I cannot write as I feel. I remember all the love which you have constantly shown me, for instance, when you had my room white-washed, and so pleasantly surprised me. It is the same with the Breuning family. If we were separated, that happened in the natural course of things; every one must pursue and try to attain distinc-tion in his calling; but the eternal unshaken foundations of virtue held us ever firmly united. Unfortunately I cannot write to you to-day so much as I wished, as I am bed-ridden, and therefore confine myself to answering certain points of your letter.

You write that I am somewhere spoken of as a natural son of the late King of Prussia; I, likewise, heard of this long ago, but have made it a principle never to write anything about myself, nor to reply to anything written about me. So I willingly leave it to you to make known to the world the uprightness of my parents, and especially of my mother. You write about your son. I need not say that if he comes here he will find in me a friend and father, and if I can help or be of service to him in any way, I will gladly do so.

I still have the silhouette of your Lorchen, from which you will see that all the goodness and affection shown to me in my youth are still dear to me.

Of my diplomas I will only tell you briefly, that I am honorary member of the Royal Society of Sciences of Sweden, as well as of Amsterdam, and also honorary citizen of Vienna. A short time ago a certain Dr. Spiker took with him my last great Symphony with chorus to Berlin; it is dedicated to the King, and I had to write the dedication with my own hand. I had already sought permission through the Embassy to be allowed to dedicate this work to the King, and it was granted. At Dr. Spiker's instigation I was obliged myself to hand over to him the manuscript for the King, with the corrections in my own handwriting, as it was to be placed in the Royal Library. Something has been said to me about the Red Order of the Eagle, 2nd class; what will come of it, I do not know, for I have never sought such tokens of honour; yet in these times they would not be unwelcome to me for many reasons.

Moreover, my motto is always: *Nulla dies sine linea*, and if I ever let the Muse sleep, it is only that she may awaken all the stronger. I hope still to bring some great works into the world, and then, like an old child, to end my earthly career amongst good men.

You will also soon receive some music from Schott Brothers of Mayence. The portrait which you receive enclosed, is certainly an artistic masterpiece, but it is not the last which has been taken of me. With regard to tokens of honour, which I know will give you pleasure, I may also mention that a medal was sent to me by the late King of France with the inscription: *Donné par le Roi à Monsieur Beethoven*, accompanied by a very obliging letter from the *premier gentilhomme du Roi Duc de Châtres* [sic].

My dear friend, for to-day, farewell. For the rest, the remembrance of the past takes hold of me and not without many tears will you receive this letter. A beginning is now made, and you will soon get another letter, and the more frequently you write, the more pleasure will you give me. No inquiry is necessary on either side concerning our friendship, and so, farewell. I beg you to kiss and embrace your dear Lorchen and the children in my name, and at the same time to think of me. God be with you all!

As always, your true friend who honours you.

BEETHOVEN.

[In connection with the silhouette, Wegeler remarks: "The silhouettes of all the members of the Breuning family, also of intimate friends of the house, were taken in two evenings by the painter Neesen at Bonn; and that is how I came into possession of the one of Beethoven, who was at that time about sixteen years old."]

440. To TOBIAS HASLINGER

[October 1826.]

Be - ster   To - - - - - - - - - - -

There is no time to-day for the remaining consonanting and vowelling. I only beg you to hand over the enclosed letter at once.

You, of course, forgive me for troubling you; but as you are the proprietor of an art post-office, one naturally can do no less than make use of it.

You see from this that I am here in Gneixendorf. The name somewhat resembles a breaking axe. The air is healthy. Concerning anything else one must make the *Memento mori*.

To the most astonishing, first of all Tobiases, to his Grace of the Art and Post-office

we commend ourselves,

BEETHOVEN.

[The *Memento mori* soon became a sad reality. The following letter shows the state of things at Gneixendorf; not entirely unfavourable to brother Johann:

GNEIXENDORF, November 1826.

My dear Brother! it is impossible for me to remain quiet any longer about Carl's future destiny; he is getting quite out of the way of all industry, and will only be brought to work again with the greatest difficulty the longer he lives here so idly. When he left the hospital, Breuning gave him only a fortnight to recuperate, and now it is two months. You see from Breuning's letter that he certainly intends Carl to return to his profession; the longer he is here, the more unfortunate for him, for the more difficult will work appear to him, and thus something bad may happen. It is a crying shame that this talented young man should so fritter away his time, and who but ourselves will be blamed for it, for he is still too young to guide himself. Therefore it is your duty, if you do not wish to incur reproach later on from yourself and from others, to get him to return at once to his profession. When that takes place, much may be done for him and his future, but as he is now, nothing can be done. I see from his behaviour, that he would gladly remain with us, but then his future would be lost, so that this is impossible, and the longer we hesitate, the more difficult will the leaving us become; I therefore implore you to take a firm resolution, and not allow yourself to be influenced by Carl. Let it therefore be *next Monday*, for you cannot wait for me in any case. I cannot leave here without money, and it will be long before I receive enough to enable me to go to Vienna.

Let us leave this until the day when you go away. Faugh! the old woman (of Johann?)

she has her share
she will get no more.

Schindler remarks as follows: "The above letter shows that Johann van

Beethoven must have had his good points, so that one feels somewhat reconciled to him. Certainly Ludwig van Beethoven was angry at his brother's request, and a very disagreeable scene took place between the two brothers concerning Carl's inheritance of Johann's property. . . . Ludwig wished his brother to get rid of his wife and disinherit her, but this Johann refused to do. This was the chief cause of dispute between the two brothers for the previous five or six years." Schindler also feels bound to say that the chief fault was on Beethoven's side.]

441. To B. SCHOTT & SONS, Mayence

GNEIXENDORF, 13*th October*, 1826.

I am using the rest of the summer for recreation here in the country, as it was impossible for me to leave Vienna this summer. Meanwhile, I have entirely metronomised the Symphony, and add the *tempi* here.

Allegro ma non troppo	88 =	♩
Molto vivace	116 =	𝅗𝅥
Presto	116 =	𝅗𝅥
Adagio tempo primo	60 =	♪
Andante moderato	63 =	♪
Finale Presto	66 =	𝅗𝅥
Allegro ma non troppo	88 =	♪
Allegro assai	80 =	𝅗𝅥
Alla Marcia	84 =	♩.
Andante Maestoso	72 =	𝅗𝅥
Adagio divoto	60 =	𝅗𝅥
Allegro energico	84 =	𝅗𝅥.
Allegro ma non tanto	120 =	𝅗𝅥
Prestissimo	132 =	𝅗𝅥
Maestoso	60 =	♩

You can have them specially printed. Do not forget what I pointed out to you about the second movement.

I will also send you the Mass metronomised next time.

It is to be hoped that you have already received the new quartet.

With regard to the publication of my complete works, I should be glad to have your opinion, and beg you to let me know it as soon as possible. If I had not energetically opposed it, the publication would already have been begun in part, which would have been harmful to the publisher and of no advantage to me.

The neighbourhood in which I am now staying reminds me in some degree of the Rhine districts, which I so deeply long to see again, as I already left them in my youth.

Write me soon something pleasant. As always, with esteem,

Yours very truly,

BEETHOVEN.

[The quartet in question was the one in F (Op. 135).]

442. To TENDLER & MANSTEIN, VIENNA

GNEIXENDORF, 30th October, 1826.

DEAR SIRS!

I send you through my brother my newest violin quartet composed for Herr Schlesinger, and beg you to hand to the former the honorarium of eighty ducats, deposited with you for that purpose; of which amount I hereby acknowledge receipt.

With esteem,

Yours very truly,

LUDWIG VAN BEETHOVEN.

[Nohl states that, with the exception of the signature, everything is in the nephew's handwriting. A. B. Marx in his *Beethoven*, gives a facsimile of the following:

Latest Quartet of L. v. Beethoven
Gneixendorf, October 30, 1826.]

443. To B. SCHOTT & SONS, MAYENCE

[*December* 1826.]

I hasten to send you the coat of arms of H.I.H. the Archduke Rudolph. You can also put the subscription lists of the others after the dedication.

The metronome marks will shortly follow; do wait for them. In our age such things are certainly necessary; also I hear from Berlin that the first performance of the Symphony went off with enthusiasm, which I ascribe in great part to the metronome marking. We can scarcely have any more *tempi ordinari*, for one must follow the ideas of unfettered genius.

You would be doing me a great kindness if you would send the following to one of my most worthy friends, the Prussian State Councillor, Franz von Wegeler in Coblenz: the *Opferlied*, the *Bundeslied*, the song, *Bey Chloen war ich ganz allein*; and the Bagatelles for pianoforte. Kindly send him the first three in score. I will gladly repay you the amount.

You will likewise receive the dedication of the Quartet in a few days. I have been laid up already for some weeks, but trust that God will raise me up again. Commending myself to your remembrance I am,

Yours very truly,

Ludwig van Beethoven.

444. To the Same

[December 1826.]

Indications of some written or printed faults in Beethoven's latest Grand Symphony in D minor and in his latest quartet in E flat major.

I. In the Symphony in D minor, page 65, of the score, after the pause must be written: *Dopo il Maggiore Presto* si ricommincia dal segno :𝄋: il Minore ¾ e continuando si fa la seconda parte solamente una volta fin' à questa fermata ; poi si prende subito la Coda.

Page 73. After the 8th bar is to be added: *Da capo del Segno* :𝄋:.

II. In the quartet in E flat there should come in the 3rd movement after the *Presto* ¾ measure, *a tempo* ¾; and here in the 17th bar of the 2nd violin should be written instead of , page 30 of the score. In the same quartet, in the 2nd movement in the *Adagio molto expressivo* in the 13th bar of the 1st violin it should be 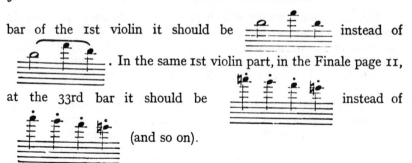 instead of . In the same 1st violin part, in the Finale page 11, at the 33rd bar it should be instead of (and so on).

DEAR SIRS!

I have already kept my bed for two months, and am suffering from dropsy—hence my silence.

Here you now receive what is still essentially wanting in the Symphony. I cannot understand why my score has not been strictly adhered to. I beg you, therefore, to make this known everywhere.

The remaining faults have still been found in the Quartet in E flat in the Paris as well as in the Mayence edition.

If you have heard that this Quartet has been published here, I can only explain this as mere gossip.

For the rest, I remain, with all esteem,

Yours very truly,

LUDWIG VAN BEETHOVEN.

VIENNA, 27th January, 1827.

P.S.—I should be very glad if you would soon send me again the *Caecilia* for my recreation.

[As the nephew had joined his regiment at Iglau, Schindler wrote this letter for the composer. Nohl only printed what is above. Here follows the missing part.]

(After the notes page 5 of the 1st violin part, line 8, bar 14).

In the same quartet (Paris edition) in the 2nd violin part, first movement, page 2, in the Allegro at the 43rd bar, instead of 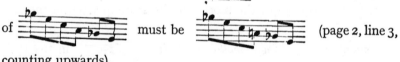 must be (page 2, line 3, counting upwards).

In the same part, in the second movement, $\frac{2}{4}$ measure, *tempo primo*, at the 15th bar, there must be

instead of

This last fault is also in the Mayence edition.

[Underneath in pencil by Schindler:]
If you like I will
see to the correction.

DEAR SIRS!
After the words in the "Mayence edition," the sentence is wanting: "In the score of the E flat quartet, page 30, line 2, the 5th bar, in the 2nd violin is missing, as already shown above."

Yours very truly,
LUDWIG VAN BEETHOVEN.

[Address also by Schindler:]
Herr W. Schott, the celebrated
Music Publisher in Mayence.

445. To MAX STUMPFF, LONDON

VIENNA, *February* 8, 1827.

. . . Unfortunately I have been prostrated with the dropsy since the 3rd December. You may imagine to what a state this has reduced me. I usually live only on the income from the work of my brain, so as to provide everything for myself and for my Carl. Unhappily for the last two and a half months I have been unable to write a single note. My annuity is sufficient to cover my rent, and then a few hundred gulden remain over. Remember that the end of my illness is still uncertain, and at length it will be impossible to fly up in the air on Pegasus with full-spread wings. Physician, surgeon, apothecary, everything must be paid. I remember quite well that several years ago the Philharmonic Society wished to give a concert for my benefit. It would be fortunate for me if they would again entertain this idea, I might perhaps still be saved from all the difficulties which lie before me. I am writing about this to Sir G. Smart, and if you, my worthy friend, can do anything for the furtherance of this object, I beg you to co-operate with him; Moscheles will also be written to on the matter, and I think that by the combination of all my friends, something may still be done for me.

[The harp manufacturer Stumpff, who had sent Beethoven an edition of Handel's works, sent an answer, in which he says: "That the works of Handel which I sent caused you great pleasure is a sufficient reward to me, for that was my sole object. In conformity with your wish and without the slightest delay I won Messrs. G. Smart and Moscheles for the good cause, I also acquainted the directors of the Philharmonic Society with the matter, whereupon it was at once resolved to hand over a sum of one hundred pounds to Baron Rothschild here, with a request that it should be forwarded by the first post to the Rothschild in Vienna with the direction that the money could be drawn by you through Herr Rau, tutor in the house of Baron Eskeles, in smaller or greater sums as you might require it." He also describes how Moscheles kindly saw to the carrying out of the matter.]

446. To Dr. F. G. WEGELER, Bonn

VIENNA, *February* 17, 1827 (¹).

Fortunately I received your second letter through Breuning. I am still too weak to answer it, but you may believe me that everything in it is welcome and desirable (²). My recovery, if I may call it so, is very slow; a fourth operation is to be expected, although the doctors do not say anything about it, I am patiently thinking that every evil has sometimes its good. But now I am astonished to see from your last letter that you have not received anything. From the present letter you will perceive that I wrote to you already on the tenth of December last year. With the portrait it is the same, as you will see from the date when you receive it (³). "Frau Steffen said" (⁴) in short, Steffen wished to send you these things if some opportunity offered, but they remained lying here up to this date; moreover, until now, it was difficult to send them back. You will now get the portrait by post through Schott and Co., who also send you the music. I should like to tell you still much more but I am too weak, thus I can only embrace you and your Lorchen in spirit.

With true friendship and affection to you and yours, I am,

Your old, true friend,

BEETHOVEN.

[This last letter of the dying composer to his old friend Wegeler is only signed by Beethoven. I here give Wegeler's notes to this letter in full:

(1) Therefore a month before his death.

(2) I proposed to him to fetch him and take him to the Bohemian Baths, and on the way to go along the Upper Rhine as far as Coblenz, when he ought to find himself quite strong.

The Schwarzspanierhaus, Beethoven's Deathplace

From a drawing by Herbert Railton

(3) On the portrait, above his name, stands written in Beethoven's hand: "To my old, honoured, beloved friend, F. Wegeler." But there is no date.

(4) Beginning of the second verse of the well-known song: "Zu Steffen sprach ein Traum," etc.]

447. To SIR GEORGE SMART, London

February 22, 1827.

I remember that the Philharmonic Society made the offer to me some years ago to give a concert for my benefit. In consideration thereof I beg to state to you that it would be very welcome to me if the Philh. Society would now renew the proposal, as I have been laid up since the first days of December with dropsy, a very wearisome illness, the end of which cannot be foreseen. Besides, as you know, I am living only on the proceeds of the works of my brain, and shall not yet be able to think of writing anything for a long time yet, and my income is so insignificant that I can scarcely pay the half-year's house-rent with it. I beseech you, therefore, kindly to use all your influence to further this object and quite convinced of your kind disposition towards me, I hope you will not take amiss my request. I shall also write to Herr Moscheles who, I am quite sure, will very willingly join you in furthering this object. I am so weak that I cannot write any more and this only by dictating the letter. I shall be very glad to receive an answer soon that there is hope of the realisation of my request. In the meanwhile receive the assurance of my greatest respect, and I remain, etc.

448. To IGNAZ MOSCHELES, London

I am sure you will not take amiss my troubling you as well as Sir G. Smart, for whom I enclose a letter with a request.

The matter, in short, is thus. Already some years ago the Philharmonic Society in London made me the handsome offer to arrange a concert for my benefit. At that time, thank God, I was not in a position to make use of this noble offer. But now it is quite different; as I have been laid up nearly 3 whole months with a tedious illness, viz., dropsy. Schindler, in his enclosure, will tell you more about it. You have known me a long time, you also know how and by what I live. For a long time I shall not be able to write anything, and this being so, I might, I am sorry to say, become in want of the necessaries of life. You have not only a large circle of acquaintances, but are also of great importance in the Philharmonic Society.

I therefore ask you to do your best, so that the Society may again adopt this resolution and carry it out. The enclosed letter to Sir George Smart is to the same purport, as well as the one I already sent to Herr Stumpff. I beg you to hand this letter to Sir George Smart and to unite with all my friends to further this object.

Your friend,

BEETHOVEN.

449. To B. SCHOTT & SONS, MAYENCE

VIENNA, February 22, 1827.

DEAR SIRS,

Your last letter I received through Capellmeister Kreutzer and I only answer now what is necessary. Before The *Opus* (Quartet in C sharp minor) which you have, comes the one of Matt. Artaria; from that you can easily fix the *Opus* number. *The dedication is to my friend, Johann Nepomuk Wolfmayer.* But now I approach you with a very important request. My doctor ordered me to drink very good old Rhine wine. Now to get it here, unadulterated, is not at all possible even by paying the highest price, and should I receive a small number of bottles, I will show my gratitude by contributions to *Caecilia*. At the excise office they would, I think, favour me a little, so that the transport would not be so very high. As soon as my strength permits me, you will also receive the metronome marks for the Mass. I am just about to undergo a 4th operation. The sooner, therefore, I receive the Rhine, or Moselle wine, the better it will be for my present state. I therefore pray you heartily to do me this favour for which I shall be most gratefully obliged.

With the greatest respect,

I am, dear Sirs,

Your most devoted,

BEETHOVEN.

[The letter, written by Schindler, is signed by Beethoven, but in a shaky hand. The Brothers Schott naturally hastened to fulfil the wish of the dying hero.]

450. To ANTON SCHINDLER

[*End of February* 1827.]

Of your accident, since it has already happened, when we meet. I can send somebody to you without any inconvenience. Accept this—here some Moscheles, Cramer, without your having received a letter. It will give an extra reason for writing on Wednesday, and again to urge my request. If you are not well by that time, one of my [servants] can post it and get a receipt. *Vale et fave*—I need not assure you of my sympathy at your accident. Accept, please, *this food from me*, I give it with all my heart. Heaven be with you.

Your sincere friend,

BEETHOVEN.

[Schindler gives the following explanation: "When Beethoven wrote this letter, he could no longer think consecutively; hence the broken sentences. *It is the very last letter which he wrote.*" The words, "here some Moscheles, Cramer," mean that Beethoven sent piano music, not only by Cramer but also by Moscheles, to his sick companion for study.]

451. To SIR GEORGE SMART, LONDON

[*March* 6, 1827.

I do not doubt that you, dear Sir, have received through Herr Moscheles my letter of the 22nd of February; but as I have found by chance among my papers S.'s address, I do not hesitate to write direct to you and recall my request again to your mind.

Up to now I cannot look forward to an end of my terrible illness; on the contrary, my sufferings and with it, my cares, have still increased. On the 28th of February I underwent my 4th operation, and it may be, perhaps, my fate to undergo a 5th or even more. If this continues, my illness will surely last till the middle of summer, and what will then become of me? How shall I then manage to live till I have recovered strength enough to gain my own living by my pen? In short, I will not trouble you further with my complaints, and refer only to my letter of the 22nd of February, asking you to use all your influence to induce the Philharmonic Society to carry out their former resolution concerning the concert for my benefit.

[According to Schindler; printed by Nohl. The letter was not written to Stumpff, as Schindler states, but to Smart; this was already pointed out by Nohl.]

452. To B. SCHOTT & SONS, MAYENCE

VIENNA, *March* 10, 1827.

DEAR SIRS!

According to my letter, the quartet ought to be dedicated to somebody whose name I already sent you. Some event has taken place which necessarily compels me to make an alteration. It has to be dedicated to Field-marshal Lieutenant, Baron Stutterheim, to whom I am under great obligation. If you should have already printed the first dedication, for heaven's sake have it altered. I will gladly pay the expense. Do not take this as mere promise, but it is of such importance to me that I am ready to pay any compensation for it.

The title is enclosed.

As regards the parcel to be sent to my friend, the R. Prussian Government Councillor, v. Wegeler in Coblenz, I am glad to release you entirely, as an opportunity is offered to forward everything to him.

My health, which will not be restored for a long time yet, compels me to ask you again for the wine which will certainly refresh me, and give me strength and health.

I am, with great esteem,
Your devoted,
LUDWIG VAN BEETHOVEN.

[To this letter, written by Schindler, Beethoven added his signature in full, and the writing is wonderfully clear. The answer arrived three days after the composer's death.]

453. To IGNAZ MOSCHELES, LONDON

VIENNA, March 14, 1827.

MY DEAR MOSCHELES!

Some days ago I found out through Herr Lewinger that you inquired in a letter to him of the 10th of February regarding the state of my illness, of which so many different rumours have been spread about. Although I have no doubts whatever that my letter of the 22nd of February has arrived, which will explain everything you desire to know, I can but thank you for your sympathy with my sad lot, and beseech you to be solicitous about the request which you know of from my first letter, and I am quite convinced that in union with Sir Smart and other of my friends, you will succeed in bringing about a favourable result for me at the Philharmonic Society. I have once more written to Sir Smart about it.

On the 27th of February I underwent the 4th operation and there are visible symptoms that I shall have to suffer a fifth. What does it tend to, and what will become of me if it continues for some time longer? A hard lot, indeed, has fallen upon me! However, I submit to the will of fate, and only pray to God so to ordain it in His divine will that I may be protected from want as long as I have to endure death in life. This will give me strength to bear my lot, however terrible it may be, with humble submission to the will of the Most High.

Therefore, my dear Moscheles, I entrust once more my affair to you, and remain with greatest respect ever

Your friend,

L. VAN BEETHOVEN.

Hummel is here and has called on me several times.

454. To ANTON SCHINDLER

[Beethoven's last lines to Schindler, 17 March, 1828.]

WONDER ·/. ·/. ! [=Wonder, Wonder, Wonder]

The very learned gentlemen have been beaten both of them; only through Malfatti's knowledge shall I be saved. It is necessary for you to come to me this forenoon just for a moment.

Yours,

BEETHOVEN.

[Schindler spoke of the former letter written to him as the "very last written by Beethoven"; he probably meant the last letter of any importance, and regarded the above only as a short note. The two learned gentlemen were the Doctors Wawruch and Seibert. Nine days after this ray of hope Beethoven breathed his last.]

455. To IGNAZ MOSCHELES, LONDON

VIENNA, *March* 18, 1827.

With what emotion I read your letter of the 1st March is not be described in words. This magnanimity of the Philharmonic Society, with which they anticipated my request, has touched my inmost heart. I therefore ask you, dear Moscheles, to be the organ through which I can express my most heartfelt thanks to the Philharmonic Society for their sympathy and help. Tell these worthy men that, if God restores me to health, I shall try practically to show my gratitude by works, and that I leave it to the Society to choose what I shall write for them. A whole sketched Symphony [the 10th] is in my desk, also a new Overture or even something else. As regards the concert which the Philharmonic Society has resolved on giving for my benefit, I beg the Society not to give up this intention. In short, I shall try to fulfil any wish expressed by the Society, and never have I undertaken a work with such ardour as will now be displayed. May it only please God to restore me soon again to health, and then I shall prove to these magnanimous Englishmen that I know how to value their sympathy to me in my sad condition.

I was compelled to accept the whole sum of 1000 fl., since I was then in the disagreeable position of having to draw out invested money.

Your noble behaviour I shall never forget, and I shall soon render my thanks in particular to Sir Smart and Herr Stumpf. The metronomised Ninth Symphony please hand to the Philharmonic Society. Enclosed find the markings.

Your most devoted friend,

BEETHOVEN.

[This letter was dictated to Schindler.]

456. CODICIL. TESTAMENTARY DISPOSITION

My nephew Carl shall be my sole heir; the capital of my estate shall, however, descend to his natural heirs, or to those appointed by him through a will.

LUDWIG VAN BEETHOVEN.

VIENNA, *March* 23, 1827.

[This was signed by Beethoven three days before his death, when, to Breuning's surprise, Beethoven changed the word "legitimate" into "natural," and refused to restore the word originally written.]

457. To B. SCHOTT & SONS, MAYENCE

April 12, 1827.

In place of a formal necrology, we give the following letter to the music publishers Schott of Mayence, which, on account of the news contained therein concerning the last hours of Beethoven's earthly existence, will certainly be of great interest to the admirers of this most remarkable and distinguished composer.

VIENNA, *April* 12, 1827

I would already have liked to take the liberty of forwarding to you the enclosed document in the name of our Beethoven as his dying request; but after the passing away of our friend, there was so much business to attend to that I found it impossible. Unfortunately it was not possible to get the document legalised; for that

Beethoven would have had to sign it at the law court, which was utterly impossible. Beethoven, however, requested Court Councillor v. Breuning and myself to add our names as witnesses, as we were both present. We therefore believe that it will serve the purpose for which it was drawn up. I must further mention that in this document you possess the *last* signature of this immortal man; for this was the last stroke of his pen.

I cannot now refrain from telling you something about the last hours when he was still conscious (namely, on the 24th of March from early morning until about one o'clock in the afternoon), for to you, sirs, this will surely be of great interest. When I came to him on the morning of the 24th of March I found his face quite drawn; moreover he was so weak, that with the greatest effort he could only utter two or three intelligible words. The *Ordinarius* soon arrived, and, after watching him for a few moments, said to me: Beethoven's end is rapidly approaching. As the business of the will had been settled, so far as was possible, the previous day, there remained for us only one ardent wish, to get him reconciled with heaven, in order that the world might also be shown that he ended his life as a true Christian. The Professor Ordinarius wrote it down, and begged him in the name of all his friends, to partake of the sacrament for the dying, whereupon he answered calmly and steadily: I will. The doctor went away, leaving me to see to this. Beethoven then said to me: My only request is that you write to Schott and send him the document; he *will need it*. And write to him in my name, for I am too weak, and say that I much desire him to send the wine. Also, if you have still time to-day write to England. The clergyman came about 12 o'clock, and the religious ceremony took place in the most edifying manner. And now for the first time he seemed to feel that his end was approaching, for the clergyman had scarcely gone when he said to me and to young v. Breuning: *Plaudite amici, comœdia finita est!* Have I not always said that it would be thus? He then, once again, begged me not to forget Schott, also again to write in his name to the Philharmonic Society to thank them for their great gift, and to add that the Society had comforted his last days, and that even on the brink of the grave he thanked the Society and the whole English nation for the great gift. God bless them.

At this moment the chancellery servant of v. Breuning entered the room with the case of wine and the decoction about $\frac{1}{4}$ to one o'clock. I put the two bottles of Rüdesheimer and the two other bottles of the decoction on the table at his bedside. He looked at them saying: 'Tis a pity, a pity, too late! These were his last words.

Immediately after commenced the death throes, so that he could not utter a sound. Towards evening he lost consciousness and became delirious, which lasted up to the evening of the 25th when visible signs of approaching death appeared. Nevertheless he did not actually die until the 26th at a quarter to six o'clock in the evening.

This death struggle was terrible to behold, for his physique, especially his chest, was like that of a giant. Of your Rüdesheimer he kept taking a few spoonfuls until he passed away.

Thus I have the pleasure of acquainting you with the last three days of our unforgettable friend.

In conclusion accept the assurance, etc.

ANTON SCHINDLER.

Together with the above there is the following declaration:

According to which I hand over to the publishing firm B. Schott, the sole copyright of my last quartet in C sharp minor, as well as the sole right of performance. And, further, they are free to print and publish, as their own property in Paris as well as in Mayence and also at all places, the above-mentioned firm may think proper

LUDWIG VAN BEETHOVEN.

[His very last signature.]

Anton Schindler,
Music Director
as invited witness.

VIENNA, *March* 20, 1827

Stephan v. Breuning
Imperial Court Councillor
as invited witness.

The English nation and the firm of Schott and Sons of Mayence were therefore the last remembrances of the dying Beethoven.

BEETHOVEN AUTOGRAPH

BELOW is my translation of an autograph in the Royal College of Music, but there seems to be no record of the person by whom it was presented; very likely it was the late Sir George Grove. Dr. Lionel D. Barnett, Superintendent of the Oriental Department of the British Museum, kindly advised me to look through the "Upanishads" in vol. xv. of the *Sacred Books of the East*, edited by Max Müller, and in them I found many sentences very similar to those in the Beethoven document. Dr. Barnett also pointed out a book in German, on Indian Philosophy, published at Jena in 1816, and here again there were sentences of a similar kind. Only the *first two sentences* appear to have been published. They are among the extracts from Beethoven's diary, published by Ludwig Nohl in *Die Beethoven-Feier* (Vienna, 1871). In a footnote Nohl states that specialists had not been able to trace the source whence they were derived. It seems as if Beethoven must have taken them from some essay or newspaper article. It is, indeed, very probable that he may have had his attention drawn to the subject by Baron Hammer-Purgstall, who wanted the composer to set to music a poem presenting the religious system of the Hindus; the above may, indeed, be an extract from that poem.—EDITOR.

DOCUMENT

God is immaterial ; as he is invisible, he can therefore, have no form. But from what we are able to perceive in His Works we conclude that he is eternal, almighty, omniscient and omnipresent. The mighty one, He alone is free from all desire or passion. There is no greater than He, Brahm; his mind is self-existent. He, the Almighty, is present in every part of space. His omniscience is self-inspired, and His conception includes every other. Of His all-embracing attributes the greatest is omniscience. For it there is no threefold kind of being— it is independent of everything—O God! thou art the true, eternal, blessed, unchangeable light of all time and space. Thy wisdom apprehends thousands and still thousands of laws, and yet thou ever

393

actest of thy free will, and to thy honour. Thou wast before all that we worship. To thee is due praise and adoration. Thou alone art the true, Blessed (Bhagavan), Thou the best of all laws, the image of all wisdom, present throughout the whole world, Thou sustainest all things. Sun, Ether, Brahma.

[These three last words have a line drawn through them.—ED.]

HYMN

SPIRIT of spirits, who, spreading thyself through all space and through endless time, art raised high above all limits of upward struggling thought, from riot didst thou command beautiful order to arise. Before the (worlds) heavens were, thou wast, and before systems rolled below and above us. Before the earth swam in heavenly ether, thou alone wast, until through thy secret love that which was not, sprang into being, and gratefully sang praises to thee. What moved thee to manifest thy power and boundless goodness? What brilliant light directed thy power? Wisdom beyond measure! How was it first manifested? Oh! direct my mind! Oh! Raise it up from this grievous depth.

THE END

LIST OF LETTERS

INDEX OF PERSONS

INDEX OF WORKS